Beyond the Tricolour

Historical Materialism Book Series

The Historical Materialism Book Series is a major publishing initiative of the radical left. The capitalist crisis of the twenty-first century has been met by a resurgence of interest in critical Marxist theory. At the same time, the publishing institutions committed to Marxism have contracted markedly since the high point of the 1970s. The Historical Materialism Book Series is dedicated to addressing this situation by making available important works of Marxist theory. The aim of the series is to publish important theoretical contributions as the basis for vigorous intellectual debate and exchange on the left.

The peer-reviewed series publishes original monographs, translated texts, and reprints of classics across the bounds of academic disciplinary agendas and across the divisions of the left. The series is particularly concerned to encourage the internationalization of Marxist debate and aims to translate significant studies from beyond the English-speaking world.

For a full list of titles in the Historical Materialism Book Series available in paperback from Haymarket Books, visit: www.haymarketbooks.org/series_collections/1-historical-materialism.

Beyond the Tricolour

*Internationalism and the French
Left from Dreyfus to Algeria*

Ian Birchall

Haymarket Books
Chicago, IL

First published in 2025 by Brill Academic Publishers, The Netherlands
© 2025 Koninklijke Brill NV, Leiden, The Netherlands

Published in paperback in 2026 by
Haymarket Books
P.O. Box 180165
Chicago, IL 60618
773-583-7884
www.haymarketbooks.org

ISBN: 979-8-88890-803-7

Distributed to the trade in the US through Consortium Book Sales and
Distribution (www.cbsd.com) and internationally through Ingram
Publisher Services International (www.ingramcontent.com).

This book was published with the generous support of Lannan
Foundation, Wallace Action Fund, and the Marguerite Casey Foundation.

Special discounts are available for bulk purchases by organizations and
institutions. Please call 773-583-7884 or email info@haymarketbooks.org
for more information.

Art and design by David Mabb. Cover art is a section from *Variant 1,
Morris, Trellis / Stepanova, Optical*, paint on wallpaper mounted on canvas
(2006).

Printed in the United States.

Library of Congress Cataloging-in-Publication data is available.

In Memory of Bel Druce

Contents

The Struggle for Internationalism

The world we live in is, more than at any previous time in history, a single integrated unit. The changing fortunes of a market economy determine the chances for life – and death – of human beings in states all around the planet. The rich and powerful move themselves, their money and their goods, across frontiers as they please; the poor and deprived, driven from their homes by war and poverty, are maltreated by border-guards and people-smugglers. Yet the populations of the world's cities contain an ever richer mixture of races and nationalities. The same films are watched and the same music is listened to in countries around the world. E-mail and Twitter [X] enable conversations that span the earth. Destructive climate change recognises no national frontiers; it threatens global disaster and requires a global solution.

This does not mean that nationalism is obsolete; it remains a powerful force. National governments, often faced with a decline in electoral support which undermines their legitimacy, need to appeal to a national interest in order to continue levying taxes and sending young people to fight their foreign wars. Individual capitalists may evade taxes; they still depend on taxation by nation states to provide the infrastructure services they require – police, schools, etc. The attempts in 2014 to glorify the First World War and defend the motives for which it was fought are just one example among many of the promotion of nationalism. Repeated concessions to the rhetoric, and sometimes the policies, of the far right show a dangerous trend. New political forces have risen, and sometimes fallen, like UKIP and the Reform Party in Britain and the Rassemblement National [formerly the Front National] in France, which look to the illusory utopia of 'national independence'. Such movements inevitably focus on controlling frontiers and hence channel hostility towards immigrants.

Historically the response of the left has been to assert internationalist values. Yet in recent years the very notion of internationalism has become feeble and confused. In the debate about Brexit in Britain the label of internationalism has been appropriated by the partisans of the European Union, a neoliberal alliance of nation states pitted against the rest of the world, its frontiers closed to refugees and migrants. A generation earlier, internationalism was used to justify the interests of the Russian state, so that the language of proletarian internationalism was used to legitimate, for example, the Russian invasions of Hungary and Czechoslovakia. French Communist leader Maurice Thorez compared the role of the Russian army in Hungary in 1956 to that of the International Brigades in the Spanish Civil War.[1] In 1965 Communist historian Eric Hobsbawm argued that the French Communist Party had 'opted for internationalism (in the only available form, loyalty to the October Revolution as embodied in the USSR)'.[2] Now many on the left seem to have given up on internationalism completely, claiming to replace the negative aspects of nationalism with a more positive 'patriotism' (though the definitions offered tend to be extremely vague).

This book examines the theme of internationalism. I understand the term as it has been used historically in the socialist, and especially the Marxist, tradition. Internationalists have been those who see that the world forms a single unit, whose problems can be analysed and confronted only in a global framework. Internationalists have no allegiance to any nation state, and see all states as the instruments of ruling classes. For them the oppressed and exploited – the vast majority of the world's population – share interests across national boundaries that are far more significant than any common interests they might have with their national rulers. Internationalists identify with victims of oppression throughout the entire world rather than with their own nation state. But since political activity is usually defined within the framework of a particular nation, they often find themselves in direct conflict with that state, and in some circumstances they cooperate with the enemies of their own country. They envisage a future in which nation states become obsolete and the world is organised as a harmonious federation of peoples.

Internationalists refuse to support wars between nation states. They oppose attempts to foment racial divisions, or to oppress particular races. They reject the oppression – military, political or economic – of weaker nations by more powerful states, supporting struggles for national independence against their own state. Internationalists do this in the interests of the oppressed within their own nation, who cannot fight to liberate themselves if they believe they have a shared interest with their own ruling class. If they blame foreigners for their problems, they cannot see the real causes. As Engels put it in a speech on Poland in 1847: 'A nation cannot become free and at the same time continue to oppress other nations'.[3]

The history of internationalism has been a tortuous one, with many contradictions. In 1848 Marx and Engels concluded the *Communist Manifesto* with the optimistic exhortation 'Working men of all countries unite!'[4] By 1864 in the

---

1   Bulaitis 2020, p. 239.
2   Hobsbawm 1977, p. 22.
3   Engels 1976, p. 389.
4   Marx and Engels 1976, p. 519.

Inaugural Address of the Working Men's International Association, Marx noted rather more soberly: 'Past experience has shown how disregard of that bond of brotherhood which ought to exist between the workmen of different countries, and incite them to stand firmly by each other in all their struggles for emancipation, will be chastised by the common discomfiture of their incoherent efforts'.[5]

Authentic internationalism has always been a minority current within the socialist movement, though not an insignificant one. In the aftermath of the First World War, following the Russian Revolution and the founding of the Communist International, it seemed for a few years as though internationalism might become a force in mainstream politics. It was not to be.

In this book I trace the history of the internationalist left in France from the Dreyfus affair in the 1890s to the end of the Algerian war in 1962, and show how it differed from the republican nationalism which characterised the politics of the mainstream left. It was a stormy period of continuing violence, in which France went through two world wars, a foreign occupation and two savage struggles for colonial independence.

Much has been written on this period, but I hope to approach events from a somewhat different perspective. I have traced a part of the history by looking at some of those women and men, often neglected by mainstream histories, who struggled for internationalist principles and clarified and defined what internationalism might mean. I have let them speak in their own words, quoting from their declarations and writings. In standard histories names such as Alfred Rosmer, Robert Louzon, Marguerite Thévenet, Hadj-Ali Abdelkader, Daniel Guérin, Jean-René Chauvin, Henri and Clara Benoits and others appear only at the margins of the narrative, if they are mentioned at all. I have tried to bring them to the centre of the story.

I have made no attempt to construct a unitary tradition – what Peter Sedgwick called 'an Apostolic succession from the ideas of certain revered forerunners to those of their (usually self-enthroned) successors in the present day'.[6] The internationalist left contains a range of different political traditions – in Tony Cliff's words 'ideas are like a river and a river is formed from lots of streams'[7] – and no one stream has a monopoly of truth. Syndicalists, anarchists, Trotskyists, left social democrats, dissident Communists, existentialists, Christians – all have a part in the story. Not all were consistent internationalists; some were forced to adopt an internationalist stance by the logic of

---

5 Marx 1985, p. 12.
6 Sedgwick, 1960–61, p. 25.
7 Cliff 2001, p. 135.

their situation. I have tried to rescue them, not so much from what Edward Thompson called the 'condescension of posterity',[8] as from posterity's neglect.

It may seem odd to write the history of internationalism within the framework of a single country. Yet concrete internationalism always comes into existence in conflict with a particular nationalism. Those who fight for internationalism find themselves pitted against their own nation state – opposing its plans for war or supporting the liberation struggles in its colonies. In the words of German socialist Karl Liebknecht during World War I, 'the main enemy is at home'.[9] France may have particular lessons of relevance to a wider world. The French Revolution of 1789 launched values of liberty, equality and fraternity which have had an influence around the globe. As the one-time head of the second largest empire in the world, France's racist colonialism generated an opposition that can continue to inspire.

All historians have their own history, and I should briefly note how I have come to the subject. For three decades I taught French language, literature and history. I lived in France for a year at the very end of the Algerian war, and have visited France on innumerable occasions; I have known, and discussed with, many comrades and friends from different currents of the French far left. Yet I remain an outsider, and am perhaps capable of looking at French history without the ties of identity that a French-born historian might have. I am neither Francophile nor Francophobe. I admire and identify with the struggles of the French working class, from Babeuf's conspiracy and the Paris Commune to the great general strike of 1968; I esteem those French intellectuals who fought for justice and human emancipation, from Voltaire and Zola to Sartre. But I despise the arrogance of French rulers, from Marie-Antoinette to de Gaulle, and I detest the brutality of the French military from the persecutors of Dreyfus to the torturers of Algeria.

It is a vast subject, and I have covered only a few of the many people and events that deserve to be recorded. There is much more work to be done, and hopefully some of the many gaps I have left – sometimes as a result of culpable ignorance – will stimulate others to further research. I have selected individuals whom I found particularly interesting and who seemed to me to illuminate the central theme. I have also, to provide context, looked at a few periods when internationalism seemed, albeit briefly, to be extending beyond individuals and inspiring collective action.

---

8 Thompson 1980, p. 12.
9 Liebknecht 1952, pp. 296–301.

In her important book *Insurgent Empire* Priyamvada Gopal examines some British critics of their own country's colonialism. She rejects the widespread notion that their opposition to Britain's imperial rule came from essentially British values, and argues convincingly that 'Britain's enslaved and colonial subjects were not merely victims of this nation's imperial history … but rather agents whose resistance … put pressure on and reshaped some British ideas about freedom and who could be free'. There was an educational process 'in which metropolitan dissidents came to learn something from their colonial interlocutors and the movements they represented'.[10]

The same is true of France. Opposition to French colonialism did not grow out of the 'republican values' so dear to French President Emmanuel Macron. French critics of their own nation's colonialism were inspired and educated by those in the colonies who fought bitterly and courageously for their own liberation. Many French citizens discovered the reality of colonialism by visiting the colonies, either voluntarily on a journey of investigation, or involuntarily as conscripts.

French colonialism was brought to an end because the inhabitants of the colonies, above all Indochina and Algeria, fought long, bloody wars against an obstinate colonialist resistance that was ultimately futile. It was their courage and determination that brought the French Empire to an end, and their history should not be forgotten.[11] The Europeans who campaigned for colonial independence, or gave practical support ['carrying suitcases': see Chapter 11], gave a helping hand to that main struggle.

Yet those European allies were not irrelevant. The wars of colonial liberation exposed deep conflicts within French society. The European population of France was not one reactionary mass – the oppressed of the colonies could legitimately count on the support of at least a minority. The role of that minority is also a part of history.

Vital for an understanding of this process is, as Gopal stresses, the notion of solidarity. Activists in France who supported those fighting for national independence did not do so out of some feeling of benevolence for the victims of oppression. Rather they recognised that they too were victims of the same system of oppression; that the working class in an imperialist country is exploited by the same people who are oppressing the colonies. As Jean-Paul Sartre told a largely Muslim audience at a meeting on Morocco in 1948: 'Those who are oppressing you are oppressing us for the same reasons'.[12]

---

10   Gopal 2020, pp. 5–6, 24.

11   For Algeria, see for example Evans, 2012, Harbi 2001, Stora 1982 and 1991.

12   Lamouchi 1996, pp. 56–7. See *La Gauche* RDR 8, November 1948.

In this book I have confined myself largely to those born in or living in mainland France [ignoring the colonial fiction that Algeria was an integral part of France]. I have not dealt with those colonial subjects who campaigned, and fought, against French imperialism. Theirs is an important story, but it has been told elsewhere. I have, however, written about colonial subjects who came to France and were active there in the movement for social change – well-known figures like Ho Chi Minh and Messali Hadj, and those who deserve to be better known like Lamine Senghor and Hadj-Ali Abdelkader. Often such activists had an influence on those they encountered in France. Henri Benoits, a Renault worker active in solidarity with the Algerian struggle, recalled how his internationalism could be traced back to his experience of demonstrating alongside Algerian and Vietnamese comrades on May Day 1945.[13]

Our understanding of history changes as the world changes around us. Victor Schoelcher is often remembered as a campaigner against slavery who made connections between the fate of slaves and the exploitation of the working class. Yet in 2021 in Martinique a statue of Schoelcher was attacked by supporters of the National Front for the Liberation of Martinique, who rejected the idea that the end of slavery was granted by benevolent French people, and who opposed the racist institutions which replaced slavery.[14] My book is a small contribution to a continuing debate about the reassessment of past struggles.

As I write, the tide of nationalism is rising again in both Britain and France. Reza Zia-Ebrahimi has shown the continuities, parallels and entanglements between Islamophobia and the anti-Semitism which blighted Europe in the 1930s – for example, the accusation of 'islamo-gauchisme' [islamoleftism], so widely current on the right, clearly echoes the 'judéo-bolchévisme' [judeo-Bolshevism] thrown around by anti-Semites in the 1920s and 1930s.[15] In the 2022 French presidential election, it was the far right, and its obsession with immigration, which set the agenda for all the other candidates. As a weakened left strives to reorient itself, it may draw some sustenance from the history of those who fought, against the stream, for genuine internationalism.

---

13   Benoits 2014, pp. 33–4.

14   Sansom 2021.

15   Zia-Ebrahimi 2021, p. 134.

Acknowledgements

This book has been a long time in the making; many people, too many to list by name, have helped me to formulate my ideas and extend my knowledge.

In the early 1960s I worked for a year in a French secondary school, and began to discover something about the importance of *laïcité* [the closest translation is secularism] in the French education system. Then for nearly thirty years I taught French at Middlesex Polytechnic [previously Enfield College of Technology and subsequently Middlesex University]. My teaching included topics from French history and intellectual life; often I learned as much from students' questions and disagreements as I taught them. Although I am not a historian by training, I worked alongside historians and social scientists and I learned a lot about approaches to history from discussions and arguments with Norah Carlin and other colleagues.

For some fifty years I was a member of the Socialist Workers Party [earlier the International Socialists]. Among my activities was speaking to large numbers of meetings on topics from the history of the socialist and working-class movement. I also spoke most years over four decades to the SWP's annual Marxism event. Audience responses were extremely valuable to me. Another of my responsibilities at certain times was dealing with the party's international contacts. In the course of such work I met a number of activists from different currents of the French far left, including such veterans as Alain Krivine, Denis Berger, Jean-René Chauvin, Daniel Mothé and Jakob Moneta, who are mentioned in these pages. In its earlier years I learned from the IS/SWP – from Tony Cliff, Mike Kidron, Peter Sedgwick, Alasdair MacIntyre, Chris Harman and others – an undogmatic, critical Marxism which has provided a framework for my historical writing.

For over twenty years I was a member of the editorial board of the journal *Revolutionary History*. I helped to edit two issues – on Alfred and Marguerite Rosmer and on the Algerian War – and have written and translated a good deal of material. Contact with my fellow board members has given me access to a vast amount of knowledge about the international revolutionary movement.

Over a similar period of time I have been a member of the London Socialist Historians Group; I have given a number of papers to its seminars and conferences, and have written for its *Newsletter*. I have also learned much from regular contact with other members of the group with their wide range of specialisms.

I have given papers on historical topics at a number of conferences where I enjoyed an exchange of views with historians concerned with the socialist movement. In particular I have taken part in a number of the London Historical Materialism conferences, three conferences at Norwich organised by the Socialist History Society, the University of East Anglia and the Chicago Institute of Working-Class History, a conference on Daniel Guérin at Loughborough and one on Blanqui at Kingston University, and two conferences of Penser l'Émancipation at Lausanne and Nanterre.

I have written articles and reviews on topics related to the themes of this book for a wide range of publications: *International Socialism, Socialist Review, Socialist Worker, Historical Materialism, New Left Review, Jacobin, Contretemps, International Socialist Review, RS21, Weekly Worker, Country Standard* and other academic and political journals. Parts of such articles have been adapted and incorporated into the present volume.

In London I have researched at the British Library [including the old newspaper library at Colindale] and at the London Library. In Paris I have worked in the Bibliothèque Nationale, the Bibliothèque de l'Arsenal, the BDIC and the CER-MTRI. I am most grateful to staff who have helped me to locate material. There have been many other spoken or written exchanges with comrades, friends and colleagues who have helped me to track down information or refine my arguments.

There are a number of references in the text to J. Maitron and C. Pennetier, *Dictionnaire biographique du mouvement ouvrier français* [https://maitron.fr/], but in addition to these I should express a general debt to this work, an indispensable tool for anyone working on the history of the French working class. The Marxists Internet Archive has also been invaluable.

Translations from the French are my own except where otherwise stated.

In writing this book I have been constantly reminded that so many of those whom I have discussed lived in circumstances that were harsh and dangerous to an extent that is, for one born in more fortunate times, almost impossible to imagine, and that they displayed a degree of physical and moral courage which I have never been required to show. I have made critical judgements – that is what historians are for, if we are to learn from our past – but I hope I have done so with appropriate humility.

In recent years I have suffered from health problems which have made it impossible for me to visit libraries and pursue research. As a result the book is less comprehensive than I had originally intended, but I hope it will still serve some purpose. My thanks to Andrew Wright and others who have helped me get access to published material. Sebastian Budgen has given me both practical assistance and encouragement. My son Danny Birchall has helped in many ways, notably in dealing with my inadequate computing skills. I could not have finished the book without the assistance of various carers who have enabled me to live something approaching a normal life.

A number of people have read drafts at various stages and made valuable comments; these include Carolyn Cahalane, Steve Cushion, David Drake, Jean-Numa Ducange, Annie Nehmad, Selim Nadi, George Paizis, Jim Wolfreys and Leo Zeilig.

Finally there was Bel Druce. Bel and I only met late in life – we were both in our seventies – but we became 'soulmates' in the true sense of that cliché. Bel read much that I wrote, including early drafts of some sections of this book, and gave me what a writer needs – sharp criticism combined with unreserved encouragement. I called her my Muse; she knew of my plans for this book, and I promised that it would be dedicated to her. She will never read it, but it is her book.

Ian Birchall

Abbreviations

AGTA   *Amicale Générale des Travailleurs Algériens* General Association of Algerian Workers [organised by FLN].

ALN   *Armée de Libération Nationale* National Liberation Army [military wing of FLN].

ARAC   *Association Républicaine des Anciens Combattants* Republican Association of Ex-Servicemen [ex-servicemen's association].

ATTAC   *Association pour la Taxation des Transactions financières et pour l'Action Citoyenne* Association for the Taxation of Financial Transactions and Citizens' Action [founded 1998].

BDIC   *Bibliothèque de Documentation Internationale Contemporaine* Library of International Contemporary Documentation [Nanterre].

CCI   *Comité Communiste Internationaliste pour la Construction de la IVe Internationale* Internationalist Communist Committee for the Construction of the Fourth International.

CDRN   *Comité de Défense de la Race Nègre* Committee for the Defence of the Negro Race [1926].

CERMTRI   *Centre d'Etudes et de Recherches sur les Mouvements Trotskyste et Révolutionnaires Internationaux* Centre for Study and Research on International Trotskyist and Revolutionary Movements [Paris].

CFTC   *Confédération Française des Travailleurs Chrétiens* French Confederation of Christian Workers [Catholic Trade-Union Federation].

CFDT   *Confédération Française Démocratique du Travail* French Democratic Confederation of Labour [founded 1964].

CGT   *Confédération Générale du Travail* General Confederation of Labour [founded 1895].

CGTU   *Confédération Générale du Travail Unitaire* Unitary General Confederation of Labour [1922–36].

CNT   *Confederación Nacional del Trabajo* National Confederation of Labour [Spain, founded 1910].

CRUA   *Comité Révolutionnaire d'Unité et d'Action* Revolutionary Committee of Unity and Action.

DST   Direction de la Surveillance du Territoire Directorate of Territorial Surveillance [1944–2008].

ENA   *Étoile Nord-Africaine* North African Star [1926–37].

FA   *Fédération Anarchiste* Anarchist Federation.

FCL   *Fédération Communiste Libertaire* Libertarian Communist Federation.

FIARI   *Fédération Internationale de l'Art Révolutionnaire Indépendant* International Federation of Independent Revolutionary Art [founded 1938].

FLN   *Front de Libération Nationale* National Liberation Front [Algeria, founded 1954].

FO   *Force Ouvrière* Workers' Strength [split from CGT 1948].

FTP-MOI   *Francs-Tireurs et Partisans Main d'Oeuvre Immigrée* Irregulars and Partisans Immigrant Labour Force.

FUA   *Front Universitaire Antifasciste* University Antifascist Front.

IFOP   *Institut Français d'Opinion Publique* French Institute of Public Opinion [polling organisation].

IFTU   *International Federation of Trade Unions* [1919–45 The Amsterdam International].

ITUCNW   *International Trade Union Committee of Negro Workers* [founded 1928].

IWMA   *The International Workingmen's Association* [The First International 1864–74].

JS   *Jeunesses Socialistes* Socialist Youth [SFIO youth organisation].

KPD   *Kommunistische Partei Deutschlands* Communist Party of Germany [founded 1919].

LCR   *Ligue Communiste Révolutionnaire* Revolutionary Communist League [Fourth International 1974–2009].

LDRN   *Ligue de Défense de la Race Nègre* League for the Defence of the Negro Race.

MLP   *Mouvement de Libération du Peuple* People's Liberation Movement [French Christian workers organisation].

MNA   *Mouvement National Algérien* Algerian National Movement [Algerian nationalist movement led by Messali Hadj, rival of FLN].

MOI   *Main d'Oeuvre Immigrée* Immigrant Labour Force.

MRP   *Mouvement Républicain Populaire* Popular Republican Movement [French Christian Democrats 1944–67].

MTLD   *Mouvement pour le Triomphe des Libertés Démocratiques* Mouvement for the Triumph of Democratic Freedoms [legal wing of the PPA].

NATO   *North Atlantic Treaty Organization* [founded 1949].

NPA   *Nouveau Parti Anticapitaliste* New Anticapitalist Party [founded 2009].

OAS   *Organisation Armée Secrète* Secret Army Organisation [against Algerian independence].

PCA   *Parti Communiste Algérien* Algerian Communist Party.

PCF   *Parti Communiste Français* French Communist Party [founded 1920].

PCI   *Parti Communiste Internationaliste* Internationalist Communist Party [Trotskyist: founded 1944].

POF   *Parti Ouvrier Français* French Workers' Party [founded 1880].

POI   *Parti Ouvrier Internationaliste* Internationalist Workers' Party [Trotskyist 1936–44].

POSR   *Parti Ouvrier Socialiste Révolutionnaire* Workers' Revolutionary Socialist Party [1890–1905].

POUM   *Partido Obrero de Unificación Marxista* Workers' Party of Marxist Unity [Spanish left anti-Stalinist party].

PPA   *Parti du Peuple Algérien* Algerian People's Party [founded 1937].

PS   *Parti Socialiste* Socialist Party [founded 1969].

PSA   *Parti Socialiste Autonome* Autonomous Socialist Party [founded 1958].

PSOP   *Parti Socialiste Ouvrier et Paysan* Workers' and Peasants' Socialist Party [1938–40].

PSU   *Parti Socialiste Unifié* United Socialist Party [founded 1960].

RDR   *Rassemblement Démocratique Révolutionnaire* Revolutionary Democratic Alliance [1948–9].

RILU   *Red International of Labour Unions* [1921–1937].

RPF   *Rassemblement du peuple français* Alliance of the French People [Gaullist, 1947–55].

SCALP   *Sections Carrément Anti-Le Pen* Solidly Anti-Le Pen Sections.

SFIO   *Section Française de l'Internationale Ouvrière* French Section of the Workers' International [French Socialist Party 1905–1971].

SouB   *Socialisme ou Barbarie* Socialism or Barbarism [1948–67].

SPD   *Sozialdemokratische Partei Deutschlands* Social Democratic Party of Germany [founded 1875].

STO   *Service du Travail Obligatoire* Compulsory Labour Service [1942–44].

SWP   *Socialist Workers Party* [Britain].

TPPS   *Toujours Prêts Pour Servir* Always Ready to Serve [founded 1935].

UDSR   *Union Démocratique et Socialiste de la Résistance* Democratic and Socialist Union of the Resistance [1945–1964].

UEC   *Union des Étudiants Communistes* Union of Communist Students.

UGS   *Union de la Gauche Socialiste* Union of the Socialist Left [founded 1957].

UGTA   *Union Générale des Travailleurs Algériens* General Association of Algerian Workers [FLN trade-union body].

UIC   *Union Inter-coloniale* Intercolonial Union.

UJRF   *Union des Jeunesses Républicaines de France* French Union of Republican Youth.

UKIP   *United Kingdom Independence Party* [founded 1993].

UNEF   *Union Nationale des Étudiants de France* French National Students' Union.

USA   *United States of America.*

USSR   *Union of Soviet Socialist Republics* [1922–91].

VE   *Victory in Europe* [VE Day 8 May 1945].

VO   *La Vie Ouvrière* Workers' Life [founded 1909].

VO   *Voix Ouvrière* Workers' Voice [founded 1956].

Some Key Dates

1871 March–May	Paris Commune.
1882 28 March	Ferry laws on education.
1885	Colonisation of Indochina.
1886 1 May	First May Day.
1889	Founding of Second International.
1891 1 May	Fourmies massacre.
1895 5 January	Dreyfus condemned.
1895	Founding of CGT.
1898 13 January	Zola *J'accuse*.
1905	Founding of SFIO.
1906	Amiens Charter.
1907 June	Troops used against vinegrowers.
1909 13 October	Execution of Ferrer.
1912 November	Basel Conference.
1914 3 August	Germany declares war on France.
1915 5–8 September	Zimmerwald Conference.
1917 March	Fall of Russian Tsar.
1917 May–June	French mutinies.
1917 6–7 November	Bolshevik Revolution.
1918 11 November	End of World War I.
1919	Black Sea mutinies.
1919 2 March	Founding of Communist International.
1919 28 June	Treaty of Versailles.
1920 September	Baku Congress of the Peoples of the East.
1920 December	Founding of French Communist Party.
1923	Occupation of Ruhr.
1924 21 January	Death of Lenin.
1924–25	Rif War.
1926	Founding of Étoile Nord-Africaine,
1927	Defeat of Chinese Revolution,
1928	Sixth Congress of Communist International – 'Third Period'.
1931 May–November	Colonial Exhibition in Paris.
1933 30 January	Hitler comes to power in Germany.
1936 4 June	Popular Front government.
1936 July	Beginning of Spanish Civil War.
1938 8 June	Founding of PSOP.

1938 September	Founding of Fourth International.
1939 1 April	Victory of Franco.
1939 23 August	Hitler-Stalin Pact.
1939 September	Outbreak of World War II.
1940 June–July	French surrender; formation of Vichy government.
1940 21 August	Murder of Trotsky.
1941 22 June	Germany invades Russia.
1944 August	Liberation of Paris.
1945 May	Sétif massacre.
1945 September	End of World War II.
1946 November	Bombardment of Haiphong.
1947 May	Renault strike – PCF ousted from government.
1947–48	Madagascan rising.
1949	Formation of NATO.
1954 May–June	Dien Bien Phu defeat – French withdraw from Indo-china.
1954 1 November	Beginning of Algerian War.
1956 October–November	British-French invasion of Egypt.
1956 October–November	Hungarian rising.
1958	Return of de Gaulle – Fifth Republic established.
1962 5 July	Algerian independence.
1968 May–June	General strike.

CHAPTER 1

The Myth of France

That something called 'France' exists may seem self-evident. Millions of people live there and it can easily be visited; it is clearly visible on the map and there are many thousands of books chronicling its history, society and culture. Millions have died defending France and the French 'national interest'. Yet defining a nation can be problematic. The obvious criteria – territory, race, language, culture – crumble under critical examination.

There is no difficulty locating French territory on the map; its inhabitants sometimes refer to it as the Hexagon. One might imagine that God himself had given France one of the primary geometrical shapes. In fact French territory acquired its present form only as the result of a long process. Alsace-Lorraine, the object of such passion on the part of French nationalists after its annexation by Germany in 1871, became French only in 1697; Lorraine had its own ruler, a duke, until 1766 and its legal and customs arrangements remained separate throughout the eighteenth century. Until 1870 the majority of the population spoke German – as do many in Alsace today.

Alsace and Lorraine returned to France at the end of the First World War. They had been under German rule for nearly fifty years. At the start of the war some 87 percent of the population saw German as their mother tongue, and it was estimated that four fifths of the population would have voted to remain German. During the war the German military authorities were harsh, and while a proportion of the population certainly welcomed the return of French rule, the French state did not leave its popularity to chance. In the immediate post-war period there were massive purges in Alsace and Lorraine. Identity cards based on ethnicity were used to strengthen that section of the population which wanted to be French. A system of prioritisation was established to identify reliable inhabitants and thousands had to attend hearings to face accusations of sympathy with Germany; some ended up in internment camps. About 200,000 Germans, some of whom had lived in Alsace or Lorraine for decades, were expelled or forced to leave. Education and language were at the centre of the French state's strategy. The French language was imposed in schools on a generation educated entirely in German; over 900 teachers were removed from their positions.[1]

---

1 Boswell 2000, pp. 119–52.

Algeria was for many years an integral part of French territory, though for most of that time the majority of its inhabitants did not have the rights of citizenship; only when it became clear that the long war to keep Algeria French was unwinnable did France withdraw within its European frontiers. Minor anomalies – Monaco, Andorra, the Channel Islands – exist to this day. In fact the territory of a nation state has no other basis than what it is able to secure – militarily, administratively and ideologically – at any particular moment. As a resolution of the 1908 congress of the CGT trade-union federation put it: 'In view of the fact that geographical frontiers can be modified at the whim of the possessing classes, workers recognise only economic frontiers, those separating the two enemy classes: the working class and the capitalist class'.[2] The enemy was not other nations but an international system.

Race is an even more slippery concept. French schoolchildren have been taught about 'Our ancestors the Gauls'. [The idea that today's French population are directly descended from the Gauls colonised by Julius Caesar's troops is satirised in the popular cartoon series *Astérix*.] The notion of unalloyed descent from the historical Gauls is scarcely plausible – as well as a large Celtic population in Brittany, Auvergne and elsewhere, France has absorbed successive waves of immigrants. If any inhabitant of France today could trace their parentage back for 500 years they would have over a million ancestors. Even the most ardent advocate of racial purity would discover that they had a rich mixture of bloods – racial purity is a superstition of the innumerate. When opponents of Jean-Marie Le Pen in 2002 chanted the slogan 'We are all the children of immigrants' they were proclaiming the literal truth.

In an important study, the historian Suzanne Citron produced a critical analysis of the 'national myth',[3] showing how an oversimplified version of French history has been taught in schools, omitting, for example, the mutinies of 1917 or the crimes of French colonialism, in order to legitimise the existing unitary nation state.

During the Nazi occupation of France the anti-Semitic authorities found it necessary to organise an exhibition to instruct people how to recognise Jews,[4] and they compelled Jews to wear yellow stars so that they might be recognised. The existence of race was central to the ideology of the Nazis and their French allies, yet such elaborate assistance was necessary to enable people to be aware of it.

---

2   Quoted by Rosmer 1936, p. 27.
3   Citron 2019.
4   Walter 1960, p. 181.

Nor is the French language a unifying factor. It was, until the time of the French Revolution, a pool of mutually unintelligible dialects. Literary French, the language of classical playwrights like Racine and Molière, was a dialect of educated Parisians, incomprehensible to the mass of the French population. Before the Revolution only a minority of the population spoke anything recognisable as French. At the end of the eighteenth century, out of a population of 24 million, only 12 million spoke French at all, and only a quarter of them spoke it 'correctly'.[5]

Even in the twentieth century a French writer writing in a language other than French won the Nobel Prize for Literature – Frédéric Mistral, the great Provençal poet. In 1905 the syndicalist Griffuelhes poured scorn on the definition of nation by language:

> Do they claim that differences in manners and language justify the existence of homelands? But in France the manners of the North are not those of the South or of Brittany; the language of the South is not that of the North, or of Brittany. There are still many Southerners and Bretons who can't speak French.[6]

Even in the early twenty-first century there are 1.5 million speakers of Occitan and 0.5 million of Alsatian [a German dialect]. It is the state which imposes the French language. Thus Breton parents recently had to fight a two-year legal battle for the right to spell their child's name with a tilde [a diacritical mark used in Breton but not in French].[7]

Only with the arrival of radio and television did a single language begin to be imposed on the French population – but paradoxically this also meant the increasing exposure of French citizens to external cultures. Despite efforts to banish *franglais*, the French are constantly subjected to such messages as 'le hot dog' or 'à Burgerking, avec chaque menu enfant, un gadget tortue Ninja'. When Beatle George Harrison died in 2001, the daily paper *Libération* [assuming its target audience would get the point] headlined in English: 'George in the sky with Lennon', a reference to *Lucy in the Sky with Diamonds*.[8] And within the French language there are many different variants, corresponding to different individuals and groups, including the versions of French spoken by those with other first languages.

---

5   Balibar and Laporte 1974, pp. 31–2.
6   Griffuelhes 1905.
7   Agence France-Presse 2019.
8   *Libération*, 1 December 2001.

If language is problematic as a criterion, culture is even more so. The ambiguity of the term's meaning – stretching from aesthetic production to a whole way of life – is notorious. There is no nation in which peasants and factory-workers, bankers and beggars share a way of life – nor is there one in which they read the same books.

The plays of Racine, recognised as one of the peaks of French culture, reached an audience of no more than 20,000 in a population of 20 million.[9] Even after the advent of universal education, the average worker or peasant might know a few phrases from Molière and Victor Hugo, but little more. A genuinely shared culture arrived only with radio and television, but at the same time this inducted France into a cosmopolitan culture. Despite the achievements of French directors, a substantial proportion of films showing in Paris at any given time are dubbed or subtitled versions of English-language movies. The twentieth century has seen practices that were previously limited to one nation or even one locality become part of an international way of life. When Daniel Guérin visited Naples in 1923 he was introduced to a local delicacy unknown even in Rome – a pizza![10]

Nations do not arise spontaneously from some pre-existing national identity. On the contrary, national identity is imposed, not natural. The nation states of the modern world and the nationalist consciousness which maintains them are the product of hard political work. Nationalism is to a considerable extent the product of the state machine [though nationalism is also sometimes invoked by the oppressed seeking liberation from those same state machines]. As Neil Davidson argued: 'National*ism* is a more-or-less active participation in the political mobilization of a social group for the construction *or* defense of a state'.[11]

The creation of the French nation was the result of a long process extending over several centuries. Louis XIV and his ministers established a centralised state on the principle of 'One king, one faith, one law'. Efforts were made to develop a national culture, albeit one accessible only to a small minority. The Académie française became the arbiter of correctness in the standard version of the French language.

The crucial turning-point was the Revolution of 1789. This was a world historical moment of social emancipation, opening up the possibility of a world based on liberty, equality and fraternity rather than on authority and hereditary power. It was a profoundly contradictory process, involving struggle between

---

9   Lough 1979, p. 97.
10   Guérin 1964, p. 153.
11   Davidson 2016.

different social layers. As Alex Callinicos has observed, since then there has been a 'process of permanent revolution in which a succession of new political subjects – workers, slaves, women, colonial subjects, people of colour, oppressed nationalities, lesbians and gays, disabled people ... emerge to stake their claim to the liberty and equality won by earlier struggles'.[12] The Revolution proclaimed the 'Rights of Man', but these did not extend to French women, who only got full rights of citizenship over 150 years later. The right to vote for men was limited to those wealthy enough to pay taxes; only the Constitution of 1793 – never implemented – accepted the principle of universal male suffrage.

Before the Revolution the term *patrie* [homeland] could simply refer to the particular territory where an individual had been born;[13] after 1789 it came to mean the revolutionary nation. A 'patriot' was one who supported the Revolution and the nation state that embodied its gains; the patriots were people of the left, not of the right. As late as 1893 Engels was finding it necessary to explain to French Marxist Paul Lafargue why he, unlike others on the left, refused to use the term patriot: 'That word has a limited meaning – or else such a vague one, depending on circumstances – that for my part I should never dare to apply that title to myself'.[14]

The tricolour and the *Marseillaise* have continued to be presented as the symbols of the Revolution of 1789. As historian Maurice Dommanget has shown, there was a parallel history, that of the red flag, which over two centuries and more represented an internationalist alternative to the nationalism of the tricolour.

> But in the country which gave birth to the red flag and gave it its internationalist character, there are still implacable veterans or young people overflowing with enthusiasm who see it as an atrocity to combine it with the tricolour. They recognise only one banner which symbolises together Socialism, labour, the liberation of the working class, the fraternity of peoples, and the redemption of humanity together with the glorious series of class battles written by history in its folds: and that is the red flag.[15]

The Jacobin faction embodied the radical wing of the Revolution. As the ideology of the artisan class, it was socially radical, defending small property and in

<hr>

12   Callinicos 2000, p. 24.
13   Hobsbawm 1990, p. 90.
14   Letter of 27 June 1893 to Paul Lafargue; Engels 2004, p. 157.
15   Dommanget 2006, pp. 488–9.

favour of an equitable division of wealth. It was vigorously anticlerical, seeing the church as the traditional ally of the rich and powerful. Since Jacobinism was formed in the course of the revolutionary wars, it was necessarily nationalistic. The Jacobin tradition would remain hegemonic over the French left for the next two centuries.

During the Revolution stronger measures than an Academy were used against the luckless speakers of German, Breton and other non-French languages. A decree of 20 July 1794 established what has become known as the 'linguistic terror'. This declared among other things that any public official who issued a document in a language other than French would be sentenced to six months' imprisonment. The Jacobins of Alsace were forbidden to hold meetings in German, although that was their native language.[16]

In terms of nation-building Napoleon carried forward the achievements of the Revolution. He and his administrators built a centralised state machine; the Code Napoléon simplified and structured the legal system, eliminating relics from earlier times. A centralised education system laid the basis for future developments.

It was one thing to establish a centralised nation state, quite another to create a sense of national identity in the population. The task of instilling patriotism into the peasantry who composed most of the French population in the nineteenth century was a long and difficult one.

Official figures as late as 1853 showed that nearly a quarter of the French population spoke no French. Eugen Weber, in his book *Peasants into Frenchmen*, has shown the processes of transformation which ensured that in 1914 France was able to effectively mobilise a substantially peasant army. In 1900 45 percent of the French working population were farmers and peasants, and as late as 1930 the figure was still 35 percent.[17]

The question of the army was vital. In 1848 and 1871 it was peasant soldiers who had suppressed risings by Paris workers. In the succeeding decades the army was used repeatedly against strikers. Among the peasantry any sense of national identity was decidedly weak. Peasants identified with their village or their province far more than they did with the French nation. From Brittany to Provence many peasants spoke languages or *patois* other than French; official figures from 1863 show that up to a quarter of the population spoke no French.[18] Theodore Zeldin recounts:

16　　Balibar and Laporte 1974, pp. 96–8.
17　　Weber 1979, pp. 67–8.
18　　Weber 1979, pp. 67–94.

In 1864, an inspector of education, touring in the mountains of the Lozère, asked the children at a village school: 'In what country is the Lozère situated?' Not a single pupil knew the answer. 'Are you English or Russian?' he demanded. They could not say. This was in one of the remoter parts of France, but the incident illustrates how Frenchmen only gradually became aware of what it was that distinguished them from other men.[19]

Central to this process was the establishment of compulsory secular primary education in 1882; the basic principle of this was *laïcité* [secularism], which became, and remains, essential to the ideology of French nationalism [see Chapter 3]. Thus a major theme of Jules Ferry's educational reforms in the 1880s was strengthening the sense of French identity. The moral and civic education which replaced religious instruction gave considerable importance to instilling ideas of patriotism and national identity. In many other countries, in Europe and elsewhere, the state coexisted with religion, the two reinforcing each other. But in the particular circumstances of France, with its history of revolutions, republican rule had to assert its independence of the church.

In the 1920s, with the founding of the French Communist Party [PCF], it briefly appeared that a section of the French left had broken with republican imperialist ideology. By the time of the Popular Front of the 1930s the PCF had reverted to the republican family. The Popular Front found its symbolism in the tricolour and the *Marseillaise*, not the red flag and the *Internationale*. During the German occupation [1940–44] national independence became a major theme for the PCF.

1945 saw the establishment of a new world order, which would last until 1989, in which international politics was dominated by the confrontation between the USA and the USSR. It was the beginning of the end for the colonial empires of Europe, which had largely disappeared within 20 years. Before 1940 the French Empire had covered nearly one tenth of the world's land area, and 5 per cent of the world's population.

France desperately attempted to cling onto its imperial possessions; the result was two extended and blood-soaked wars, in Indochina and Algeria [see chapters 10 and 11]. The principal factor that shaped French political choices after 1945 was the republican tradition which dominated French political thinking, especially on the left. This easily accommodated the notion that France's role in the world was a progressive one, bringing enlightenment to

---

19   Zeldin 1980, p. 3.

more benighted territories, the so-called 'civilising mission'. This was a non-sense. In 1830, before French colonisation, Algeria had a higher literacy rate than France.[20]

As Gilles Martinet argued, many Socialist Party supporters refused to recognise the legitimacy of the Algerian demand for independence because they believed that nothing was superior to being a citizen of the Republic, and that an African could hope for nothing better than to become simply French.[21]

After 1962 France was finished as a colonial power. Yet France's imperial past continued to haunt it, and nationalist republicanism was still at the heart of the ideology of France's ruling class. Only in 1999 was it officially acknowledged that there had been a 'war' in Algeria.

'Republican values' and in particular *laïcité* continue to be seen as part of the heritage of the left, even of the far left. For a long time *laïcité* has been a diversion; appeals to the tradition of eighteenth-century philosopher Voltaire are wholly inappropriate. In Voltaire's day the church was the ally of a highly repressive state; blasphemers could face the death penalty. In more recent times it can scarcely be seen as the main enemy. While freeing education from church control was undoubtedly progress, the way in which *laïcité* replaced religious values with nationalist ones merely introduced new forms of oppression.

In recent decades *laïcité* has found a new target. France now has a substantial Muslim population. These are not some alien invaders. Some are Algerian workers who came to France in the 1950s, when Algeria was an integral part of French territory; many more are their children and grandchildren. Increasingly Muslims have been demonised. That such Islamophobia should emanate from the far right is scarcely surprising. What is more alarming is that similar attacks are frequently heard from the political left.

Islamophobia is not unique to France, but it has taken a particularly virulent form in France, precisely because it comes not only from the right, but also from the left in the name of secularism. Any manifestation of Muslim culture, notably in the form of female dress conventions, is seen as a challenge to the authority of the republic.

Muslims are believed to have a dangerously divided loyalty; the parallel with attitudes to Jews in the late nineteenth century is obvious. *Laïcité* becomes an insistence that there must be no ideological rivals to the authority of the republican state. In recent years *laïcité* has served as a justification for a variety of things – ranging from banning headscarf-wearing mothers from accompany-

---

20   Ruedy 1992, pp. 103 ff.
21   Martinet 1962, p. 140.

ing their primary-school children on school outings to telling Muslim – and Jewish – schoolchildren that they must eat pork or go hungry.[22]

Laïcité is not just a value inside people's skulls; it has a very material embodiment in the French educational system. In France today around a quarter of the population are involved in the education system, as students or employees.[23]

In 2015 France suffered two horrific terrorist outrages. In January twelve people, mostly members of the editorial team of the satirical publication *Charlie Hebdo*, were murdered in the magazine's offices. In November over a hundred people were killed in random attacks. The response of France's rulers was to invoke 'republican values'.[24]

France has a long record as a brutal imperialist power, and that record should not be forgotten. It is necessary to analyse and understand the ideology through which that brutality was exercised. Republican values, especially *laïcité*, have been inextricably linked to French imperialism for over a century. That history needs to be demystified, which means rediscovering the voices of the minority who, even in the most difficult times, resisted the lure of republican nationalism and argued for internationalism. It is to that rediscovery that this book is devoted.

---

22   Chrisafis 2015.

23   See statistics at http://www.education.gouv.fr/cid57096/reperes-et-references-statistique s.html.

24   See Wolfreys 2015.

Precursors

When the French trade-union confederation, the Confédération Générale du Travail [CGT] published its antimilitarist pamphlet *The New Soldier's Manual*[1] in 1902 [see Chapter 5] it included quotations from writers going back to the fourth century CE. The aim was to show that antimilitarism had a long history. The proletarian internationalism that flourished from the beginning of the twentieth century had many precursors.

France's development as a nation state coincided with a period of expansion of trade and commerce, and increasing contact with the non-European world, notably the American continent. The result of such contact with other cultures was to encourage a spirit of relativism, of recognising that French, and indeed Christian, civilisation was not necessarily superior. As Pascal was to put it, 'truth this side of the Pyrenees, falsehood the other'.[2]

One of the earliest manifestations of this new sense of relativism was Montaigne's essay on *Cannibals* [1580], where he gave an account of what was known of non-European peoples [the alleged cannibals]. He used the existence of alternative patterns of civilisation as a basis for criticism of the assumptions of his own society; he noted that native Americans visiting Europe could not understand how the poor, in face of the huge differences in wealth that existed, 'could tolerate such injustice without taking the others by the throat or burning down their houses'.[3]

In the eighteenth century most peasants never travelled more than a few miles from their native village – unless they were drawn into the army, their one opportunity to visit foreign lands. The privileged classes and their intellectual hangers-on travelled widely; it was among intellectuals that the first notions of internationalism emerged.

Voltaire, the most influential thinker of the Enlightenment, was no revolutionary; he maintained a friendship with king Frederick the Great of Prussia. Yet he made sharp criticisms of many of the dominant ideas of his age, and envisaged a world that would be more rational and humane. His version of internationalism was a simple one. He saw the best hopes of human progress as lying in free trade, and recognised that this could not function if obstructed

---

1   Fédération des bourses du travail 1902.
2   Pascal 1964, p. 151.
3   Montaigne 1580.

by barriers of faith, race or nation. He took the London Stock Exchange as an instance of how trade led to the establishment of human fraternity:

> Go into the London Stock Exchange, a more respectable place than many courts; you will see assembled the representatives of all nations for the utility of men. There the Jew, the Muslim and the Christian trade with each other as if they were of the same religion, and they apply the term infidel only to those who go bankrupt; there the Presbyterian trusts the Anabaptist and the Anglican accepts the Quaker's promise.[4]

Voltaire understood that those excluded from the rights of property could hardly be expected to show loyalty to a national entity. In the article *Patrie* [Homeland] of his *Philosophical Dictionary* he recounted the following anecdote:

> A young pastry-cook's boy, who had been at college and still knew a few phrases of Cicero, was one day affecting to love his homeland. 'What do you mean by your homeland?' asked his neighbour; 'is it your oven? is it the village where you were born, and which you have never seen again? is it the street where your mother and father lived, who are ruined now, and who have left you reduced to putting little pies in an oven to earn your living?' ... The pastry-cook's boy didn't know what to say. A thinker who was listening to this conversation concluded that in any reasonably sized country there must be several million men who have no homeland.[5]

Here Voltaire seems to anticipate the claim by Marx and Engels that 'the working men have no country. We cannot take from them what they have not got'.[6]

In 1789 revolutionary nationalism adopted the language of internationalism; France claimed to be spreading the gains of the Revolution to the oppressed of all lands, with the slogan [coined by Sébastien-Roch Nicolas de Chamfort] 'War on the castles, peace to the cottages'. There was a continuing contradiction between the notion of the Revolution as an essentially French event, establishing the French nation on a new basis, and the idea that the French nation was the agency of universal emancipation, bearing the principles of liberty and equality throughout the earth. So the French Revolution contained within itself

---

4   Voltaire 1964, p. 29.
5   Voltaire 1961, p. 594.
6   Marx and Engels 1976, p. 502.

both the notion of the 'civilising mission' – later to be used to justify the worst crimes of French colonialism – and the seeds of revolutionary internationalism.

The decision by the revolutionary government in 1794 to emancipate slaves in the French colonies was more complex than it might appear at first sight. The decision had been prepared by pre-Revolutionary critics of slavery like the *abbé* Raynal, and later by the anti-slavery *Amis des Noirs* [friends of the Blacks]. While motivated by an Enlightenment ideal of human equality, they were also concerned to preserve France's colonial possessions; as Robin Blackburn has pointed out, Raynal was 'concerned that huge aggregations of plantations of slaves endangered the colonial order ... he was not sympathetic to colonial independence'.[7] Only after the slaves took things into their own hands with the 1791 rising in Saint-Domingue was slavery legally abolished. In the Caribbean black slaves saw the demand for liberty and equality as applying to them too and the revolt of Toussaint L'Ouverture marked the first stage of a movement which would lead to the abolition of slavery and to the struggle for black emancipation. Slavery was re-established in 1802. A group of black students who had been admitted to the École Polytechnique were excluded, despite a declaration by the remaining students that they would always see them as brothers.[8]

As early as 1789 Gracchus Babeuf, later to lead the Conspiracy of the Equals, rejected the whole idea of European superiority implicit in colonialism. He argued that it was Europe which had transmitted into a previously innocent hemisphere the terrible vices which had degraded its own society.[9] Babeuf's followers argued that in a society based on true equality there would be no drive to war and conquest.[10]

Babeuf had never visited the French colonies. One of the other leaders of the Conspiracy of the Equals, Robert-François Debon, had more direct experience. Born in Caen around 1755, he had difficulty finding suitable employment, and in 1779 went to England where he worked as a teacher. In 1787 he went to the French colony of Saint-Domingue, where he worked for two years. In the colony there were over 400,000 slaves, ruled by a white population of some 30,000. In his brief account of his life Debon did not explicitly mention slavery, but Saint-Domingue was entirely based on slave labour. He simply described it as a 'hell of the living'.

---

7   Blackburn 1988, p. 170. For an analysis of the question in general, see Blackburn 1988, pp. 167–81, 191–5.

8   Alexandre-Debray 1983, p. 47, citing Holcroft 1802.

9   Daline, Saitta and Soboul 1977, p. 206.

10   Buonarroti 1957, Volume I, p. 176.

When invited to continue working there he responded that 'to become rich one had to become hard, unjust and cruel'. He moved to New Orleans and travelled in the United States, where he met native Americans who welcomed him. In 1791 he went to London where he defended the principles of the Revolution and expressed support for the execution of the French king. Returning to France, he joined Babeuf's movement; we can only imagine what parallels he may have seen between colonial slavery and the oppression of the poor in France.[11]

One militant who emerged in the new radical societies, over which Babeuf's comrade Philippe Buonarroti exercised a significant influence until his death in 1837, was Théophile Joachim René Guillard de Kersausie.[12] Born into an aristocratic family, in the 1820s he became a member of the *carbonari*, an Italian-based network of clandestine revolutionary organisations.

In 1834–35 Kersausie and François-Vincent Raspail [another member of the *carbonari*] published a journal called *Le Réformateur*, which was exceptional on the left in defending the independence of Belgium – Belgium had become independent in 1830, but most of the republican left in France wanted it to be re-annexed. They were almost unique in asserting the right of self-determination, arguing that those Belgians who spoke French had as much right to remain Belgian as those Alsatians who spoke German had to remain French. It was Belgium which must be consulted first of all on its own future.[13] Kersausie left France and involved himself in various struggles for national rights. He supported Polish independence and presented the Italian republican Garibaldi with the sword of honour belonging to his great uncle La Tour d'Auvergne.[14]

In the period after 1830 there was considerable enthusiasm for the national aspirations of the oppressed nations of Europe – Greece and above all Poland; between 1772 and 1795 Poland was carved up between Russia, Prussia and Austria and ceased to exist as an independent state. The popularity of the Polish cause owed something both to humanitarianism and to the presence of Polish exiles in France. Among the unemployed workers of Paris it had a more material basis. They knew that war meant jobs – through recruitment to the army and through orders for military supplies.[15]

---

11   Schiappa 1990.
12   For a full account see Birchall 2002.
13   *Le Réformateur*, 10 November 1834, quoted by Darriulat 2001, pp. 36–7.
14   Trévédy 1906, pp. 243–4.
15   Faure 1974, p. 74.

The *carbonari* operated in Italy, France and to some extent in Germany, and carried forward the traditions of Babeuf. It was in Lyon that the most significant developments took place. There had been German printworkers in the city from the sixteenth century onwards, and in the seventeenth and eighteenth there were many foreign workers. The city developed a tradition of cosmopolitanism, and was effectively the birthplace of proletarian internationalism. The *carbonari* had been active in Lyon, seeking, among other things, to use it as a base for sparking off a rising in Piedmont. The city had seen considerable activity by the followers of the utopian socialist Claude-Henri de Saint-Simon during the 1820s, and their notions of universal fraternity had begun to enter into the consciousness of a section of the working class. The silk-workers [*canuts*] of Lyon depended on silk from Tonkin in Indochina.

Between 1831 and 1834 struggles by the silk-workers rose to the level of strike and insurrection. In 1834 soldiers sent to control the situation fraternised with workers.[16] One expression of the rapid development of working-class political awareness was the launching of a working-class newspaper, *L'Echo de la Fabrique* [the echo of the factory]. A major contributor was François Arlès-Dufour; a follower of Saint-Simon, he was far from revolutionary, and urged co-operation between workers and employers. He also advocated a European federation based on the alliance of England, France and Germany.[17] On 27 May 1832 Arlès-Dufour contributed to *L'Echo de la Fabrique* an address to English workers, urging them to remain united and organised, since they and French workers shared the same enemies.[18]

The same issue contained an article by Antoine Vidal, another Saint-Simonian, arguing for international fraternity. His reasoning reflected Enlightenment optimism; he believed that industry, by uniting employers and employed, would break down national barriers and prejudices. He argued that anyone obliged to earn their living by hard labour could not see as enemies those who suffered the same condition, just because they were born in a different country. They were all *industriels*; the Saint-Simonian term *industriel* meant one engaged in production, whether employer or worker. They should therefore seek the association of peoples and reject the rivalries of nations, for it was the blood of workers that was shed in wars.[19] In September 1840 the French Christian Socialist newspaper *L'Atelier* [the workshop] reported what

---

16   Bruhat 1952, pp. 256–7.
17   See Jeanmichel 1993.
18   Rude 1982, p. 108.
19   Rude 1982, pp. 108–9.

was probably the first financial contribution from British workers in support of a foreign strike; English tailors sent a small sum of money to their fellow-workers in Paris.[20]

In 1839 the *Travailleurs égalitaires* [egalitarian workers] included in their membership ritual the claim that they recognised no frontiers and no *patrie*, that all communists were their brothers and all aristocrats their enemies.[21] The workers' paper *La Fraternité de 1845* [fraternity of 1845] protested at the expulsion of German asylum seekers from France, including one Karl Marx.[22]

In sharp contrast to William Wilberforce in Britain, who was conservative and indeed anti-working class,[23] the leading anti-slavery campaigner in France, Victor Schoelcher, described himself as a socialist, and argued that 'the extinction of slavery and reform of the proletariat are sisters'.[24] In 1844 he organised an anti-slavery petition signed by over 3000 working men and women in Paris.[25] In his election address of 1848, he wrote of:

> ... the emancipation of our brothers, black men, members of the race which monarchical governments put into slavery, and which the republic will soon liberate. This task has not, however, been exclusive for me, and has never prevented me from thinking of my white brothers; since I was first old enough to do so, I have worked to defend the interests of the poor, the proletarians, the labouring classes and the oppressed.[26]

In 1848 one of the first acts of the Provisional Government established after the overthrow of the monarchy was to abolish slavery, this time definitively; Schoelcher became President of the Commission on Slavery. However it was the activity of the slaves themselves which made the decision irreversible; as Robin Blackburn records: 'Slaves simply abandoned the plantations and groups of slaves were seen everywhere discussing the situation. The slave order was simply decomposing as blacks took their fate into their own hands'. This was before news of the detailed decree emancipating slaves had reached the West Indies.[27] In August 1848 elections with universal male suffrage, in which

---

20   Collins and Abramsky 1965, p. 6.

21   Maillard 1999, p. 315.

22   Maillard 1999, pp. 95–6.

23   Blackburn 1988, p. 151.

24   Letter of October 1843, Alexandre-Debray 1983, p. 106.

25   Martin 1948, pp. 41–2.

26   Alexandre-Debray 2006, p. 138.

27   Blackburn 1988, p. 498.

all races voted, were held in the French colonies. Schoelcher, elected in both Guadeloupe and Martinique, withdrew in Guadeloupe in order that a black deputy should sit in the National Assembly. However in 1849 the National Assembly, with Schoelcher's support, voted substantial compensation for former slave-owners, worth around half the price of their slaves.[28] There was no compensation for the slaves themselves.

While Schoelcher was undoubtedly a genuine radical reformer, who saw colonial slaves and French workers as having common interests, it is important to distinguish between Schoelcher himself, and the myth which has been constructed around him in more recent years. French republicanism created a cult of Schoelcher; roads were named after him and statues erected. As Pierre Jean-Christophe put it, 'The cult of Schoelcher was accompanied by total ignorance of the major facts of the slaves' struggle. The aim was to make people believe that the blacks owed their freedom to a white man because they would have been incapable of winning it for themselves'.[29]

As Françoise Vergès has concluded: 'Schoelcher was neither a slave trader nor a slave owner and was behind the decree making the abolition of slavery in the French colonies final and definitive. [But he] represents a past that offered absolutely no repair for the crimes, damages and wounds of the slaves and that facilitated and justified post-slavery colonisation'.

In the years before the 1848 revolution Paris had become a home for many political exiles, and the 1840s saw the foundation of a number of clubs of émigrés from various countries – Poles, Germans and Italians. Many Parisian workers had direct contact with exiles and became sympathetic to their cause. In 1848 thousands of Parisian workers were prepared to demonstrate in defence of the national interests of the Poles. Internationalism had taken to the streets. If the minorities, in the clubs and secret societies and small workers' newspapers, had not been campaigning on the question of Poland over the previous two decades, then the Polish question would not have acquired the significance it did in 1848.

Inspired by the memory of 1793, when war had pushed the government into taking more radical social measures at home, radical activists believed that the question of Poland was inextricably linked to the direction the regime was taking on domestic issues. If the Provisional Government formed in 1848 was prepared to help Poland, then it could also be expected to take radical measures in favour of the unemployed and for the redistribution of wealth; if, on

----

28   Blackburn 1988, p. 501.
29   Jean-Christophe 2020.

the other hand, the Provisional Government was willing to let the question of Poland drop, it would probably renege on its promises with regard to social questions.

Things came to a head on 15 May. The radical clubs organised a petition to the National Assembly calling for military intervention against Russia in defence of Polish national independence. They were supported by a massive demonstration, perhaps as many as 50,000, led by representatives of the Polish émigrés in Paris, and supported by thousands of unemployed workers from the National Workshops. A rising in occupied Poland had just been bloodily suppressed by Prussian troops, and feelings were high. This appealed to those elements in the working class who tended to take a lead from the most radical republicans, such as Auguste Blanqui. From the 1830s until his death in 1881, Blanqui was the best-known and most influential of the radical republicans, committed to egalitarianism and the building of clandestine organisations. That he was perceived as a serious threat was confirmed by the fact that he spent over half his adult life in jail.

The demonstrators invaded the National Assembly. The leaders who made speeches directly linked Poland to the progress of the revolution.[30] Radical leaders, including Blanqui and Armand Barbès [a republican activist involved in secret societies before 1848], were arrested and the left was beheaded politically.[31]

A few weeks later, when the government closed the National Workshops for the unemployed and then shot down workers who protested at their closure, it was clear that the left leaders had been right to link Poland to the progress of the revolution. The French bourgeoisie did not intend to go to war in support of the oppressed nations of Europe.

In 1850 London typefounders went on strike. The employers sought to recruit substitute labour in Paris. The London trade unions received the following message from the organisation of Parisian typefounders:

The Founderie [*sic*] Typographique Française, recognising that in all the countries of the world the maintenance of wages is a question of primordial principle, seeing that it is the integral maintenance of our property, declares that it will refuse all concurrence, and will accept of no propositions, however advantageous they may be, proceeding from master founders of foreign countries, which may tend to bring about a com-

---

30   Agulhon 1975, pp. 143–5.
31   See Guillemin 1967, pp. 340–52.

petition to the injury of their fellow workmen, especially as regards the acceptance of work at a reduced scale of wages.[32]

In the early 1860s links were made between British, French and German workers – gas-workers, building workers, tailors – to prevent strike-breaking and provide financial support for strikes. In the London building workers' strike of 1861 the sum of £5.18.0 – perhaps £700 at today's prices – was received from France; a small sum, but one which had considerable political importance as a symbol of international solidarity.

In 1864 a number of working-class organisations of varying political alignments formed the International Workingmen's Association [IWMA, later known as the First International]. During the Paris bronze workers' strike of 1867 the IWMA persuaded the London Trades Council to help organise the reception of a delegation of French trade unionists who came to London and visited the executives of about twenty unions. A financial donation from English workers led the employers to retreat.[33] In the same year London tailors sent a donation of £200 to striking Parisian tailors with an assurance that 'no London house would be allowed to execute work for Paris houses'. The strike was won.[34]

The IWMA was primarily a European organisation, but it set its sights beyond Europe. Paul Lafargue, Marx's son-in-law, was of mixed white, mulatto and Jewish descent; he was the only black member of the General Council of the IWMA, and was seen as a symbolic representative of black workers, for example writing an article on slavery in the USA.[35]

The International could not ignore the growing threat of war in Europe. The 1868 Brussels Conference passed a resolution urging strike action to prevent war:

> ... therefore the people can henceforward lessen the frequency of war by opposing those who make war or declare war; That this right belongs especially to the working classes, who are almost exclusively subject to military service, and that they alone can give it a sanction; ... The Congress urges the workers to cease work should war break out in their respective countries.[36]

---

32   *Red Republican*, 17 August 1850.
33   Fribourg 1871, p. 101.
34   Collins and Abramsky 1965, pp. 83–4.
35   Lafargue 1970, p. 20.
36   Palme Dutt 1964, p. 70.

When war with Prussia became imminent in the summer of 1870, most of the population rallied to support their own nation. But the internationalist current was not completely drowned out. On 12 June a number of leading working-class militants published an anti-war address to their 'brothers in Germany', saying that war was 'the awakening of savage instincts and national hatreds'.[37]

On 15 July, just before the declaration of war, a small anti-war demonstration of perhaps 200 to 300 people was held in Paris.[38] Jules Vallès, who took part, stresses the hostility it encountered:

> I was nearly murdered at a street corner, by a handful of warmongers in whose presence I had screamed my horror of war. They called me a Prussian and would probably have strung me up if I hadn't told them my name ... We took strips of cloth on which we had written with a stick of wood dipped in a cup of ink: 'Long live Peace', and we marched with them through the streets of Paris. Passers-by attacked us.[39]

Vallès later noted that this was the moment at which he moved beyond the rhetoric of the *Marseillaise*: 'It horrifies me, your *Marseillaise* of today! It has become a State anthem. Instead of inspiring volunteers, it leads herds'.[40]

Prussian success led to the fall of emperor Napoleon III. French rule now faced a challenge in Martinique, with a rising by thousands of insurgents who set plantations on fire; it was brutally repressed; the newly established republic was continuing the colonialism of the empire.[41]

In the elections of February 1871 some workers' clubs nominated as a candidate Wilhelm Liebknecht, the German socialist – an internationalist gesture at a time when Prussian troops were besieging the city.[42] As French troops arrived in Montmartre, local people, especially the women, fraternised, offering them breakfast and wine. When soldiers were ordered to fire into the crowd they refused. Paris declared itself an independent state, the Paris Commune. For just over two months a revolutionary government held power and began to introduce measures in the interests of the working class.

A generous internationalism was displayed by the *communards*. Foreigners and exiles were welcomed: a Hungarian goldsmith who had travelled around

---

37 Rabaut 1975, p. 15.
38 Guillemin 1956, p. 103.
39 Vallès 1964, pp. 200–1.
40 Vallès 1964, p. 203.
41 Couti 2021.
42 Lissagaray 1970, p. 80.

Europe to improve his skills, Léo Frankel, was elected to the Commune and became a member of its labour and finance commissions;[43] a Pole, Jaroslaw Dombrowski, was appointed a general and died defending the Commune. Walery Wroblewski, a veteran of the Polish rising of 1863, was also a general who organised the defence of southern Paris.

Despite the efforts of the *communards*, the rising remained confined to Paris; communes in other French cities lasted only for a few days. Yet the events made an impact internationally, and there were expressions of support from socialists, anarchists and republicans in Britain and elsewhere.

Though the Commune was crushed by the end of May it remained an inspiration to a new generation. One expression was the *Internationale*, composed by a *communard*, Eugène Pottier, while in hiding after the defeat.[44] The fifth stanza, doubtless inspired by the events of 18 March, was sharply antimilitarist:

> Les rois nous soûlaient de fumées,
> Paix entre nous, guerre aux tyrans!
> Appliquons la grève aux armées,
> Crosse en l'air et rompons les rangs!
> S'ils s'obstinent, ces cannibales,
> A faire de nous des héros,
> Ils sauront bientôt que nos balles
> Sont pour nos propres généraux.[45]

> No more deluded by reaction
> On tyrants only we'll make war!
> The soldiers too will take strike action
> They'll break ranks and fight no more!
> And if those cannibals keep trying
> To sacrifice us to their pride,
> They soon shall hear the bullets flying
> We'll shoot the generals on our own side.

For those like Vallès, disgusted by what the *Marseillaise* had become, there was now an alternative

---

43   See Chuzeville 2021.
44   See Dommanget 1971.
45   Pottier 1966, p. 101.

Laïcité and Its Critics

The crushing of the Commune was a massive defeat for the left. The following decades saw a regrouping of the socialist movement, and also important developments for republican nationalism.

The surviving *communards* had been scattered around the world as they went into exile. Gustave Courbet, the painter, had proposed the demolition of the Vendôme Column, erected by Napoleon I to honour French military victories, and which he had earlier described as 'a monument ... tending to perpetuate by its expression the ideas of war and conquest of the past imperial dynasty, which are condemned by a republican nation's sentiment'.[1] Now he was jailed for six months. He went into exile in Switzerland to escape having to pay personally for the rebuilding of the Vendôme Column, and died in 1877 without seeing France again.

Louise Michel, who fought with the *communards* in their last stand in the Montmartre cemetery, was deported to New Caledonia in the South Pacific, where she remained for seven years. She was one among a minority of the deported *communards* who supported the 1878 rising by indigenous Kanaks.

Jules Vallès, revolutionary journalist – his *Le Cri du Peuple* was the most widely read daily paper of the Commune – was sentenced to death in his absence, and spent the following decade in exile in London and Brussels, much of it in poverty.

Eugène Pottier, author of the *Internationale*, was condemned to death in his absence; in 1873 he went to Boston in the USA, where he worked as a draughtsman and as a French teacher. In 1880 he returned to Paris, where he died in 1887. Ten thousand people attended the funeral – the police attacked the procession to grab a red flag carried by one of the demonstrators.

The *communards* had been crushed, but they had continued their struggle, in various forms and in different parts of the world. When, after a campaign by radical republicans, an amnesty was declared in 1880, the survivors were ready to encourage a new generation. Exile had merely served to strengthen their internationalism.

The first Bourse du Travail [labour exchange] in Paris dated from 1887. The labour exchanges provided a means whereby workers could find employ-

---

1   Quoted by DD 2015.

ment, but also became centres of working-class organisation. The Fédération nationale des syndicats [National Federation of Trade Unions] was created in 1886, and in 1895 merged with the Federation of Labour Exchanges to give birth to the Confédération générale du travail [CGT], which for over a century would be France's main trade-union body.

It was only with the amnesty that socialists were able to resume activity in France. In 1880 Jules Guesde and Paul Lafargue formed the Parti Ouvrier Français [POF – French Workers' Party]. The POF programme was written by Guesde with input from Marx, Engels and Lafargue. In 1882 Laura and Paul Lafargue moved to Paris.

A central issue facing the left was the question of educational reform, and in particular the principle of *laïcité*. *Laïcité* is often seen as a value defended by the left, but the reality of its origins show that it was much more ambiguous.

By the 1880s the republican left was growing in strength, and it was able to introduce radical reforms. In particular the laws of 1881 and 1882, promoted by Jules Ferry, established the principle that primary education in France would be free, compulsory and secular. Church education was not abolished, but its influence was restricted. Church schools continued to exist, but their teachers had to be qualified and they received no state finance. Moral and civic education replaced religious instruction in the state schools.

Partly such reforms were, as elsewhere in Europe, a response to the need for literacy in a modernising economy. The defeat by Prussia in 1870 was sometimes attributed to low educational standards in France. But there was another factor. France was a large, and mainly rural, country. A great many peasants had only the vaguest notion that they were French citizens. Yet in every village there was a priest. The rulers of the republic were afraid that too many peasants would follow the politics of the Vatican rather than of Paris. The schools were designed to give children a sense of the nation they belonged to.

Hence the stress on *laïcité* was of great significance. From the seventeenth century until 1870 – with a short interval during the Revolution – the French state had always worked closely with the Catholic Church. The French king was often referred to as the 'eldest son of the Church'. Under the Second Empire there seemed no contradiction between the Vatican and French foreign policy.

The politicians who controlled the Third Republic had started out as members of the opposition under the Second Empire. They tended to be anticlerical and distrustful of the Catholic Church. The clergy's loyalty was obviously divided between the French state and the Papacy; the Papacy had its own foreign policy which did not necessarily coincide with that of France. There was a fear that Catholic teachers might not always choose Paris before Rome. At the time of the Franco-Austrian war in 1859, the priest in one village had told his parishioners to pray for the Austrians because they were Catholics.[2]

In 1870 the Papacy lost its territory in Italy, but continued to actively pursue international relations, asserting itself as a political as well as a spiritual power. Under Leo XIII [1878–1903] the Papacy was friendly towards France, but also cultivated good relations with the German Empire, France's main rival. Leo also encouraged Catalan nationalism and supported Chile in a war with Bolivia and Peru.

Faced with the possibility of another European war, Jules Ferry [prime minister 1880–81, 1883–85] and his supporters believed that such an important task as the education of the new generation could not be left to potentially unreliable allies in the Church, but that it should be taken over by direct employees of the French state. That their belief had some basis was confirmed in 1914, when the Papacy refused to endorse either side in the war.

Ferry's periods in power are remembered for two things, the educational reforms and the French takeover of Indochina. The two were closely connected as part of the project of building an imperialist nation, the 'civilising mission' which generations of politicians have invoked in defence of French national interests in the world.

As Antoine Richard wrote in an article in *La Révolution prolétarienne* to commemorate the fiftieth anniversary of the laws on *laïcité*, 'colonisation, the Republic and the homeland are a whole, ... linked to the same national and democratic mystique'. Ferry had combined secularism and colonialism 'because it's the same social order which needs schools and colonies'.[3]

While aware of widespread public support for a new war with Germany, Ferry himself did not favour military retaliation. His preferred option was the expansion of France's colonial empire. He was a paternalist racist who argued that 'superior races ... have the duty to civilise inferior races'.[4]

The colonising of Indochina proved unpopular. The take-over was badly managed, and the military costs were not justified by economic gains. Only rarely were the inhabitants of the colonised territories seen as of any significance in the argument. Frédéric Passy, an economist who advocated legislation in defence of workers' rights, and was a campaigner for peace [he was the first winner of the Nobel Peace Prize], argued for the principle of self-determination in the National Assembly in 1885:

---

2 Magraw 1970, p. 177.
3 Richard 1931.
4 Ferry's speech in the Chambre des députés, 28 July 1885, quoted by Keiger 1983, p. 10.

> While in Europe you don't recognise to any power the right to take from another a single shred of its territory, that is to say of its national flesh, you claim to have not only the right but the duty to dominate, enslave and exploit other peoples which are perhaps less advanced than ourselves in civilisation, but which nonetheless have their personality, their nationality, like ourselves, and are no less attached to their independence and to that of their native soil.[5]

Certainly the separation of church and state, achieved in France in 1905, had been a long-standing demand of the left. When Marxist Paul Lafargue was elected to the National Assembly in 1891, his first act was to move, unsuccessfully, a resolution calling for the separation of Church and State.[6] The Commune's commission on education, on which Vallès served, did not have time to elaborate an alternative view of education, but it is worth mentioning a manifesto, which Vallès helped to draft, which invoked 'the rights of the child'.[7] The idea that the child had rights, and that education should be conceived in terms of those rights, was very different to the way education was envisaged by the advocates of *laïcité* in the Third Republic, who saw education primarily in terms of promotion of the national interest.

Moreover the *communards* did not much use the term *laïcité*, considering themselves materialists rather than neutral on the question of religion. As Kristin Ross has shown,[8] the Commune did not see itself as a state but rather as pursuing local autonomy within an international framework. It certainly did not see education as preparation for military service. The Commune represented an internationalist tradition quite different from that developed by the partisans of *laïcité*.

Undoubtedly it was an important step forward for schoolchildren to be freed from the direct influence of the clergy and religious ideas. Yet *laïcité* as it was implemented in practice was a double-edged phenomenon, with conservative as well as progressive aspects.

For Ferry and his fellow republicans the central task of the new secular schools was to create and reinforce a sense of national identity. It is states which create nations, rather than the other way round, and the French state still had a lot of work to do.

---

5 Quoted by Pisani-Ferry 1962, p. 40.
6 Larue-Langlois 2007, p. 102.
7 Comité des 20 arrondissements 1871.
8 Ross 2015.

The question of the army was central. In 1848 and 1871 it was peasant soldiers who had suppressed risings by Parisian workers. Yet the peasantry's sense of national identity was weak, so a central theme of the educational project was strengthening the sense of French identity. The moral and civic education which was to replace religious instruction gave great importance to instilling ideas of patriotism and national identity.

The specifically military component of the new educational system was particularly important. The basic syllabus included military training for all boys. [Girls were to do needlework.[9]] As one historian has described it:

> It was the time of the 'school battalions'. A republican invention made by Paul Bert and launched in 1882. It meant taking advantage of the entry of pupils into primary schools in order to inculcate them with notions of 'patriotic citizenship' through military exercises. The children practised marching with a toy gun with a wooden bayonet, but they also practised with live ammunition, outside the school, in army rifle ranges.[10]

It was the practice in state schools for the teacher to write certain sentences on the blackboard; the pupils would recite them in chorus and the words would remain there for the rest of the day. Typical examples were:
– A good Frenchman must know how to die for the flag.
– You exist only for the homeland, you live only for her.
– A good little Frenchman must prepare to become a good soldier.[11]
One book used in schools explained that 'military service is the apprenticeship for war. It is necessary in order to form a solid army, capable of defending us against criminals within and enemies abroad'.[12] 'Criminals within' clearly refers to the use of the army against strikers.

A book by Charles Dupuy, a former prime minister, was a best-seller. This asked pupils: 'How shall we demonstrate our love for our homeland? – By obeying its laws, even if they inconvenience us and by defending its territory and its independence against the foreigner, even at the cost of our own blood'.[13]

---

9   Journal officiel, 29 March 1882, available at: http://www.senat.fr/evenement/archives/D42
        /1882.html.
10   Yves Gaulupeau in Le Monde de l'éducation, July–August 2000, quoted in Boulangé 2004b,
        p. 17.
11   Quoted in Janvion 1907, p. 7.
12   Janvion 1907, p. 8.
13   Quoted in Franchet 1903, p. 54.

Internationalist ideals were mocked: 'Perhaps you will hear around you idle and selfish people saying there's no point in being a citizen of one's country, that one should be a citizen of the world, what is called a cosmopolitan; that one's native land is everywhere where one is at ease; that the homeland is only a word, an abstraction which should not deceive positive and practical minds'.[14]

Textbooks supposedly devoted to teaching morality directly advocated hatred and lying:

> I know one can love one's native land without thereby detesting other peoples and desiring or preparing their ruin. But for soldiers there are cases when it is necessary to be able to hate, to hate the envious pitiless enemy who, after having misused force, having robbed us of our brothers in Alsace-Lorraine, is ever on the look-out for an opportunity to strike the final blow.
>
> As long as hatred remains alive for the conqueror of our homeland, then the defeated one cannot forgive or forget.
>
> So hate past injustice, the injustice which still threatens. Yes, in order to avenge the one and to ward off the effects of the other, hatred is a force, French people, hatred is a duty![15]

In the schoolbook *Tu seras soldat* [You will be a soldier], Émile Lavisse urged his youthful readers to envisage a future as spies. He told the schoolchildren that the end justified the means and that lying and dissimulation were entirely legitimate:

> The spy who serves his country in times of peace is a cunning, brave and bold man who goes to a foreign country to study its defences and war preparations in order to make them known to his homeland.
>
> All means are legitimate to achieve his end. He conceals his nationality and adopts a false name; he speaks the language of the country and hides his task by working in various professions.[16]

Support for *laïcité* thus meant supporting the state against the church. So the sharpest critique of *laïcité* came from those sections of the left which had an understanding of the state as representing the interests of one class against another, and which therefore did not see the strengthening of the state as being

---

14   Franchet 1903, p. 55.
15   Franchet 1903, p. 59.
16   Quoted in Franchet 1903, p. 63.

an advance for socialism. This meant the Marxists, the anarchists and the syndicalists. As Marx had put it: 'Government and church should rather be equally excluded from any influence on the school ... the state has need, on the contrary, of a very stern education by the people'.[17]

The first significant independent Marxist thinker in France was Paul Lafargue, working closely with his wife Laura, Karl Marx's daughter. Until 1895 the Lafargues were in regular correspondence with Engels. There is no reference to the Ferry laws anywhere in the Engels-Lafargue correspondence for 1882;[18] apparently neither Engels nor the Lafargues saw *laïcité* as a significant step forward for the left.

Paul Lafargue was an atheist, strongly opposed to church influence. He was also sceptical of those who stressed anticlericalism. Having been formed and influenced by the thought of Marx and Engels – notably Marx's *Critique of Hegel's Philosophy of Right* [1843–4] – he was well aware that Marx saw religion as the product of an unjust social order; he was therefore hostile to any attack on religion which was an end in itself, believing that the question of religion could only be resolved by the transformation of society.[19]

In the 1883 programme of the Parti Ouvrier, written by Lafargue and Jules Guesde, there was a disdainful reference to bourgeois free-thinkers who wanted 'the suppression of state subsidies to the churches and ... the separation of Church and State'. They pointed out that in the USA there was separation of Church and State, so that religions were a 'private industry like a grocery or a pork butcher's shop'; but that this 'does not prevent religious leprosy eating away the great American republic more than any power on earth'.[20]

In 1886 Lafargue published a satire entitled *La Religion du capital* [The Religion of Capital].[21] In it he imagined a conference in London with economic and political representatives of European capitalism – French Radical politician Clemenceau, the French Baron de Rothschild of the famous banking family, British politician Gladstone, British philosopher Herbert Spencer, German general von Moltke, etc. Among those attending were Ferry and also Paul Bert, who as education minister had been one of Ferry's main allies in establishing *laïcité*. Their concern was to enable the survival of capitalism; for that a religion of some sort was required. In the satire Bert declared that he was a non-believer himself, but that he was in favour of religion for the working class.

---

17   Marx 1989, p. 97.
18   Engels and Lafargue 1956–9, tome I.
19   Tevanian 2013, pp. 17–28.
20   Guesde and Lafargue 1883, p. 62.
21   Lafargue 1970, pp. 192–238.

'The workers must believe that poverty is the gold which buys heaven ... I am a very religious man ... for other people'.[22] The problem was that Christianity was no longer credible. In a passage of Voltairean mockery, Lafargue noted that it was no longer possible to get people to believe 'that a pigeon slept with a virgin and that from this union, condemned by morality and physiology, was born a lamb'.[23]

The delegates agreed that a new religion was required, based on the worship of Capital and a catechism imposing the duty of labour on workers. Lafargue was mocking the role of *laïcité*, which he saw as a doctrine that could play a role which the obsolete teachings of Christianity could no longer fulfil.

The anarchist position could be summed up as 'neither the church nor the state'. As Sébastien Faure put it, the Christian school was 'organised by the Church and for it', while the 'école laïque' [secular school] was 'organised by the state and for it'. He contrasted the idea of 'the school of the future ... organised for the child'.[24] André Lorulot put it rather more crudely, calling state schoolteachers 'intellectual cops of the capitalist class'.[25] The formulation reflected a certain reality, but was hardly tactful if one were attempting to unionise the teachers.

Various attempts were made by anarchists to set up libertarian schools that would be independent of both church and state; one such venture received financial support from Emile Zola and other writers, though in the end it came to nothing.[26]

The anarchists had a low opinion of Ferry. Emile Pouget's journal *Le Père Peinard* [Tired Old Man] combined radical opinions with very direct popular, often vulgar, language. Pouget's opinion of Ferry was aggressively hostile:

> If there's one swine who revolts me, it's Ferry. What a dirty brute this animal is, he's the biggest scoundrel in France ... I'd like to see someone wring his neck; you could kill him with no more compunction than crushing a bug.[27]

---

22   Lafargue 1970, p. 196.

23   Lafargue, 1970, p. 196.

24   Quoted by Maitron 1975, tome I, p. 359.

25   Quoted by Maitron 1975, tome I, p. 352.

26   See Maitron 1975, tome I, pp. 355–6.

27   Pouget 1976, p. 181.

Pouget had a novel take on the argument about whether priests should be allowed to work as teachers. He argued that in order to protect pupils and to demonstrate their commitment to celibacy, they should be castrated.[28]

A number of anarchist publications put the case against *laïcité*. The pamphlet *The School: Antechamber of the Barracks and the Sacristy*[29] bore no author's name but seems to have been written by Émile Janvion, one of the founders of the CGT, who claimed to have been the initiator of the first libertarian school in France. The main thrust of his argument was that *laïcité* merely constituted an alternative dogma to that of the church. He cited republican politician Léon Gambetta's claim 'Clericalism is the enemy', and retorted 'Religions (whether of state or church) are the enemy'.[30] He concluded with the observation: 'Our anticlericals have a priestlike spirit. Our atheists are pious people'.[31] Antonin Franchet's *The Secular Good Lord*[32] pursued similar arguments but focussed more specifically on the textbooks used in secular schools.

One of the most devastating attacks on *laïcité* came from a young anarchist who would later be known under the name Victor Serge. He was just nineteen and had never been to school. In an article in *l'anarchie*[33] he set out a critique of *laïcité* undoubtedly derived from the anarchist circles he had frequented since coming to Paris from Belgium.[34] As an anarchist individualist he believed secular and religious schools had the same function, to prepare children for social life by suppressing initiative and revolt. The task of schools was to produce servile automata for society's barracks and factories. Even if they wanted to, secular teachers could not produce independent individuals within the framework of state education. So there was no reason to take sides in the dispute between the secular and the religious.

The young Serge returned to the attack a couple of years later, with an article that challenged the whole idea of a secular morality:

> Secular morality is not an advance on Christian morality. It suppresses the individual more than the latter. ... There is really nothing more boring than the sermons of secular moralists.[35]

---

28   Pouget 1976, p. 304.

29   Janvion 1907.

30   Janvion 1907, p. 4.

31   Janvion 1907, p. 27.

32   Franchet 1903.

33   *l'anarchie*, 20 January 1910. English translation in Serge 2015b, pp. 48–50.

34   See Maîtrejean 2005.

35   *l'anarchie*, 6 December 1911.

The anarchist critics had their own contradictions – Pouget and Janvion in particular were anti-Semites.[36] And the anarchist critique often underestimated the positive value of education for the working class. Yet their observations on *laïcité* help to make clear that it was not as unambiguously progressive as is often claimed.

Despite the opposing voices, *laïcité* achieved what it set out to do. In 1914 the French working class – and above all the peasantry – was successfully mobilised in defence of the alleged national interest. Historian Eugen Weber described how the education system had established a sense of national identity. 'In August 1914 it was not surprising to hear a young peasant from the Var and his friends leaving for the front "happy (as he wrote to his parents) to go and defend our country, France"'.[37]

Of course a similar process of the development of state education occurred in other European countries where there was a different relationship between state and religion. In Britain, for example, the state was able to co-exist happily with the Church of England, which had no external loyalties. But in the specific conditions of France *laïcité* played a key part in the way the ideological process worked itself out.

Yet the critics were not silenced and their successors would re-emerge in the period after World War I.

---

36   See Janvion 1912 for his anti-Semitism.
37   Weber 1985, p. 237.

Dreyfus: The First Test Failed

By the early 1890s many socialists were organised in the Parti Ouvrier Français [POF] led by Jules Guesde with the support of Paul and Laura Lafargue. Guesde's followers recognised the nation state as embodying ruling-class interests, and believed that state primary education poisoned the population with patriotism,[1] thus distinguishing themselves from the republican tradition, which saw secular state education as a positive achievement.

The Guesdists took as their starting point Marx's statements in the *Communist Manifesto* on the essentially international nature of capital. Capital constantly crossed national frontiers in search of profits, and in so doing it undermined the nation and created an international working class. The Guesdists can be accused of excessive optimism in believing that the nation state and nationalist consciousness were withering away, but their analysis ensured that they made few compromises with nationalism.

The Guesdists advocated self-determination for Alsace-Lorraine, and showed that French industrialists had greatly profited from the fact that the lost provinces were now behind a tariff wall, so that French manufacturers were protected from competition from imports. So hostile was the party to nationalism that one branch expelled members for celebrating Bastille Day.

Likewise they were perceptive as to what a future European war would mean, namely the massacre of hundreds of thousands. Their mistake was to believe that such a prospect would be enough to prevent the ruling class from launching a war. They condemned the arms trade and believed that capitalism was producing arms for a war that would never happen in order to counteract the falling rate of profit. They were firmly antimilitarist, pointing to the way that the army was used for conquest abroad and to repress the working class at home. Guesde's anti-war line was so sharp that on occasion he was accused of being in the pay of the German government.[2]

The emerging working-class movement faced a number of obstacles and threats. Most important of these was the anti-Semitism widespread in French society; in the France of the 1890s, there was nothing unusual in a popular newspaper taking the title of *L'Antijuif* [the anti-Jew]. A working class divided

---

1   See Stuart 2006, p. 39, quoting Lafargue 1900.
2   Stuart 2006, p. 44.

on racial lines and encouraged to see Jews as the source of its ills would be unable to fight its real enemies.

Édouard Drumont's *La France juive*[33] [Jewish France 1886] was one of the best-selling books of the age; it was reprinted 200 times by 1914. Drumont was an extreme conservative, who believed that electric light was a dangerous modernising innovation. Thus the anti-Semitism of this period was very different to such later versions as that of Adolf Hitler, who was subsidised by Henry Ford and was a fervent promoter of motorways and private car ownership. It was nonetheless an insidious threat to working-class unity.

The connections between anti-Semitism and *laïcité* are complex. Some of the most virulent anti-Semites were Christians who blamed Jews and protestants for the establishment of secular education; this joined with the traditional anti-Semitism of the Catholic Church which saw Jews as the killers of Christ. At the same time anti-Semitism was growing in the context of a state-led drive to strengthen the sense of national identity. The notion of the Jew as a non-French outsider contributed to the power of French nationalism by giving the nation an other to define itself against.

The POF had a reasonably good record of opposing anti-Semitism and frequently found itself in conflict with the anti-Semitic far right. Anti-Semitism was more common in the syndicalist milieu. Often this was based on a stereotype of the rich Jew exemplified by the Rothschild banking family.

At the same time conflict between the working-class movement and the state was growing. Things came to a head at Fourmies on 1 May 1891. Fourmies was a small town of 15,000 inhabitants in North-Eastern France, dominated by the textile industry. In the spring of 1891 preparations were being made to celebrate May Day, which was becoming recognised as an international workers' day, in commemoration of the events in Chicago in 1886, when a general strike for the eight-hour day begun on 1 May had met savage repression. When the Socialist International was founded in 1889 it adopted a proposal that international demonstrations should be held on 1 May.

Paul Lafargue noted his impression, from making propaganda tours around the country, that May Day was regarded in a different way to other events and commemorations:

> Every worker who demonstrates on 1 May is convinced that the workers of the whole world are acting and feeling as he does. He may feel isolated in one particular corner of the country but he knows that the demonstration

---

3   Drumont 1886.

is a response to the famous slogan launched by Marx and Engels: 'Workers of the world unite'; internationalism puts a special, almost mystical stamp on the demonstration. It is moving to see workers who have never left their own small locality, and who have no contact with any agitation, informing themselves about the May demonstrations in other countries, of which they scarcely know the name and whose geographical location is certainly unknown to them.[4]

In 1891 conditions for workers in Fourmies were deteriorating. Wages were falling while the working day was often of twelve, sometimes even fifteen hours a day, six days a week. The POF had some influence in the region and called for strike action on 1 May in support of demands for the eight-hour day and wage increases. The POF stressed that action should be peaceful, but the town's employers insisted that there would be no concessions, and the mayor requested that troops be sent to preserve order. The local organiser of the POF, Hippolyte Culine, had arranged for workers to take their demands to the town hall in the morning.

There was a scuffle with the demonstrators, and four arrests. After this demonstrators demanded both the eight-hour day and the release of their comrades. More troops were sent in, armed with the deadly new Lebel rifles. A crowd gathered and stones were thrown by the unarmed crowd. The troops fired in the air, but the demonstrators did not disperse. The commanding officer gave orders for the troops to open fire; the three warnings required by law were not given. Within a minute there were nine dead and 35 wounded. Among the dead were four women aged 20 or under, and two boys of 14 and 11. A tenth victim died of his wounds the following day. Numerous soldiers, including some officers, had refused to fire. When one soldier refused to shoot, his officer threw him to the ground; he responded that he could see his mother in the crowd. It was clear that the state was prepared to be ruthless in confronting the rising working-class movement.

Politicians from across the political spectrum attempted to use the Fourmies events to support their own preoccupations. Georges Clemenceau, still a figure of the left, spoke in parliament on 8 May 1891 condemning the shootings. Drumont, while claiming to be defending the workers, used the whole episode as a pretext to attack Jews.

Paul Lafargue argued that the responsibility extended to 'the officers who executed the will of the capitalist class, and also the manufacturers, their rep-

---

4   Lafargue 1891.

resentatives and the municipal councillors, who had called in the army and sent the soldiers and officers against the workers'.[5]

The authorities arrested, not only Culine, but Lafargue, who had not been at Fourmies, but was accused of incitement to murder for a speech made at Wignehies on 14 April 1891. The two men were tried together and found guilty; Lafargue was sentenced to a year in jail. Culine appealed for a pardon, but Lafargue refused to do so, instead standing for election in nearby Lille while in jail. His pro-government opponent put up posters calling Lafargue a 'candidate without homeland' and urging voters to 'send back to Germany where he belongs the candidate Lafargue, son-in-law of the Prussian Karl Marx'. Despite press attacks Lafargue won the election by a majority of 6420 to 5175 and was released from jail.[6]

Lafargue had challenged the power of the state. French political life was dominated by two essentially nationalist forces. On the one hand there was anti-Semitic reaction with its vile fantasies. On the other there was anti-clerical republicanism, committed to the reinforcement of national identity. Now there was an emerging third force, a current of internationalist socialism, partly nourished by the inspiration of an international movement embodied in the Second International founded in 1889. Then in 1894 the whole process was disrupted by a series of events which would transform the French political landscape for the next decade.

French intelligence services kept a close watch on the German Embassy in Paris which maintained spies and informers. In the summer of 1894 French intelligence obtained a document recovered from the waste paper basket of the military attaché at the German Embassy. This listed various French military documents dealing with new weapons and troop movements. An initial investigation concluded that a French officer was passing information to the Germans.

Some rather unreliable studies of handwriting were made by men of questionable competence; suspicion fell on Captain Alfred Dreyfus. Dreyfus was a promising young officer; his family origins were in Alsace, now German territory. More significantly he was Jewish. Anti-Semitism was widespread in the senior ranks of the French army, and many of Dreyfus's fellow officers found his guilt all too plausible. In October 1894 he was arrested and imprisoned; he vigorously protested his innocence.

When the trial opened on 19 December it was behind closed doors, which meant that the weakness of the prosecution case could be covered up. The

---

5   Lafargue 1891.

6   Willard 1957, pp. 70–79.

seven officers who were both judges and jury took three days to reach the unanimous verdict that Dreyfus was guilty of collusion with a foreign power.

On 5 January 1895 Dreyfus was subjected to a ceremony of degradation; he was put on board ship and on 22 February 1895 sailed for French Guiana. On 14 April he was transferred to Devil's Island, where he was confined in a stone hut; he and his guards were the only inhabitants of the island.

The response of the anti-Semitic right to the accusations against Dreyfus was scarcely surprising. They were more interested in punishing a Jew than in their claimed defence of France's military interests against its enemies. They seemed unconcerned by the fact that if the verdict were unsound it would mean that the real culprit was still at large, and presumably continuing to engage in espionage on behalf of the enemies of France.

The anti-Semitic jubilation was an indication that Dreyfus's fate represented a clear danger to the whole working-class movement. The only legitimate response to the sentencing of Dreyfus could be a principled internationalist rejection of anti-Semitism in all its forms. Such a response was largely absent.

One of the few socialists to grasp the significance of the Dreyfus trial was Maurice Charnay, an activist in the Parti ouvrier socialiste révolutionnaire [POSR] led by Jean Allemane. He had played an important part in the party's antimilitarist activity; he was the author of *The Soldier's Catechism*,[7] in which he stated that the *patrie* was 'a false idea and a lie'. This had earned him six months in jail in 1894.

Immediately after Dreyfus's degradation he wrote an article in the Allemanist paper *Le parti ouvrier* under the headline 'Suppose he was telling the truth?'[8]

> Captain Dreyfus was degraded on Saturday, to the great joy of those for whom patriotism is combined with a taste for public spectacles and a worship of brutal force ... But suppose it were true that Dreyfus was innocent, that he hadn't passed over anything to Germany, that he was the victim of fate, of an accident or of a terrible plot? That they had decided to persecute the Jew in him ... Suppose the government had invented a travesty of treason, manufactured documents, – sacrificing Dreyfus, when its choice could have fallen on anybody else – political motives know no law – in order to whip up chauvinism, to make a useful diversion at a time when socialism is beginning to penetrate into the army! ... shouting with the

---

7   Charnay 1893.
8   Charnay1895.

crowd, whipped up by journalists and our rulers, would for socialists be the worst kind of cowardice.

It was a remarkable analysis which foreshadowed much that would be said and written in the coming years. Sadly it was an isolated contribution. Over the next few years Charnay continued to take up Dreyfus's cause in the pages of *Le parti ouvrier*; in January 1898 he criticised the socialist deputies for failing to speak out in defence of Dreyfus. Later that year he was injured in a duel after being challenged by one of Dreyfus's opponents.[9]

The overall response of the French left to the verdict on Dreyfus was dismal. There were some gross examples of left anti-Semitism, especially but not exclusively in syndicalist circles. While such anti-Semitism was wholly to be condemned, it was not the central problem. Rather the French left in this period was guilty of what might be described as 'ultra-classism'. Many French socialists stressed class questions to the exclusion of all other forms of oppression. The left remained indifferent, since Dreyfus was an army officer of conservative disposition. This failure to distinguish between a single individual and the army as an institution revealed a left whose class consciousness was still on the level of gut response rather than serious social analysis.

A blatant example of this was Emile Pouget. Pouget played an important part in the development of French revolutionary syndicalism; he was a tireless activist, an influential writer and had a major role in the early years of the CGT. He saw himself as an internationalist, recognised the international nature of the class struggle, and opposed colonialism. He had spent time in Britain, and took a keen interest in the British and Spanish labour movements.[10] Unfortunately his anti-Semitism was in contradiction to his other positions, and his comments on Dreyfus were trivialising and callous:

> The patriots are furious.
>
> One of their richest officers, an Alsatian Yid called Dreyfus, a big cheese in the Ministry of War, has flogged a whole bundle of secrets to Germany.
>
> O ho, bourgeois, you don't surprise us; the military have that in their blood.

---

9   Charnay 1898. Maitron and Pennetier 1964–2023 article2106, notice CHARNAY Maurice Revu et complété par Julien Chuzeville, version mise en ligne le 30 juin 2008, dernière modification le 17 août 2020.

10   Bantman 2009.

The instinct for treachery is a bloody sight more common in their knapsacks than marshals' batons.[11]

The Guesdists in the POF largely kept free of anti-Semitism, but they stood aloof from the movement in defence of Dreyfus. They argued that workers should not take sides in a dispute that was increasingly dividing the nation.[12]

Socialist leader Jean Jaurès [see Chapter 5] was no anti-Semite. Yet his initial response to the trial was disappointing. When he spoke in the National Assembly following the verdict on Dreyfus, he made a legitimate point about the difference in the way military law affected officers and private soldiers; Dreyfus had not been sentenced to death, whereas private soldiers were shot for far lesser crimes.[13] His primary aim was to propose a resolution in favour of abolishing the death penalty in the army. This brought down on him the wrath of the Chamber; he was suspended from parliament.[14] Yet Jaurès seemed to disregard the possibility that a military tribunal might be mistaken; his indignation at Dreyfus's treason sounded odd in the mouth of a socialist, and his words could even be interpreted as calling for Dreyfus's execution.

The weakness of the left's response to the Dreyfus verdict can therefore be explained by an oversimplified notion of class. Dreyfus was seen as an individual who happened to be a wealthy army officer. There was no recognition of the fact that an attack on Dreyfus led quite directly to an attack on all Jews – something that the anti-Semites grasped much more clearly. To defend Dreyfus meant, not defending one individual, but defending all Jews against the nationalist onslaught.

Moreover, there was an acceptance of lazy stereotypes. While there were undoubtedly some very wealthy Jews in France, most Jews were poor workers, often immigrant victims of persecution in Eastern Europe. In Zola's last novel, *Vérité* [Truth, 1903] the hero, Marc, reflected 'How many even more wretched Jews were dying of hunger in foul cesspits ... There was no Jewish question, just the question of piles of money, poisonous and rotten'.[15]

Initially Dreyfus's brother Mathieu almost single-handedly carried the burden of trying to get a reversal of the sentence. It was left to individuals outside the ranks of the socialist movement to initiate a campaign. The first to play an important role was Bernard Lazare. In 1894 he had published a study

---

11   *Le Père Peinard* 4, November 1894, quoted in Maitron 1975 tome I, p. 331.
12   Stuart 2006, pp. 112–14.
13   Boussel, 1960, pp. 67–9.
14   Miquel 1972, pp. 28–9; Auclair 1954, pp. 301–3.
15   Zola 1903, pp. 178–9.

of anti-Semitism, offering an alternative to the work of Drumont. His book, *Anti-Semitism, its history and causes*, was a refutation of Drumont's doctrines. The central thrust of his argument was to deny any validity to the concept of 'race'.

> Race is, however, a fiction. No human group exists that can boast of having had two original ancestors and having descended from them without any adulteration of the primitive stock through mixture; human races are not pure, i.e., strictly speaking, there is no such thing as a race. ... Semitic blood has mingled with Aryan blood and Aryan blood has mixed with Semitic blood.[16]

Racial mixing had been so extensive that racial identity was impossible to establish. Hence the very notion of race should be abandoned, thus undermining the whole anti-Semitic case.

Lazare's perception of the role of anti-Semitism persuaded him, after some hesitations, to take up the defence of Dreyfus, and he was one of the first public figures to do so. His pamphlet *A Judicial Error*[17] made a detailed analysis of the accusations against Dreyfus, and began to turn the tide in Dreyfus's favour. In 1899 he published another pamphlet, *Antisemitism and Revolution*, in which he dealt explicitly with the relation of anti-Semitism to socialism and the working class. He pointed out that the great majority of Jews were not the likes of Rothschild, but poor working people:

> Do you think you would have made any progress if you had driven out of France – or killed – little Jacob, my neighbour whom you know, who is an upholsterer and earns five francs a day when he's not out of work, which happens a hundred days in the year? ... [O]ut of eight million Jews, there are seven million who are in little Jacob's position, or are even worse off. In Russia, in Galicia, in Romania, in Serbia, in Turkey, in London, in New York, in certain districts of Paris they are in terrible poverty. Most of them are artisans and as such they are victims of the social condition.

If some Jews were wealthy capitalists they were no worse than their Christian counterparts. Was it the Jews, he asked, who:

---

16   Lazare 1894, pp. 248, 271.
17   Lazare 1896.

> ... drew up the new law on unions and strikes; do they cause unemployment, or cuts in wages; is it only the Jews who refuse to accept the eight-hour day and systematically reject all our demands?

So he urged workers to recognise that

> ... there are no Aryans and no Semites: there are the poor and the rich, exploited and exploiters.[18]

In exposing the reactionary nature of anti-Semitism and in showing the close links between the struggle against anti-Semitism and the interests of the working class, Lazare made a significant contribution to the job which should have been done by the working-class movement.

Lazare's intervention had little impact on public opinion. He was an obscure intellectual with anarchist sympathies; moreover he was Jewish. He could be safely disregarded. Now, however, there were developments inside the army itself; the botched corrupt conviction of Dreyfus was causing problems. When Lieutenant Colonel Georges Picquart became head of the army's intelligence section he re-examined relevant documents and observed that some letters from a Major Esterházy were in the handwriting that had been attributed to Dreyfus. Esterházy was charged, but was acquitted after a travesty of a trial.

At this point Emile Zola took up where Lazare had left off. Zola was probably France's best-known living writer. He was an exceptional figure in the French literary milieu, for he was almost unique in having no truck with the prevalent anti-Semitism. His willingness to put his head on the line for Dreyfus was deeply rooted in his life and work.

Zola had an Italian father and a Greek grandmother, a fact of which his enemies did not cease to remind him. The historian Jacques Bainville denounced him as 'half Italian, quarter Greek, three or four times half-breed', and when he was named in the Senate in December 1897 there were cries of 'Italian! Dago!'[19] When he was an adolescent, the family moved from the Marseille area to Paris, and Zola later told Paul Alexis that in Aix-en-Provence he was derided as a Parisian, but in Paris he was mocked by his school-fellows as a *marseillais*.[20] These childhood experiences may have helped to shape his opposition to racism.

---

18 Lazare 1899, pp. 11, 12, 15.
19 Guillemin 1960, pp. 11, 39.
20 Alexis 1882, p. 36.

Zola had no organisational links with the French socialist movement, though since the 1880s he had considered himself in some sense a socialist. He was the author of a savagely antimilitarist short story, *Le Capitaine Burle* [Captain Burle], which described the degeneration of the French army after the defeat of 1870, when a period without war led officers into debauchery and idleness. Burle was a widower who lived with his ultra-patriotic mother and his son. To pay for his pastimes he fiddled the books, and was only saved from disgrace by his friend Laguitte. Outwardly reformed, Burle had a squalid liaison with the maid – and carried on fiddling the books. This time the only way Laguitte could save his reputation was to challenge him to a duel – and kill him. His son, whom the grandmother was determined to make into a soldier, died – apparently of typhoid. In fact, Zola explained, 'he died of fear'.[21] Contempt for the officer class ran through every page of the story.

Zola was a known opponent of anti-Semitism. This was clear from his 1891 novel *L'Argent* [Money]. In the middle of one of the anti-Semitic diatribes by the unscrupulous financier Saccard, he inserted the comment of Mme Caroline: ' "What a peculiar thing!" Mme Caroline murmured gently, with her vast knowledge and her universal tolerance. "As far as I'm concerned, Jews are people like anyone else. If they are separate, it's because we made them separate".'[22] The judgment carried obvious authorial approval; Zola identified strongly with Mme Caroline and in his preliminary notes he wrote 'Put myself entirely into her'.[23]

In 1896, before being involved with Dreyfus, Zola had published an article entitled 'In Defence of the Jews' [Pour les Juifs], which appeared on the front page of *Le Figaro* on 16 May. He described anti-Semitism as 'a monstrosity, I mean something outside all common sense, all truth and all justice, a blind, stupid thing which would take us back to centuries gone by'. He argued that there was no Jewish problem, only a problem of anti-Semitism: 'The Jews, as they exist today, are our work, the product of our 1800 years of imbecile persecution'.[24] Because of this article Zola was approached to intervene in the Dreyfus case.

His article 'J'Accuse' [I accuse] appeared in *L'Aurore* of 13 January 1898. Over a hundred years later it is remembered as a classic example of what campaigning journalism in defence of human rights looks like. The impact was

---

21   Zola 1883, p. 60.
22   Zola 1962, p. 483.
23   Hemmings 1966, p. 251.
24   Zola 1896, pp. 203, 206.

immediate – *L'Aurore* normally printed around 30,000 copies, but 300,000 of this issue were sold.[25] The article dealt with the structure of power and ideology behind the condemnation of Dreyfus. Zola denounced religious bias and class prejudice; he lambasted anti-Semitism, described as the 'persecution of "dirty Jews", which dishonours our age', Anti-Semitism was the very negation of the principles of the French Revolution: 'It is a crime to corrupt the weak and the humble, to inflame the passions of reaction and intolerance, by sheltering behind the detestable anti-Semitism which will kill the great liberal France of the Rights of Man, if it is not healed of it'. Zola invoked French values which he saw as positive, but insisted: 'It is a crime to exploit patriotism in the cause of hatred'.[26]

After Zola's intervention nothing could be the same again. There were twists and turns ahead; Zola himself would be prosecuted and obliged to go into exile in England for a year.[27] But it was now impossible to remain silent, to evade the issue.

The socialist movement was not yet pulled out of its sectarian torpor. Jaurès and Guesde were personally convinced of the case for Dreyfus, but were held back by their more reformist colleagues such as Alexandre Millerand;[28] they backed Dreyfus within the parliamentary group, but accepted the majority position. On 18 January 1898 – *after* Zola's intervention – a statement signed by all socialist deputies urged workers not to take sides in a 'bourgeois civil war'. Jules Guesde abandoned support for Dreyfus after poor election results in May 1898, and in July the POF [led by Guesde and Lafargue] argued that 'workers ... have no place in this battle which is not theirs'. The same year the syndicalist CGT issued a pamphlet declaring 'We workers, eternally exploited, should not take sides in this conflict between Jews and Christians!'[29]

If the left had moved in Dreyfus's defence earlier, at the time of Charnay's neglected article, the socialists could have defined the terms of the debate and transformed the campaign to defend Dreyfus into one which could have not only defeated the reactionaries in the army hierarchy, but also built the socialist movement by mobilising the powerful enthusiasm for justice behind socialist values.

Paul Lafargue was Guesde's long-term ally, and the shrewder political brain. He too had lapsed into ultra-classism, but eventually recognised reality and

---

25   Swardson 1998.

26   Zola 1898.

27   Rosen 2017.

28   Fiechter 1965, p. 238.

29   Cahm 1994, pp. 129–30, 145.

wrote to Karl Kautsky describing the abstentionism of the socialist movement as inexcusable and inexplicable.[30] It is unfortunate he had not developed this position a little earlier.

At long last the left began to move. Jaurès now turned his powerful propagandist talents to the campaign. His book *The Proofs* [1898] collected his eloquent journalism on questions related to the affair. He argued forcefully that the case was a class issue:

> So who today is the most threatened by the arbitrary power of the generals, by the constantly glorified violence of military repressions? Who? The proletariat. It therefore has an overriding interest in punishing and discouraging the illegalities and violences of the courts martial before they become some sort of universally accepted habit. It has an overriding interest in provoking the moral discredit and fall of this reactionary army which is ready to strike it down tomorrow.[31]

Yet Jaurès remained trapped in left republicanism. Rather than oppose the right-wing nationalists with a clear internationalist message, Jaurès got into the game of claiming to be a better nationalist than the nationalists. While scorning the 'so-called defenders of the French race' and 'professional patriots', he contrasted them to those who, like himself, were authentically concerned with France's interests and reputation.[32]

Many of the younger generation looked to the syndicalist and anarchist milieu for a more thorough-going revolutionary response. For those just coming to political activity Dreyfus was a powerful source of inspiration. Pierre Monatte was still at school, though already a member of a socialist youth group, when his history teacher discovered in his desk a copy of Zola's pamphlet *Letter to Youth* [1897], which recalled how the idealism of the Latin Quarter had supported the 'oppressed peoples' of Poland and Greece.[33] He was summoned to the headmaster who stopped short of expelling him only because he was a good student from a highly regarded family.[34]

Alfred Rosmer's earliest involvement in politics was also in support of Dreyfus. Over half a century later his niece recalled: 'I can still hear him reading

---

30 Letters of 28 July and 15 September 1898, quoted by Croix 1967, p. 69. See also Derfler 1991, p. 222.

31 Jaurès 1898, p. 13.

32 Jaurès 1898, pp. 253, 279–80.

33 Zola 1897, p. 4.

34 Chambelland 1999, p. 15.

Zola's letter *J'Accuse* to the whole family, and demanding that grandfather [Rosmer's father, a hairdresser] should leave *L'Aurore* in the shop so that the customers could read it'.[35]

Throughout his life Rosmer continued to invoke the Dreyfus case as a point of comparison, for example describing Stalin's Moscow Trials of the 1930s as 'new Dreyfus cases'.[36] Rosmer and Monatte were to be among the most intransigent internationalists of their generation, and the role of the Dreyfus case in radicalising them and their contemporaries was crucial.

Another group from the younger generation who were deeply affected by the Dreyfus affair were those around Lucien Herr, the librarian at the École Normale Supérieure, including Charles Andler and future prime minister Léon Blum. Like Charnay, Herr and Andler were members of the POSR.[37]

Herr was working on a book on intellectual progress; Andler summarised his views as follows:

> National frontiers themselves are called into question, inasmuch as they are artificial barriers whereby nations protect their own wealth. Justice does not stop at a geographical boundary. Human truth no longer permits big nations to exploit small ones, as it no longer allows powerful and rich individuals to exploit the weak. The exploitation of men or conjunctures by a class of men or a nation is obsolete. 'We can measure the level of civilisation by the level of cosmopolitanism'.[38]

Slowly the tide began to turn in favour of the *dreyfusards*, though there would be setbacks. Esterházy's guilt became evident and Colonel Henry, who had forged documents to make Dreyfus appear guilty, committed suicide. In 1899 Dreyfus was brought back to France for a new trial. He was again convicted of treason but with extenuating circumstances, and sentenced to ten years' imprisonment. The government now had little alternative but to offer him a pardon – which he accepted – and he was released. This was followed by an amnesty for all others involved in the affair. After his horrific sufferings it is hard to criticise him – but many of his supporters were deeply disappointed at this inconclusive result. In 1906 he was fully rehabilitated and restored to his rank in the army.

---

35   Gras 1971, p. 28.
36   Gras 1971, p. 388.
37   Andler 1932, pp. 91–5.
38   Andler 1932, p. 74.

The country seemed threatened with political instability. In 1902 elections returned a left-of-centre republican majority. This took advantage of the post-Dreyfus situation to pursue the cause of *laïcité*; in particular the separation of Church and State was carried through in 1905. In 1906 Clemenceau, who had played a creditable role in the defence of Dreyfus, became prime minister, and Picquart, another defender of Dreyfus, became army minister.

Clemenceau's record in government was unambiguously reactionary; as one historian sums it up: 'For three years he presided over a government that arrested union leaders, fired protesting teachers, and used soldiers to break strikes from Paris to the wine-growing regions of the Midi. In the end twenty workers were killed and nearly seven hundred wounded'.[39]

Half a century later Alfred Rosmer recounted his memories of the Dreyfus case and the state of the left following it [Millerand had been the first Socialist in the Third Republic to join a bourgeois government under Waldeck-Rousseau]:

> The Dreyfus Affair ... ended badly for those fighting on both sides, who, for several years, had been violently opposed. The military judges insisted on finding him guilty, despite the clear evidence of innocence. Dreyfus accepted a pardon: he was not the hero required by the circumstances so that the battle could be fought out to a conclusion. ... The pro-Dreyfus government of Waldeck-Rousseau proposed nothing more substantial than clipping the claws of clericalism; ... It was a derisory conclusion to a battle in which such efforts had been expended, and making Millerand a minister added nothing. Quite the reverse; it was a provocation which was confirmed by his personal policy of bribing workers' organisations.[40]

Rosmer's pessimistic assessment was largely correct. By its slowness in responding the socialist left missed the opportunity of taking the lead in the struggle for justice, and thus winning to socialism many of the young people radicalised by the case. As late-comers, the socialists could take only a defensive stance. It was the republican radicals, focussing on *laïcité*, who came out on top and thus defined the core values of the left. The more thoroughgoing internationalism which the socialists could have advocated remained marginal to French political life.

---

39   Burns 1992, p. 322.
40   Rosmer 1951, p. 1.

Certainly the Dreyfus affair had a massive impact. A whole generation of young people were radicalised by their involvement. The campaign around Dreyfus made many people more aware of other cases of injustice. If Zola's intervention changed the course of events, it is also true that the Dreyfus case changed Zola; his involvement led to a radicalisation of his own political stance. After Dreyfus, Zola rethought a whole range of political questions. Thus he took up the case of anarchists sentenced to penal servitude; following his intervention, a vigorous campaign ended up with five being released.[41] In his writings following the Dreyfus case – his final novel cycle, the *Four Gospels* – Zola came to develop a growing interest in questions of internationalism. *Travail* [Work, 1901] ended by describing the future establishment of a world order which made war impossible. In *Justice*, incomplete at the time of his death, Zola looked forward to a time when 'nothing remains but the great human homeland. The United States of Europe. The alliance of all nations'.[42] The last books were a clear indication of just how far the Dreyfus case had shifted his thinking. And while it is unlikely that there will ever be definitive proof, it seems very possible that he paid the ultimate price for his courage, since there are indications that his death may have resulted from the deliberate act of an enraged anti-dreyfusard.[43]

The heritage of the Dreyfus case weighed on the French left for half a century. The Dreyfus affair created the modern French right, the authoritarian anti-Semites who were to achieve their victory in Vichy. It thus pushed the left into defending the republic, and helped to reinforce the myth of republican unity, which became such a dangerous inheritance in 1914. A poisonous legacy remains on the French far right. Éric Zemmour, far right candidate in the 2022 presidential election, though himself a Jew, drew heavily on the rhetoric of the anti-dreyfusards, redirecting it against Muslims.[44] As Jim Wolfreys has argued, the failure of the left to build a socialist alternative to republicanism at the time of the Dreyfus case has affected the development of the left throughout the following century, notably making it less effective in opposing Islamophobia.[45]

Might things have been different in 1914 if the French left had acquitted itself better over the Dreyfus case? The point should not be overstated – the factors that led to the capitulation of the French left in 1914 would still have been present. The fact that the process was virtually identical in the other European

---

41   Méric 1909, p. 28.
42   Leblond 1927, p. 10.
43   Bedel 2002.
44   Abidor and Lago 2022.
45   Wolfreys 2018, p. 165, quoting Kergoat 1997.

nations, which had not suffered a Dreyfus case, suggests that France would still have gone to war. However the left might have been a bit stronger and more self-confident, there might have been a few more Rosmers and Monattes. After the catastrophe of 1914 France saw a growing anti-war movement and in 1920, the founding of a mass Communist Party. Some of the seeds sown during the Dreyfus affair were coming to fruition.

In The Shadow of War

At the beginning of the twentieth century the French working-class movement was becoming stronger. The dominant current within the CGT, formed in 1895, was syndicalism, a distrust of parliamentary politics and a belief that trade-union action alone would suffice to transform society in workers' interests; this was embodied in the Amiens Charter of 1906. In 1905 the various groupings of the French socialist movement were finally united into a single party which showed the importance it accorded to the Socialist International by taking the name *Section française de l'internationale ouvrière* [SFIO – French Section of the Workers' International]. That the emerging labour movement was a force to be reckoned with in French society was shown by various repressive responses of the government.

There were a number of factors which contributed to a growing awareness of France's place in an ever more interconnected and interdependent world. Travel and communication were being transformed. A network of railways brought together the whole of Europe, and the telegraph meant that news from all parts of the world could appear within hours in the daily newspapers.

Workers would cross state boundaries in search of employment, and often they would make contact with the labour movement in the country they moved to. Many rank-and-file workers felt themselves to be a part of an international movement. For example, Bolshevik Alexander Shlyapnikov left Russia in 1907 and came to work in Western Europe, for a time in an automobile factory at Asnières-sur-Seine on the outskirts of Paris. Here he encountered syndicalist ideas which may have helped him develop a critical perspective on Bolshevism in power.[1]

One example of how at least some of the French working class saw themselves as part of an international movement was the response to the execution of the Spanish activist Francisco Ferrer in 1909. Ferrer was a syndicalist and educational reformer. He had had close links with the French syndicalists in the CGT, having translated their material. After a failed workers' revolt in Barcelona in 1909 he was executed, though his role in the events had been minimal. The young Victor Serge, active in anarchist circles, described the demonstrations:

---

1   Allen 2016.

The movement in Paris was spontaneous. From all the suburbs came hundreds of thousands of workers and ordinary people, aroused by a terrible sense of indignation, flocking towards the city centre. The revolutionary groups didn't lead these crowds, but rather tailed behind them. The editors of revolutionary papers, surprised by how influential they had suddenly become, launched the slogan: 'To the Spanish Embassy!' ... Two days later the government authorised a legal demonstration, led by Jaurès, where we marched, half a million of us, accompanied by republican guards on horseback, who were now subdued, as they were evaluating the rise of this new power.[2]

The founding of the Second International in Paris in 1889 had marked a decisive advance on the First International [IWMA]. It was a federation of mass socialist parties, a centralised and disciplined body. When the various congresses of the Second International passed resolutions in favour of taking measures to prevent war – above all the Basel Conference of 1912 which urged workers to 'exert every effort in order to prevent the outbreak of war by the means they consider most effective' – these were taken seriously as a commitment to action.

There were two areas in which the need for internationalism confronted the French working-class movement in concrete terms. The first was the question of immigrant labour. By the 1890s 10 percent of the French workforce was foreign. Obviously there was racial friction within the working class, and this was sometimes reflected in socialist and trade-union publications. An article in *Le Socialiste* in 1893 pointed to the danger of France being swamped by Chinese workers brought in by employers seeking cheap labour, and the parallel threat of China becoming industrialised and flooding France with cheap imports. It warned that French workers could be 'submerged by a real invasion by the yellow race'.[3]

This was an exception. In general the POF took a more principled position. Its programme contained the demand that it should be legally required for employers to pay foreign workers at the same rate as indigenous employees.[4]

Much of the POF's propaganda and activity revealed a positive internationalism. It advocated full legal rights for immigrant workers, so that they could not be used to weaken class organisation or depress wages. It organised in the West Indian colonies of Guadeloupe and Martinique, so it had many black members. When a young Algerian Muslim called Hadj-Ali Abdelkader [later a lead-

---

2 Serge 2001, p. 523.
3 'L'invasion chinoise', *Le Socialiste*, 30 April 1893.
4 'Les ouvriers étrangers', *Le Socialiste*, 13 May 1893.

ing Communist] came to Paris in the early years of the century, and obtained French citizenship, he was able to participate actively in the SFIO from around 1910.

The POF showed unqualified opposition to anti-Semitism; POF street fighters frequently came into conflict with anti-Semites. When the latter attacked a Jewish shop in Nantes, POF militants were among local inhabitants who defended the shopkeeper. The police arrested the defenders![5]

The second challenge for internationalists was the threat of European war. The rivalry between Europe's imperialist powers was visible to all, and the risks it posed were widely discussed. France's alliances with Russia [1892] and Britain [1904] showed the line-up that a coming war would produce. The Franco-Prussian war of 1870 was still in living memory and in some quarters there was enthusiasm for winning back Alsace-Lorraine; as had been clear at the time of the Dreyfus case, Germany was regarded as the main potential enemy.

Few could foresee the full horror of four years of trench warfare across Europe. Paul Lafargue predicted the possibility of 'slaughterhouses many kilometres square where hundreds of thousands of men will be massacred without glory and without heroism'.[6] Often, however, the prediction of doom was tempered by the over-optimistic view that such a prospect would be enough to deter the ruling class from launching a war, or that fear of mutiny and revolution would mean that the bourgeoisie would not dare to mobilise workers.[7]

The decade before 1914 was punctuated by a series of international crises – Fashoda, Morocco, Trieste – which brought Europe to the brink of war. In each case war was averted, and in each case strong anti-war feelings were manifested by the working-class movement. There were forces built into the capitalist system that were pushing irresistibly towards war, but there was no inevitability that war should break out in just the way it did at the time it did.

By 1910 the SFIO had 75 deputies [out of 595] in the National Assembly, and by 1914 its membership was some 70,000. Its best-known figure, nationally and internationally, was Jean Jaurès. a great orator who wrote in a vivid prose style. He was a major intellectual figure, whose most important contribution was his *Socialist History of the French Revolution*. Jaurès saw modern socialism as emerging directly out of the French Revolution, writing of 'the burning stream of socialism that came from the Revolution and democracy as if from a furnace'.[8]

---

5   Stuart 2006, p. 102.
6   Lafargue 1895.
7   Stuart 2006, p. 42.
8   Jaurès 1969, p. 159.

Jaurès underestimated the need for a qualitative break with the values of the bourgeois revolution. In 1914 one of the key arguments used by French labour leaders to persuade their followers to support the war was that France was the homeland of the Revolution, and that by defending its territory they were defending the republic which was inextricably tied up with the interests of socialism. Jaurès's integrity in opposing the drift to war in 1914, at the cost of his life, cannot be questioned; yet the ideas embodied in his history of the Revolution may have contributed to winning popular support for the war, since they spread far beyond those who actually read his books.

Jaurès's position on nationalism was clearly marked by the tradition of the French Revolution. He argued that workers have no *patrie* as long as they are split up and scattered in capitalist society, but the more they develop as a class, the more they have a country.[9] Hence, he argued, 'a little internationalism leads us away from the *patrie*, but a great deal of internationalism brings us back to it'.[10]

Jaurès was undoubtedly a sincere lover of peace, who blamed war on the capitalist system. Yet he also drew up detailed proposals for legislation to replace the professional army with a citizens' army based on mass conscription, a peculiar mixture of utopianism and reformist realism.

Jaurès exercised an enormous influence, but he did not break with the republican tradition that dominated the French left. Had he lived it seems likely he would have found the appropriate patriotic rhetoric from the Jacobin tradition to defend the war. The very fact that we cannot be sure how he would have responded had he lived even a few days longer shows that his position involved a balancing act between different social forces.

Jaurès's main rival in the leadership of the SFIO was Jules Guesde, who in the 1893 election had been denounced by his opponents as the 'Prussian candidate' because of his internationalism.[11] Guesde and his followers took as their starting point Marx's writings in the *Communist Manifesto* on the essentially international nature of capital. Hence there was a vigorous current of internationalism on the revolutionary wing of the SFIO, which found expression especially in the journal *La Guerre sociale*, in which the driving force was Gustave Hervé. Hervé signed his articles 'Un Sans-Patrie' [one without *patrie*] to emphasise his rejection of patriotism. His opposition to militarism led him into constant conflict with the authorities and several spells in jail.

---

9   See Hirou 1995, p. 253.
10   Jaurès 1911, p. 571.
11   Stuart 2006, p. 79.

There was an element of ultra-left swagger in many of Hervé's writings. In 1901 he caused a sensation by an article in which he advocated a ceremony in which 'after having gathered all the filth and dung from the barracks, ... the colonel, in full regalia and to the sound of a military band, should stick the regimental flag into the dung-heap'.[12] Such language was designed to appeal to the more committed of his supporters rather than to win over those beyond. In the more sober eyes of Alfred Rosmer his impact was only a 'superficial and transient effervescence'.[13]

In 1912, when Hervé had renounced his antipatriotism, Rosmer wrote a sharp critique of him, pointing out that Hervé's linguistic extremism was in sharp contrast to serious antimilitarist work like the 'sou du soldat' [see below] which had to be carried out with 'the necessary discretion'.[14] In 1914 Hervé became a fervent patriot.

A more serious contribution was made by Paul Louis, a member of the SFIO. In 1905 he published a short book entitled *Le Colonialisme* [colonialism], in which he examined the expansion of colonial empires in recent decades, and their significance for the working-class movement. He argued that colonialism was a product of capitalism and that it aggravated and universalised social conflicts.[15]

Another notable campaigner against colonialism was Paul Vigné, known as Vigné d'Octon [1859–1943]. As a young man he served as a doctor in the naval medical service in the West Indies and Senegal, where he was able to observe the brutality of colonialism at first hand. He became a writer and published several novels in which he took the side of the colonised populations. In 1893 he was elected to the National Assembly, where he sat for thirteen years, not aligned with any party though close to the POF. He used the National Assembly to denounce colonialism, notably in Madagascar, and incurred the enmity of the colonialists. After leaving parliament he took part in an official enquiry in North Africa; when his report was not published he gave it to Hervé's *La Guerre sociale*. He wrote newspaper columns and gave lectures on what he called 'colonial robbery'.[16]

The most important theoretical contribution to the French socialist movement before 1914 came from Paul and Laura Lafargue. Born in Cuba, Paul Lafar-

---

12   Quoted by Kriegel and Becker 1964, p. 8.
13   Rosmer 1936, p. 44.
14   Rosmer 1912a.
15   Louis 1905.
16   Maitron and Pennetier 1964–2023 article134542, notice VIGNÉ Paul, dit Vigné d'Octon par Jean Sagnes, version mise en ligne le 30 novembre 2010, dernière modification le 26 mars 2011.

gue claimed that the blood of three oppressed races ran in his veins. His grandmother was a mulatto, and his mother was half Jewish, half Caribe Indian. He stated that he was proudest of his black origin.[17] 'They have thrown in our faces, as an insult, the term *homme de couleur* [man of colour]. It is up to us revolutionary mulattos to pick up the term and make ourselves worthy of it'.[18]

Lafargue's aim was not simply to repeat the ideas of Marx and Engels, but to extend the application of the Marxist method, notably to the cultural field. For him socialism was not, as it was for Jaurès, merely icing on the republican cake. Socialist politics and socialist organisation had to be counterposed to the republican tradition.

One work in which Lafargue pursued this argument was his essay 'The Legend of Victor Hugo'.[19] Hugo, who had gone into exile in opposition to Napoleon III, was something of a hero to the republican left. Lafargue gave a devastating account of Hugo's actual political stances, including his support for the crushing of the June 1848 workers' rising in Paris and his lack of support for the Paris Commune. His conclusion was harsh: 'The libertarian Hugo was not one to hesitate to restrict any liberty that worried the possessing class and disturbed stock exchange prices. ... By heaping up anger on individuals, on Napoleon and his acolytes, he diverts the people's attention away from the causes of social suffering, which are the appropriation of the wealth of society by the capitalist class'.

Lafargue was obliged to fight consistently for internationalist principles. As Laura Lafargue wrote to Engels,[20] the Marxists had been the only anti-chauvinist party in France, while the Blanquists and others had exploited the unpopularity of the Marxists' internationalism. During the recent elections Paul Lafargue had been applauded when he spoke in favour of international solidarity.

At the 1907 SFIO Congress Lafargue spoke against the use of the army to repress strikes: 'The Third Republic holds the European record for the brutal and ferocious repression of strikes. You know this as well as I do; but do the capitalists need to be so impudent as to blame socialists and workers for being antipatriotic, when it is they who teach antipatriotism by having the children of France massacred by French soldiers ...'[21]

---

17   Derfler 1991, pp. 14–15.
18   Lafargue 1970, p. 20.
19   Lafargue 1885.
20   Letter of 27 December 1888, Engels and Lafargue 1956–9.
21   Hirou 1995, p. 46.

1   **Antimilitarism**

There was a significant antimilitarist current within the SFIO. From the beginning of the century socialists worked alongside syndicalists and anarchists in producing a paper called *Le Conscrit* [the conscript], of which 100,000 copies were printed each year when the annual batch of recruits was taken into the army.[22] When the SFIO was founded, members became involved with *Le Conscrit*.

While warning against 'individual and sterile rebellions' it predicted that the bourgeoisie would see the army it had created being turned into an enemy: 'We shall turn the weapons that it has given us back against it'.[23] It told its readers that the whole edifice of patriotism was a fraud: 'the army, the flag and national defence are just so many lying pretexts to perpetuate the enslavement of the class you belong to. *Patrie* is a word without any meaning. Those they call your enemies and whom they want to turn you against are in reality simply unfortunate people like yourselves, workers having the same interests as you'.[24]

The main antimilitarist campaigning came from the CGT. The CGT was France's main trade-union confederation, and was seen as a threat by successive governments. It had, however, only around 300,000 members, as compared to 2,5 million trade unionists in Germany or 4 million in Britain. While the CGT did excellent work among the working class, a substantial proportion of the French population were peasants or self-employed artisans, and these went largely untouched by antimilitarism.

The political philosophy of the CGT was revolutionary syndicalism. The French syndicalists did not make an artificial separation of trade-unionism and politics. As Alfred Rosmer pointed out, the whole point of the CGT's Amiens Charter of 1906, which laid down the principles on which French syndicalism was based, was a reaction against the Second International tradition of a division of labour between the socialist parties and the trade unions, the former occupying themselves with political matters and the latter with economic ones. As Rosmer put it, this was 'the decrepit, thoroughly rotten and mendacious Second International, whose principle was as follows: "You shall concern yourself with political matters and we with economic matters; don't stick your nose in our affairs and we won't worry about yours"'.[25] The CGT banned party politics in the organisation because it claimed that the union

---

22   Rabaut 1975, p. 73.
23   *Le Conscrit*, January 1900.
24   Le Conscrit, February 1906.
25   Rosmer 1921.

was adequate for both economic and political tasks. As Rosmer later noted: 'Its weakness lay precisely in the fact that it was something of a hybrid, both a trade-union organisation and a political party, and a party even more than a trade-union organisation'.[26]

Syndicalism explains both the strengths and the weaknesses of the CGT's antimilitarism. The strength of syndicalism was that it put its emphasis on direct action by workers – the use of their own power, through strikes, sabotage etc. – rather than on proposing changes to be legislated into existence by parliament. Its antimilitarism was less verbal than that of the SFIO's antimilitarists, far more oriented to how workers could be organised.

The weakness of the CGT was precisely that it was, in Rosmer's term, a 'hybrid' organisation, half-union, half-party. Because the CGT acted as a party as well as a union, it was harder for it to present itself as the organisation of all employed workers, as unions in Germany and Britain did. Hence unionisation levels were much lower in France. The union was seen not as the organisation of the whole class but as an 'active minority'. As a result the proportion of the working class it could reach was limited, and its ability to act effectively was restricted.

In some ways the CGT was cutting with the grain in its antimilitarism. In the early twentieth century the army was very unpopular in France. One factor in this was the widespread circulation of largely autobiographical novels of army life. One of the most read was *Biribi* by Georges Darien, an antimilitarist activist and prolific writer, who had spent 33 months in a disciplinary battalion in Tunisia. Darien described life in such a battalion; the marches in the hot sun [with an army doctor who refused to recognise exhaustion] and the soul-destroying boredom; the cruelty and corruption of the officers and the sheer brutality of the NCOs. Harsh punishments were imposed for such minor offences as smiling inappropriately and buttoning a greatcoat incorrectly.

Darien pointed unambiguously to the social role of the army: 'The army is the cornerstone of the present social structure; it is the power which enables forcible conquests; it is a barrier much less against invasions from abroad than against the demands of the citizens. The soldiers, these sons of the people armed against their father, are no more nor less than policemen in disguise'. As one of his characters put it: 'If war ever breaks out and we're led by people like these [their officers], it won't be the Prussians who'll be the first to be shot down'. Darien concluded: 'The army is a social cancer, an octopus whose

---

26   Rosmer 1936, p. 36.

tentacles are draining the blood of the peoples, who will have to cut off their hundred arms with an axe if they want to live'.[27]

An equally bleak picture of army life was found in *Au Port d'Arme* [Carrying a weapon] by Henry Fèvre.[28] Pierre Guerbert had joined the army hoping for a career, but came up against the sergeant Lacassègne, who hated him and systematically bullied him because he had had an education. Lacassègne set up a situation where Guerbert was provoked to a fight in a brothel and lost his rank as a corporal; he also seduced Guerbert's lover. Eventually Guerbert was driven to trying to kill Lacassègne by using a live bullet on manoeuvres, but failed and was executed by firing squad. The sergeants were shown as bullies, while the senior officers condoned their conduct. One soldier speaking of the adjutants said: 'I don't know where they find these people, thieves and pimps; in civilian life they'd have been in jail long ago'.[29]

Antimilitarist songs came into circulation. One – *Les Insoumis* [Those refusing to be conscripted, draft-dodgers] – was sung to the tune of the *Marseillaise*, bringing out the deep divide between the Jacobin tradition and antimilitarist internationalism:

> *Allons enfants des prolétaires,*
> *On nous appelle au régiment.*
> *On veut nous faire militaires*
> *Pour servir le gouvernement.*
> *Nos pères furent très dociles*
> *A des règlements incompris.*
> *Nous, nous serons moins imbéciles,*
> *Les insoumis, les insoumis. (bis).*
>
> *On nous dit d'avoir de la haine*
> *Pour les Germains envahisseurs,*
> *De tirer Alsace et Lorraine*
> *D'entre les mains des oppresseurs.*
> *Que nous font les luttes guerrières*
> *Des affameurs de tous pays?*
> *Nous ne voulons plus de frontières,*
> *Les insoumis, les insoumis. (bis)*

---

27   Darien 1890, pp. 90, 123, 283.
28   Fèvre 1887.
29   Fèvre 1887, p. 190.

Onward children of the working class,
We've been called to the army.
They want to make us into soldiers
To serve the government.
Our fathers were very docile
To rules they didn't understand.
We shall be less stupid,
The draft-dodgers, the draft-dodgers. (repeat)

We're told that we should feel hatred
For the Germanic invaders,
That we must snatch Alsace-Lorraine
From the oppressors' hands.
What do we care about the wars
Between those who starve all countries.
We want no more frontiers,
The draft-dodgers, the draft-dodgers. (repeat)[30]

The main factor in the CGT's commitment to antimilitarism was the use of the army against workers' organisations and especially against strikes. In the 25 years before 1914 there were some notorious examples of the use of the army – but also of soldiers refusing to obey orders. In 1907 the Clemenceau government sent troops against demonstrating winemakers in the Languedoc; about 500 soldiers mutinied and fraternised with demonstrators. In July 1908 troops opened fire on striking workers at Villeneuve-Saint-Georges, leaving four dead and a large number of wounded.[31] Following this nearly all the leadership of the CGT was imprisoned.

Claire Sainte-Soline, an anarchist, recalled the army being sent to break a strike in the Nord region in 1911. 'They were given orders, they stood there, without moving a step forward, as though they had suddenly become paralysed and deaf'.[32]

The syndicalist antimilitarists constantly linked the anti-working class role of the army within French frontiers to the preparation for war abroad, showing that the class struggle at home and internationalist opposition to war were inextricably connected. Syndicalist propaganda made ample reference to the need to forestall a new European war.

---

30   Rabaut 1975, p. 99.
31   Julliard 1965.
32   Sainte-Soline 1955, p. 100.

The CGT produced an enormous quantity of antimilitarist propaganda. The most important and influential was the *Nouveau manuel du soldat* [New Soldier's Manual] produced on the basis of a decision taken by the Tenth Congress of Labour Exchanges [Fédération des Bourses du travail] held in Algiers in September 1902. Eventually around 200,000 copies were distributed.[33]

The pamphlet was short [32 pages] and clearly argued, but it did not patronise its readers and drew on a wide range of literary references. It began by denouncing the whole idea of the *patrie* – 'one of the words which has caused the greatest loss of human blood'. It went on to note that 'our first playthings were sabres, guns, helmets and flags'. It insisted that a country could not be defined by a flag, a succession of kings or an extent of territory, but only in terms of 'men grouped together in order to produce and consume what is necessary for their lives'.[34] While workers had patriotism instilled into them, employers were quite happy to use foreign labour and buy foreign goods if they were cheaper. Soldiers defended the interests of a minority, not of the whole nation, in particular when they were sent to attack demonstrations and to replace striking workers.

Extracts from Zola's novel *La Débâcle*, dealing with the Franco-Prussian war of 1870, were quoted, describing corpses on a battlefield, to warn potential conscripts of the realities of war. The pamphlet went on to expose the inadequacy of peace congresses, concluding that 'only the workers can impose peace'.

The final appeal was to workers' self-activity: 'Religion and *patrie* are as bad as each other. To make the sign of the cross or to salute the flag is evidence of the same sad mentality. What is required is for us to count on ourselves'.[35]

The pamphlet concluded with some concrete advice to those about to be conscripted into the army. It did not come down firmly on the question of the choice between desertion and agitation within the army, leaving this to the discretion of the individual in terms of how he envisaged the prospects of what he could achieve in the army: 'If you think you won't be able to stand the vexations, the insults, the imbecilities, the punishments and all the squalid experiences which await you in the barracks: *Desert!* That is better than serving as a source of amusement to the drunken thugs and raving lunatics who will take care of you in the military prisons'.

Deserters were promised moral and financial support, and assistance to leave the country. But those who believed they could agitate within the army were also encouraged:

---

33 Brossat and Potel 1976, p. 78.
34 Fédération des bourses du travail 1902, pp. 2, 3, 5.
35 Fédération des bourses du travail 1902, pp. 19–20, 21, 29.

But if the affection of those who surround you, if the fear of the unknown, of all the troubles and sufferings that await you in a land whose language and customs you know nothing of; if other reasons too are stronger than your horror of the regiment: *Go into the army!* But do your best to remain a man while you are there. Overcome your disgust. Make yourself liked by your unfortunate companions in slavery and make propaganda to them individually. Make the school of crime into a school of revolt.

There was no ambiguity about the final recommendation:

> If you are sent to a strike: *Don't shoot!*
>
> Do they want to make you into killing machines? ... Rebel! The ones who should tremble are those who dare to arm you against your brothers, for *your only enemy is the one who exploits you, oppresses you, gives you orders and deceives you!*
>
> If they insist on making you murderers with guns in your hands, *then don't be fratricides!*[36]

The implication was clear: soldiers should shoot their own officers.

The *Manuel* thus set out a clear position: the army was a tool of the ruling class, and the working class had nothing to gain from supporting it; they should work for its destruction, either by undermining from within or by evading conscription. This overall message reached – if not the whole working class – a significant minority among them.

The themes of the *Manuel* were followed and reinforced by a whole range of propaganda. In 1905 the Association Internationale Antimilitariste [International Anti-militarist Association], involving many syndicalists, produced a poster whose message was even more explicit:

> When you're ordered to fire your guns at your brothers in poverty – as happened at Chalon, in Martinique, at Limoges –, workers, soldiers tomorrow, you won't hesitate, you won't obey. You'll shoot, but not at your comrades. You'll shoot at the troopers with stripes who dare give you such orders.
>
> When you're sent to the frontier to defend the money-boxes of the capitalists against other workers who have been deceived like you, you won't

---

36   Fédération des bourses du travail 1902, pp. 30, 32.

go. All wars are criminal. You'll respond to the mobilisation order with an immediate strike and insurrection.

The poster led to a trial which ended with 26 people being sentenced to a total of 36 years in jail.[37]

In 1905 the syndicalist journalist Hubert Lagardelle conducted a survey of trade-union activists in *Le Mouvement socialiste*.[38] Those polled were for the most part working members of their trades and leading figures in the union at a local level. The vast majority of those interviewed rejected the notion of patriotism, and while the majority in favour of strike action in the army was smaller, it was also quite a large proportion.

Within the ranks of the organised minority of the working class antimilitarist ideas had achieved a real penetration. Yet that influence remained among a minority, as some of the most perceptive syndicalists warned. In responding to the *Mouvement socialiste* survey, Alphonse Merrheim, later to be one of the first opponents of the 1914 war, pointed out:

> Now anyone who says: 'the mass of workers are more and more antimilitarist and antipatriotic, and therefore, completely *internationalist*', is making a grave error, for there are many who, out of hatred for the barracks and the loss of freedom that they bring, for the brutality, the discipline and the officers, are antimilitarists and call themselves antipatriots; but try talking to them about internationalism! Immediately their old prejudices are reawakened, and if they are willing to be against the army, they refuse to be internationalists and remain patriots.

Merrheim concluded that only the continued experience of economic reality would finally convince workers of the necessity of internationalism.[39] As he recognised, antimilitarism was not necessarily internationalist, but it prepared conditions in which internationalism could develop.

---

37   Rabaut 1975, p. 73.

38   'Enquête sur l'idée de patrie et la classe ouvrière', *Le Mouvement socialiste*, August 1905, pp. 433–70, September 1905, pp. 36–71, October 1905, pp. 201–31, November 1905, pp. 320–38.

39   *Le Mouvement socialiste*, November 1905, pp. 331–2.

2 Le Sou du Soldat

The CGT did not confine its antimilitarist activity simply to propaganda. It also developed a more concrete form of organisation known as the *sou du soldat* [the soldier's *sou*]. A *sou* was five centimes – one twentieth of a franc; at this time a worker's daily wage might vary between three and six francs a day.[40] This was a fund established in 1900.[41] The idea was stolen from the Catholic Church which had been running a similar scheme for some years.[42] The aim was to ensure that trade-union members who were called up for military service were kept in contact with the movement during their time in the barracks, and that they should be encouraged to feel loyalty towards their fellow-workers rather than to their officers.

In the Paris building workers' union, conscripts who had previously been trade unionists would receive three times a year a letter containing a monetary gift of between five and fifteen francs, enough to buy a few luxuries that would make barracks life a little more agreeable. Soldiers who accepted promotion out of the ranks or who agreed to act as officers' servants did not receive the money.[43] The gift was accompanied by a circular which, in guarded terms, reminded the conscripts of their allegiance to the working class. They were told that the employers, whose exploitation they had fought against, were now arming workers to defend their privileges. The trade-union conscripts were urged to take on the task of educating their fellow-soldiers, and of helping them to understand where their true interests lay. They were encouraged to cooperate with other trade unionists in the army.[44]

The impact of the *sou du soldat* was uneven. In some places at least it allowed activists to make antimilitarist propaganda within the army. An article in *La Vie ouvrière* by a serving soldier described how antimilitarists like himself were able to operate in the army.

The army authorities became aware that soldiers were receiving money and antimilitarist literature through the post. After a vain search for subversive literature the officers attempted to stamp out antimilitarist ideas; every day they gave lectures about anarchists and CGT agitators. Most of the soldiers did not understand a word; afterwards they asked the trade unionists to explain. Obvi-

---

40 Tillon 1969, pp. 38, 71.
41 Gravereaux 1913, pp. 115–17.
42 Becker 1973, p. 23.
43 Lacour 1911, p. 402.
44 'Le Procès Viau, Dumont et Baritaud', *La Vie ouvrière*, 20 January, 1912, pp. 146–8.

ously this provided an excellent opportunity for the antimilitarist soldiers to spread their ideas.

Subsequently orders were given to break off all relations with the soldier in question. There was a punishment of eight days' imprisonment for anyone who spoke to him. The parents of his associates were asked to warn their sons against frequenting antimilitarists. All this merely increased the sympathy that most soldiers showed him.

He also pointed out that the antimilitarists tended to be the best soldiers; they were the cleanest and did not drink – though they were denounced as drunkards. On one occasion the regiment was supplied with new machine-guns. The trickiest jobs in handling these weapons had to be entrusted to anti-militarists, as they were the most able.[45]

Military service was unpopular; it disrupted the life patterns of both peas-ants and workers, and the army's rituals provoked a spontaneous anti-authoritarianism. Louis Lecoin, who was to become a lifelong antimilitarist act-ivist, described the low level of morale in the French army at this time. Military service was 'a long and unpleasant burden, even for the volunteers who quickly regretted their mistake. Most of the young lads of twenty desired more than anyone else to see the army disappear'.[46]

Lecoin was to be one of the most remarkable antimilitarist campaigners over some sixty years. He did his military service, but was jailed for refusing to take part in strike-breaking. He was jailed again in 1913 for antimilitarist pro-paganda, and spent eight years in prison. He described himself as an 'anarchist-communist'. He was not opposed to all violence – he once went armed to a CGT Congress! – but rejected all forms of war. As he wrote to the military governor of Paris in 1917: 'The war fomented by world capitalism is the worst of the crimes perpetrated on the working classes'. After World War II he was involved in cam-paigning for the right of conscientious objection to military service [no such right existed in France until 1963], including a hunger strike at the age of 74. He was nominated for the Nobel Peace Prize, but withdrew in favour of Martin Luther King.[47]

In 1910 *La Vie ouvrière* carried an article by Robert Louzon, who had recently done a month's military service as a reservist. He reported that:

> Last year I spent 23 days with a Paris regiment. Half the reservists called up with me were peasants from Normandy, half were Parisian workers. I must

---

45   Lacour 1911, pp. 405–6.
46   Lecoin 1965, p. 48.
47   Lecoin 1965.

say first of all that if the peasants certainly hated war and the officers, they hated urban workers just as much. But as for the Parisian reservists, they were all very clearly antimilitarist, sympathetic to socialism or anarchism ...

What I'm certain of is that any small thing, a minor incident or a moment of enthusiasm, would have been enough to make the fifteen or so reservists with me side unanimously with a workers' insurrection.

It's very rare for someone coming back from a period with the army not to report some antimilitarist incident. Sometimes it's acts of collective indiscipline, making it impossible for the officers to impose punishments, sometimes the singing of the *Internationale* breaks out in the middle of manoeuvres, sometimes antimilitarist publications are distributed widely in the barrack rooms, and those responsible are never discovered, thanks to the complicity of everyone.[48]

This suggests that antimilitarist propaganda was at least getting a sympathetic hearing. Jean-Jacques Becker's assessment, based on an analysis of state papers, was that the *sou du soldat* affected, even if it did not wholly convince, many young soldiers. The police took it very seriously.[49]

The enemies of antimilitarism recognised that it was having a real impact on the armed forces. On 30 November 1912 in the National Assembly Adolphe Messimy, formerly minister of war, launched a fierce attack on the *sou du soldat* and the *Manuel du soldat*, which he described as a 'true catechism of desertion and cowardice'.[50] Messimy professed to be a defender of secular education and to be concerned that the *sou du soldat* was a threat to its principles.[51]

In support of his argument Messimy produced statistics which showed that since the introduction of the *sou du soldat* levels of desertion and evasion of conscription had increased massively. 'While before 1900 the average figure for desertions was 1900, and that for draft evasion was 4000, between 1900 and 1904 desertions increased to 2200 and draft evasions to 5000, and in the most recent period, when propaganda is becoming more and more intense, there are 2600 desertions and 10,000 draft evasions, some three times as many as formerly'.[52]

---

48   Louzon 1910.
49   Becker 1973, p. 46.
50   *Le Temps*, 1 December, 1912.
51   Becker 1973, p. 34.
52   *Le Temps*, 1 December, 1912.

When there was a revival of the *sou du soldat* around 1910 it came into more direct conflict with the French state. The builders' union, known for its militancy on wages and in support of a shorter working day,[53] was prosecuted for its involvement in the *sou du soldat*, and three of its members were jailed. They received very substantial support, with a demonstration on the day of the trial attracting thousands.[54]

Even more serious, in the eyes of the authorities, was the decision in August 1912 by the primary school teachers' union to support the *sou du soldat*.[55] This seemed to be a threat to the principle of *laïcité*. The state school system was designed to encourage a sense of national identity, so the teachers' decision threatened to undermine the work of the school system. As critics pointed out, if there were 6,000 antimilitarist teachers, that meant 120,000 pupils exposed to the ideas of antimilitarist teachers. This was particularly serious because many of these pupils would be peasants, the main source of army recruitment, and hitherto largely untouched by the antimilitarist agitation. The initial panic soon evaporated; only 5 percent of teachers were unionised,[56] and in the end nothing came of it.

3   *La Vie ouvrière*

One of the most significant political currents within the CGT was *La Vie ouvrière*, a journal which also represented a political tendency; it drew around it the most consistent internationalists in the confederation. It was launched by Pierre Monatte.[57] Monatte was a young syndicalist activist, jailed for a month for supporting a miners' strike and then obliged to take refuge in Switzerland to avoid arrest. It was not the journal of an organisation, but rather was produced by a *noyau* [nucleus] of writers whom Monatte gathered around himself. Notable members of the nucleus were Alfred Rosmer, Robert Louzon, Alphonse Merrheim, Georges Dumoulin and Francis Delaisi.

La Vie ouvrière appeared twice monthly. Each issue had 64 pages, occasionally more. Its content was geared to the syndicalist milieu, and the main substance of most issues consisted of analyses of strikes in France and reports

---

53   Becker 1973, p. 28.
54   *La Vie ouvrière*, 20 January, 1912, p. 152; Becker 1973, p. 31.
55   Salabelle 1912.
56   Miller 2002, pp. 178–9.
57   For a biography of this remarkable militant, see Chambelland 1999.

from trade-union conferences. There were also economic analyses, historical articles, book reviews and polemics with the SFIO and its newspaper *L'Humanité*.

The journal was aimed at what might be called worker intellectuals – active trade unionists, many of them with only the minimum of formal education, people who had, through their political and trade-union activity, acquired a serious interest in ideas. It was free from jargon, other than the normal terminology of trade-union life, and it did not talk down to its readers. It assumed that they were intelligent people who wanted solid but accessible information. In 1914, the number of subscriptions was over 1900, close to Monatte's target of 2000.[58] The whole thing was a shoestring operation, kept going by Monatte's dedication and enthusiasm.[59]

La Vie ouvrière aimed to be a current within the CGT, not to juxtapose itself to the CGT organisation; its function would be educational. Effective international coverage was at the heart of the project. In almost every issue there were reports on struggles and situations around the world, from Sweden to South Africa, Spain to Switzerland, Guadeloupe to New Zealand. At a time when most international communication still relied on the postal services, it was not possible to have up-to-the-minute news from abroad, and some articles were clearly worked up from reports in the mainstream press. Monatte built up a small network of international contacts; well-known militants like Tom Mann from Britain and William Z. Foster from the United States contributed articles.

In 1911, when the journal had 1607 subscribers, *La Vie ouvrière* published a geographical breakdown of its circulation. As well as 38 subscribers in North Africa, there were another 79 scattered around the globe. There were 29 in Belgium, 28 in Switzerland [probably including the future President of the Communist International, Zinoviev], six in the United States and just two in England.[60]

Monatte advocated a view of the world which argued that the exploited and oppressed in various countries had more interests in common with each other than they did with the exploiters and oppressors in their own countries. His argument can be taken as a programmatic statement of how internationalism would be dealt with in the journal:

> Our first task is to become closer morally, to get to know each other better, to be mutually informed. Internationalism, like all sentiments, because

---

58   *La Vie ouvrière*, 20 June 1914, p. 730.
59   Rosmer 1951.
60   'Entre Nous', *La Vie ouvrière*, 5 March 1911, p. 317.

that is what it is first of all, needs to be nourished, and it can only be nourished on one condition, namely that we should follow the great struggles
carried out by each other, that we should be stirred by the successes and
the setbacks of our distant friends, that we should drive home the simple
truth which cannot be hidden for long: that everywhere workers experience their exploitation, and everywhere, with sudden outbursts or tenacious efforts, they are striving to raise their heads and stand upright.[61]

Behind the rather moralising language there was an insistence that it was consciousness, and not forms of organisation, that was primary.

The underlying spirit of the international reports in *La Vie ouvrière* was not
simply to accumulate information, but to show that the struggles of working
people in different parts of the world were fundamentally the same, for better
wages and conditions, for workers' rights, and ultimately for the overthrow of
capitalism.

One fairly obvious example was the campaign being waged in pre-1914
France for the 'English week', that is, the five-and-a-half day week, with Saturday afternoon off. This had been achieved by some British workers, and the
aim was for French workers to emulate them.[62]

Parallel to this was a study of how employers in various countries used different tactics in opposition to the working-class movement. Henri Amoré wrote a
short survey of German employers' organisations, showing how they confronted strikes. Methods included: financial aid to employers affected by strikes,
blacklisting, the organisation of strike-breaking and the use of lock-outs.[63] The
aim was to urge the need for effective organisation on the trade-union side. The
English trade unionist Tom Mann, who had lived in Australia for nine years,
contributed an article on arbitration in that country.[64]

There were also important lessons to be drawn from workers' struggles. Francis Delaisi [writing as Cratès] contributed a two-part article on the Barcelona
insurrection of 1909. This had begun in opposition to the war in Morocco and
the recall of reservists. It was initially very successful, spreading out from Barcelona, and it seemed briefly as if 'the Revolution had begun'. The government
succeeded in crushing the revolt by using troops. Cratès concluded that the les-
son was the need for effective organisation.[65]

---

61   Monatte 1909, p. 338.
62   Various authors, 'La Semaine anglaise en France', *La Vie ouvrière*, 5 May 1912, pp. 161–73.
63   Amoré 1909.
64   Mann 1910.
65   Cratès 1909b; Cratès 1909c.

La Vie ouvrière also carried articles analysing the pressures leading to war. In the first issue Cratès wrote an analysis of the Spanish war in Morocco. He began by noting the fundamental division of views on the question of patriotism:

> Some consider that as soon as the flag is involved, it must be defended unquestioningly. Others, who think that the homeland is an outdated concept, keep their devotion for 'humanity' and their energies for the 'social war'.
>
> But very few know by what means ingenious financiers and crafty politicians induce hundreds of thousands of men to risk their lives for interests they know nothing of and which in any case do not concern them.

Cratès then explained the origins of the conflict. French explorers had discovered iron deposits in Morocco and had set up a company to exploit them. A Spanish company and a British company had decided to do the same. When the companies found they were in conflict, they turned to their national governments. Meanwhile the native inhabitants of Morocco were unhappy with developments, knowing from the experience of Algeria that their land would be grabbed and any rebellion suppressed by force of arms.

Conflict broke out, as the indigenous inhabitants attempted to block the exploitation of the mines at Melilla:

> A group of workers on their way to work fell into an ambush; three or four were killed. A serious matter! Immediately the Melilla garrison was mobilised.
>
> It is curious to observe how the skin of workers, which is so cheap in their home countries, increases in value when it is exported. In France as in Spain it is not highly valued; regularly hundreds of workers are killed in strikes or in dangerous work; some are murdered each day in various points of the globe, without diplomatic incidents being caused.
>
> But when the skin of proletarians covers some big financial scheme, then it becomes an infinitely precious object for governments.

He concluded with a historical anecdote: 'It is said that on the evening after the battle of Rosbach, the Prussian King Frederick II was crossing the plain where thirty thousand corpses lay, and said with a smile to his attendants: "Gentlemen, there are thirty thousand men who got themselves slaughtered for something which didn't concern them."'[66]

---

66   Cratès 1909a.

It was a devastating critique of imperialist war, and the basic arguments were repeated in many contributions to *La Vie ouvrière*.

La Vie ouvrière also took up the situation in the French colonies. In 1910 it published a series of letters from a correspondent in Guadeloupe, where three strikers on a sugar plantation had been killed. The letters stressed the brutality and poverty of life in Guadeloupe; a concluding editorial note was added: 'Workers earning 85 centimes a day, who are shot and burned, that is the balance-sheet, in Guadeloupe, of fifty years of French colonialism'.[67] In France a worker's wage was often between three and six francs per day.

A further piece by a black militant provided more details on the poverty and oppression of working people in Guadeloupe, citing a factory manager who stated that 'if he had arrived in Guadeloupe ten years earlier, the blacks would never have worn shoes'.[68]

A major advance in *La Vie ouvrière*'s reporting of international matters came when Monatte recruited Alfred Rosmer. Rosmer had been born in the USA and spoke fluent English. He would go on to be a leading anti-war activist, and play an important part in the early years of the French Communist Party and the Communist International.

Rosmer travelled to Britain in 1910 to report on developments there. In 1912, at the time of the Balkans War, he tried to disentangle the situation. He began by saying 'Being neither turcophiles nor turcophobes, but being solely concerned with truth and the concern to prevent the Balkans War from degenerating, as a result of the greed of the great rival powers, into a European slaughter, we want to show in a true light what these Balkan populations are and expose those who are really responsible for the conflict'.

He insisted that the real responsibility for the situation lay with the great powers of Europe and not with the Turks. He was scathing in dismissing the various national and racial myths which were evoked in trying to explain the war. The mixture of races in the Balkans meant it was impossible to determine racial characteristics: 'How many of these ferocious Christians, pursuing the infidel, have Muslim blood in their veins?'

His conclusion pointed clearly to the European war that was now only a couple of years away: 'And now the really serious phase of the conflict is beginning. It is the great powers and groups of great powers who are fighting with each other, and it is more than ever necessary that the European proletariat should indicate clearly and forcefully its determination to oppose by all means a European slaughter'.[69]

---

67   'Grèves et politique à la Guadeloupe', *La Vie ouvrière*, 5 May 1910, pp. 520–24.
68   Rosso 1910.
69   Rosmer 1912b.

Rosmer also wrote about South Africa. He reported a major strike by white gold-miners, and also noted the terrible conditions suffered by black workers and the appalling death rate as a result of accidents. He pointed out that the strike had become general because the black workers refused to work in the absence of the white miners.[70]

La Vie ouvrière had little sympathy with the ideas of Jaurès on the reform of the national army. An example of this came with a report on the Swiss army. Jaurès had praised the Swiss system for organising national defence in the form of militias. Jean Wintsch gave a scathing account of the reality:

> The officer corps is made up, in fact, of rich bourgeois and various types of aristocrat; there is a mass of young failures and idlers who have been incapable of pursuing a liberal, commercial, industrial or any other occupation in civilian life. So the arrogance of these individuals has become unbearable, with the result that they are generally thoroughly detested by their soldiers. There is no shortage of examples of brutality, vulgarity, stupidity, negligence and extortion in the upper levels of the military.

As a result the Swiss army was extremely unpopular among working people. As he pointed out, 'it was Switzerland which was the first to use the army against strikers. During the last ten years there have been no less than twenty such interventions'.[71]

The most important contribution to the discussion on the impending war was a series of four articles by Alphonse Merrheim.[72] Merrheim was a leading member of the *La Vie ouvrière* grouping; in some senses he represented a reformist trend within revolutionary syndicalism, since he believed that workers were not yet sufficiently prepared for a revolutionary confrontation with the capitalist state. From 1920 he became violently anti-Bolshevik, producing a flood of polemics, but nothing can detract from his intransigent internationalism before and during World War I.

The articles appeared in 1911 under the title 'The Approach of War'. He argued, 'we are on the eve of a gigantic European conflict'. He warned that war 'can break out in ten years' time, in five years, perhaps earlier'. It would be just three and a half.

He then tried to analyse the factors driving towards war. In the present world overproduction led to commercial expansion, with capitalist nations compet-

---

70   Rosmer 1913.
71   Wintsch 1910.
72   See Papayanis 1985.

ing to take over new countries. 'But as the new countries are penetrated and saturated with products, competition becomes keener and the situation gets more tense. Slowly but surely the sword comes out of the sheath'.

Merrheim saw the main commercial rivalry as between England and Germany. Both sides would try to draw France into the conflict. England needed French soldiers, Germany needed French finance. 'For us, who need peace in the world in order to pursue our task of national and international organisation, in order to prepare the struggle of the whole proletariat against capitalism, there is not a minute to lose'.

The arms race could not continue indefinitely, yet disarmament was impossible. A limitation of individual production would have serious consequences, since it would lead to unemployment and wage cuts, and hence to social unrest. As a result 'the capitalist regime is between two abysses: war or revolution'.

French workers would not be able to ignore the impact of an Anglo-German war. In particular, England had the problem that it could not impose conscription, because workers thought an army would be used against them. So England would need French soldiers to complement its navy. Merrheim correctly predicted that Germany would not respect Belgian neutrality, and that this would become a major issue in pro-war propaganda:

> What will be necessary to make France go to war? To persuade it that it is in danger, that national rights have been trampled underfoot. Belgium invaded by Germany is the violation of the neutrality of small countries! Our chauvinistic press, well bribed, will find it easy to howl that French intervention is necessary. Our Northern frontier is unprotected. We must go to war.

He added: 'Fortunately for the peace of the world there is one force whose opinion they take good care not to ask. It's the French working class; in fact its opinion is known in advance; it does not intend to be knocked to pieces either for the King of Prussia or for the King of England'. [A French idiom 'working for the king of Prussia' means working without reward.]

Since the French working class had no interest in taking sides, it must stand by the decision made at CGT congresses: 'Insurrection sooner than war! General strike as a response if mobilisation is ordered!'

Merrheim ended on a cautiously optimistic note:

> Already English workers seem to have understood their duty. Their trade unions are active. There is a complete reversal going on inside them; they

will soon stand up against war. There are still the German workers. Will they understand their duty? Will they draw their leaders along with them? We hope so.[73]

4   Impending War

That there was a significant antimilitarist current within the French working class in the years before 1914 is not in doubt, though opposition to colonialism, especially in Algeria, was less visible. Any evaluation of that current has to be set against the fact that it was a failure. In 1914 the entire French labour movement, with a few tiny and isolated exceptions, went over to support for the war.

That there was still a real anti-war current in the working class was shown by the mass demonstrations that took place in Paris in July 1914. On the evening of 27 July there was a huge march on the Paris boulevards. A demonstration estimated by supporters as at least a hundred thousand, predominantly workers from the suburbs, marched from the place de la République to the place de l'Opéra. Around nine o'clock a crowd gathered outside the offices of *Le Matin*, a particularly pro-war newspaper; the *Internationale* was sung and there were chants of 'Down with war'. The police were unable to disperse the demonstration, despite increasingly brutal attacks; eventually there were some five hundred arrests.[74] Clearly at least the most militant elements of the Paris working class were not reconciled to war.

The following day came the Sarajevo events, and the rapid developments leading to the German declaration of war on France on 3 August. The leaders of the working-class movement throughout Europe backed the war, and the vast mass of their followers went with them. The anti-war left was powerless; the collapse was sudden and unexpected. It was not just the Second International which collapsed – in France the capitulation of the syndicalist leaders of the CGT was equally important.

The reason for the collapse is a question that has engaged historians ever since 1914. In his *Age of Imperialism* Eric Hobsbawm argued that: 'The socialist parties which accepted the war often did so without enthusiasm, and chiefly because they feared to be abandoned by their followers, who flocked to the colours with spontaneous zeal'.[75] It is too simplistic an account. Zeal there certainly was among at least some of those recruited to the armed forces in the

---

73   Merrheim 1911.
74   *L'Humanité*, 28 July 1914. See also Rosmer 1936, pp. 102–3.
75   Hobsbawm 1987, pp. 108–9.

heady atmosphere of the summer of 1914. It is very questionable whether it was spontaneous.

It would be unwise to try to establish a single factor which led to the collapse of the internationalist left in 1914. On the contrary, it was a coming together of various events and processes which produced the defeat, and in each country there were particular factors, of history and ideology, to explain the capitulation.

In the French case, in the first place there was a long-term ideological offensive, operated primarily through the *laïc* school system. In the three decades since Ferry's reforms of the 1880s the *laïc* school, despite the best efforts of a minority of antimilitarist teachers, had done its job of, in Eugen Weber's phrase, converting peasants into Frenchmen.[76] Processes such as the imposition of the French language on peasants who spoke other dialects and languages were combined with the specific tasks of the glorification of war and military training.

While the CGT had concentrated on the industrial working class, organised in trade unions, the ideologues of the *laïc* school realised very clearly that it was the peasantry which was central to France's ability to mobilise an army. Peasants were crucial, since many key industrial workers, from well unionised sectors such as miners, railway workers and engineers, were withdrawn from fighting because they were needed for the war effort at their original jobs.[77]

At the time of the outbreak of war the long-term ideological offensive was reinforced by rumours and outright lies which created a climate combining fear and patriotic fervour. Rosmer described the mood in Paris at the outbreak of war, where violence and intimidation were not spontaneous but encouraged by the regime:

> There was no sign of life, except around the stations and sometimes in the streets, where there were marches by howling mobs, chanting: 'To Berlin! To Berlin!' and singing the *Marseillaise*. In order to feed their patriotic fervour, those leading them here and there launched them against 'boche' shops. ... A German-sounding name on a shop was enough to provoke destruction and looting. Henceforth our 'brothers' from Alsace were not spared, and it was enough for a bakery to be 'Viennese' for it to be pillaged. The government let things take their course – that is, if we assume

---

76   Weber 1979.
77   Rosmer 1936, p. 537.

that it did not actually instigate these patriotic displays.[78] [*boche* was a xenophobic term for a German.]

There was also direct intimidation by the state authorities. Central to this was the existence of the 'Carnet B'. This was a list of people known for antimilitarist activities, including CGT leaders, who could be rounded up in case of a national emergency. Adolphe Messimy, War Minister at the outbreak of war, warned:

> Give me the guillotine and I guarantee victory ... These people shouldn't imagine that they will simply be sent to prison. They must know that we shall send them to the front line; and if they won't go, well, they'll be shot from in front and behind. Then we shall be rid of them.[79]

But in August 1914 the government made clear that it would not use the Carnet B, believing that if it avoided confrontation with the labour movement, the CGT leadership could be won over to support for the war. It thus encouraged the CGT leadership to shift to a more accommodating position. However in some provincial areas – notably the Nord, which was close to the combat area – trade-union activists, some of whom had been involved in antimilitarist activity, were arrested and imprisoned.[80]

Then came the assassination of the SFIO's best-known leader, Jean Jaurès. On 31 July Jaurès met a member of the government who asked him what the Socialist Party would do if the moves towards war continued. When he replied that they would continue to campaign against the war he was told: 'You wouldn't dare do that; you would be killed on the next street corner!' Two hours later he was shot dead.[81] The far right began to mobilise on the streets, threatening and attacking socialists and syndicalists. A mob marched through the streets, chanting 'Down with Jaurès! Up with war!' and brandishing the tricolour in the face of trade-union activists.[82]

Added to this intimidation was a climate of rumours and lies. In the ensuing months public sensibility was inflamed by numerous unsubstantiated atrocity stories. This should have been resisted by a working-class leadership with daily newspapers at its disposal. But there were deep problems within the SFIO and CGT leaderships.

---

78   Rosmer 1936, p. 209.
79   Rosmer 1936, p. 109.
80   Rosmer 1936, pp. 156–9.
81   Rosmer 1936, pp. 91–2.
82   Rosmer 1936, pp. 116–17.

For the other crucial factor in the collapse of opposition to the war was the failure of the leaders of the working-class movement, in both the SFIO and the CGT, to offer any effective alternative. Both organisations were essentially reformist, committed to achieving change within the limits of the French nation state. Within a few days at the beginning of August both organisations transformed their positions. In his history of the labour movement in the First World War Alfred Rosmer traced the dramatic way in which the CGT capitulated, showing the shifts in the CGT's daily paper, *La Bataille Syndicaliste*, between 1 August and 4 August. On Saturday 1 August it still had a staunchly anti-war stance; by the following Tuesday it was telling its readers that '... against Germanic militarism, we must save the democratic and revolutionary tradition of France'.[83]

Within a very short time the labour leaders were lining up to back the war. Jules Guesde went over to full support for the war, and became a government minister. One-time antimilitarist campaigner Gustave Hervé took such an enthusiastic pro-war position that he was eventually excluded from the SFIO. Socialist Albert Thomas became Minister of Labour, and was highly commended for his efficient work. Léon Jouhaux, secretary-general of the CGT, worked closely with Albert Thomas, and took a strongly pro-war line in the union.

Before 1914 a number of international crises had brought Europe to the brink of war. A strong enough response by the working class in August 1914 and war could have been postponed yet again. In retrospect all defeats are inevitable, but for those who actually live through the process of alternative possibilities the experience varies enormously.

An important factor in the labour leaders' capitulation was the invocation of the French revolutionary tradition. Rosmer provides a number of examples, from both socialists and syndicalists, of appeals to the legacy of 1789 and contrasts with the alleged militarism of Germany. Prime minister Viviani told the National Assembly that France was 'the daughter of the seething Revolution', and was applauded by the Socialist deputies.[84] Rosmer provides extensive evidence to show the double nature of the revolutionary tradition, and demonstrates the way in which the republican-nationalist interpretation of the revolutionary tradition was deployed in a reactionary fashion.

In a state of emergency it was very easy for revolutionary defence to slide into nationalism and even ethnic stereotyping. On 6 August a prominently placed article in the *Bataille syndicaliste* stated: 'In the present conflict the ethnic ques-

---

83   Quoted by Rosmer 1936, p. 144.
84   Rosmer 1936, p. 206.

tion has some importance. The Germans have heavier blood and hence a more submissive and resigned temperament, and thus lack our spirit of independence'.[85]

Rosmer's own account of the defeat focussed on the psychology of working people in the period immediately preceding the outbreak of war. He noted that in the weeks before the outbreak of war, people had been alternately threatened with war, then told there was a hope for peace. 'The anxious populations were systematically tossed between war imposed by the enemy and peace which had been finally preserved. In a single day it was war, then peace, then war again. All that interspersed with emergencies, rumours, denials. Already in ordinary times the power of the press over opinion is considerable. In such times of anxiety it takes over completely. After a week of such battering, the strongest heads can take no more; the state of nervous tension is such that people ask for nothing but a way out. Peace, certainly, would be welcomed with joy, but even war is better than this maddening uncertainty'.[86] He summed up the experience with the judgment: 'when war starts, it means the working class has already been defeated'.[87] The time to stop wars is before they start.

A more extensive analysis of the causes of defeat came from another member of the *Vie ouvrière* team, Georges Dumoulin. A miner from north-eastern France, Dumoulin had been a leading figure in the pre-war revolutionary syndicalist movement and was closely associated with *La Vie ouvrière* from its inception. By 1914 he was deputy secretary of the CGT. On the afternoon of 2 August he attended a meeting of the confederal committee of the CGT, at which there was a total lack of direction, and where one half-drunken delegate launched a patriotic tirade of anti-German abuse. That same evening Dumoulin left on a train for the front with the very first batch of soldiers to be mobilised; syndicalist morality required that he share the fate of his fellow-workers. In February 1916 he was at the battle of Verdun; he wrote to his friend Monatte:

The ends of my fingers are frozen, my lips are burnt, my feet sore and my shoulders bruised. In the scrap I lost my underwear, my papers, my notes, my most useful possessions. I've aged several years in eight days. My body is covered with lice and filth. My heart is full of malice and

---

85   Quoted by Rosmer 1936, p. 118.
86   Rosmer 1936, p. 86.
87   Rosmer 1936, p. 9.

> hatred. And the funny thing is that I don't have the heart to resent any-
> body other than the traitors, our own people who have betrayed us so
> much.[88]

After three years in the army, Dumoulin, aged forty, was sent back to mining
in the Loire valley. Having seen what the war had meant to the working class,
he was able to draw his thoughts together and attempt an explanation of why
the CGT had collapsed so abysmally. In the summer of 1918 he produced a short
pamphlet entitled 'The French syndicalists and the war'.[89]

The tone of the pamphlet was bitter, but it attempted a sober assessment
of the limitations of the CGT's antimilitarism and the reasons for its failure.
Looking back to the pre-war period, he dismissed the influence of Hervé's antipatriotism as a mere 'breath of wind'. Within the CGT he identified two currents.
One, which he associated with Merrheim and *La Vie ouvrière*, he saw as seriously concerned to study the economic developments of the period which were
producing the drive to war.

The other current, that of Griffuelhes and Jouhaux, had no interest in knowledge; 'those who studied were abused as being petty bourgeois, arid doctrin-
aires and unrealistic'.[90] Among the leading clique there was jealousy and hostility towards the German union leaders, which easily spilled over into anti-
German feeling pure and simple.

The spread of opportunism among the leadership was paralleled by divisions among the rank and file of the union. Without any clear political guidance
from the CGT leadership, each group of workers became preoccupied with
purely sectional interests. Dumoulin observed a disappearance of the moral
commitment which had been central to all that was best in revolutionary syndicalism. He gave a horrifying depiction of the state of the CGT on the eve of
war:

> An ignorant proletariat which cannot read, doesn't want to read, or reads
> filth. Militants who play cards endlessly with their comrades in bars. In
> Paris, a gang of adventurers hanging around the Labour Exchange buying
> drinks for the full-time officials. Working-class journalism as corrupt as
> the other which lives in the filthy sewer of the Croissant [a printworks in
> the rue de Croissant, Paris]. Drunks and profligates who correct the faulty

---

88   Chambelland, 1999, p. 102.

89   The full text is reproduced in Rosmer, 1936, pp. 524–42, from which all quotations are
      taken.

90   See Rosmer 1936, p. 525.

grammar of the top officials and talk up their conference speeches. And war is on its way.[91]

With the loss of moral integrity at the top, the union was seen, by members and non-members alike, as merely an economic instrument. Hence, faced with the challenge of impending war, the leadership lost its nerve.

Dumoulin was withering about Jouhaux, who was in full health, but who was not called up, and devoted himself to charitable work in the framework of the 'sacred union' [the unity of all political forces in support of national defence]. It was not simply the top leaders who collapsed in 1914; it was the whole apparatus of union activists.

For Dumoulin the real source of the CGT's weakness lay not in the failings of individuals, but in the limited influence of the CGT before 1914. Whereas the German unions had two and a half million members, the CGT had only 300,000.[92] Antimilitarist propaganda had been vigorous, but confined to a limited section of the working population. Genuine antimilitarist propaganda had been carried out in about forty labour exchanges [the local centres of union activity]. 'Meetings always reached the same audience'.[93] As a result a minority congratulated itself on its antimilitarist rhetoric and left the mass of workers untouched.

Antimilitarist propaganda had been shallow and unpolitical. The analysis of the roots of war in capitalist society was not developed; antimilitarism merely reflected the gut feelings of the proletariat rather than offering an enhanced understanding:

> We thought it was enough to detest the barracks and loathe the NCO for war not to come. The workers do not hate the state of affairs which they suffer because they do not hold it responsible for war. The sacred union was possible because capitalism had not been seen as guilty by the mass of the exploited ... I hear poor buggers saying: 'There will always be wars because there always have been wars'. They don't know the history of the past wars which they identify with the present and the future.[94]

Hence the CGT resolutions calling for general strike action were futile. The 300,000 unionised workers were a small minority amid a much greater mass

---

91   See Rosmer 1936, p. 527.
92   See Rosmer 1936, p. 532.
93   See Rosmer 1936, p. 532.
94   See Rosmer 1936, p. 533.

of workers and peasants. On the eve of war they had neither the means to win over the mass of workers, nor the ability to act independently of them.

As Dumoulin knew from his own experience, the majority of workers went enthusiastically to war. He described his own experience in the troop train leaving on the first evening of war. Everywhere there was singing, shouting and the chalking up of crude nationalist slogans. The small minority who did not share the enthusiasm were condemned to remain silent, all the more intimidated because they had no alternative to look to. As a result it took those who survived a long time to come to terms with reality, and even then they lacked political understanding.

He concluded that while the CGT leaders would look to cooperation with pro-war union leaders abroad and the international bourgeoisie, 'we shall go towards the workers of all lands to rebuild the workers' international'.[95]

Sadly Dumoulin himself did not move in this direction. Broken by his wartime ordeal and unable to respond to the new prospects offered by the Russian Revolution, he made no further contribution to the internationalist left. After the war he moved to the right of the CGT; in 1940 became a collaborator with the Nazis. Sentenced to death in 1945, he hid till his sentence was quashed and spent his last years as a Catholic. As Rosmer pointed out, his subsequent faults should not conceal what was 'great and heroic'[96] in his conduct after 1914. In looking with total honesty at the movement to which he had devoted the best years of his life, he made clear not only the moral power which was the legacy of the best of syndicalism, but the political weaknesses which condemned its highest aspirations to failure. The most useful epitaph is the one which helps future generations to learn to do better, and as such Dumoulin provided the best epitaph for pre-1914 syndicalism.

Yet that epitaph should not be entirely negative. If syndicalism failed to prevent the war, it was from among the syndicalists that some of the first and most tenacious opponents of the war were to come. And after the war the role of syndicalists in forming the French Communist Party has often been underestimated. As the next two chapters will show, there was much that was valuable in syndicalisms's contribution to the development of the French working class.

---

95   See Rosmer 1936, p. 542.
96   Rosmer 1936, pp. 10–11.

From Slaughter to Mutiny

There had been many predictions of the world war that erupted in August 1914, but the reality was more horrific than most of them. For four years venal politicians and inept military leaders sent increasingly reluctant soldiers to their deaths in numbers that are almost impossible to grasp. The Western Front ran through France and Belgium, and a significant part of the war was fought in North-Eastern France, disrupting communities and economic life, and leaving some areas under foreign occupation.

At the outbreak of war the few remaining internationalists found themselves completely isolated. Alfred Rosmer gave a vivid account of the situation during the first few days of the war:

> In this Paris, which was deserted and overwhelmed – overwhelmed in spirit, that is – Monatte and I undertook to seek out what little islands of resistance might exist. ... Monatte and I were not subject to the call-up. We set out to look for people. Our first visit was to James Guillaume [a Swiss veteran of the First International]. *La Vie ouvrière* had had no more devoted friend; he was always ready to help in whatever fashion, even taking on humble translation jobs, for which there were never many volunteers. But it was a hopeless visit. His deep hatred for social democracy, his persistent bitterness going back to the time of the First International, were bound to draw him into a war against Prussian militarism.[1]

They had many similar experiences:

> Meanwhile Monatte had gone to *Le Libertaire* [the main anarchist journal]. There he had met Pierre Martin [a long-standing anarchist weaver], who was very solid, but who was convinced that nothing could be done until women from the suburbs took to the streets. This was quite a common feeling. We observed it in the case of several syndicalist militants. They believed nothing could be done. Things must be allowed to take their course. It was a passivity encouraged by the belief – or the hope – that the war would be short. What could be observed in the poor dis-

---

1 Rosmer 1936, pp. 210–11.

tricts also tended to support it. Left to themselves, the workers who remained behind had not been able to swim against the stream. The same ones we had seen in the Pré-Saint-Gervais, in all the anti-war demonstrations, had now been carried away by the crusade against Prussian militarism.[2]

There was one notable exception:

One day, on returning from our disappointing wanderings, we found a note from Marcel Martinet. He had only recently been associated with us, but he was very well informed about working-class matters and activities, and he had immediately given us active support. The few lines he had written said, in effect: 'Is it I who am mad? Or the others?' We visited him without delay. It was the first time we had landed on solid ground and we felt great joy. From then on Martinet was involved in all our activities, closely associated with our work; he was to be the poet of these 'accursed times'.[3]

Marcel Martinet [1887–1944], poet and novelist, was the author of anti-war poems which would be published in Switzerland in 1917 under the title *Les Temps maudits* [accursed times]. In a savage poem of shock and anger, dated 30 July 1914, Martinet saw the coming war for what it was – a confrontation of workers who had everything in common except their national allegiance:

Travaille, travailleur.
Fondeur du Creusot, devant toi
Il y a un fondeur d'Essen,
Tue-le.
Mineur de Saxe, devant toi
Il y a un mineur de Lens,
Tue-le.
Docker du Havre, devant toi
Il y a un docker de Brême.
Tue et tue, tue-le, tuez-vous.
Travaille, travailleur.

---

2 Rosmer 1936, p. 212.
3 Rosmer 1936, pp. 211–12.

> Worker, set to work.
> Smelter from Le Creusot, before you
> Stands a smelter from Essen,
> Kill him.
> Miner of Saxony, before you
> Stands a miner from Lens,
> Kill him.
> Docker from Le Havre, before you stands
> A docker from Bremen,
> Kill and kill, kill him, kill each other,
> Worker set to work.[4]

The capitulation of the CGT was shameful, but not total. There was opposition even within the CGT leadership body. Alphonse Merrheim opposed the war from the start, though the atmosphere of the CGT was such that he used to take two large dogs with him to meetings.[5] Soon an anti-war current began to develop within the metal-workers' union, under the leadership of Merrheim and Raoul Lenoir. Lenoir confronted other unions in the CGT, insisting on the principles of the CGT and asserting that the war 'was not our war'.[6]

La Vie ouvrière had been obliged to suspend publication; for the moment Rosmer, Monatte, Martinet and other *VO* supporters could act only as individuals. In November 1914 Monatte resigned from the Confederal Committee of the CGT, following the CGT's refusal to attend a conference called by socialists in neutral countries. He justified his action by arguing that so-called syndicalists were speaking 'a language worthy of pure nationalists'.[7]

Only in November 1915 was Rosmer able to issue a circular to all the former subscribers to *La Vie ouvrière*. This provided an acute internationalist analysis of the war. He began with a contemptuous dismissal of the various justifications given for supporting the war:

> A war of liberation, a war of civilisation against barbarism, a war of races, a war for the rule of law, the need to crush enemy militarism, a war to end all wars, a war for the principle of nationalities, for the independence of small nations – we saw none of that in the enormous conflict which had

---

4 Paizis 2007, pp. 66–69 [translation by George Paizis].
5 Rosmer 1936, p. 182.
6 Rosmer 1936, p. 174.
7 Rosmer 1936, p. 177.

been unleashed. We recognised the clichés which governments produce at the beginning of every butchery, and which they use against each other. A few months ago, in his letter to Clemenceau, Georg Brandes [a Danish literary critic] recalled that in 1870 it was already said that this war would be the last. But amid the disarray into which they had been plunged by the collapse of socialism and syndicalism, many workers clutched onto one or another of these explanations, which seemed to them like a last hope. They were offered a counterfeit ideal. They accepted it. A unanimous press imperceptibly distorted judgements.

He showed no sympathy for those labour leaders who argued that Germany bore sole responsibility for the war, and rejected the arguments of those who believed that German militarism could be crushed by military victory and the removal of some of Germany's territories; this would merely reinforce militarist attitudes inside Germany. As he pointed out, 'German militarism can be defeated only by the Germans themselves'. If the syndicalist leaders were now arguing that Germany bore all responsibility for the war, they were repudiating all their activities from the period before the war: 'What strange forgetfulness that would be'.

While not denying that the German regime had its share of responsibility for the war, he insisted that the main blame lay with the whole imperialist system:

> There is for us only one possible attitude: to say that the war results from a conflict of rival imperialisms and resolutely refuse to identify with our governments which all bear their share of responsibility. And if we are told we are pro-German because we do not accept the official explanation of the war, we shall reply as Noah Ablett [Welsh miners' leader] replied to the English jingoes in the name of the Welsh miners: 'We are not pro-German, but we are working class!' … Imperialism must be defined as the economic struggle between great powers for the conquest of markets, to acquire spheres of influence in non-industrialised countries where they can sell off their products, obtain concessions and exercise a sort of protectorate. It lies at the foundation of all modern wars: the USA against Spain, for Cuba and Panama; Japan against Russia, for Manchuria and Korea; Britain against the South African Republics, for the exploitation of the mines.

Thus Rosmer stated his sympathies with the English people, while utterly rejecting the policies of British imperialism:

I was and I remain an Anglophile. But the England without soldiers, the England of individual freedom, the England which welcomes refugees, this England is in process of dying, and it will not be Germany which has killed it, but its own imperialists. One of my friends, alarmed by the changes which he is observing, wrote to me: 'Poor old England, we shall not see her again!'

He therefore repudiated the whole policy of 'sacred union'.

What was to be done? In the present situation the internationalist left was weak, and its response could only be a defensive one, though he looked to the example of the anti-war wing of the Italian Socialist Party and to the British Independent Labour Party:

In the state of disarray produced by any great war, above all when the socialist and workers' leaders go over to the government, there is a period in which one can think only of saving and preserving what exists. The task which then faces revolutionaries is, for them too, to stand fast. That is what the Italian Socialists have done. It is what our comrades in the Independent Labour Party have done from the very first day, and have not ceased to do ever since. If we had had a similar attitude to theirs, the government would have felt the existence of a great force hostile to its policies, a great movement which it could momentarily paralyse, but not destroy, and that would have been a salutary reminder for it.

He concluded with some very modest proposals for collecting and circulating information among the anti-war left:

I thought I could support this action by supplying as often as possible information on the international socialist and labour movement. In France we know nothing of what is *really* happening abroad. We don't even know what is going on in France. Who knows, for example, that Louise Saumoneau [a feminist pacifist member of the SFIO jailed for anti-war activity] has been in prison since 2 October?

For that I shall need moral and material assistance. You can give moral support by writing to me, and material support by sending me subscriptions. For the moment there can be no question of fixing a subscription rate, since these Letters are appearing irregularly and their form is provisional. But even with this limited form, it will be possible for me to say many things which I think are useful. I shall not be short of subject matter. Today I am making a start using my own resources, to break our long silence. But I do not need to say that I shall delightedly welcome the cooperation of all those who want to help me. With the assistance I receive along the way, it will be possible to create the instrument for our propaganda.[8]

Rosmer's circular got a widespread welcome from his correspondents,[9] but both Rosmer and Monatte were now in the army and their activity was limited. It was only after the war, in April 1919, that *La Vie ouvrière* was able to resume publication.

Rosmer had already made one attempt to circulate information within the working-class movement. In 1915 the metal-workers' union had decided to bring out a special issue of its newspaper for May Day. Government censorship strictly controlled any published material hostile to the war. Rosmer, working with Merrheim of the metal-workers' union, helped to prepare an issue with articles critical of the war, including a piece by himself about the strikes on the Clyde in February 1915, about which French workers knew nothing, and an anti-war statement by German socialists including Luxemburg, Liebknecht and Zetkin.

The proofs were submitted to the censors, who demanded the removal of the offending articles. A few papers were run off with the appropriate blank spaces, and a large number with the full version. They were then carefully packed up, with the censored papers at the top and the rest underneath, and put into the post. Some 17,000 papers were distributed to members of the metal-workers' union and to former subscribers to *La Vie ouvrière*.[10]

1   Romain Rolland

The revival of the internationalist left was encouraged by the intervention of Romain Rolland, a well-known novelist. He had no record of involvement in political activity, and his positions could best be described as well-meaning but confused. His socialism was essentially pantheistic, a pantheism in which Spinoza, Tolstoy and Wagner replaced the Catholicism of his youth. He had no interest in the self-emancipation of the working class and had little time for Marxism, which he regarded as deterministic.

---

8   Rosmer 1936, pp. 543–51.
9   Rosmer 1936, pp. 402–11.
10   Rosmer 1936, pp. 254–8.

If war had not come in 1914 Rolland would have continued on the same road, establishing himself a small place in the history of French literature but little else. The cataclysm of 1914 threw him into another world, in which he acquired a certain significance.

In 1914 Rolland was 48, too old for combat. He withdrew to Switzerland, where he produced a series of articles collected under the title *Au-dessus de la mêlée* [Above the Struggle]. Rolland continued to believe that France was defending legitimate interests against 'Prussian imperialism'. He had no concrete proposals for bringing the slaughter to an end, and was positively opposed to mutiny. All he aspired to do was to humanise the war, by denouncing the more virulent forms of chauvinism and the lies about atrocities, by opposing particularly brutal weapons such as poison gas and by giving assistance to prisoners of war.

Yet even in these modest proposals there was a passionate denunciation of a war which Rolland believed was unnecessary and disastrous. He blamed the 'heads of state who are the criminals responsible' for wars, and insisted that 'love of my country does not mean that I should hate and kill pious and loyal souls who love other countries'. He mocked the socialists who backed the war, in France and Germany: 'these men, who don't have the courage to die for their beliefs, are brave enough to die for the beliefs of others'. Anticipating Liebknecht's assertion that 'the main enemy is at home' he wrote: 'The worst enemy is not beyond our frontiers, it is inside each nation, and no nation has the courage to fight it'.[11]

Amid the conscious manufacturing of war-fever even the mildest criticisms of the war seemed like treachery and were met by vilification. Criticism of the war, however restrained, by a prominent public figure created a space which anti-war activists could occupy.

The anti-war left did not take a negative attitude to Rolland, but welcomed his contribution to their struggle. A key figure in the process was Amédée Dunois. Dunois came from an anarchist background but joined the SFIO in 1912 and was with Jaurès when he was murdered. He was also involved with *La Vie ouvrière* and recruited Rosmer to write for the journal. Later he was a founder-member of the Communist Party, which he left in 1927; he rejoined the SFIO and died in Belsen in 1945 as a result of his Resistance activities.

Dunois published brief extracts from Rolland's articles in France, in *L'Humanité*, paper of the pro-war Socialist Party, in order to defend Rolland

---

11   Rolland 1915, pp. 25, 29–30, 33.

against an attack from the historian Alphonse Aulard.[12] For the tiny minority of socialists who opposed the war his words provided enormous encouragement; Pierre Monatte described spending whole nights copying Rolland's critique.[13] The copying was done by typewriter and by hand.[14] This was activism of a type utterly foreign to Rolland, but through it he became a symbolic figure for the anti-war left. Marcel Martinet began a correspondence with Rolland, who was later to assist with the publication of Martinet's anti-war poems, *Les Temps maudits*, which he held in the highest esteem. Martinet reciprocated the esteem, and offered to dedicate the volume to Rolland.[15]

Another source of encouragement for the French internationalists was the presence in France of foreign anti-war activists, in particular the Russian *Nashe Slovo* [our word] group in Paris, who worked closely with Rosmer; because of government bans the paper actually had three names, *Golos*, *Nashe Slovo* and *Natchalo*. This group produced a modest daily paper in Paris – just a single two-sided sheet – despite censorship and repression. The *Nashe Slovo* group included a number of individuals who went on to join the Bolsheviks and play a significant role in post-revolutionary Russia. While Trotsky is the best-known name, others involved included Lunacharsky, Ryazanov, Kollontai and Radek.

2   Zimmerwald

The French internationalists played their part in the process that led to the Zimmerwald conference of September 1915, when a small number of anti-war activists gathered in Switzerland. In Trotsky's words, 'half a century after the founding of the first International, it was still possible to seat all the internationalists in four coaches'.[16] Among the participants were Lenin, Trotsky and Zinoviev; in just over two years they would be in power in Russia.

----

12   Dunois 1914.
13   Wohl 1966, p. 59.
14   Rosmer 1936, p. 215.
15   Maitron and Pennetier 1964–2023 article 129462, notice ROLLAND Romain, Edme, Paul-Émile par Bernard Duchatelet, version mise en ligne le 30 novembre 2010, dernière modification le 28 avril 2020; article 120684, notice MARTINET Marcel par Jean Prugnot, version mise en ligne le 30 novembre 2010, dernière modification le 28 juin 2021; article 23355, notice DUNOIS Amédée [Catonne Amedee Gabriel dit]. Pseudonymes DANKIN, AME-DUNE, DANHINX Raphaël, DUNOIS Raphaël, MOREAU Nicolas par Justinien Raymond, version mise en ligne le 25 octobre 2008, dernière modification le 6 novembre 2022. See also Paizis 2007, pp. 44–6.
16   Trotsky 1930, p. 194.

Zimmerwald marked the first significant turning-point for the anti-war movement in France. The report back, and the building for the follow-up conference at Kienthal the following spring, gave the internationalist left an opportunity to pull together their support and lay the foundations of an anti-war organisation. Various committees were set up which would later enable the left to grow in the period after the Russian Revolution.

The *Vie ouvrière* nucleus, now somewhat expanded, provided the base for those in France who wished to attend the conference. Rosmer was centrally involved in organising for the conference, the first attempt to regroup anti-war forces on an international level. He himself was not able to attend because he had been called up into the armed services, but he was closely involved in mandating the two delegates from *La Vie ouvrière* and in publicising their reports. One of these was Merrheim; the other was Albert Bourderon, a follower of Allemane and an activist in the coopers' union, the CGT and the SFIO.

The internationalists remained a tiny minority. But slowly a changed mood was developing which would offer a larger audience for their ideas. However, while anti-war feeling was beginning to develop behind the lines, the army was a different matter. Since many industrial workers had been exempted from military service because they were needed for war production, this was largely a peasant army, pretty much untouched by trade-union antimilitarist propaganda.

The experiences of Pierre Monatte show what was, and was not, possible for an individual within the army.[17] Monatte was initially declared unfit for service, but when he resigned from the Confederal Committee of the CGT, denouncing the union's support for the war, the authorities changed their mind and called him up. Monatte made no attempt to evade or refuse military service; he believed that the place of a revolutionary was alongside his fellow-workers in the army. He also made it clear from the outset that under no circumstances would he fire his gun against the enemy; he insisted that he could not continue as a militant if he had killed a fellow-worker. For a short time he was threatened with execution.

After a period of training he was sent to the front line. In his correspondence he noted that since his trench was close to the Germans, artillery from both sides passed overhead. Later there are references to heavy losses and a grim allusion to the fact that soldiers had to wear wristbands 'to identify corpses'. The

---

17   See Monatte 2018.

real enemy was not the Germans, he wrote; 'our enemy is mud'.[18] He became a
signaller and was commended for repairing telephone lines under fire.

In an army that was largely peasant, not working-class, there was not much
that Monatte could actually achieve. He seems to have had little success in
arguing for his position with his fellow-soldiers. He felt isolated, seeing those
around him 'not daring to reason with their good sense and incapable of thinking other than according to their newspapers'. But he insisted that the main task
was to change public opinion and that individual expressions of opposition
were necessary to begin a process of change in opinion. He asserted his belief
in internationalism and looked forward to the 'United States of the World'.[19]
He knew that ideas could change in many ways; Monatte was far removed
from the facile clichés of *laïcité*, recognising that 'people who have a faith
are closer to us' than superficial supporters who seemed to share syndicalist
ideas.[20]

As Robert Louzon had reported in *La Vie ouvrière*,[21] peasants tended to dis-
like Parisians as much as they hated the officers. This distrust was increased
by war; soldiers suffering in the trenches felt that those behind the lines were
having a relatively easy time of it. As the war continued discontent grew
among both soldiers and civilians, but there was no simple way of bringing
the struggles together. Civilians might complain that sugar was rationed or coal
expensive; soldiers would be contemptuous of such grumbling, since they were
without sugar and means of warmth.

3   Trench Warfare

The initial euphoria of the troops who believed they were heading straight for
Berlin wore off rapidly as soldiers encountered the grim reality of trench warfare. Georges Dumoulin, who had travelled to the front with the first batch
of recruits, noticed how their consciousness had evolved after the experience of a year and more in the trenches: 'When I met them again at Verdun,
they blamed everyone: journalists, members of parliament, socialists, Parisians, police, everyone at the rear. The strongest and clearest impression they
had was of brain-washing, lies, exaggeration and untruth'.[22]

---

18   Monatte 2018, pp. 74, 67.
19   Monatte 2018, pp. 31, 25.
20   Monatte 2018, pp. 65–66.
21   Louzon 1910.
22   Rosmer 1936, p. 536.

This was not as yet an evolution towards revolution or mutiny, nor even anti-militarism. It was simply a deep distrust of everyone who did not share their own circumstances. There was little scope here for outside agitators, even if they had managed to make contact with the soldiers. To organise politically in the trenches was difficult, since the heavy rate of casualties meant that establishing any kind of stable organisational form was virtually impossible.

One form of organisation that did develop was the production of trench newspapers. Newspapers like *Le Ver luisant* [the glow-worm], *La Fusée* [the rocket] or *Le Canard du boyau* [the communication trench rag] did not express anti-war sentiment; indeed, hatred of the enemy was a dominant theme, but they did enable soldiers to give some expression to their discontents and reflected a growing sense of distrust of those who had sent them to fight.[23] They contained poetry, jokes, and competitions; and they reflected the dangers and miseries of trench life in a way the national press did not. There was no explicit criticism of the government or its war strategy; *La Fusée* explicitly titled itself as a paper that was 'anti-*boche*, anti-political and anti-sad'. There was hostility, not only to Germans, but to black soldiers fighting for France and to civilians who failed to appreciate the realities of life in the front line.

At most such journals permitted themselves the occasional ironic comment on the war. In a mock reply to queries, *Le Canard du boyau* told a reader: 'No, you are not entitled to a supplementary food ration for the lice and fleas you are rearing'.[24] *La Fusée* published an imaginary satirical interview with a general from a neutral country who promised that this war would be the last: 'all wars have been the last; why should this one be any different from the others?'[25] Through such publications soldiers began to develop a consciousness in some ways independent of the official ideology.

Trench fighters developed various means of subverting the intentions of their officers. In a study based on official records as well as the recollections of combattants, Rémy Cazals has shown that there were frequent instances of tacit truces and even fraternisation between French and German soldiers.[26] Often there seemed to be an unspoken agreement by both sides to minimise enemy casualties in order to avoid reprisals – what Tony Ashworth, in a study

---

23   See Ferro 1969.
24   *Le Canard du boyau*, October–November 1916, p. 4, available at: https://gallica.bnf.fr/ark:/
      12148/bpt6k111435v/f38.item.
25   *La Fusée*, 20 June, 1917, p. 1, available at: https://gallica.bnf.fr/ark:/12148/bpt6k1040667h?rk
      =21459;2.
26   Cazals 2006, pp. 87–205.

of the British army, has called the 'live and let live' system.[27] Sometimes front-line soldiers were within a few metres of the opposing trenches, and they could hear German soldiers talk, sing and laugh. They recognised that German soldiers faced the same problems as themselves, especially in bad weather; as one soldier put it: 'The enemy isn't Fritz, it's the winter'.[28] Sometimes there was even direct contact between the two trenches, with handshakes and exchanges of cigarettes, wine and coffee. Of course the military authorities threatened severe penalties for contact with the enemy, but in practice punishments were quite light, and junior officers knew what was going on.

Some insight into the evolving consciousness in the army is provided by various novels written on the basis of the experience of combatants. Of these the most remarkable is *Under Fire* [Le Feu] by Henri Barbusse. Most of the well-known novels of the First World War were written and published after the end of hostilities. *Under Fire* was published in 1916 and won the prestigious Goncourt Prize the same year. Barbusse was aged 41 in 1914, over the age for military service, but he volunteered to fight. His initial motivation may have been a mixture of patriotism and a desire to share the fate of his compatriots, but he became determined to be a witness to the reality of war.

There is no romanticisation or glorification of war here – as he puts it, 'Don't talk to me about military virtue because I've killed Germans'.[29] The realities of death and injury are described in detail, and the coarse speech of soldiers is vividly rendered.

Barbusse shows no hatred for the Germans, whom he describes as 'poor dupes who have been vilely deceived and stupefied',[30] victims of the same system as their French opponents. The war is blamed essentially on those who 'cannot or will not make peace on earth; all those people who, for one reason or another, cling on to the old order'.[31] In one of the most striking passages of the book Barbusse depicts a French soldier expressing his admiration for Karl Liebknecht, seen as a representative of the German anti-war movement, who will 'shine for the beauty and force of his courage'.[32]

Under Fire circulated widely among serving soldiers and was read in the trenches by men who found in it an authentic representation of their own condition. Henry Poulaille, who between the wars was a well-known proletarian

---

27   Ashworth 1980, p. 19.

28   Cazals 2006, p. 136.

29   Barbusse 2007, p. 398. See also Ares 2016.

30   Barbusse 2007, p. 397.

31   Barbusse 2007, p. 397.

32   Barbusse 2007, p. 297.

novelist, wrote an obituary of Barbusse in which he recalled: 'I read *Under Fire* in the trenches of the Chemin des Dames, and I nearly got myself killed by going to dig it out of the mud in a corner of the passage between trenches'.[33]

Raymond Lefebvre made his first contact with left-wing ideas as a student in Paris before 1914 – he took part in the 1909 demonstration against the execution of Francisco Ferrer – and he was radicalised by his experience of military service, moving just before the outbreak of war towards the circle around *La Vie ouvrière*. He opposed the war from the outset – called up as a medical auxiliary he made propaganda to the wounded he was responsible for. At the outbreak of war he had attended some of the meetings of the tiny anti-war group, together with Monatte, Rosmer, Martinet, Merrheim, Trotsky and others. In his book *L'Éponge de vinaigre* [The Vinegar Sponge] he described how

> we confined ourselves to sadly stirring up the cold ashes of the International, and drawing up, with a bitter memory, the huge list of those who had failed us; and glimpsing with futile accuracy the length of a war of attrition in which civilisation would be the only loser ... Here, in the heart of Paris, we knew that we were among the last Europeans of the fine intelligent Europe which the world had just lost for ever, and at the same time the first men of a future International of which we remained confident. We formed the link between two centuries.[34]

He volunteered to fight at the front, so that, if he survived, he could 'undermine the glory with all the authority of someone who had been there'. In 1915 he joined the SFIO to support the anti-war current in the party. He was wounded at Verdun and returned to Paris. He later attended the Second Congress of the Communist International as a delegate of the Committee of the Third International, and died at sea on his way back from Russia.[35]

As well as various articles and pamphlets Lefebvre left two books in which he summed up his experience of the war. One was *L'Eponge de vinaigre*. This is simply a short [79 pages] memoir of his own childhood in Bayeux, and his subsequent return there from the trenches, contrasting civilian notions of war with the experience of the front. The whole tone is bitter; he describes the reactionary milieu in which he grew up. As a child he had supposed that the words

---

33 Poulaille 1935.

34 Lefebvre 1921, pp. 5–6.

35 Maitron and Pennetier 1964–2023 article117117, notice LEFEBVRE Raymond par Nicole Racine, version mise en ligne le 24 novembre 2010, dernière modification le 17 mai 2021. See also Mazuy and Pernot 2023.

'socialist', 'anarchist' and 'assassin' were synonyms; and that Jaurès was a high-way robber. He also describes the German teacher, Catherine, who taught him as a child; he didn't grasp that she was one of the Germans of whom so much ill was spoken, so that the children would cheerfully talk in her presence of 'killing all Germans'.

The other was a more conventional novel, *Le Sacrifice d'Abraham*.[36] [Abraham's Sacrifice]. Édouard Testut, a prosperous scholar of Celtic civilisation, living in Eastern France, is forced to abandon his home and move to Paris. He earns a living by writing articles supporting the war and attacking German intellectuals. His son, Mathieu, joins the army. A government minister offers to find him a post away from the fighting, but Testut refuses without consulting his son. Mathieu is seriously injured and his father travels into the combat zone to visit him; he sees his son in delirium die drinking his own urine. Mathieu has left writings about the horror of war with anti-war sentiments. His father publishes these, making a good income for himself. He returns home, resumes his studies and takes little interest in the further course of the war. Again the tone is bitter; the main theme is the contrast between the realities of life at the front and the continuing life of civilians. The ignorance of the civilians is satirised: thus Testut and his friend interrogate a soldier returning from the front, and ask if he has heard dying soldiers shouting 'Long live France!' He assures them he has never heard any such thing.

Marcel Martinet's novel *La Maison à l'abri*[37] [The Sheltered House], which was short-listed for the Goncourt Prize in 1919 – the year it was won by Proust – takes a different perspective. There is no direct representation of the war; Martinet shows the war's impact on the civilian population by tracing the fortunes of a cluster of people, mostly workers, living in a house in Paris. There is no unifying plot, just a series of parallel narratives.

Martinet depicts the changing and contradictory patterns of consciousness. Despite the war fever, one worker remembers the Germans he had worked with before the war broke out: 'They worked with us, like us. Oh yes, they were people like us'.[38] Their lives are torn apart by the war; we see the sufferings and grievances of the non-combattants. A war widow goes to work in a munitions factory, where she helps to organise a petition for a wage increase. Three days later she is sacked without explanation, and leaves the factory wondering how she will feed her child.

---

36   Lefebvre 1919.
37   Martinet 1919.
38   Martinet 1919, p. 64.

Between 1914 and 1918 up to 900,000 men from the French Empire were drawn into the European conflict – over half a million soldiers, at least 250,000 from North Africa and many thousands more from Indochina, plus some 220,000 workers.[39] Asians, Africans and West Indians were sent to the slaughter even more callously than native French workers. Of 157,000 black African troops sent to Europe some 30,000 were killed, a very high proportion. Some Senegalese troops literally died of cold, as the French army had provided no alternative to the tropical clothing they had worn at home. After the French mutinies of 1917 greater use was made of African troops in order to spare white soldiers.[40]

There is a remarkable reconstruction of the experience of African soldiers in David Diop's novel *Frère d'âme* [translated as *At Night All Blood is Black*].[41] He shows the sheer brutality of trench warfare, and the folly of a conflict into which African soldiers are flung but which has nothing to do with their experience or their interests. We see the power of the white officers, who seek to exploit the alleged savagery of the African troops in order to intimidate the Germans; but there are also moments of solidarity from white soldiers.

The involvement of African trrops in the war helped to change the way French workers perceived those originating from the colonies, of whom they had hitherto known little. At the same time, by enabling colonial workers and soldiers to see life in France, military service gave them new perspectives and aspirations.

An important part of the ideology imposed on the troops in the trenches was the dehumanisation of the enemy. Although the Germans were often only a couple of hundred metres away, troops were discouraged from recognising that the Germans were similar to themselves, suffering similar hardships. Many of the peasant soldiers had never travelled outside France or met a German, so it was easy to demonise the enemy.

One way in which some human contact was established was the taking of prisoners. French soldiers who were taken prisoner by the Germans, or who had the responsibility of looking after German prisoners, were able to make direct contact, and to see that the enemy were very like themselves.

Maurice Wullens [1894–1945] was a schoolteacher who had helped to launch the magazine *Les Humbles*, with a fierce hostility to intellectual snobbery. He was called up at the outbreak of war; in training he was constantly told of

---

39   Liauzu 1982, p. 100.
40   See Kiernan 1977, pp. 20–39.
41   Diop 2018.

'German atrocities' – 'heads and hands cut off, bodies torn in pieces, twisted corpses' – and assured that the Germans were instructed to kill their prisoners.

So when he was wounded, lying unable to move in a trench as the Germans advanced, he feared the worst. Instead a young German soldier greeted him as 'comrade' [Kamerad] and got him medical assistance. 'I shake his hand warmly in an impulse of gratitude and gentle humanity'.

As a prisoner of war he had good conditions; when a German officer found copies of *Les Humbles* in his possession he enquired if he was a social democrat and shook his hand. When he wrote home to say he was being well treated, it was assumed he was lying. On being repatriated to France, he was interrogated by the police, who tried unsuccessfully to get him to say that he had been ill-treated – 'this worthy (!) official thinks I am more stupid than he is'. It was only in 1920, after the end of the war, that he was able to publish an account of his experiences.[42] Wullens later became an activist on the far left throughout the interwar period.[43] Such episodes reveal how dangerous fraternisation could have been for the established order.

4   **The Home Front**

Anti-war and even revolutionary ideas circulated at the front, but strict military discipline and above all the murderous level of combat and the high casualty rate made it impossible to give any organisational form to the discontent. Up to the end of 1916 the development of an opposition to the war was mainly on the home front.

Issues began to arise in various industries which led to the revival of industrial conflict. By 1916 and 1917 strike action was quite extensive in France. A significant factor was the introduction of large numbers of women into industrial production; they played a central role in strikes in the latter part of the war. Another factor was the relatively high wages which workers in the munitions industry were able to earn. The fact of rising wages in wartime was a reflection of the labour shortage, and of the fact that workers continued to sell their labour power as a commodity, despite the grip of nationalist ideology.

Various sectors of French society were radicalised by the impact of the war. It is true that the system of secular primary education was designed to strengthen national consciousness, and doubtless the majority of primary school teachers

---

42   Wullens 1939, pp. 82, 83, 184.

43   Maitron and Pennetier 1964–2023 article135428, notice WULLENS Maurice par Jean Prugnot, version mise en ligne le 30 novembre 2010, dernière modification le 13 mars 2021.

[*instituteurs, institutrices*] carried out their role loyally and effectively. However, as was shown by the affiliation of the primary school teachers' union to the *sou du soldat*, there was a small but significant minority of teachers who detested the pro-war propaganda included in schoolbooks and who wanted to pass on an anti-war message to their pupils.

To become a primary teacher was one of the few careers open for a woman seeking to get an education; the same was true for many men from under-privileged backgrounds. When war broke out, a number of *instituteurs* became anti-war activists. Some of those to the forefront of the adoption of the *sou du soldat* by the teachers' union, for example Marie and François Mayoux and Louis and Gabrielle Bouët, became anti-war activists after 1914.

In 1917 the Mayoux couple published a pamphlet entitled *Syndicalist teachers and the war*,[44] a devastating attack on the war and those advocating its pursuit. It was not just a general critique; their argument was rooted in their situation as education workers. They indignantly rejected the attempt to make teachers defend the war to their pupils, repudiating 'this claim by the government of the Republic to transform us into political agents of the lowest kind, into "anti-boche" propagandists, into missionaries of the blindest hatred, even – shame and infamy! – into brainwashers of our own pupils'.

This was explained by a more general critique of governmental power: 'in the upper levels of French society popular emancipation is seen as dangerous'. As they pointed out, French colonialism had been guilty of all the crimes of which the Germans were accused: 'theft, arson, destruction, rape, mutilation of children and the wounded, slave-trading'. They quoted the 'prophetic lines' of lawyer and journalist Urbain Gohier: 'The blood we allow to be shed will fall on our own heads'.

As internationalists they stressed that *all* countries were responsible for imperialist violence – including Belgium, often presented as the innocent victim of German invasion: 'Russians, English, Germans, Spanish, Italians, Austro-Hungarians, Turks, etc. – all, all, even the Belgians whose horrors in the Congo are perhaps worse than those committed by the other colonial killers'.

So they vowed that in their teaching they would tell the truth about war: 'If we speak of war to our kids, we shall confine ourselves to general considerations of human, historical fact, accepted by all who are not misled by chauvinistic folly. War is immoral, inhuman and ruinous'. They looked forward to a future when conflict would be replaced by 'the united states of the world'.

------

44   Mayoux 1917.

The pamphlet was published in a form which enabled it to be sent by letter – to members of the armed forces among others. The state could hardly disregard such a direct challenge and they were sentenced to two years in jail. Their furniture was sold to cover court costs. They were released in 1919, but allowed to resume teaching only in 1924. They would become founder-members of the Communist Party, but were expelled in 1922 for their syndicalist positions.[45]

The emerging opposition to the war saw the involvement of a significant number of women, some of whom became life-long internationalist activists. Neither the republican nor the syndicalist traditions had been particularly encouraging to the struggle for women's rights, but many women activists moved from feminism to a total opposition to war and the social system that produced it.

Hélène Brion, born in 1882, was an orphan; she trained as a teacher and became an *institutrice* from 1905; she joined the SFIO and the CGT teachers' federation as soon as it was formed, evolving from feminism to revolutionary syndicalism. She rose into the union leadership at the time of the crisis caused by support for the 'sou du soldat' in 1912. Initially she backed the pro-war majority in the SFIO but in 1915 agreed to accept the anti-war line of the Syndicat des instituteurs. In 1916 she wrote a 'feminist statement for the resumption of international relations' which began 'We who have not been able to do anything to prevent war because we have no civil or political rights, we are fully with you in wishing to put an end to it'. She distributed pamphlets in support of Zimmerwald; her home was searched and her mail intercepted. In 1918 she was given a three-year suspended jail sentence for distributing anti-war propaganda. She would join the Communist Party at its foundation but left in 1925 in solidarity with Rosmer and Monatte after they were expelled. She remained a feminist activist till her death in 1962.[46]

Born in 1879, Marguerite Thévenet abandoned her original aspirations to become a pianist, and worked as a railway employee. She was a family friend of Pierre Monatte and bride's witness at his wedding. Before and during the war she organised holiday camps for working-class children. She was involved in anti-war activity from 1915 onwards, and met Alfred Rosmer at a pacifist meeting in 1916; they were to remain a couple for the rest of their lives.

---

45   Maitron and Pennetier 1964–2023 article121350, notice MAYOUX Marie et François, dits
      BOUGON Joséphine et BOUGON Constant par René Bianco, version mise en ligne le 30
      novembre 2010, dernière modification le 8 mai 2020.

46   Maitron and Pennetier 1964–2023 article17968, notice BRION Hélène, Rose, Louise par
      Henri Dubief, Julien Chuzeville, version mise en ligne le 20 octobre 2008, dernière modification le 7 septembre 2020.

During the war Thévenet took responsibility for accompanying groups of children from the regions worst affected by war. This meant frequent journeys to Switzerland, and in the course of these she first began to develop her skills in smuggling anti-war literature across frontiers. She brought into France issues of *Demain*, the anti-war review published in Switzerland by Henri Guilbeaux during 1916 and 1917.

Thévenet helped to maintain contact between the French opponents of the war and Romain Rolland in Switzerland. Rolland, who liked women to be demure, was taken aback by her manner:

> Mlle Marguerite Thévenet came to see me (for the first time) on 5 March 1916 ... She brought me news from friends. I didn't much like the *carbonaro* style which she gave to an exchange of matters of no great importance. She produced a letter from her hat, and two or three more from her bodice; I was expecting to see her take off her stockings.[47]

Roger Hagnauer recalled seeing her at the end of the war, on May Day 1919, on the Place de la République, giving out Communist International leaflets to soldiers until an officer warned her that there were police behind the military cordon.[48] [For her subsequent development see Chapter 7.]

Lucie Colliard was born into a peasant family in 1877. She worked as an *institutrice* from the 1890s and joined the SFIO in 1912. She was a pacifist from the outbreak of war; she supported Zimmerwald and met Lenin in 1916. She was imprisoned for a month in 1918 for infringing war-time press laws. She would be a founder-member of the Communist Party and later a follower of Marceau Pivert on the left of the Socialist Party.[49]

Louise Saumoneau, born in 1875, was a seamstress; she was a socialist feminist from 1900, and a founder member of the SFIO. She founded the Socialist women's group of the SFIO in 1913. She gave French lessons to foreigners, especially Russian political refugees. From July 1914 she devoted herself full-time to publishing and distributing pamphlets against the war. In January 1915 she circulated Zetkin's *Appeal to Socialist Women of All Lands*, which stated: 'The longer the war continues, the more are the masks torn down that have deceived so many people. It is presenting itself in all its naked ugliness as a war of cap-

---

47   Rolland 1952, p. 685.

48   Hagnauer 1962.

49   Maitron and Pennetier 1964–2023 article20365, notice COLLIARD Lucie [née PARME-LAND Lucie, Claudine] par Jean Maitron, Claude Pennetier, version mise en ligne le 25 octobre 2008, dernière modification le 24 février 2021.

italist conquest and world domination'. She attended the clandestine women's peace conference in Berne, March 1915, organised by Clara Zetkin, an initiative which preceded Zimmerwald, and which declared: 'An end to the war can be brought about only by the clear and unshakeable determination of the popular masses in the countries at war'.[50] She was arrested in October 1915 for anti-militarist activity. She welcomed the Russian Revolution, and was critical of the support given to Woodrow Wilson [see chapter 7], urging that the American President be greeted with shouts of 'Long live the Bolsheviks', 'Long live the German Revolution', 'Long live the Workers' International'. She did not join the Communist Party, remaining in the SFIO, but broke with it on pacifist grounds at the beginning of the Second World War.[51]

In 1914 all the main socialist and syndicalist publications had gone over to support for the war. *La Vie ouvrière*, the one small bastion of internationalism, was forced to suspend publication. As discontent with the war began to spread, in the armed forces and on the home front, publications which reflected this changing mood began to appear. Government controls and censorship were rigorous, and expression of anti-war views could lead to imprisonment. In October 1915 several publications – *L'Oeuvre, La Guerre sociale, Le Rappel, Le Radical* – faced suspension.[52] Despite this the circulation of critical ideas could not be prevented.

The publications that emerged did not automatically adopt an internationalist stance. There were many contradictions and inconsistencies, which reflected the slow emergence of an opposition to the war. A striking case of such contradiction was the figure of Miguel Almereyda, the pseudonym of Eugène Bonaventure Jean-Baptiste Vigo. Initially an anarchist, he was a provocative and ambiguous figure. His pseudonym was an anagram of 'y a la merde' [there is shit]. In the pre-war period he became a successful radical journalist who worked closely with Gustave Hervé and was involved in anti-militarist activity. He founded the paper *La Guerre sociale* [social war] and later the organisation *Les Jeunes gardes révolutionnaires* [revolutionary young guard], created to counter the Camelots du Roi, the violent youth organisation of the far right Action Française, and mainly active in the Latin Quarter of Paris.

In 1914 Almereyda launched *Le Bonnet rouge* [red bonnet], which became a daily paper shortly before the outbreak of war. While vigorously opposed to the

---

50   Rosmer 1936, pp. 308–9.

51   Maitron and Pennetier 1964–2023 article130564, notice SAUMONEAU Louise, Aimée par Justinien Raymond et Charles Sowerwine., version mise en ligne le 30 novembre 2010, dernière modification le 14 août 2020.

52   *Le Canard enchaîné*, 15 October 1915.

far right of the Action française, it also had close links to a government minister, Joseph Caillaux. When war broke out, *Le Bonnet rouge* initially took the position of defence of the republic, calling the war 'a holy war'. Although he suffered from health problems – which presumably explains why he did not fight himself, but merely encouraged others to fight – Almereyda did very well out of the situation and enjoyed a luxurious life-style. For a time *Le Bonnet rouge* was secretly subsidised by the Ministry of the Interior.

After visiting battlefields Almereyda picked up on disillusion with the war and decided to reflect this in his paper. He praised Romain Rolland and commented favourably on Zimmerwald. This meant that he fell out with the government and lost his financial support; his paper faced increasing censorship and eventual closure. Finally he was jailed on the accusation of possessing documents prejudicial to national security, and died in prison in circumstances that remain obscure; it is at least possible he was murdered. Though he was undoubtedly a dubious character, his paper had an influence on the emerging anti-war mood.[53]

Pierre Brizon was a teacher who became an SFIO deputy in 1910. Initially he supported the war, but moved to an oppositional stance. In 1916, when other French delegates were banned from attending the Kienthal conference [the follow-up to Zimmerwald], Brizon was able to attend by virtue of parliamentary immunity. Brizon was repudiated by the SFIO leadership, refused to vote for war credits and was suspended from parliament. He became involved in the Committee for the Resumption of International Relations [Le Comité pour la reprise des relations internationales] – set up to bring together the supporters of Zimmerwald in France – and in January 1918 launched the weekly *La Vague* [the wave], which described itself as 'socialist' and 'feminist'.[54]

It was not possible to isolate the armed forces from the civilian population. Soldiers had family and friends and went on leave or convalescence from injury. Barbusse's *Under Fire* circulated widely at the front, as did various publications critical of the government, some of them openly anti-war. Such publications were often passed around the trenches or on board ship, and so reached a large readership. It is impossible to evaluate exactly what impact was made, and many soldiers perished before the ideas could ripen in their skulls.

---

53   Maitron and Pennetier 1964–2023 article155252, notice ALMEREYDA Miguel [Eugène, Bonaventure, Jean-Baptiste Vigo, dit] [Dictionnaire des anarchistes] par Guillaume Davranche, version mise en ligne le 6 mars 2014, dernière modification le 3 février 2019.

54   Roy 2004.

Because Marcel Martinet's poems were banned in France, they were published in Switzerland and smuggled across the border into France where handwritten copies were circulated. A translation was distributed in Germany in hand-written form.[55]

5   Mutiny

In May and June 1917 there were widespread mutinies in the French army, reaching a peak around 2 June. It is very difficult to calculate exactly how many men were involved – one recent estimate puts the figure at between 30,000 and 80,000 mutineers,[56] out of a total army strength of a little under 2 million. Many more who did not actively mutiny were touched by the general mood of discontent.

Among those who mutinied in France were many of the Russian soldiers who had been sent to fight on the western front. They had heard news of the fall of the Tsar and refused to fight. The authorities were very keen to isolate them from French soldiers so that revolutionary ideas would not spread. Eventually they were taken away and shelled into submission. Many of the survivors who remained intransigent were then deported to Algeria.[57]

Also involved were some of the troops brought from the French colonies to assist with the war. When a mutiny broke out among Senegalese troops in August 1917, the authorities made some concessions, being afraid that too heavy repression might have a disastrous impact on other Senegalese, Madagascan and Indochinese troops.[58]

Mutiny is a fateful decision for soldiers. Strikers can walk out and, if they fail to win, go back to work. Failed mutineers face execution or long jail sentences. But with a high mortality rate and a war which seemed to be continuing interminably, many soldiers came to feel that they had nothing to lose by mutiny. As one soldier [carpenter Henri Kuhn] put it: 'Shoot me, but I won't go back to the trenches; in any case it amounts to the same thing'.[59]

What remains a matter of dispute is how far the mutinies were political. Were the soldiers simply in revolt against poor conditions and a military strat-

---

55   Paizis 2007, pp. 47–8.
56   Loez 2010, pp. 196–7, 235.
57   Adam 2007.
58   Rolland 2005, pp. 301–2.
59   Loez 2010, p. 9.

egy which seemed wasteful of human life, or were they committed to bringing the war to an end?[60]

The truth seems to lie somewhere in the middle. Those involved in the mutinies had a variety of motives; an eye-witness reported of one mutiny that some wanted peace, some wanted to go on leave, and others were singing the *Internationale*.[61] Consciousness was very fluid. Soldiers who had decided to reject military discipline were entering uncharted waters. Even if their initial motivation derived from specific discontents, they were moving into a situation where they were open to new ideas; the old certainties that had held their world together were collapsing. Those who survived the next year and a half of fighting would return to civilian life profoundly radicalised.

The mutinies were often simple, apparently spontaneous, refusals to obey orders. A couple of incidents are recorded as follows:

One battalion was due to make its way to the trenches:

> The men had formed up without incident. But when the signal from the battalion leader sounded, nobody moved. The companies remained lined up behind stacks of rifles and kit bags.
>
> There were a few seconds of anguished expectancy ... The whistle was blown a second time, and again there was no movement. The situation was suddenly obvious.
>
> The whole troop remained in a state of immobility which might seem concerted, in order, but refusing to obey.

In another incident:

> The battalion was stationed in a mushroom farm with the divisional headquarters. When they were told to pick up their kit bags, nobody moved, the candles went out and it was pitch dark. Every time an officer lit a candle, it was immediately put out. It was impossible to assemble the troops. When orders were given, the men replied with sneers and insults. The divisional officers tried to intervene and exhort the men to do their duty, but they were shouted down.[62]

Pure spontaneity is a myth. In any revolt there is always someone who takes an initiative, sets an example that others take up and follow. Obviously the

---

60   See Pedroncini 1967 for the argument that the mutinies were non-political, and Smith 1994, for a critique of this position.

61   Loez 2010, p. 382.

62   Rolland 2005, pp. 58, 299.

initiative in the mutinies was often taken by individuals, some of whom were probably politically motivated, or may have been influenced by the extensive anti-militarist propaganda carried out by the trade unions in pre-1914 France. There was no central political leadership to organise the movement, which was often extremely volatile. Rumours and false information undoubtedly played a significant part.

The soldiers rapidly improvised forms of organisation – for example the use of flying pickets to spread the action to other sections of the army.[63] Without any political coordination it was too little, too late.

One demand that arose in a number of places was the idea of a march on Paris. Clearly this represented a recognition of the need for a political solution, a wish to force the government to bring the war to an end. Without political leadership it was unclear how this could be achieved. The authorities had little difficulty in sealing off the railway stations and suspending the train service to Paris.[64]

The authorities, headed by General Pétain, were able to regain control. Repression was severe; there were 629 death sentences,[65] though most were commuted; there were between 26 and 57 executions [it is difficult to disentangle which were directly linked to the mutinies and which were for other offences].[66] Many mutineers were sentenced to imprisonment; most were amnestied in 1921 or 1925, but a few stayed in jail till 1933.[67]

Pétain and the government recognised that the mutinies had shown a serious threat of the breakdown of discipline; they responded with both stick and some rather small carrots. All soldiers were to be guaranteed seven days' leave every four months, with additional rest periods away from the front line. The quality of food was to be improved, with kitchens as near as possible to the trenches.[68] Pétain abandoned the strategy of *offensive à outrance* [large frontal offensives pushed to the limit] which had led to particularly heavy casualties, but life at the front did not change much.[69]

---

63   Loez 2010, pp. 304–5.
64   Loez 2010, pp. 260–64.
65   Pedroncini 1967, p. 192.
66   Loez 2010, p. 513.
67   Rolland 2005, pp. 388–92.
68   Pedroncini 1967, pp. 235, 237, 242.
69   Smith 1994, p. 215.

6   Revolution in Russia

So the slaughter continued. The war seemed to stretch indefinitely ahead, with no end in sight. When hope did become visible, it was from an unexpected direction. The February Revolution in Russia had clearly had an impact on the summer's mutinies. In early November came news of another revolution in Russia [the so-called October Revolution in the Julian calendar]; the Bolsheviks had taken power.

To most people in France it was something of a mystery what this might mean. The French press understood little, and in any case was not minded to give its readers any explanation of what was going on. For the mass of war-weary soldiers and civilians, the news remained vague, but seemed to offer a promise. The Russian Revolution was opening up a new road, an alternative direction which France and the other combatant nations could take.

The new regime was fragile and had many enemies. Its only hope of survival was for the revolution to spread to other countries as rapidly as possible. From the time of Zimmerwald and the April Theses Lenin had insisted that the old Socialist International was bankrupt and that it was necessary to build a new International. Over the next few years this strategy would lead to splits in several mass working-class parties. Initially there was an important role to be played by individuals who could participate in the restructuring of the international labour movement.

A meeting in August 1918 led to the formation of the Moscow-based Anglo-French Communist Group [Groupe communiste anglo-français], initially consisting of members of the French Military Mission in Russia; it was part of the Federation of foreign groups [Fédération des groupes étrangers] set up by the Bolsheviks as part of their preparation for a new International. The group produced a weekly two-page paper *La IIIe Internationale* [Third International].[70]

There were a number of French military personnel in Russia, and also journalists and others. Some of these, having been witnesses of the working-class upsurge which culminated in the Revolution, decided to throw in their lot with the Communist cause. Their political backgrounds were diverse, an indication of the way that the principles of the October Revolution exercised a magnetic attraction.

Lieutenant Pierre Pascal was a member of the French military mission in Russia, who had come over to the Revolution. He was a practising Catholic; according to Rosmer, who knew him well, he 'had come to the side of the

---

70   See Body 1988.

Revolution, not despite his Catholicism but because of it ... It was precisely the Spartan character of the regime that attracted him'.[71] For some years he worked hard and devotedly for the revolutionary cause. In particular he worked on a publication aimed at French troops invading Russia. Later he translated the secret correspondence of Izvolsky, the Tsarist Russian ambassador in France.[72]

René Marchand had been the Russian correspondent of French daily newspaper *Le Figaro*; he had gone over to the Revolution because he was appalled at the various machinations of Britain and France at the start of the Revolution. He explained this in a short book called *Why I went over to Bolshevism*.[73] He went on to dig up details of the diplomatic correspondence between France and Russia. In the early twenties he helped look after French delegates to the Comintern congresses.[74]

Henri Guilbeaux, a poet, had frequented anarchist circles in France before 1914. Early in the war he attended meetings of the *Vie ouvrière* group in Paris before moving to Switzerland in 1915. He became part of the pacifist circle around Romain Rolland. In 1916 he launched the journal *Demain* [Tomorrow] as an organ of the anti-war movement. His aim, he said, was to 'defend the territory of thought everywhere abandoned to the nationalist enemy thanks to the treachery of the intellectuals'. He was at the Kienthal conference, then later was expelled from Switzerland and made his way to Russia through Germany in February 1919; in France he was condemned to death in his absence for alleged contacts with Germany. He was a delegate at the founding conference of the Communist International on behalf of the French Zimmerwaldian left.[75]

Marcel Body had been a French soldier. He was sent to Odessa where leaflets and pamphlets were distributed to French troops who had been sent to intervene against the Russian Revolution. Later he worked as a translator for the Communist International before being expelled from the French Communist Party.[76]

---

71   Rosmer 1953, section 1920 chapter XX.

72   Maitron and Pennetier 1964–2023 article125018, notice PASCAL Pierre par Jean-Louis Panné, version mise en ligne le 30 novembre 2010, dernière modification le 17 août 2019.

73   Marchand 1919.

74   Mazuy 2002, p. 93.

75   Maitron and Pennetier 1964–2023 article114483, notice GUILBEAUX Henri, Louis, Émile. Pseudonymes: James BURKLEY, CARTIGNY, COBRAT, DALOU, André SASTOR, WOLF par Nicole Racine, version mise en ligne le 24 novembre 2010, dernière modification le 27 janvier 2020.

76   Body 1988, p. 24; Maitron and Pennetier 1964–2023 article50851, notice BODY Marcel [BODY Jean, Alexandre dit Marcel]. [version DBK] par Anne Manigaud, version mise en ligne le 16 juillet 2009, dernière modification le 16 juillet 2009.

Henri Barberet, son of a French teacher living in Moscow, joined the Bolsheviks at the age of seventeen in October 1918. Sent to Sebastopol in 1919, he organised the distribution of revolutionary literature on French ships, but in August 1919 was killed in Odessa defending the town against counter-revolutionaries.[77]

The French Communist Group soon degenerated; its members came from diverse political backgrounds, and there were constant disagreements.[78] But for a brief period it offered a vision of a new internationalist current.

Many political leaders in Britain and France were now anxious to get the war with Germany over as quickly as possible so that they could devote themselves to what they saw as the more important task of crushing the Russian Revolution before the infection could spread to the rest of Europe. In France it was prime minister Clemenceau who became the scourge of Bolshevism. French soldiers and sailors were among the armies from fourteen foreign states which invaded Russia to take part in the wrongly named civil war.

The world war finally ground to a halt in November 1918, just one year after the Russian Revolution. Though France was on the winning side, the popular mood was not one of triumphalism, but rather of anger and aspiration. Among the surviving soldiers there was a deep bitterness about what they had been made to undergo.

Both ex-soldiers and civilians started to turn to the established organisations of the left, the CGT and the SFIO, in the hope of radical policies. Often organisational attachments were somewhat fluid – Jacques Duclos, later a French Communist leader, recalled that he had attended, and spoken at, SFIO meetings without ever being a member.[79]

Not all the members of the armed services were being demobilised. Clemenceau and the French government had been quick to join the alliance of Western states determined to crush the Russian Revolution before it could offer a model to working people around the world. On 30 October 1918 an armistice was signed with Turkey, opening up the Dardanelles to the Allies. On 16 November, five days after the world war had ended, Allied ships entered the Black Sea. A large number of French warships were sent to the Black Sea and the ports of Odessa, in Ukraine, and Sebastopol, in Crimea, were occupied by French troops who were intended to assist the counter-revolutionary forces in Russia. The French armed forces were in contact with, and offered support to, the counter-revolutionary leader Denikin.[80]

---

77   Maitron and Pennetier 1964–2023 article97918, notice BARBEREY Henri (ou Barberet Henri), version mise en ligne le 3 novembre 2010, dernière modification le 13 mai 2017.
78   Rosmer 1953, section 1920 chapter XX.
79   Jacques Duclos in *L'Humanité*, 15 December 1970, quoted by Ferrette 2011, p. 39.
80   Marty 1999, p. 35.

There was now a widespread feeling among the rank and file that they had done the job they joined up for, and that they should go home. Among troops sent to Ukraine was the 58th infantry regiment, originating from Avignon, which had a revolutionary action committee. Some of these were soldiers who had mutinied on the French front in 1917 and had been deported to the Eastern army. In early February, it was the first regiment to refuse to fight against the Bolsheviks. The regiment was disarmed and sent to Morocco, where its men were drafted into disciplinary companies.

The Bolsheviks realised that their best hope was to win support from the soldiers and sailors being sent to attack them, men who were war-weary and potentially sympathetic to the Bolshevik cause. One of the members of the French Communist Group played an important role.

Jeanne Labourbe was born in 1877 in a small town in central France. Her father was a propertyless agricultural day-labourer, who had fought in defence of the Paris Commune. Jeanne was one of the first to benefit from the new compulsory schooling; she also had to work to earn money for the impoverished family and looked after flocks of sheep. Later she earned her living doing ironing.

Her modest education gave her the opportunity to leave her native environment. She got a job in Poland, in an area then still part of the Russian Empire, as a governess and servant. She soon became involved in the left-wing political milieu. She became a friend of Rosa Luxemburg, and also met Dzerzhinsky, the future head of the Soviet secret police, and Lenin. In 1905 she joined the Bolshevik party, the first French person to do so. She did risky work for the socialist movement, using her French passport to act as a courier between illegal organisations in various countries. By 1917 she was in Moscow. Here she helped set up the French Communist Group, of which she became the secretary – so there is some justice in calling her the first French Communist.

When French ships and troops invaded, Jeanne was horrified that young Frenchmen, descendants of the *communards* of 1871, were being used in this way. Her old friend Rosa Luxemburg was murdered in January, and she knew that the future of the revolution throughout Europe was on a knife-edge. She volunteered to go to Odessa to try to persuade the troops there to refuse to obey orders. As her final letter showed, she was well aware of the risks.

She arrived in Odessa and with a few comrades began to produce newspapers and leaflets. These called on French soldiers to refuse to participate in the suppression of the Revolution, appealing to their sense of France's revolutionary history. One leaflet explained Bolshevism in terms of a direct appeal to worker and peasant conscripts, calling it socialist society in practice, the putting in power of those who have always been exploited by the rich and powerful.

She made direct contact with soldiers wherever possible. Aged forty-one, she was old enough to be the mother of many of the young conscripts, and she addressed them as if they were her children.

The French authorities could not tolerate such a threat. On 2 March 1919 ten armed men arrived at the door of the house where Jeanne and other Communist agitators were living. They were bundled into a car, tortured, driven to the nearby Jewish cemetery, and shot dead. A huge crowd [claimed to be 100,000] attended her funeral.

Her actions had not been in vain. The French authorities had to admit defeat. Just one month later it was decided that the troops were not reliable enough to hold Odessa, and the French withdrew. A pro-Bolshevik regime was re-established in the city.[81]

7   Naval Mutinies

By now there was a substantial wave of discontent in the French armed forces. From November 1918 to October 1919 there was a series of mutinies and uprisings in the French navy, involving thousands of sailors, and marked by great courage and imagination. A new generation was discovering the potential of a fight for internationalist values. Some fifty years later three participants, Marcel Monribot, Charles Tillon and Virgile Vuillemin, helped to write a vivid account of their experiences in the mutinies.[82]

The conditions of sailors were very different from those of soldiers. Soldiers in trench warfare were constantly on the move and suffered an appalling casualty rate. The possibility of developing any kind of political organisation was very limited. A large ship was a different matter. Several hundred men lived together in a confined space; unless the ship was sunk there were few casualties. Modern ships required skilled workers; many seamen were technicians and skilled artisans with some trade-union experience. There was thus much in common between a ship and a factory. Engineers were often particularly revolutionary because of the similarity between their work and that of a factory worker.

---

81   Maitron and Pennetier 1964–2023 article114903, notice LABOURBE Jeanne [LABOURBE Marie dite Jeanne] par Jean Maitron, version mise en ligne le 24 novembre 2010, dernière modification le 8 mai 2020; see also van der Motte 2009.

82   Published in *Cahiers de Mai*, 1969; English translation in *Revolutionary History* 8,2, Summer 2002, available at: https://www.marxists.org/history/etol/revhist/backiss/vol8/no2/blacksea.html. See also Marty 1999 and Perry 2020.

While there was no centralised political leadership to the struggles, there were a number of highly political activists, and radical ideas circulated widely on the warships. Of papers circulating in the French navy, the most significant was Brizon's *La Vague*, which by 1919 had a print-run of 100,000; despite military censorship each copy was often passed around many readers. Every issue had a column of correspondence from soldiers and sailors. Cuttings from it reached soldiers, inserted inside reactionary papers. In the immediate post-war period readers' groups called 'Friends of *La Vague*' [Les Amis de la Vague] were set up. *La Vague* was pacifist in its sympathies, but pointed to the roots of war in class society. In 1919 it commented on the end of the war:

> No, no, let us not celebrate 'victory' ... Victory is war. And war is death. There are too many dead. ...
>
> But war will be permanently destroyed only by the triumph of the peoples over their rulers who are based on plunder, privilege and reaction.[83]

Besides *La Vague*, the crews also read other papers, for example *Le Journal du peuple* [The People's Paper] and *Les Hommes du jour* [Men of the Day], both published by Henri Fabre and Georges Pioch, *L'Oeuvre* [The Work] and *Ce qu'il faut dire* [What Must be Said] published by the libertarian Sébastien Faure.

On the battleship *France*, René Vinciguerra had taken the initiative in organising a clandestine library of books and pamphlets, and the crew received anti-war and libertarian papers from France. A group to discuss current events met once or twice a week, under the official pretence of being a choir.[84] As a result it had been possible to develop a political leadership on some of the ships, in a way that would have been impossible in the army.

Chief engineer André Marty, on the torpedo boat *Protet*, had a long political past; he was already in his thirties. He had been a professional seaman before 1914, involved with the socialist paper *Cri du marin*; since 1917 he had been in close contact with the revolutionary syndicalists and anti-war Socialists from Paris. Like many left-wing activists at the time, he was a freemason.[85]

Marty used to give technical instruction to the mechanics and stokers, but took the opportunity to make political propaganda; he began his classes by say-

---

83   Roy 2004, pp. 190–1, 208, 239, 281–2.
84   Marty 1999, p. 114.
85   Marty 1999, p. 107.

ing that the working class would soon have to take over the running of society, and that therefore young workers should be prepared technically for the task. He helped to make the sailors aware of the world situation.[86]

Marty was above all concerned to prevent the French sailors being used to sabotage the Russian Revolution. He was in a position to sabotage his own boat. As he realised, that would achieve little; another torpedo boat would be sent. Only collective action could be effective.

> What was necessary was to *openly and publicly prevent* the ship from continuing the war against the soviet Revolution. In this case, it would no longer simply be a unit refusing to fight, but a brilliant example given to the whole fleet. And I had no doubt that it would be followed.[87]

Marty failed in his attempt. On 16 April 1919 he was arrested and imprisoned. News of his arrest rapidly became known throughout the fleet in the Black Sea, and he became an inspiration for further revolts that took place.

Marty was an experienced activist with some political experience; the wave of revolt also threw up many younger leaders. Virgile Vuillemin on the *France* was not yet twenty-one years old, but he soon developed leadership qualities and played a leading role in the mutinies. Many other young sailors were thrown into activity and had to learn to develop their political qualities very rapidly.

The issues which provoked the mutinies were multiple and complex. Sailors were weary and wanted to go home. There was widespread sympathy for the Russian Revolution, which seemed to offer an alternative to the whole social system that had dragged the world into war. Another common argument was that the intervention in Russia was unconstitutional. The constitution of the Third Republic stated quite clearly that there could be no declaration of war without the agreement of both chambers of parliament; but there had been no vote on the question.

These general political concerns converged with more immediate issues, notably the poor quality of food and the ruthless discipline imposed by the officers. On the *France*, the revolt was provoked by the way the officer in command had decided that the loading of coal would take place on 20 April, which was Easter Sunday. It was a laborious task, and there was great discontent since the crew expected that the day would be observed as a holiday. On the battle-

---

86   Marty 1999, pp. 89–90.
87   Marty 1999, pp. 88–89.

ship *Justice* the spark which set off the explosion was the fact that the sailors had been given only frozen or rotten potatoes to peel. The sailors had to invent forms of organisation to deal with the emerging situation. Delegates were elected and there were heated and lively debates.

The naval authorities responded quickly and brutally. It soon became apparent that peaceful demonstrations had no chance of success. In one case the Admiral gave the crews permission to go ashore; it was a planned ambush. A group of sailors formed a procession singing the *Internationale* through the streets of Sebastopol; they received a warm welcome from the population and the president of the Bolshevik revolutionary committee greeted them. Then Greek troops under French command opened machine-gun fire; it was a massacre with a large number killed and wounded.

This setback did not prevent the mutinies from spreading rapidly and with great success; communications were sent by boat from one ship to another to bring the sailors into action – in effect a flying picket. A new leadership emerged, and young men like Vuillemin were not afraid to confront officers who were much older and senior in rank. When senior officers tried to assert their authority, sailors threatened to throw them in the sea. On one ship an officer who had been threatening was actually thrown into the sea – then fished out again.

The crews were organised and well-disciplined. On the battleship *France* self-management was established; the sailors carried out their duties impeccably. On the *Jean-Bart* the officers ordered hogsheads of wine to be brought onto the deck in the hope of getting the crew drunk. The mutineers placed a picket around the receptacles; nobody touched them.

The demands drawn up by the various mutinies showed a coming together of immediate concerns and a political opposition to the whole French strategy of intervention. For example on the *Jean-Bart* the five demands were:

1. An end to the war against Russia;
2. Immediate return to France;
3. Less rigorous discipline;
4. Improved food;
5. Leave for the crew.[88]

The mutineers adopted the symbolism of the international working-class movement. Time and again the mutinous crews would assemble singing the *Internationale*, despite the horrified protests of their officers. On Easter Sunday 1919, on the *France* and the *Jean-Bart*, the tricolour flag was raised at the rear of

---

88   Marty 1999, p. 118.

the ships, but instead of saluting it most sailors stood facing the bow and sang the *Internationale*, while the red flag was raised on the bowsprit mast.

Some of the songs that were sung by the mutineers reflected an emerging internationalist consciousness:

> J'ai réfléchi, je ne tirerai pas,
> Je suis marin, je refuse quand même,
> Car sur mes frères révoltés là-bas
> Je ne tirerai pas, c'est indigne de moi-même.
> I've considered, I shall not shoot,
> I am a sailor, but I still refuse,
> For on my brothers in revolt over there
> I shall not shoot, it is unworthy of me.

The Committee to defend Black Sea sailors published a song with the chorus:

> Salut! Salut à vous!
> Vaillants marins de la mer Noire!
> Salut! Salut à vous!
> Petits cols bleus couverts de gloire.
> Salut! Salut à vous!
> Ennemis du capitalisme
> Qui croyait, en comptant sur vous,
> Assassiner le communisme!

> We salute you
> Brave sailors of the Black Sea!
> We salute you
> Little white collars covered with glory.
> We salute you
> Enemies of capitalism
> Which thought that, by counting on you,
> It could murder communism!

It might have been possible for the mutiny to join forces with the Russian Revolution. Such a course was envisaged by the action committee on the cruiser *Waldeck-Rousseau*. There the gunner Nouveau, a member of the action committee, threatened that if the sailors were not given satisfaction, the ship would be berthed in Odessa that very evening. It was also what André Marty had wanted to attempt on *Le Protet* before he was arrested. There did seem to be the possibility of seeing the whole fleet go over to the Bolsheviks and the Revolution. Things did not go that far, and some sailors doubtless saw the threat merely as a means of bargaining for their main aim, demobilisation. The fact that the threat was there showed just how much was at stake, and what the potential of the mutinies had become.

The action soon spread beyond the Black Sea. Charles Tillon, born in 1897, had served an apprenticeship as a metal-worker, then became a fitter; his father had had revolutionary syndicalist sympathies. He joined the navy in 1916, serving on the cruiser *Guichen*, which was used for troop transports to the East, shuttling between Italy and Greece. The crew learned of the Black Sea mutinies, and when they realised that they were being used to transport troops to Odessa, there was a mutiny in which Tillon played a leading role. The mutiny was suppressed; the *Guichen* was returned to France.

Soon the mutinies were well-known and widely discussed in France itself. In particular there was an impact in areas such as Toulon, an important military port, where anti-war newspapers were in great demand and revolutionary leaflets were circulating on the ships and in the naval barracks. A debate about the mutinies was scheduled for 6 June in the National Assembly. Just before midnight on the day before, the red flag was raised at Toulon on the mast of the *Provence* in solidarity with the mutineers. This was followed by a general rising of all ships and soldiers in Toulon, together with striking workers from the shipyards at nearby La Seyne-sur-Mer.

The French state wanted its revenge, and, more importantly, to ensure that there would be no repetition of such mutinies. There were heavy penalties for those identified as the leaders. Courts martial, some meeting on board ship, others in naval bases, imposed prison sentences of up to 20 years. The accused stood up to the military courts. Virgile Vuillemin gave evidence for two hours and effectively became a lawyer for the accused.

Punishments were exceptionally harsh. Charles Tillon was sentenced to five years hard labour, and sent to jail in Morocco. Although he was released early, he needed four months in hospital to recover. The mutineer most harshly treated was André Marty, who was sentenced to 20 years hard labour. A powerful propaganda campaign won an amnesty for the Black Sea mutineers in July 1922, but Marty was released only a year later. While imprisoned Marty was presented as an election candidate by the newly formed Communist Party and was elected, but promptly disqualified. He was even nominated and elected to the workplace committee of an arms factory in Tulle, though he had no connection with the factory.[89]

---

89   Marty 1999, p. 191.

Those who had taken part in a struggle against nationalism at such a high level were part of a new generation of leaders emerging in the French working-class movement. Marty and Tillon were to become leading figures in the French Communist Party for some thirty years – until they were purged by the party in 1952, perhaps partially because, having been leaders of real struggles, they seemed to pose a threat to those who owed their positions in the party entirely to activity within the apparatus [see Chapter 10]. Virgile Vuillemin became an anarchist, then, after involvement in the Resistance, joined the Communist Party – from which he resigned in protest at the expulsion of Marty.[90]

The horrors and sufferings of the war had devastated a whole generation. Now a new generation were emerging who were determined that such nationalist folly should never be repeated. For that they would need new ideas and new forms of struggle.

----

90   Maitron and Pennetier 1964–2023 article154234, notice VUILLEMIN Virgile, Léon, Louis [Dictionnaire des anarchistes] par Claude Pennetier, notice complétée par Marianne Enckell, version mise en ligne le 20 avril 2014, dernière modification le 11 août 2020.

A Time for Hope

Could a version of the Russian Revolution be repeated in any of the states of Europe? This was the question that was being asked, anxiously by the defenders of the old order, hopefully by millions of war-weary workers. From November 1918 until 1923 Germany seemed to be on the brink of revolution.

At the same time things were changing on a global scale. The United States had entered the war in April 1917, on the winning side, clearly aiming to pick up the pieces. It was developing its economic and political interests around the globe – but it rejected the traditional European method of doing so, namely colonialism.[1] In January 1918 US President Woodrow Wilson issued his Fourteen Points, which defined the United States' war aims and tried to set out policies that would avoid the recurrence of such destructive wars.

Wilson was no internationalist. On the contrary, he was a white supremacist who had written of the 'natural, inevitable ascendancy of the whites' in the US South.[2] But in the particular conjuncture of the aftermath of world war, his role was ambiguous. His primary project was to increase American penetration in the war-wrecked European economy; he realised that this could not be carried through without a degree of ideological camouflage. His proposals involved a settlement based on the principle of 'peace without victory' [i.e. no excessive reparations] and non-intervention in Russia [though in fact US troops had been sent to Russia]. Wilson was an effective demagogue and gave the impression of addressing himself to the mass of the people rather than to other politicians. Although the French government eventually accepted Wilson's points, they were suspicious; Clemenceau and others, eager to intervene in Russia, were hostile. This doubtless made Wilson more attractive to the French left.

Wilson came to Europe immediately after the armistice. He caught the mood of the time and was very popular. When he toured France it was clear that he was perceived as more radical than the French government. In various areas demonstrations to welcome Wilson were called by the CGT and the Socialist Party, and in some cases these were banned by the government. Trade-union bodies and groups of workers in factories passed numerous resolutions of good wishes to Wilson.

---

1 See Callinicos 2003, pp. 108–10.

2 Ali 2022, p. 147.

Many people were undoubtedly naïve and confused about Wilson's motives; he was compared to Jaurès, and since his programme included non-intervention in Russia there seemed to be no incompatibility between being a supporter of Wilson and sympathising with the Bolshevik Revolution. Undoubtedly some of those who came out to back Wilson were also supporters of the Russian Revolution; many more were part of the potential audience for the Communist Party that was to be formed in December 1920. At a CGT conference a resolution was unanimously carried, with the support of anti-war activist Merrheim, which backed both Wilson and the October Revolution.[3] The mass popularity he enjoyed was a manifestation of the widespread internationalist mood that existed in the working class.

Another expression of this post-war mood was the formation in France of the *Clarté* [Enlightenment] organisation which aimed to bring together anti-war intellectuals. A central figure in its founding was Henri Barbusse, author of *Under Fire*, and the movement took its name from his second anti-war novel, published in 1919. In that year *Clarté* groups were set up in Paris and in various parts of France; one local group in Paris had nearly 200 members. They campaigned against intervention in Russia, and urged that 'the cause of justice and equality requires the destruction of the old social barbarism'.[4] *Clarté* groups were formed in several other countries, including Germany.

As a movement *Clarté* was short-lived, but it gave birth to a journal which survived for nine years. This reflected the consciousness of a left milieu in which the problems of internationalism were making themselves felt. The editorial team was divided about its attitude towards Marxism and the Russian Revolution. The central question during its nine-year life was the perspective for revolutionary change.

With its origins in the anti-war mood of 1919, *Clarté* developed beyond the moralising pacifism of its roots towards a greater concern with the social and economic causes of war. In 1919 supporters of *Clarté* issued a statement condemning the Versailles Peace Treaty, – which they correctly prophesied would lead to future wars – supporting the efforts of US President Wilson, and proclaiming that 'only through internationalism will the unification of the masses be achieved one day'.[5]

In particular it took up the question of colonialism; as Jean-Richard Bloch prophetically warned 'The nineteenth century was dominated by the problem

---

3 Chambelland 1999, p. 109.
4 Cuenot 2011, tome I, pp. 21, 23–6.
5 *Clarté* 75, 1925, quoted by Cuenot 2011 tome I p, 20.

of nationality; the colonial problem will dominate the twentieth century. It is in the colonies that the fate of Great Britain and France will be settled'.[6]

There were also internationalist sentiments in the radical wing of the cultural milieu. Tristan Tzara's journal *Dada au grand air* [Dada in the open air] alternated between the French and German languages, a significant gesture so soon after the end of the war.

1   Founding of the PCF

The most important expression of the internationalist mood was the birth of the French Communist Party [PCF], founded at the Tours Congress of the SFIO in late December 1920. In the process of preparing the Tours Congress a crucial part was played by the revolutionary syndicalists.[7] They – especially the current around *La Vie ouvrière* – had been the most intransigent internationalists in the period before the war, and the most determined to oppose the war once it had broken out. The central debate at Tours was affiliation to the Communist International [Comintern], founded in 1919 to draw together workers' organisations committed to supporting the new revolutionary state in Russia.

Two events at the Tours Congress are worth noting. The first was a speech by a young Indochinese delegate Nguyen-Ai-Quac. This was both an indictment and a plea.[8] He told the delegates how his compatriots were 'shamefully oppressed and exploited', as well as 'poisoned' by alcohol and opium. Prisons were more numerous than schools, and freedom of the press did not exist. He urged that 'the Party must make socialist propaganda in all the colonies', and concluded with the appeal: 'Comrades, save us!'

He got a good reception, with repeated applause; but he was interrupted twice. On the first occasion, Jean Longuet, Karl Marx's grandson, called out in justification of his own reputation: 'I have intervened to defend natives!' A little later, when an unnamed delegate heckled, Nguyen responded with a cutting 'Silence, parliamentarians!' That a young rank-and-file delegate from a colonial territory should have no compunction in telling members of parliament to be quiet shows the potential for an anti-colonial orientation in the new party. Later the delegate would be better known to the world as Ho Chi Minh.

The second dramatic moment was carefully staged. Frossard, the Secretary of the SFIO, was in the middle of a speech when the lights went out; when they

---

6   Cuenot 2011, tome II, p. 34.
7   Chuzeville 2017.
8   Ho Chi Minh 1920.

came on again veteran German revolutionary Clara Zetkin was on the platform. In her speech Zetkin stressed the international nature of the tasks facing the movement:

> The job of French socialists is not only to make the revolution in France, but to assist the development of the German revolution. German capitalism's only hope of rescue is from an agreement with French capitalism.
>
> Dear friends, it is not the German bourgeoisie but the working class which will suffer under the Treaty of Versailles, this treaty of blood and iron. This treaty will not be modified by the bourgeoisie. Only the alliance of French and German workers can destroy it.[9]

The appearance of Zetkin, despite a French government ban, so soon after the end of the war, was a magnificent internationalist gesture.[10] To get her to Tours, a long way from the German border, at the time of a high-profile Congress which must have been under heavy surveillance, was an extraordinary feat.

After the congress, Zetkin wrote a personal letter to Lenin. She was well aware of the inadequacies of the Comintern functionaries. By addressing Lenin without deference, she hoped to give him a clearer picture of what was going on within the International and its constituent parties. In criticising the Comintern's intervention at Tours, she advised:

> I urgently recommend you to discuss the matter with Rosmer, who must be well-informed, but above all with his wife, who will soon be coming back to Moscow. During my stay I have learnt to value Madame Rosmer as one of the most lucid, loyal, energetic and politically intelligent 'men' in the French movement.[11]

'Madame Rosmer' was Marguerite Thévenet [see chapter 6], the lifelong partner of Alfred Rosmer [though they only found time to get married in 1932]. If ever the phrase 'hidden from history' was appropriate then it fitted the case of Thévenet. Her name never appears in her husband's account of the early years of the PCF in *Lenin's Moscow* and it is absent from virtually all histories of the party. The fact that Thévenet has left so few traces is not accidental. She shunned publicity; one of her obituaries bears the title 'Discreet Marguer-

---

9   Zetkin 1920.
10   Badia 1993, p. 216.
11   Letter written by Zetkin 25 January 1921, published in Stoljarowa and Schmalfuss 1990.

ite'.[12] That discretion was part of her temperament, and was also inherent in the activity at which she was most skilled, namely smuggling people across frontiers. Such activity required considerable discretion, and was best not discussed in too great detail even years after the event.

Along with Monatte, Martinet and Rosmer, Thévenet was one of the first to show active solidarity with the Russian Revolution. Her gifts for smuggling literature were devoted to getting material from Russia to Western Europe, despite the blockade imposed by the Western powers. She organised a route across frontiers for books and pamphlets published in Petrograd, in particular documents from the *Black Book*, which made public the diplomatic correspondence about the Franco-Russian alliance of 1910–16, discovered in the Russian archives by René Marchand.

It therefore seems probable that she played some part in organising Zetkin's appearance at Tours. Maurice Chambelland, a close associate of Rosmer and Monatte, says that she helped to organise Zetkin's visit. Other sources claim that the visit was organised by René Reynaud and André Le Troquer [later president – equivalent of speaker – of the National Assembly!], and that she was driven to the Congress in the car of Auguste Mougeot, an anarchist plasterer and painter, and a friend of the Rosmers.[13]

Behind the rhetoric and drama, the main issue at Tours was affiliation to the Communist International. Though these were never actually voted on at the Congress, affiliation implied recognition of the Twenty-One Conditions for admission to the International. These conditions were a response to the collapse of the Second International in 1914; the old International had not been sufficiently disciplined to prevent the slide into war. The new conditions, it was hoped, would be a safeguard against the Comintern being entered by opportunist elements who might make another débâcle of the 1914 type possible. The majority at the Congress accepted the conditions and became the PCF; the disssenting minority reorganised itself under the name of the SFIO.

The decisions taken were not those of a few conference delegates reflecting a passive and uninformed membership, but were the result of intense political argument prior to the Congress. Most of those involved recognised that to vote for affiliation to the Communist International was to opt in favour of the international working class and against a reformist framework which put loyalty to their own nation state first. Not everyone who supported affiliation to

----

12   Chambelland 1962b. See also Hagnauer 1962, Godeau 1963.
13   Badia 1993, p. 217. See also Chambelland 1962a.

the Comintern did so out of total commitment to the Bolshevik position; for many rank-and-file Socialists the prime issue was to defeat the right wing in their own party and break with the traditions that had led to support for the national war effort. If alignment with the Bolsheviks meant that, they would go along with it.

The conditions laid down the required activities of Communist Parties admitted to membership of the Comintern. Two conditions in particular were designed to ensure that the policies of any Communist Party were authentically internationalist. These were the fourth, on anti-militarism:

> Persistent and systematic propaganda and agitation must be conducted in the armed forces, and Communist cells formed in every military unit. In the main Communists will have to do this work illegally; failure to engage in it would be tantamount to a betrayal of their revolutionary duty and incompatible with membership in the Third International.

and the eighth, on anti-colonialism:

> Parties in countries whose bourgeoisie possess colonies and oppress other nations must pursue a most well-defined and clear-cut policy in respect of colonies and oppressed nations. Any party wishing to join the Third International must ruthlessly expose the colonial machinations of the imperialists of its 'own' country, must support – in deed, not merely in word – every colonial liberation movement, demand the expulsion of its compatriot imperialists from the colonies, inculcate in the hearts of the workers of its own country an attitude of true brotherhood with the working population of the colonies and the oppressed nations, and conduct systematic agitation among the armed forces against all oppression of the colonial peoples.[14]

The fourth condition reflected very well the experience of the CGT and the *sou du soldat*, and to implement it the PCF needed only to look back to the best traditions of the French left. The eighth condition was more problematic, since neither the SFIO nor the CGT had a particularly good record of opposing colonialism.

The formation of a mass Communist Party, committed to the principles of revolutionary internationalism and constitutionally a section of a revolution-

---

14   Lenin 1965.

ary International, was an important advance. Yet it also presented a potential problem. 'Internationalism' could now have two meanings. On the one hand it could mean recognition that the oppressed and exploited of different nations shared common interests in face of the nation states which oppressed them. On the other hand it could mean loyalty to, and acceptance of the discipline of, an international body such as the Comintern.

There was not necessarily any contradiction between the two meanings. Inasmuch as the International was a body established to put into practice the principles of internationalism, then the two meanings coincided. Yet already in the first years of the Comintern, as Zetkin was observing, the International was acquiring an apparatus which was beginning to develop interests of its own that might diverge from those of the working-class membership. Members of that apparatus would defend themselves with the assertion that the interests of the International were, by definition, the interests of the international working class. For the moment the problem was only a shadow on the horizon; it would not disappear.

Defence of a newly created socialist regime was an obligation for any internationalist. All the more reason why a great many left activists wanted to see for themselves. From the very earliest years of the Bolshevik regime, there were numerous visitors. A journey across Europe so soon after the colossal damage inflicted by the world war was not easy, and travel inside Russia was made more risky by the civil war being fought on its territory.

Throughout the 1920s revolutionary militants from France were harassed by state authorities if they attempted to visit Russia; delegates to the early congresses of the Comintern risked jail on their return. The police had good knowledge of the various routes used by militants to visit Russia; if they did not always block their journeys, they made them more difficult, which imposed a financial burden on the various left organisations.[15]

Yet there was a steady stream of visitors to the new revolutionary state, a clear indication of how important belonging to an international movement and an international organisation was to militants of this generation.

2   The Baku Congress

In the autumn of 1920 the Bolsheviks took another step forward in their struggle against imperialism and colonialism. This was the Baku Congress of Septem-

---

15   Mazuy 2002, p. 24.

ber 1920, with which the Bolsheviks made a declaration of their opposition to imperialism and attempted to lay the foundations for an organisational expression of this opposition.[16] The Executive Committee of the International invited representatives of the oppressed peoples to gather at Baku, in Azerbaijan, one of the countries of the former Tsarist Empire which had become independent in 1918, and which was 'at the junction between Russia and the East'.[17] The journey was a dangerous one – British aircraft attacked and killed delegates on their way to the Congress – but those attending came in large numbers. According to the stenographic report there were 1891 delegates, including 1273 Communists.

As Zinoviev put it in his opening address: 'We want to put an end to the rule of capital throughout the world. We are certain that we shall not be able to finally abolish the exploitation of man by man unless we light the revolutionary fire, not only in Europe and America, but in the whole world, unless we are followed by that portion of humanity which lives in Africa and Asia'.[18]

As he warned, this was not just a question of abstract solidarity; the European powers would use colonial troops against their own working classes.[19] In his concluding speech he somewhat optimistically promised 'holy war' against the common enemy, French and British imperialism.[20] The Congress was lively, sometimes chaotic, with no unanimity on crucial questions like religion, in particular Islam, and the rights of women.

Present at the Congress were Communists from the three biggest imperialist powers – John Reed [author of *Ten Days that Shook the World*] from the USA, Tom Quelch from Britain, and Rosmer from France. On the way from Moscow they had travelled across Russian territory devastated by civil war.

In his address to the Congress Rosmer made a searing attack on the hypocrisy of French imperialism:

> When the World War started, the leaders of France and Britain, and their lackeys in the press, assured us that this universal inferno would bring freedom to the peoples oppressed by German barbarism. But if it was a matter of liberating oppressed peoples, why did these great powers not begin by giving their freedom to the people they themselves were oppressing? Why did Britain not give Ireland its freedom? Why does it keep the 300 million people living in India under its rule? Why does

---

16   Collectif 2017. See also Riddell 1993.
17   Broué 1997, p. 181.
18   Collectif 2017, p. 19.
19   Collectif 2017, p. 35.
20   Collectif 2017, pp. 186–7.

France, which claimed to be fighting against German barbarism, oppress Morocco, Tunisia and Algeria, and why today is it waging war in Cilicia and Syria to expand its empire with a piece of Asia?

On the contrary, France and Britain are trying to take back from these peoples even the small reforms that they had conceded before the war. When they had to fight Germany, and to this end had to mobilise hundreds of thousands of Algerians, Tunisians and Moroccans, these latter were promised all sorts of freedoms; but today, when the representatives of Tunisia remember the 45,000 Tunisians who died in battle, and hesitantly recall the promises made by the French government, this government offers no response except to arrest and jail the 'agitators' and close down the native newspapers which dared to publish their statement.

That's how they behave in France, that's how they behave in Britain! That's how the great powers treat the countries they made use of to oppose German imperialism.[21]

Among victims of the perilous journey between France and Russia were three delegates to the Second Congress of the Comintern, Raymond Lefebvre, Marcel Vergeat and Jules Lepetit. Lefebvre, whose novels are discussed above [chapter 6], was already a Communist; Vergeat was a syndicalist and Lepetit an anarchist. All three were anxious to learn as much as they could about the realities of life in Bolshevik Russia; then, eager to return home and tell what they had seen, they embarked on a boat despite a raging storm and perished at sea.

Lepetit's biography was typical of that of many activists in the period just after the Russian Revolution. Born into dire poverty, he went to work in the Saint-Nazaire shipyard at the age of eleven. He became an anarchist and was known as a powerful orator who could captivate an audience. He worked as a navvy, was a militant trade unionist, a class fighter and, during World War I, an anti-war activist.[22]

In a letter written days before leaving Russia, Lepetit insisted:

The Revolution is giving birth in blood and tears, in pain and anguish, but the essential thing is that it is giving birth to something beautiful and healthy. I believe that, despite all its faults, the Russian Revolution, still in

---

21   Collectif 2017, pp. 87–8.

22   Maitron and Pennetier 1964–2023 article 99688, notice BERTHO Louis, Alexandre, dit LEPETIT Jules, Marius, dit également LEGRAND, version mise en ligne le 3 novembre 2010, dernière modification le 30 juin 2019.

its first phase, will, if other peoples can assist it, produce a truly beautiful society. *But that means that the workers of the West must not leave it to rely on its own strength.*[23]

3 Rosmer and the RILU

The besieged revolution needed allies in every quarter. Effective internationalism meant developing new and inventive organisational forms. One example was the task given to Alfred Rosmer after the Second Congress of the Comintern, that of building the Red International of Labour Unions [RILU]. After the 1920 Comintern Congress, Rosmer was kept in Russia for 17 months in order to work on the founding of the RILU, even though he could have played a vital role in the early development of the PCF.

Founded in 1921, the RILU[24] was an attempt to establish a rival, pro-Communist, alternative to the resolutely reformist International Federation of Trade Unions [IFTU], also known as the Amsterdam International. The RILU aimed to seek affiliation, where possible, from national federations, but also from minorities within such federations. In its first couple of years it was the focus of a vigorous confrontation between different traditions of trade unionism.

The fact that Rosmer, who came from a syndicalist, and not a Marxist background, was entrusted with such a responsible task was an indication of the relative openness of the Comintern in its early years. If a genuinely international movement were to be rebuilt, then it would mean a coming together of different political traditions from a range of different countries, with no one tradition claiming absolute correctness. It would mean a united front in which different currents would work alongside each other and learn from each other. For a brief period it seemed as if at least some in the Comintern leadership, including Lenin himself, were willing to envisage such a possibility. For example in 1920 the Comintern needed support in the main French trade-union body, the CGT. In 1920 the CGT had two million members, as against the SFIO's 180,000.[25] Anarchists and syndicalists had been the first supporters of the Russian Revolution in France.[26]

---

23   Cited in Maitron and Pennetier 1964–2023 article 99688, notice BERTHO Louis.
24   See Tosstorff 2004.
25   Kendall 1975, pp. 339, 380.
26   Maitron 1975, Volume II, p. 42.

Rosmer had a real feel for the Western labour movement in its diversity. He was a man of great perceptiveness and unquestioned integrity, who knew how to lead but also how to learn and listen. He had to carry through the work of preparing for the founding conference of the RILU, a process which took considerably longer than originally hoped.[27] He also found himself in a buffer position, as one of the few intermediaries trusted by both the Bolsheviks and by the anti-authoritarians in Russia and abroad. In addition he had to deal with Zinoviev, who often advocated a mechanical imitation of Russian methods. Rosmer had to play a double role, both conciliating the syndicalists and defending the Comintern line.

The Founding Conference of the RILU was held in July 1921. Rosmer's speech[28] was one of his major contributions to the theory and practice of the Comintern. Three basic themes emerged. Firstly he argued in defence of the syndicalist tradition. Rather than claiming universal validity for the Bolshevik model, he insisted that what had been positive in syndicalism should be maintained and incorporated into the Comintern. Secondly he rejected any attempt to separate the political and the economic. If such separation was always to be rejected, it was a positive absurdity in a period of potentially revolutionary crisis. Finally he rejected formalism. Syndicalism and Bolshevism had different traditions and used different languages; the important thing was what they had in common. Rosmer argued that the CGT in fact functioned as a party, and that its anti-party stance was no more than a question of terminology.

Yet in the end the RILU's achievement was very limited. In the words of Rosmer, who had done so much to try and make it work, 'the RILU was not a real International, for Internationals could not be made out of minorities, organisations were needed'.[29]

In 1921 Victor Serge, a former anarchist who had gone to Russia and had become an active supporter of the Bolsheviks, published two short pamphlets, *During the Civil War* and *The Anarchists and the Experience of the Russian Revolution* in the series edited by Marcel Martinet, *Les Cahiers du travail* [Labour Notebooks].[30] The previous year he had written a series of articles in *La Vie ouvrière* entitled *The Endangered* City, later collected into a pamphlet.[31]

Serge's strategy in writing the pamphlets has to be seen in the context of the situation of the French left in 1921. The winning of the Socialist Party

---

27   See Tosstorff 2004.

28   Rosmer 1921.

29   Quoted by Tosstorff 2004, p. 613.

30   Serge 1921a, Serge 1921b.

31   Serge 1924a.

to the cause of the October Revolution entailed serious problems. Many of the best militants in France had been anarchists or revolutionary syndicalists. While potentially such militants had a key role to play in building a genuine revolutionary Communist Party in France, the anarchists and syndicalists were often suspicious of the Communists – firstly because of the opportunist ex-Socialists whom they saw in charge of the French Party, and secondly because of the reports, sometimes but not always inaccurate or distorted, that they had received from the new-born soviet republic in Russia.

The aim of the pamphlets was to win anarchists and syndicalists over to support for the Communist cause. Serge argued eloquently that no revolutionary purism should keep any revolutionary away from giving full political and material solidarity to the Bolshevik regime.

At the same time, he was keenly away of the dangers that existed at the heart of the Revolution itself. His accounts were no facile attempt at public relations, but an honest appraisal of the weaknesses and mistakes of the regime. Although Serge had broken politically with the anarchism of his youth, he still believed that the moral integrity of the anarchist and syndicalist militants could make a real contribution to strengthening the revolutionary cause and providing a counterbalance to bureaucratisation and opportunism.

Solidarity with the besieged soviet republic could take many forms. While Alfred Rosmer was attempting to build the RILU on a secure foundation, his partner Marguerite was involved in activity of a very different kind. In the aftermath of the civil war, parts of Russia fell victim to a lethal famine during 1921 and 1922. This offered an opportunity to bring practical assistance to the homeland of the Revolution, and at the same time to contribute to educating French workers in the meaning of international solidarity.

In the autumn of 1921 Thévenet began preparations for a major project, that of taking a trainload of supplies to the famine-stricken areas of Russia. By the Spring of 1922 the train was in Russia and in two articles in *L'Humanité*[32] Thévenet reported on the experience so far. Involved in the work were a number of veterans from the women's anti-war organisations. As Thévenet noted, 'They have already learned a lot in Russia, much more and much better than those of our comrades who only attend congresses'.

Writing with brutal directness, Thévenet described her experiences:

> I am writing to you from our railway carriage, where I have been living since February. We have been stopped for some hours in the little halt at

---

32   Rosmer M 1922a, Rosmer M 1922b.

> Shulika, and it is the usual nightmare of stations in the starving regions;
> the weather is fine, it is hot, but we are confined in our carriage with the
> windows shut and the doors closed tight. Despite that we can hear the
> endless moaning of the little children hanging around the carriage and
> crying with hunger: 'Diadinka [little uncle], please give us'. Some of them
> repeat that very softly in varying tones for ten minutes or a quarter of an
> hour, without stopping, and then flop down on the ground when they can
> go on no longer; others concentrate their strength and shout very loud and
> frequently; their little voices become irritated and rise higher and higher,
> chilling you to the marrow; then they stop suddenly and go away to lie
> down anywhere, and sometimes they never get up again.

Thévenet made no attempt to romanticise her picture of Russia. She showed
the appalling suffering, destitution and moral degeneration of the famine victims. Doubtless that is why her reports did not receive more prominence; the
rhetoric of revolutionary success was more useful to bureaucrats in Paris and
Moscow.

Thévenet used these horrific scenes to encourage French workers to collect
money and food for the Russian famine. She clearly distinguished the activity of her train from that of traditional charity workers. Their aim was not
simply to help the victims, but to eradicate the causes of their suffering by
developing the foundations of a socialist economy; hence part of their effort
was devoted to establishing a 'soviet estate [Sovcoz]', with farming and a workshop.

4   Anti-Colonialism

In 1920 France's colonial empire ranged from Indochina in Asia and New Caledonia in the South Pacific through Central and North Africa [Algeria, Tunisia,
Morocco] to Guadeloupe and Martinique in the West Indies. The Communist
Party was committed by the eighth condition of affiliation to the Comintern to
support 'every colonial liberation movement', and to 'demand the expulsion of
its compatriot imperialists from the colonies'.

For the indigenous inhabitants of the countries of the French empire one of
the most important questions was the so-called 'Native Code' [Code de l'Indi-
génat]. This was not a single text but a collection of laws and practices. Colonial
administrators had the power to impose internment, surveillance, house arrest,
confiscation of goods and collective fines. They were able to impose punishments for words or actions that were disrespectful to a figure of authority, even

if that person was not acting in an official capacity. Any action liable to lessen the respect due to authority could be punished.

As the historian of colonialism Olivier Lecour Grandmaison has pointed out, the Native Code betrayed and undermined one of the most fundamental principles of the French Revolution, namely the principle of the universality of the law. The Native Code meant that there were two different laws, according to whether one was a settler or a member of the indigenous population. If a native proletarian were to steal a few grapes from his employer's vineyard, he would certainly end up in jail, whereas if a settler were to kill one of his native workers, he would get away with a suspended sentence of two months in prison.[33]

In its early years the PCF conducted a vigorous campaign against the Native Code. However the historian Claude Liauzu has argued with some justice that the anticolonial campaigns of the early PCF were the work of a handful of almost marginal activists who came up against the indifference of the party leaders. The French delegation to the Fifth Comintern Congress in 1924 did not contain a single party member from the colonies, which led to reprimands from the Comintern.[34]

It was in Algeria that the contradictions within the new Communist Party most quickly became visible. The party in North Africa that had been inherited from the SFIO was very much a European settler party. It was only slowly and with difficulty that it began to recruit native Algerians over the coming decade.[35] The Second North African Interfederal Communist Conference, on 24 September 1922, unanimously adopted a resolution which effectively denied that the indigenous Algerian population was capable of emancipating itself.

This began with a critique of the Comintern's eighth condition and advanced the argument that a strategy for North Africa must begin with an understanding of the particular situation in the region. Therefore tactics must be based on the specificities of the situation, which would require an analysis of the Algerian mentality. This led to a very negative analysis of the Arab masses, described as being ignorant, prone to 'fatalism and religious fanaticism', guilty of rejecting equality for women and of a low level of trade-union organisation.

A second text drew a rather pessimistic strategic conclusion: 'The emancipation of the native populations of Algeria can result only from the revolution

---

33   See Le Cour Grandmaison, 2010.
34   Liauzu 1982, p. 18.
35   Drew 2014, p. 35.

in France ...'[36] The resolution provoked the wrath of the Comintern, notably an article by Trotsky.[37] It also got a prompt response from a Muslim member of the PCF, Hadj-Ali Abdelkader. The most devastating reply came from Robert Louzon, a French member of the PCF now resident in Tunisia; it was entitled 'A Disgrace'.[38]

Louzon insisted that the document was 'a disgrace for the so-called Communist who drew it up and for those who voted for it without, I hope, having read it carefully'. Its logic was to defend the preservation of imperialist rule:

> In the opening lines it is already stated: 'There are oppressed peoples who are already now ready for sovereignty and others *who are not*'. And since the rest of the report shows clearly that for its author the natives of Algeria fall into the second category, that of peoples who are not 'ready for sovereignty', who must be maintained 'in guardianship', the practical conclusion is that the French capitalist bourgeoisie must continue to rule over the native masses of North Africa and to impose on them its 'guardianship' – if necessary with machine-guns – if they attempt to rebel.
>
> This is the most shameless justification for the present state of affairs, it is the most unmistakable condemnation made of the attempts by the native inhabitants of all the colonised countries, in Algeria as well as elsewhere, to free themselves from the yoke that Western capitalism has imposed on them; it is a proclamation of the right, for the bourgeoisie in industrial countries, to carry out 'primitive accumulation' by expropriation of agricultural peoples not yet subjected to capitalist rule.
>
> Moreover, all this is concealed under the same hypocritical phraseology as is always used by the bourgeoisie to cover up the material interests which motivate it. It is 'in order to serve as humane and impartial mentors to the colonised peoples' that it imposes itself on them.

Louzon went on to show that the author of the report failed to notice that the arguments made to show that the indigenous Algerians were unready for self-emancipation would apply equally to French workers at the time of the French Revolution ... or indeed at the present day:

---

36   Rapport présenté 1922.
37   Trotsky 1922.
38   Louzon 1923.

In 1789 or even in 1848 there were scarcely more French people who knew how to read than today there are Arabs able to do so: does therefore the author of the report consider that as a result the French people was not then ready for 'sovereignty' and that it should have remained subjected to the 'guardianship' of a monarch or a foreign people?

He made a similar point with regard to the influence of religion:

Then the report points to 'influence of the marabouts [Muslim religious leaders] and the religious brotherhoods' on the minds of the natives. Would people in Algeria be unaware of the influence of priests and monks on the minds of most French people? Would they be unaware that the number of pilgrims to Lourdes and other places are counted in hundreds of thousands every year? Would they not have noticed that during the war the number of French soldiers who did not wear some sort of amulet and who, when they were wounded, refused the chaplains' practice of exorcism, was very small?

He dealt similarly with the oppression of women:

Equality between men and women does not exist among the natives. That is true. But does it exist in France? Neither in civil rights nor in political rights is there equality between French men and French women.

and with the question of trade-union organisation:

Finally! The decisive argument! According to the author of the report the best proof that Algerian natives need 'guardianship' is that native agricultural workers are not unionised! But does the author know many trade unionists among the European agricultural workers in Algeria, and even in France, does he think that the Federation of agricultural labourers has a very high membership?

He concluded by pointing out that:

if after a century of 'guardianship' the natives are still in the backward state in which they are depicted, it is because 'guardianship' is a tool of domination, but not a tool of progress ... The necessary but not sufficient condition for a people to progress is independence. To keep natives in a state of servitude is an infallible means of preserving the soul of a slave.

He responded to the accusation of nationalism against the indigenous Algerians by making the point that there is a clear distinction between the nationalism of the oppressors and the nationalism of the oppressed:

> It is a specious argument to see all nationalisms as equal. There is no equivalence between the nationalism of an oppressor people whose nationalism consists in oppressing another people, and the nationalism of an oppressed people whose nationalism aims simply to get rid of the oppressor people. There is no equivalence between the nationalism of the English who want to go on ruling Ireland, and the nationalism of the Irish who want to rule themselves. In the first case, nationalism means *imperialism*, in the second it means *independence*.

He concluded with a reaffirmation of basic Communist principles:

> A Communist must have a Communist mentality, not an 'Algerian mentality'. He must not believe himself superior to the native because he wears a hat instead of a fez, or because he calls on the name of Jesus rather than that of Allah. ... Communism is the struggle for the emancipation of workers, of *all* workers, not for putting some of them under 'guardianship' by a foreign proletariat or a foreign capitalism. Communism has nothing in common with a politics which is only concerned with winning higher pay and privileges for *French* officials in North Africa, who are proud of wearing detachable collars and of having been to school.

In terms of a strategy for North Africa, Louzon knew what he was talking about. He had taken part in the meetings of the group around Pierre Monatte, which produced *La Vie ouvrière*, from the very outset. In 1913 he went to Tunisia in order to run a farm. He took part in the 1914–18 war as a captain in an infantry regiment, then returned to Tunisia. In 1919 he joined the Tunis branch of the Socialist Party. After the Tours Congress he became secretary of the Tunisian Communist Federation.

In November 1921, the Tunisian Federation launched a daily paper in Arabic, *Habib el Oumma*, the first Communist daily paper to be published in Arabic. Louzon, unlike many European settlers, was aware of the huge potential for colonial revolt. He wrote in a letter to his friend Amédée Dunois:

> There is here a vast indigenous movement for national demands. This movement includes all classes of the population, and all of it is extremely favourable to the Communist Party, which is seen as the only party fully

sympathetic to the political emancipation of the native population … We must take advantage [of the situation] to create, within the indigenous movement, a clearly defined class movement of workers and peasants.[39]

If Louzon recognised the significance of an Arabic-language daily paper, so too did the French authorities. The paper was soon banned. For some days new Arabic dailies were launched, each day under a different title, and each was immediately banned. Then a decree required prior permission for any newspaper in Arabic.

Louzon and his comrades now decided to replace the newspaper with a leaflet and a pamphlet. The leaflet carried a poem which used religious language to advocate Communism. This time Louzon was arrested. He and two comrades were initially prosecuted on the basis of an 1884 decree for 'attacking the rights and powers of France in Tunisia'. On top of this he was accused of inciting racial hatred – an absurd claim since the poem made no reference to race and stated that Christians and Muslims were equal. The authorities were determined to get a conviction and Louzon got eight months in jail.

He was then expelled from Tunisia and returned to France to work on *L'Humanité*; he also became a member of the party's Colonial Commission. Two years later he left the PCF after the expulsion of his friends Monatte and Rosmer [for writing an open letter to party members protesting at the manipulative methods of the leadership]. He was later centrally involved with *La Révolution prolétarienne*, a journal launched by Monatte after his expulsion from the PCF. In 1937, at the age of 54, he fought at the front with republican forces in Spain; in 1960 he signed the Manifesto of 121 in support of those who gave active solidarity to the Algerian FLN [see Chapter 11].[40]

Over the coming forty years France's history would be shaped by two great movements for national independence, in Indochina and in Algeria. Both these movements were born in Paris in the 1920s. Michael Goebel has described the Paris of the interwar years as an 'Anti-Imperial Metropolis'. He argues that the concept of the 'Third World' – a term coined in the 1950s which had an enormous influence on political thought in the 1960s – had its origins with the 'idea of

---

39 Dunois 1922.

40 Maitron and Pennetier 1964–2023 article24774, notice LOUZON Robert, Adolphe, Alphonse par Colette Chambelland, version mise en ligne le 1er mars 2009, dernière modification le 7 juillet 2020.

an anti-imperialist solidarity spanning several continents' among the migrant activists of the 1920s and 1930s.[41]

By 1930 there were some 100,000 non-Europeans living in Paris, more than in any other European city. Around three quarters of a million colonial subjects had been brought to France, as soldiers or workers, in the course of World War I, and although an ungrateful nation did its best to repatriate them, many stayed or returned. Some were students; there were also significant numbers of North African workers at the Renault Billancourt car plant and at other large factories; in 1930 around a quarter of the workforce at Renault was from overseas. There were also the Chinese worker-students who combined their studies with spells of factory work, and thus had direct contact with French and migrant workers.

For young migrants Paris offered a liberating experience; there were political organisations, meetings and also the *cafés maures*, which served North African food and where Algerian workers met to complain about their working conditions and discuss politics; they became a fertile recruiting-ground for nationalist organisations.

In this atmosphere activists from many parts of the world got their political initiation. From Algeria came Ferhat Abbas, later a leading figure in the Algerian FLN. From Vietnam, as well as the young Ho Chi Minh, there was the Trotskyist militant Tạ Thu Thâu, who had a strong following in the thirties and who was murdered by the Vietminh in 1945. From Senegal came Lamine Senghor, one of the Communist Party's most remarkable black organisers and writers. Among the Chinese 'worker-students' in Paris were future Communist leaders Zhou Enlai and Deng Xiaoping. From Indonesia there was Arnold Mononutu, who later played an important part in organising the 1955 Bandung conference of newly independent Afro-Asian nations. From Latin America came the Peruvian Marxist Mariátegui, the writer César Vallejo and Peruvian political leader Haya de la Torre.

The existence of this milieu presented significant political opportunities to the young PCF. The party took certain initiatives in this period which produced important results over the coming years, but have often been ignored by historians of the early years of the PCF.

5   *Le Paria*

The PCF established an organisation for those of colonial origin living in France – the Union inter-coloniale [UIC] – and then, from April 1922, the news-

---

41   Goebel 2015.

paper *Le Paria* [The Pariah]. *Le Paria* was somewhat scruffy and underfinanced, and its circulation was always low. Nonetheless it brought together a small group of comrades committed to the anti-imperialist struggle.

Thirty-six issues of *Le Paria* appeared between 1922 and 1926.[42] All issues except one were printed on a single large-format sheet. The heading *Le Paria* was flanked by Chinese and Arabic characters. The price per issue was 25 centimes [about the same as a daily newspaper] and subscriptions were three francs for one year [rising to five francs in 1925].

The main concern of the paper was the situation in France's colonial empire. Editor Nguyen-Ai-Quac wrote of the 'incredible cruelty' of a 'sadistic functionary' in the colonial administration,[43] and contrasted the barbarity of France's colonial practice with the traditional imagery of republican politics:

> There is a painful irony in observing that civilisation, symbolised in its various forms – liberty, justice, etc. – by the gentle image of woman, and arranged by a category of men who are reputed to be champions in politeness towards ladies, should make the living emblem suffer the most ignoble treatment and attack her shamefully in her behaviour, her modesty and her very life.[44]

Particular attention was given to economic oppression of the native populations: in 1925 Lamine Senghor reported on new regulations which effectively imposed forced labour on native workers in French West Africa. African workers were to be bound by contracts in French, although the education system did not teach them to read French.[45]

Le Paria was addressed mainly to the colonial proletariat. Max Clainville-Bloncourt argued that the colonial proletariat formed an essential part of the world proletariat and that it was necessary to destroy any illusions held by the bourgeoisie that 'the black and yellow populations of the colonial empire will agree to act militarily against the metropolitan working class struggling against

---

42   Numbered 1 to 38, with two double issues (6/7 and 36/37). This analysis is based on an incomplete file (23 issues) kept in the Bibliothèque Nationale, Paris. A combination of cheap printers and Europocentric culture meant that there were often variations and inaccuracies in the spelling of non-European names. I have standardised these in order to minimise confusion.

43   *Le Paria* 4, July 1922, p. 2.

44   *Le Paria* 5, August 1922, p. 1. Many of Nguyen-Ai-Quac's accounts of atrocities in Indochina were collected in Nguyen Ai Quoc 1998.

45   *Le Paria* 36–37, September–October 1925.

its exploiters'.[46] *Le Paria* carried extracts from a RILU document of June 1923 on the need to build unions in the colonial countries.[47]

In 1924 *Le Paria* published a vitriolic article on the 'Infamy of the Algerian bourgeoisie', referring to 'debauched *marabouts*, servile chiefs and native elected representatives, repugnant in their cowardice and treason' who were 'agents of French imperialism'. The article concluded 'It now therefore seems undeniable that the emancipation of Algerian natives will be the work of the exploited themselves'.[48]

In 1925 Lamine Senghor reported on a four-day railway strike in Senegal. The company had proposed wage increases for European workers, compensated for by cuts for native workers. 'From an admirable class consciousness' the European workers refused. The strike won the original demand of increases for both European and native workers.[49]

Le Paria argued for unity between metropolitan and colonial workers. In a 1922 'Appeal to the Colonial Populations' it urged: 'In face of capitalism and imperialism, our interests are the same; remember Karl Marx's words: Workers of all countries unite'.[50] Clainville-Bloncourt insisted: 'Colonial brothers, it is indispensable for you to realise that there is no possible salvation for you outside of the conquest of political power in Europe by the labouring masses'.[51]

In practice, things were not so simple. In an article for *L'Humanité*, addressed to the PCF's members and supporters, Nguyen-Ai-Quac recognised the ignorance and prejudice that existed among both metropolitan and colonial workers. Quoting Lenin on the need for metropolitan workers to assist struggles in subject nations, he observed sadly: 'Unfortunately there are still many militants who think a colony is nothing but a country full of sand with the sun shining down; a few green coconut trees and some men of colour, and that's all'.

Meanwhile most colonial inhabitants were either repelled by the idea of Bolshevism, or identified it purely with nationalism. The educated minority might understand what Communism meant, but they had no interest in seeing it established. Hence, he argued,

> From the mutual ignorance of the two proletariats prejudices are born. For the French worker, the native is an inferior being, insignificant, incap-

---

46   *Le Paria* 6–7, September–October 1922, p. 1.

47   *Le Paria* 20, November 1923, p. 2.

48   *Le Paria* 23, February 1924, p. 1.

49   *Le Paria* 33, April–May 1925, p. 1.

50   *Le Paria* 5, August 1922, p. 1.

51   *Le Paria* 6–7, September–October 1922, p. 1.

able of understanding and even less of acting. For the native the French – whoever they may be – are all wicked exploiters. Imperialism and capitalism do not fail to take advantage of this reciprocal distrust and this artificial racial hierarchy to obstruct propaganda and to divide forces which ought to unite.

He concluded: 'In face of these difficulties what should the Party do? Intensify propaganda in order to overcome them'.[52]

Le Paria contained humorous articles. Nguyen-Ai-Quac contributed a piece entitled 'Zoology' which claimed to describe the discovery of a new species, *coloniae Indigena*: 'Some of its practical qualities are superior to those of our domestic animals. Once tamed, it can be shorn like a sheep, laden like an ass and sent to the slaughter like a calf'.[53]

The precise relationship between *Le Paria* and the PCF was problematic. The whole thing was a shoestring operation. *Le Paria* never appeared regularly; a promise to appear twice monthly from the autumn of 1922 did not materialise.[54] In fact the frequency with which the paper appeared declined; there were only ten issues in 1924 and just five in 1925. The main explanation was financial; the paper had great difficulty in meeting its printing bills, and it seems reasonable to assume that relatively little money found its way back from the colonies. Yet in 1923 the Colonial Commission of the PCF decided to give the UIC a subsidy of just 100 francs. [At a very rough estimate, the equivalent of just under 60 euros or less than £50 in today's money.][55] Clearly many of the former reformists in the PCF did not consider stirring up discontent in the colonies as one of the party's major priorities.

The articles were short, clear and concrete, generally written in a style aimed at a relatively educated readership, in contrast to a later paper, *La Race nègre* [the Black race], launched by Lamine Senghor in 1927, which carried articles in 'français tirailleur', the spoken language of an African recruit in the French army.[56]

Le Paria's initial print-run seems to have been 1000, rising at best to 3000. The majority of these went to the colonies; out of 2000 copies of one issue only 500 stayed in France, while 500 went to Madagascar, 400 to Dahomey, 200 to the Maghreb, 100 to Oceania and 200 to Indochina. Since the circulation was

---

52 Nguyen Ai Quac 1922.
53 *Le Paria* 2, May 1922, p. 1.
54 *Le Paria* 5, August 1922, p. 1.
55 Liauzu 1982, p. 109.
56 Dewitte 1985, pp. 158–9.

clandestine, and copies were frequently seized by the authorities, it is hard to know how widely the paper was in fact distributed.[57] Yet despite its limitations, *Le Paria* was a worthy venture which briefly hinted at a genuinely internationalist alternative to the crimes and brutalities of imperialism; it deserves to be remembered.

Le Paria did not neglect the crucial question of immigrants from the colonies now living in France. There were many brief news items dealing with specific injustices – the eviction from their lodgings of a number of comrades from Guadeloupe,[58] or the revelation that an organisation established to import maids from Martinique was now being prosecuted for fraud.[59]

In an article ironically titled 'Paris … City of Light!' Ali Baba [Hadj-Ali Abdelkader] gave a description which would be recognised by many immigrant workers of later date:

> And yet there are Algerians in Paris. There are tens and tens of thousands working themselves to death in the factories, rotting away in the Grenelle district, and in the slums of the Boulevard de la Gare and de la Villette.
>
> … They live alone, without wives, steeped in their patriarchal habits. They cannot bring over the women they left over there. They prefer to live in abstinence, cutting away at the minimum they need to live in order to send money to their children, to the aged parents they have left behind and who are being trampled on by colonialism.[60]

A labourer, signing himself 'Saïd' described conditions at Renault:

> In the immense fortress which this scoundrel Renault owns at Billancourt 27,000 men and women are shamefully exploited. Among this number are 3000 colonial pariahs; they are suffering an even more miserable fate. Why?
>
> Because the majority of my Algerian comrades are less well educated. And Renault takes advantage to make them work for lower wages.[61]

An article signed 'El Djazaïri' commented on a recent press campaign insulting Algerian workers in France; this pseudonym – meaning 'The Algerian' –

---

57   Liauzu 1982, p. 110.
58   *Le Paria* 20, November 1923, p. 1.
59   *Le Paria* 23, February 1924, p. 2.
60   *Le Paria* 22, January 1924, p. 1.
61   *Le Paria* 33, April–May 1925, p. 2.

sometimes indicated Menouar Abdelaziz, a trade unionist at the Renault factory [see below]:[62] 'Already in France the Communist Party is organising North
African workers, not only politically but economically. It supports them in their
struggle against capital. Everywhere, natives are joining the unitary unions. and
showing their class consciousness thereby'. [The unitary unions were unions
affiliated to the *Confédération générale du travail unitaire* [CGTU], formed in
1922 by Communists and syndicalists after they had been expelled from the
CGT.] 'These natives have lined up alongside their French comrades in the
strikes of gasworkers, at Citroën, by taxi washers, at the Saint-Étienne mines,
in the Nord *département*, etc'.[63]

   Le Paria carried slogans exhorting its readers:

> COMRADE COLONIAL WORKER, IF YOU WANT TO EMANCIPATE YOUR-
> SELF, JOIN THE UNION FOR YOUR TRADE.
>   THOSE FROM THE COLONIES, FOR YOUR LIBERATION JOIN THE COM-
> MUNIST PARTY.[64]

However *Le Paria* rarely raised the demand for independence for the colonial territories.[65] The political perspective of the Comintern and its national
sections was still, until the failure of the German Revolution in 1923, one of
imminent revolution in Europe. In such a context it made some sense for Communists in the colonial territories not to demand immediate separation, but
rather to aspire to develop a new form of association with Europe's forthcoming proletarian states.

   Le Paria built up an enthusiastic team of activists who carried the paper.
The driving force was undoubtedly Nguyen-Ai-Quac. Born in Indochina in 1890,
the young Nguyen had received a privileged education; he apparently said that
as soon as he heard the slogan 'Liberty, Equality, Fraternity', he wanted to see
France.[66] He left Indochina and travelled first to London, then Paris. He joined
the SFIO, spoke at Tours and became a member of the PCF. He wrote copiously
for *Le Paria* and other publications, not only on Indochina but on a range of
topics to do with colonialism. He packed the copies to be sent overseas, and

---

62   Maitron and Pennetier 1964–2023 article112017, notice EL DJAZAÏRI, version mise en ligne
     le 24 novembre 2010, dernière modification le 24 novembre 2010.
63   *Le Paria* 31, November–December 1924, p. 2.
64   *Le Paria* 22, January 1924, p. 2.
65   Dewitte 1985, p. 101.
66   Trang-Gaspard 1992, p. 52.

was known as the best seller of the paper.[67] He also doubled as a cartoonist. One rather didactic drawing showed a large man reclining in a two-wheeled chair, being pulled by a very thin Asian. The passenger is saying: 'Show your loyalty, for God's sake!!!' The six spokes of the wheel are labelled 'Civilisation, Oppression, Association, Assimilation, Protection, Exploitation'.[68]

Nguyen soon came to the attention of the authorities. In August 1922 he published an ironic open letter to the Radical Minister of Colonies, Albert Sarraut, offering to save the government money spent on surveillance of Indochinese in Paris by giving a daily bulletin of his activities.[69]

Nguyen's interests extended much further than Indochina – he was for example an enthusiastic supporter of Irish independence. It should also be noted that his earliest contacts on arriving in France seem to have been with the syndicalist left. He visited the Librairie du travail on the quai de Jemmapes, at what had been the offices of *La Vie ouvrière*.

Le Paria also drew around it some other remarkable activists. Jean Ralaimongo, born in 1884, was from Madagascar; as a child he was sold into slavery, but after being trained by Protestant missionaries he became a schoolteacher. He fought in World War I with the Madagascar infantry out of enthusiasm for the French cause; yet when he asked to stay in France after the end of the war he was refused six times before a friendly deputy intervened. He too was a founder-member of the PCF.

Samuel Stéphany, the first business manager of *Le Paria*, was also born in Madagascar in 1890 into an intellectual family. He fought in World War I and was gassed in Serbia. He remained in France and became tutor in Malagasy at the École des langues orientales. He was a member of the SFIO and joined the PCF after Tours.

By 1924 the PCF was changing. The attempts by the Comintern under Zinoviev's leadership to impose a supposedly 'Bolshevik' style of organisation led to further conflicts and purges and prepared the way for the PCF's total Stalinisation by the end of the decade. *Le Paria* did not survive the process. It virtually disappeared after September 1925, with just one final issue in April 1926. There were growing conflicts between the party's tiny colonial cadre and the bureaucratic apparatus.

The enthusiastic group of activists which had built *Le Paria* were dispersed. Stéphany had already returned to the SFIO by 1923; Ralaimongo went back

---

67   Liauzu 1982, p. 108.
68   *Le Paria* 5, August 1922, p. 1.
69   *Le Paria* 5, August 1922, p. 1.

to Madagascar in 1922 and later set up his own paper, *L'Opinion*. Nguyen-Ai-Quac/Ho Chi Minh was whisked off to Moscow in 1923 and transformed into a lifelong Stalinist.[70]

The PCF continued to build organisation among immigrant workers. In the early 1920s some 200,000 immigrants per year were entering France, mainly from central Europe and Italy. In 1926 the PCF took the initiative in establishing the Main d'Oeuvre Étrangère [Foreign Labour Force], later known as the Main d'Oeuvre Immigrée [MOI – Immigrant Labour Force] within the CGTU. This was subdivided into linguistic groups, and produced publications in German, Italian, Hungarian, Russian and Yiddish. It survived into the following decades and played a significant role in the Spanish Civil War and during the Nazi occupation [see chapter 9].

The 21 Conditions required Communists to be active in opposing war and militarism, when necessary using illegal means. Though some in the SFIO had campaigned vigorously against war, it was the syndicalists, with the *sou du soldat*, who had actually challenged the frontiers of legality with their organisation in the army. The fact that a whole generation had experienced the horrors of trench warfare had shifted the mood and made the possibility of serious antimilitarist work more acceptable.

The PCF's response was to create a paper directly addressed to soldiers, called *La Caserne* [the barracks]. This was launched in May 1923 and followed very much in the tradition of the *sou du soldat*. It had four pages, appeared fortnightly or monthly, was titled 'Antimilitarist Organ' and was published by the Communist Youth. Like any such agitational paper *La Caserne* had to strike a balance. If it merely made abstract political propaganda then it would appeal only to a small minority of politicised soldiers. It had to take up the day-to-day concerns of soldiers – food, pay, accommodation, hygiene, working hours and conditions, discipline and opposition to the extension of the service period. It also raised the question of political rights, in particular the right of soldiers to vote and join a trade union, and gave advice on how to organise in the army; there were regular letters from serving soldiers on these topics. At the same time the paper had to take up political questions – the nature and role of the army in the modern world, and the particular ways in which the army might be used. As well as reports there were cartoons, and stories by the satirical author Courteline.

A letter from a young soldier in Morocco told how 'we did forty kilometres without a drop of water. ... We make our food ourselves. We've no bread. They

---

70   See Ngô Văn 1995.

give us flour and we get by'.[71] At Worms in Germany soldiers went on hunger strike, leading to a violent clash with NCOs. 'After four days of strike and protests, the normal provision was noticeably improved'.[72]

Only by achieving this balance between immediate grievances and a broader political framework was it possible for *La Caserne* to intervene effectively when a political crisis erupted – as it did in Germany.

By 1922 the KPD [German Communist Party] was growing and there seemed to be a real hope that it could make a bid for power in the not too distant future. There was growing friction over the failure of Germany to pay the massive reparations being demanded by the victorious powers, and there was a real danger that this could spill over into armed conflict.

In September 1922 Victor Serge, using the pseudonym 'R Albert' as a Comintern journalist in Germany, addressed[73] an appeal for international solidarity to French workers. Serge had been politically active in France before 1914, and had many contacts there. French troops were already occupying the Rhineland, and as the economic crisis made Germany unable to pay the reparations, the threat of an occupation of the Ruhr became more real.

Serge began his letter to a French comrade by describing the terrible poverty that was afflicting the working class in Germany, and in particular the catastrophic inflation. In less than two months the average cost of living in Germany had more than tripled, and the prices of essential goods such as shoes and clothes had gone up five times. The price of bread was due to be quadrupled. As a result in the working-class districts of Berlin young faces bore the marks of tuberculosis and hunger.

He went on to argue that the German working class was not just a victim; over the last few years it had shown its remarkable capacity to fight back, second only to the Russian working class in its contribution to the liberation of humanity. As the German working class moved towards revolution, it imposed responsibilities on French workers to support the German proletariat.

This was not just a moral obligation; the future of the French working class was intimately tied up with that of its German comrades. The alternatives facing workers in France and Germany were either a catastrophic defeat, which would have terrible consequences in France and Italy, with the consolidation of fascism in Italy, and in France the rule of a military caste in the service of financiers – or else revolution.

---

71   Un jeune soldat 1923.

72   Anon 1923d.

73   *Correspondance internationale* 72, 23 September 1922.

Serge's short-term prediction was wrong; the failure of the German revolution in 1923 was not a definitive defeat. In the longer term he was accurate. Hitler's triumph in 1933 established a dictatorship, and for France the eventual consequence was German occupation and the Vichy regime.

He warned French workers that the fate of the whole European working class would depend on the struggles developing in Germany. Only working-class unity, going beyond traditional alignments, could achieve a successful outcome to the impending struggles. Thus he professed indifference as to whether his reader was a Communist, a syndicalist or a libertarian; whatever their personal opinions their duty was to support the German Communists. The vital task was to build the revolutionary organisation which could enable the French proletariat to save the German revolution.

Serge was arguing that, at this crucial turning-point in history, internationalism was not just an aspiration. It was an essential factor which could determine the physical survival of the working class. If French workers failed to see their shared interests with German workers, they would pay a heavy price.

6   Occupation of the Ruhr

When the crisis came to a head at the beginning of 1923, the PCF was prepared for the challenge. The party already had a soldiers' newspaper and a small, but very capable, cadre of activists from the colonies. The membership were prepared for the combination of legal and illegal work that would be necessary.

Germany in 1923 was a society about to collapse. Since 1914 four years of war had been followed by five years of bitter class struggle. Then it was hit by catastrophic inflation. French troops were already occupying the Rhineland; early in 1923 French prime minister Raymond Poincaré decided to occupy the Ruhr Valley, the main coal and iron producing region of Germany, to enforce German payment of reparations for the 1914–18 war.

Whatever the retrospective analyses of historians, Germany in 1923, with mass inflation and the invasion of the Ruhr, *looked* like a revolutionary situation. As Paul Vaillant-Couturier wrote in *Clarté*, 'For the whole of Germany, the time of the workers' and peasants' government has come. Germany's only choice is now between the proletarian gun and the fascist grenade'.[74]

It was only five years since the end of the First World War and anti-German feeling doubtless still existed in many sections of the population, but the PCF's

---

74   Vaillant-Couturier 1923.

campaign adopted a resolutely internationalist approach. On 3 January 1923 a mass meeting attended by thousands was held in a hall at La Grange-aux-Belles in northern Paris. It was jointly sponsored by the PCF and the CGTU trade-union federation, as well as by the ARAC [an association of ex-servicemen] and the Anarchist Federation. The German Communist Party was represented on the platform by Rosi Wolfstein, a former comrade of Rosa Luxemburg's, who had been brought into the meeting unannounced. She was welcomed with enthusiasm by the mass audience of Parisian workers.

She told how a strike at Ludwigshafen was defeated through the use of French troops [there were already French troops in the Rhineland]. As she pointed out, the French generals had shown that for them 'the enemy ... was, first of all, the proletariat, whether German or French'. She affirmed that German workers 'have sworn that if they take arms again, it will not be to shoot at their brothers across the frontier'.[75]

When the Ruhr was invaded a few days later the PCF and the German Communist Party immediately moved to co-operate. An international conference was held to co-ordinate the activities of the various parties involved [Belgian troops were also involved]. On Sunday 7 January a major international meeting was held at Essen in the Ruhr to protest against the invasion; Clara Zetkin, Marcel Cachin [editor of *L'Humanité*], Belgian Communist Édouard Van Overstraeten, Gaston Monmousseau [secretary of the CGTU] and other comrades spoke. As he came down from the platform Monmousseau was dragged away to the police station. The ten thousand people attending the meeting simply decided to go and get him. The German police hastened to release the prisoner.[76]

Further meetings were held in France, and the PCF ran a campaign of opposition to the war with posters and leaflets, and in *L'Humanité*. The French authorities recognised that the activities of the PCF constituted a serious danger to the successful carrying out of their plans for occupation, and the party was subjected to considerable harassment. Leading members were arrested and imprisoned, and the offices of *L'Humanité* were searched. Many hundreds of rank-and-file Communists were engaged in making propaganda against the war.

The propaganda put out by the PCF achieved some real response from sections of the working class. The PCF also attempted to form a united front with the SFIO by following up the call of the Communist International for joint

75   Martinet 1923.
76   Anon 1923a.

action with social democrats on this issue. If the attempt to call a general strike at the end of January 1923 came to nothing it was a viable move to attempt it.[77]

On the ground the PCF co-operated closely with the German Communist Party in running a campaign which called on French soldiers not to obey orders in the repression of the German population, while at the same time trying to dissuade German nationalists from terrorist attacks on French soldiers. The two went hand in hand; the only effective argument against the nationalists who claimed that all French soldiers were the enemy was to show that there were French workers and soldiers prepared to oppose the occupation.

Leading members of the PCF, including parliamentarians like Marcel Cachin [who was jailed],[78] were sent into the Ruhr to address public meetings. Most of the basic work on the ground was done by members of the Youth Section of the PCF, a contingent of whom went into Germany to carry out a campaign of agitation and propaganda.

In a report written for the Communist International after the occupation was over, the Yugoslav Communist Voya Vuyovitch analysed the work done by the Comintern in this period. He noted in particular that the PCF was still deeply entrenched in the habits of legality, and that its members found it difficult to engage in serious clandestine work; the main burden of the campaign had been borne by the youth, who were somewhat freer of parliamentary illusions.[79] The intervention showed that Communist Parties could collaborate when their own ruling classes were in dispute, and that they could make their message heard by a section of the working class and the armed forces.

Many French soldiers sent to the Ruhr were unhappy about their role; this was especially true of veterans of the First World War, who wanted nothing less than to be plunged into a second war against Germany. When a contingent of soldiers were due to leave the Gare de l'Est in Paris for the Ruhr many of them dropped their rifles on the floor and broke them as if by accident, or found that their back-packs had mysteriously been badly buckled so that they fell off. Amid the chaos caused by such accidents large numbers of soldiers broke into the singing of the *Internationale*.[80] Clearly an atmosphere existed in which it was possible to do serious internationalist agitation.

The PCF's activity met with a positive response from a large number of soldiers. *La Caserne* was distributed illegally in the barracks. In many cases French soldiers refused instructions to tear down Communist posters that had been

---

77   See *L'Humanité*, 25, 26, 31 January 1923.
78   Wohl 1966, pp. 317–20.
79   Vouïovitch 1924, p. 35.
80   Anon 1923b.

flyposted in the area of the barracks. Leaflets and stickers were distributed widely – it was claimed tens of millions of stickers were put up 'on the barracks walls, on telephone posts, in trains, on urinals'.[81]

Stickers bore slogans such as:

Soldiers, Fraternise with the German workers!
Soldier, Never shoot at your brother worker!
Soldiers, Support the German Revolution!
Soldiers, Follow the example of the Black Sea Sailors.
[for the Black Sea mutiny see Chapter 6]
Soldiers! To defend the Revolution in Germany is good, to make it in
    France is better.
Soldiers! The German worker is your brother.
Soldier! The German worker wants bread and work. Help him get
    them![82]

One particularly striking poster depicted a French soldier and German workers joining together to attack the representatives of the French and German bourgeoisies, personified by the German industrialist and war profiteer Hugo Stinnes and the French industrialist and government minister Louis Loucheur. The caption – in both French and German – to the poster cited Liebknecht's insistence that the enemy was in one's own country.[83]

The young Communist agitators adopted many imaginative tactics for spreading propaganda to the French troops. Balloons were used in order to drop copies of *L'Humanité* and *La Caserne* into the barracks.[84] On one occasion young Communists made their way into the projection room of a cinema where a large number of French troops were present and slid a message onto the screen in French and German, urging French soldiers to fraternise with the German working class.[85]

There were a number of mutinies and acts of disobedience among the French troops in the Ruhr, and the authorities took them seriously enough to respond with severe repression. In February French troops sent to Datteln refused to go because they were being used against civilians.[86] At Duisburg four

---

81   Vouïovitch 1924, p. 20.
82   Vouïovitch 1924, p. 21.
83   Köller 1963, p. 121.
84   Köller 1963, p. 303.
85   Köller 1963, pp. 121–2.
86   Anon 1923e.

mutineers were shot,[87] and many other soldiers suffered severe punishment for involvement in allegedly subversive activities.

La Caserne reported that 'at Essen, at Bochum, at Dortmund, at Düsseldorf French soldiers did not fire on the working class, at Neustadt Moroccan soldiers did not shoot their guns, at Duisburg Belgian soldiers led a demonstration against the abolition of the eight-hour day, singing the *Internationale* with the crowd'.[88] Vuyovitch reported: 'During September, October and November, we saw numerous cases where soldiers refused to fire on workers'. At Essen soldiers were called to help the German police, but their commanding officer was obliged to tell the Germans that 'French soldiers don't fire on starving workers'.[89]

Desertion in the French army rose to such a level that the authorities were seriously worried. A penalty of ten years' jail was decreed for any civilian who provided civilian clothing for a French soldier in order to enable him to desert.[90]

Just five years after the end of the world war, it would have been very easy for nationalist passions to rise again, but the PCF's actions made it much harder for the German far right to whip up anti-French feeling.

One particular issue raised by the Ruhr occupation was the use of troops from the French colonies, often in circumstances when it was feared white troops could not be relied on.[91] For many on the left, in Germany and internationally, this provoked what was effectively a racist response – that the French were in some way insulting the German people by using these allegedly savage troops for the occupation. The Communists had to dissociate themselves from such racism while at the same time arguing that the black troops should indeed not be there. A special leaflet put out to black troops made this clear:

> You are here to pillage and steal in favour of the same French imperialists who murder and rob you in your homelands.
> German workers are your brothers and are fighting for freedom as you do in your countries!
> Up with the liberation of Algeria and Morocco!
> Up with the freedom of the peoples oppressed by French imperialism![92]

---

87   Anon 1923c.
88   *La Caserne*, January 1924.
89   Vouïovitch 1924, p. 26.
90   Köller 1963, p. 125.
91   Vouïovitch 1924, p. 11.
92   Vouïovitch 1924, p. 11.

There were serious problems in getting propaganda to soldiers from the colonies, for there was a very low rate of literacy – given poor educational provision in the colonies perhaps only two or three percent could read; special leaflets with drawings were directed at them.[93] Propaganda distributed to the Senegalese tried to link the struggle of German workers to that of the Senegalese people for national independence. In a pamphlet published shortly after this time the PCF raised the general slogan that there should be no white troops in the colonies and no troops of colour in France.[94] Morgan Philips Price noted that in the Rhineland the middle class responded with racial hostility, but that workers fraternised with troops whom they saw as 'not an enemy but a friend'; off-duty black troops used to play with German working-class children.[95] Some success seems to have been achieved by this propaganda, since after these leaflets were distributed the black troops were withdrawn from the Ruhr and moved to other areas of Germany.[96]

The PCF produced a bilingual publication, in French and Arabic, called *La Caserne/El Kazirna* [The Barracks].[97] Some of the PCF's Algerian members played a major part in this work. Abdelaziz ben Mohamed Menouer was born in Algiers in 1893. During World War I he lived in the USA; he worked in a porcelain factory in New York, where he helped to organise a union and took part in two strikes. He returned to Algeria where he became a Communist; his potential was recognised and he was sent to the Communist University of Toilers of the East in Moscow. Moving to France, he played a leading role in the PCF and the CGTU.[98]

Ben Lakhal Mahmoud was part of the small cadre that had been built up around *Le Paria*. Born to a prosperous family in Algiers in 1894, he was one of a group of Algerians who used to frequent the shop owned by Hadj-Ali Abdelkader, an Algerian who played a leading role in *Le Paria* [see below]. Ben Lakhal joined the PCF in 1921, and became a member of the editorial committee of *Le Paria* from 1923. He was given responsibility for propaganda among North African troops in the Ruhr.

---

93   Vouïovitch 1924, p. 11.

94   Doriot 1924, p. 34.

95   Price 1999, pp. 108–9.

96   Vouïovitch 1924, p. 11.

97   Drew 2014, p. 34.

98   Maitron and Pennetier 1964–2023 article121650, notice MENOUER Abdelaziz ben Mohamed ou Ab-del-Aziz, dit souvent MENOUER Ali, écrit parfois MENOUAR dit ALI, ou ALI ou MENOUAR Ali, écrivit aussi sous le nom de El DJAZAIRI (l'Algérien) par René Gallissot, Michèle Velay, version mise en ligne le 30 novembre 2010, dernière modification le 28 février 2011.

As a result of his activity in appealing for fraternisation, Ben Lakhal was imprisoned from 18 December 1923, and in June 1924 at a trial in Mainz he was sentenced to five years in jail. He had been arrested as a result of the betrayal of a Tunisian corporal, Mustapha Matari, and false evidence presented by the adjutant Bognon. After his arrest Ben Lakhal suffered appalling abuse; the colonel of the 28th infantry kicked and thumped him while calling him a 'dirty Arab' and a 'dirty *bicot*' [a term of racist abuse]. When Ben Lakhal told the colonel that it was French people who had taught him Communism, the colonel screamed at him: 'They are bad Frenchmen'. In the military prison at Siegburg he was deprived of food for several days.[99]

Nor did the lawyers appointed for the defendants do much of a job. In his final speech M[e] Neumann, the defence lawyer, effectively conceded the case to the prosecution: 'He explained that all the accused, some fanatical Communists, the others very young and rather thoughtless, were only carrying out orders. He asked the judge to disregard the attitude of the accused, who had maintained complete silence only because the defence lawyers they had chosen had withdrawn'.[100]

Ben Lakhal and the other defendants were released on 13 August 1924, after a vigorous campaign by the PCF; *Le Paria* claimed with some justice that Ben Lakhal's freedom had been won by the action of the French working class.[101]

In 1925 Monatte's journal *La Révolution prolétarienne* published an assessment of the opposition to the invasion of the Ruhr. Signed only 'A Witness' it seemed to have been written by a serving soldier who had seen the activity from within. It was quite critical of some aspects, and did not share the over-optimism which sometimes characterised accounts issuing from the Comintern. Nonetheless it showed that, despite difficulties, the Communist opposition had been worthwhile:

> The army's spirits were affected. If it was not altogether won over, at least we had partially destroyed its nationalist prejudices; the junior officers were worried by how long the occupation was lasting; whole regiments were feeling proletarian influences; ... But the general staff and the government no longer expected general passive obedience, and they were right. Their fears, and the repression provoked by them, were a testimony to the Communist propaganda.[102]

---

99   Anon 1924a.
100   Anon 1924b.
101   *Le Paria* 29, September 1924, p. 1.
102   Un témoin 1925.

The failure of the expected German Revolution was a turning-point for the international Communist movement. In the immediate aftermath of the October Revolution it had been reasonable to hope that revolutions throughout Europe would follow the Russian pattern. A second successful European revolution would have irrevocably changed the course of world history.

Historians have given many explanations of the German débâcle in 1923.[103] Some anxious French Communists probably looked to *Clarté*, a journal at this time close to, but not wholly controlled by, the PCF, though it had a very small print-run – around 11,000.[104] *Clarté* was fortunate in its German correspondent, Victor Serge, who had followed events for *Inprekorr* and had an acute political judgment.

Serge's account shows that in 1923 the Communist movement, in France and elsewhere, was still a movement in which it was possible to ask honest questions and expect honest answers:

> To talk of mistakes after the situation has been wound up is all too easy. But it must be done. We need constant, vigorous, detailed self-criticism. For us yesterday's retreat is never anything but a roundabout route to tomorrow's action. We leave to the old democratic parties the cult of irresponsibility. Let us ask the question clearly: does the responsibility for the October retreat fall on the leaders of the KPD, and to what extent?

The KPD had been made illegal – though the ban would last only three months. Serge insisted that '*The October retreat was not a defeat* … The threshold has not been crossed. We have even taken a step back. But we are still at the threshold. The situation in Germany remains profoundly revolutionary'.[105] There were many lessons, general and detailed, to be drawn from the German experience. The most fundamental point was a recognition that the road ahead would be longer and more complicated than had been believed. Far more than a simple imitation of the Russian model would be required.

The year 1923 saw not only the German setback, but major changes within the leadership of the Comintern. Lenin's health meant that he played virtually no role in events after March 1923. The recognition that the revolutionary process was going to be more protracted than had been supposed meant that Stalin's idea of 'socialism in one country', first put forward after Lenin's death in 1924, now had a certain plausibility.

---

103   See Broué 2005, Harman 1982.
104   Cuenot 2011, tome I, p. 125.
105   Serge 1924b.

The more immediate danger came, not from Stalin, but from Zinoviev. For Zinoviev the answer to the problems of the isolated Russian Revolution would come from what he termed 'Bolshevisation', a strategy promoted by the Fifth Congress of the Comintern in June–July 1924. This meant imposing on the sections of the Comintern structures and practices allegedly derived from the history of the Russian Bolshevik party. In fact Bolshevisation served as a means of tightening central control from Moscow on the various sections of the International; often this entailed purges of dissident elements. In France, under the pretext of rooting the party in the working class, there was a strengthening of central control, sometime referred to as 'military centralism'.[106] As a result many of the individuals who had made a major contribution to the founding of the PCF were expelled or driven to resignation. Rosmer and Monatte were gone by the end of 1924, Loriot and Souvarine by 1926.

There was considerable confusion among members and former members of the PCF. Things were changing to such an extent that the very idea of what constituted internationalism was becoming problematic. Historian Pierre Broué tells us that by 1924 the Comintern had 'a single, centralised and disciplined apparatus of professional militants, reproduced on the model of the Soviet party, led from Moscow and in conformity with Soviet foreign policy'.[107] This was the beginning of a process which would ensure that by the 1930s the Comintern was a direct instrument of the Russian state.

For those who continued to give their political loyalty to the Comintern the question was fairly straightforward; the International was the concrete embodiment of internationalism. So to be an internationalist meant following the line of the International. They no longer saw the organisation as a means to the end of putting internationalist principles into practice, but rather determined those principles in terms of the organisation.

For those outside the International, by choice or by expulsion, things looked different. Internationalism continued to mean what it had meant before 1917, the unity of the interests of working people in the different nations of which they happened to be inhabitants. An organisation might, in some circumstances, embody this principle – thus Trotsky and those around him eventually came to advocate the building of a new International. There was also the question of workers in Russia – did they share the same interests as their leaders? If not, as became increasingly apparent, what did that tell us about the nature of Russian society? From very shortly after the Russian Revolution there

---

106   Robrieux 1980, pp. 187–8.
107   Broué 1997, pp. 384–5.

were those – both anarchists and Bolshevik oppositionists like Sapronov – who argued that Russian society was a new variant of capitalism. By 1931 Lucien Laurat [Otto Maschl] was arguing that Russia was neither capitalist nor socialist, but a 'new form of the exploitation of man by man'.[108] The two concepts of internationalism would come to define two radically different currents within the socialist movement.

7   Hadj-Ali Abdelkader

The changed situation after 1923 produced a new set of problems for the small group of colonial activists gathered around *Le Paria* and the UIC. They were now, in a more long-term perspective, able to exploit the possibilities of operating in a legal framework. One of the PCF colonial activists who played an important role in this process was an Algerian called Hadj-Ali Abdelkader. Hadj-Ali was born in Algeria in 1883. His family were land-owners but the once prosperous family found itself plunged into poverty. Hadj-Ali's grandfather had him sent to the city of Mascara, where he got a job in an ironmonger's shop.[109] From his family's misfortunes and his experiences in the city, he became increasingly aware of national oppression, and he resented French rule.[110]

In 1905 he decided to move to France.[111] The rest of his life would be spent in mainland France, but he never forgot his identity as an Algerian and a Muslim. He joined both the CGT and the SFIO. In 1911 he successfully applied for French citizenship.[112] In April 1912 he married for a second time. Perhaps with financial help from his new wife, he bought his own ironmonger's shop. One of the rooms became a meeting-place where Hadj-Ali engaged in political discussion with his Algerian friends. A number of future activists gathered here and the idea of an Algerian revolutionary party was discussed.[113]

At the beginning of 1921 he joined the newly-formed French Communist Party. He soon became a regular contributor to *Le Paria* under various pseudonyms such as 'Ali Baba' and 'Hadj Bicot'. 'Bicot' is a particularly offensive racist-

---

108   Laurat 1931, p. 178; see van der Linden 2007, pp. 69–73.
109   Righi 2006, pp. 39–40.
110   Righi 2006, pp. 41–3.
111   Righi 2006, pp. 45–6.
112   Righi 2006, pp. 48–50.
113   Righi 2006, p. 51.

epithet applied to North Africans, so he became a pioneer of the technique of subverting racist language and turning it back against those who used it.

At the party congress in January 1924 Hadj-Ali was elected a member of the Central Committee, a position which he held for just one year.[114] After his involvement in the Ruhr agitation [which included chairing a meeting in the campaign for the release of Ben Lakhal], his next activity was strictly constitutional. In May 1924 the PCF presented Hadj-Ali as a candidate in the parliamentary elections for the second sector of Paris. As one of the few Algerians who had French citizenship he was eligible for election. A statement in the PCF daily *L'Humanité* set out the Party's aims:

> All our comrades must indeed be convinced that whatever may be a worker's origin or colour, he belongs first and foremost to the working class. Racial prejudice is something which any conscious worker must totally reject. By neglecting, or even worse despising, the worker recruited in the colonies because he has different habits, the French worker is playing his exploiter's game.
>
> Capitalism is precisely trying to sharpen these racial antagonisms in order to more effectively break the workers' class action.
>
> French capitalism is holding in reserve its colonial subjects, as strikebreakers, as troops to be used, if necessary, against French workers.[115]

Claude Liauzu has argued that the decision to stand Hadj-Ali was imposed by a small group of activists, and that the Communists of the second sector were unwilling to accept it.[116] There is some evidence for this. When the PCF announced that on May Day, less than a fortnight before the elections, there would be sixteen simultaneous rallies in Paris, each with around six speakers, Hadj-Ali was not billed to speak at any of them. Only in the last week of the campaign did he address at least four public meetings in his own constituency.[117] He campaigned in distinctive North African clothing, wearing a *burnous* [cloak] with a *chechia* [Maghreb brimless cap] on his head.[118]

Two Communists were elected for the eleven-member constituency; Hadj-Ali obtained the lowest total on the list. [Voting was by a complex list system.] The two Communists elected got 41,601 votes and 40,805 votes respectively; the

---

114 Righi 2006, p. 97.
115 Anon 1924c.
116 Liauzu 1982, p. 18.
117 See reports in *L'Humanité*, 28, 29 April, 7, 8, 9 May 1924.
118 Righi 2006, p. 104.

average for the list was 40,781, and Hadj-Ali obtained 40,569.[119] Very few of his voters would have been North Africans, since the vast majority of them did not have citizenship.

The result was quite a success. Hadj-Ali achieved 99.48 percent of the average for the list. For Algerians in France the important thing was how well he had done.[120] It now seemed possible to envisage an Algerian being elected to the French parliament on the basis of support from French workers.

The election campaign was to have another result, of significance for the history of Algerian independence. One of those drawn in by the campaign was a young Algerian from Tlemcen called Messali Hadj. He recalled in his *Memoirs* that one day on leaving work he stopped to read election posters and immediately noticed an Arab name on the list, that of Hadj-Ali. Messali was delighted and went to the meeting close to the factory where he worked. He was very impressed by the presentation, and afterwards they spoke briefly and arranged to meet again.[121] [Messali's *Memoirs* were edited and pruned after his death from an unfinished manuscript. Nonetheless they constitute a very valuable source.[122]]

They – and their wives – soon became firm friends. Initially Hadj-Ali was very much the teacher and Messali, some fifteen years younger, the pupil. They had many discussions about Lenin and the Third International.[123] Messali was impressed by Hadj-Ali's grasp of Communist theory.[124]

Throughout this time Hadj-Ali remained a practising Muslim. Indeed, the defence of his native land's religion and its cultural traditions was an important component in his advocacy of Algerian rights. One of his main charges against French imperialism was the way it had weakened Islam by school closures, the introduction of other religions and the encouragement of alcohol.[125] As Messali Hadj noted, the long time Hadj-Ali had spent in France and his membership of the Communist Party had not detracted from his Arabic identity or his Muslim faith.[126]

In 1924 Hadj-Ali wrote an article for *Le Paria* in which he argued that Communists should adopt a non-polemical position towards Islam.[127] There seems

---

119   See results in *L'Humanité*, 13 May 1924, p. 1; see also *Le Temps*, 13 May 1924.
120   Stora 1986, pp. 52–5.
121   Messali 1982, p. 136.
122   See Simon 2003, pp. 292–3.
123   Messali 1982, p. 138.
124   Messali 1982, p. 137.
125   Righi 2006, p. 206.
126   Messali 1982, p. 137.
127   *Le Paria* 25, April–May 1924.

to have been no pressure on him to disavow or play down his religious heritage. The PCF at this time considered that religious belief was a matter for personal choice.

Hadj-Ali has now largely disappeared from histories of the PCF. Yet he should be remembered. The fact that he was able to be active for several years within the party and campaign for radical anti-imperialist and anti-racist policies shows that, for a few years at least, the party had moved beyond the tricolour.

The migrant activists were cooperating closely with the French working-class movement, which they saw as their natural ally. Many had developed personal relations with French activists; often they considered that reform was the way forward rather than the establishment of national independence. Only slowly did the independence demand emerge.

For many migrants economic demands were more important than what must have seemed the remote prospect of independence. Algerian workers in France could not collect child benefits if their children lived in Algeria, since this was deemed to be a foreign country, even though constitutionally it was an integral part of France. Likewise colonial ex-servicemen received lower pensions than their French counterparts. Migrants expected their organisations to fight on such immediate questions. French imperialism squeezed out the middle ground so that more radical elements came to the fore; by rejecting those who advocated moderate reform, French imperialism paved the way for a bloodier future.

It was the Comintern rather than Algerian activists in France who took the initiative in launching a movement for Algerian independence. PCF strategy towards North Africa was very much influenced by the positions adopted by the Communist International. In China the emerging Chinese Communist Party was instructed by the International to subordinate itself to the nationalist Guomindang, an alliance which lasted until the Communists in Shanghai were massacred by Guomindang forces in April 1927.[128] In the course of 1925 there was discussion in the PCF about the establishment of a North African Guomindang, which led to the formation of the Étoile Nord-Africaine [North African Star – ENA].[129]

The ENA first acquired a public face at a meeting held in June 1926.[130] It involved workers from Tunisia and Morocco as well as Algeria.[131] The initial

---

128   See Isaacs 2009.
129   Simon 2003, p. 64.
130   Righi 2006, pp. 132–4, 142–6.
131   Righi 2006, p. 142.

core consisted of some 8000 North African workers unionised in the CGTU [out of a total of over 100,000 North African workers in France]. That even this degree of unionisation had been achieved was the result of the hard work of Hadj-Ali and his comrades over the preceding three years.[132]

In the course of 1926 and 1927 the ENA held a number of large public meetings in the Paris area, the biggest attracting several hundred. There was also a banquet for students. The main campaigning issues were the abolition of the Native Code, free movement between Algeria and France and freedom of the press and assembly.

Historically the name of Messali Hadj is associated with the ENA; he was for many years its leader and the leader of its successor organisations. Hence there have been claims that he was in effect its founder. The name of Hadj-Ali has largely vanished from history. Yet it is clear that at the time of the foundation it was Hadj-Ali who played the key role, and that he was the organisation's leader in its first years.

By 1926 divergences were appearing between Hadj-Ali and the PCF. Hadj-Ali had been a trusted member of the PCF, who combined a good grasp of Marxism with his nationalist and religious ideas. But in the last resort it was the question of Algeria that motivated him. Hadj-Ali favoured the establishment of an autonomous party of colonial subjects, independent of the PCF, rather than the Communist International's strategy of creating a North African revolutionary nationalist party on the model of the Guomindang. In 1926 he was removed from the party's Colonial Commission.[133]

In February 1927 Hadj-Ali and Messali attended a world congress of oppressed peoples in Brussels, organised by the League Against Imperialism and Colonial Oppression, which was backed by the Communist International. This marked the beginning of Messali's career as a political leader when he made a powerful speech denouncing French imperialism's role in Algeria.[134]

Meanwhile the PCF, which in its early years had encouraged the self-organisation of colonial activists, was becoming more manipulative, concerned to exercise party control over organisations in its orbit. Increasing friction between the PCF and the leaders of the ENA was becoming inevitable.

Hadj-Ali's position seems to have been that the ENA should be an autonomous organisation independent of PCF control, although he was quite open about his own commitment to Communism. The minutes of an internal PCF

132   Righi 2006, p. 73.
133   Righi 2006, pp. 92–3.
134   Simon 2003, p. 95.

meeting from 1926 record him as saying that if asked, he would say: 'I am a Communist, but I am also a Muslim, and that is why I have joined the ENA'.[135]

He continued to advocate the formation of an autonomous Communist Party – or at least a North African Communist Party in France – and the creation of a revolutionary nationalist party in Algeria. He was accused of wanting to create a party within the party; differences with the PCF leadership became ever sharper. There were increasingly stormy meetings of the ENA. At a meeting of North African militants and workers in 1928 those attending were asked if they wanted to be dependent on the PCF or to form an independent organisation on a national basis. There was unanimous support for the latter formulation.[136]

Meanwhile important changes were taking place within the Comintern. In 1928 the International abandoned the strategy of the united front. For the leaders of the ENA it meant an inevitable parting of the ways with an increasingly manipulative Communist International.

Hadj-Ali was expelled from the PCF, probably in 1930, for having stood as a candidate in municipal elections without party permission.[137] It was the final consummation of a break which had been developing for some time. He remained active in the ENA, which was facing considerable difficulties because of state repression and the withdrawal of PCF support. In October 1930 he played a key role in the founding of the paper *El-Ouma* [The Nation], of which he was the first editor. But he seems to have withdrawn from activity by the beginning of 1932.[138]

8   The Rif War

Between 1924 and 1926 the PCF had to confront the challenge of the Rif war in Morocco. This required a major mobilisation of the party membership and a combination of legal and illegal activity. In assessing the strengths and weaknesses of the PCF in this period it is important to remember that the party was in a transitional phase. It had lost some of its best members, and was increasingly hampered by its links to Moscow, but it was not yet the fully Stalinist party which emerged after 1930.

---

135   Righi 2006, p. 58.
136   Kaddache 1980, p. 230.
137   Righi 2006, pp. 97–8.
138   Righi 2006, pp. 120–23.

In 1912, Morocco had been divided into French and Spanish protectorates. In 1921 there was a Berber uprising in the Rif Mountains in northern Morocco, leading to the establishment of the Republic of the Rif. The leader of the insurgency was Abd el-Krim. His aim was to establish an independent state for Morocco; in social terms he had no particularly radical ideas. His peasant army was able to inflict repeated defeats on the Spanish troops.

By 1924 Spain was facing defeat. France's rulers feared that if Spain were driven out of Morocco it would endanger French rule in that country and, possibly, the rest of North Africa. Large numbers of French troops were sent to Morocco, where they found themselves facing a much tougher task than they had expected.

Robert Louzon, who had some experience of organising in North Africa, wrote in support of the Moroccan struggle, showing its implications for the whole future of French colonialism: 'The question of the Rif is closely linked to the whole problem of North Africa, it has a decisive importance for the recent movement that has grown up in Tunisia and Algeria'. He concluded by looking to 'the day when there is in North Africa a native republic developing normally free from all European interference, this example will achieve more than any propaganda ... It will speed the day when the North African peoples, having regained their freedom of development, will be definitively carried along by the general stream of civilisation'.[139]

The Rif war faced the French Communist Party with a challenge as sharp as that presented by the Ruhr occupation.[140] Similar tactics were adopted. Mass rallies against the war were called; one meeting in the Luna-Park Hall in Paris drew in as many as 15,000.[141] On 12 September 1924 Hadj-Ali spoke alongside Jacques Doriot at a meeting in opposition to the Rif war. He made a rousing appeal for 'the unity of *all* the exploited, whatever race they belong to, against *all* exploiters'.[142]

Local meetings were held, prepared with systematic fly-posting. Where posters were torn down, the organisers would send out teams into the working-class suburbs with horns and metal pots to attract attention so that the meeting could be announced. The importance of involving women in the movement was emphasised; as André Marty argued, no-one could put the case against war better than bereaved mothers and wives.[143]

---

139   Louzon 1925.

140   See Le Guennec 1972, Slavin 1991.

141   Semard 1925, p. 80; Anon 1925b.

142   Anon 1924b.

143   Le Guennec 1972, p. 43.

Support for the Moroccans was open and aggressive. French Communists Doriot and Semard caused a scandal by making public a telegram to Abd el-Krim which urged him to continue 'the struggle against all imperialists, including French, until the complete liberation of Moroccan territory',[144] When this was read to the National Assembly on 30 September 1924 – Doriot was a deputy – it caused outrage and the Communists were accused of treason.[145]

PCF propaganda attempted to link the war to the economic attacks being made on French workers. *L'Humanité* claimed the occupation of Morocco had already cost French workers and peasants 4,000 million francs, and that 'only a little clique of bankers and capitalists is getting the profits'.[146] It was a valid attempt to link the war to domestic issues. The action committees set up to oppose the war also campaigned in support of the wages struggle.

On 12 October 1925 the PCF and the CGTU called a one-day general strike against the war. In line with party strategy the war was linked to increased taxation [largely to pay for the war] and to the increase in the cost of living. Systematic work was done to build the strike, despite harassment by the authorities and the refusal of the reformist CGT and the SFIO to cooperate [though some Socialist Party members were won to a united front].[147] *L'Humanité* campaigned consistently to build the strike. In line with its concern to win support from immigrant workers it published appeals to support the strike in Italian, Polish, Armenian, Czech and Romanian, which it asked its readers to show to fellow-workers who spoke those languages.[148]

The results of the strike were mixed. Different sources give varying estimates of the extent of the support. The correspondent of the London *Times* who declared it to be a 'fiasco' was a little too gleeful in reporting failure to be considered a reliable source.[149] *L'Humanité*'s claims of success, however, may have contained an element of triumphalism.[150]

While it was a long way short of a general strike, with at best a total of 900,000 strikers, it did have an effect in some areas.[151] By general consent the biggest impact was in the Paris working-class suburb of Saint-Denis, which had a tradition of militancy. Here the strike and associated demonstration spilled

---

144 Broué 1997, p. 390.

145 Le Guennec 1972, p. 41.

146 Le Comité Central du PCF 1925.

147 Semard 1925, p. 62.

148 *L'Humanité*, 4 October, 1925. p. 6, carried pieces in Italian and Polish; the issue of 8 October, p. 6, had pieces in Romanian and Italian.

149 *The Times*, 13 October 1925.

150 Vaillant-Couturier 1925.

151 Le Guennec 1972, p. 52.

over into violence and the police opened fire on the crowd. At Suresnes in the
Paris suburbs a Communist worker was killed. Certainly the evidence would
suggest that there was some base for launching industrial action against the
war. However, while a militant section of the working class was mobilised, it
appears that the PCF was not able to involve a broader proportion of workers. If there was certainly support in Paris, the strike was less successful in the
provinces.

Pierre Monatte judged that while there had been some local successes, the
strike as a whole had been a failure – 'it was a demonstration of our impotence, that of the party and that of trade unionism'. A good part of the blame,
he argued, fell on the failure of the PCF leadership to win wider support: 'they
gave a clear impression of pursuing the party's interests rather than an end to
the war in Morocco'.[152]

There was also some success in organising opposition to the Rif war among
intellectuals. In particular this involved writers connected to the journal *Clarté*
and the emerging group of surrealists who were increasingly moving beyond
artistic revolt to a recognition of the need for political revolution.[153]

Among soldiers the PCF's central demand was for fraternisation.[154] While the
demand had had a real resonance during the Ruhr occupation, it was considerably less successful in Morocco, although there were a few instances. A French
defector, Placide Goux, assisted the Riffians; he was later sentenced to ten years
forced labour.[155]

There was some discontent in the army; *L'Humanité* carried a report from a
conscript of how a trainload of soldiers bound for Morocco had chanted 'Down
with the war in Morocco' and 'Up with the Riffians!' and had sung the *Internationale*.[156] There were a number of naval mutinies.[157] But there seems to have
been no direct agitation among troops on the scale of the work done during the
Ruhr occupation. It was obviously more difficult to send militants to Morocco
than it had been to slip people across the frontier into Germany; moreover the
Party was now smaller and suffering from bureaucratisation under the influence of 'Bolshevisation'.

Some critics of the Party argued that in the concrete circumstances the fraternisation demand was ultra-left and sectarian, and that by raising the demand

---

152   Monatte 1925b.
153   See Drake 2006.
154   Treint 1925.
155   Broué 1997, p. 391, citing Oved 1984, pp. 394–5.
156   Anon 1925a.
157   Le Guennec 1972, pp. 46–7.

for fraternisation rather than a more basic slogan like the immediate with-drawal of troops the PCF was sabotaging the possibility of united front work with the SFIO and the CGT. There were critics inside the Party – including André Marty – who argued that the fraternisation line had not been properly implemented, and in particular that the party had not done enough to defend servicemen subjected to disciplinary measures.[158] The war ended in 1926 with the surrender of Abd el-Krim.

One element in the situation, which may show the potential for internationalist agitation, was the role of Jacques Doriot. Doriot was at the time one of the leading figures in the Communist Youth, which had played a notable role in the Ruhr campaign, and was one of the most popular leaders of the party. He played a public role in the street fighting in Saint-Denis in October 1925, and received a heavy jail sentence for his part in the anti-war campaigning.

His subsequent evolution to the extreme right, recruiting soldiers to fight with the Nazis on the Eastern Front in World War II, should not eclipse his achievements in his days as a Communist – those stand in their own right. Doriot's evolution needs to be explained in terms of the development of the PCF in this period rather than on the basis of a claim that he was rotten from the start. Victor Serge, who had known Doriot in the 1920s, believed he had been a genuine revolutionary, and that his defection to the far right resulted from the triumph of Stalinism and fascism.[159] When Doriot's rejection of the discipline of the PCF led to a savage response from his former party, it is perhaps not surprising that his position rapidly became anti-Communist. Doubtless his personal ambition was encouraged by his electoral popularity, and unlike others who dissented from the PCF line, he did not turn to the marginal and divided far left.

Doriot was a member of a delegation sent to convey solidarity to Abd el-Krim. They were unable to enter Morocco, but he made repeated public declarations in which he called for fraternisation and physical support to the rebels in the Rif. He was vilified in the right-wing press as a traitor to his country.

All this seems to have had no adverse effect on his popularity with his working-class supporters. On the contrary for the next ten years Doriot enjoyed enormous popularity with rank-and-file Communists and with working-class voters. In the early thirties he was elected as deputy and mayor for the proletarian Paris suburb of Saint-Denis, and was re-elected in 1935 and 1936 despite opposition from the Communist Party with which he had by then broken.[160]

---

158   Le Guennec 1972, p. 57.
159   Serge 2012, pp. 601–04.
160   Maitron and Pennetier 1964–2023 article22865, notice DORIOT Jacques, Maurice. Pseud-

He built a massive Communist base there, one which survived until the 1980s. Certainly his popularity was enhanced by his concern to defend local workers and to provide facilities for the inhabitants, but his reputation as a traitor does not seem to have impaired his working-class support. Only in 1937 did he find himself defeated in his own fiefdom by an orthodox Communist. It is evidence that anti-imperialism is not necessarily such a vote-loser as is often alleged.[161]

In 1926 the General Strike in Britain offered a brief hope that the movement in Europe was reviving. If it had ended in victory, the course of history might have been different. Only a narrow stretch of water separated France from Britain, and the question of international solidarity was posed in very concrete terms.

L'Humanité, the daily paper of the PCF, gave extensive coverage to the strike – there was a major item on the front page for every day of the strike.[162] One of the first concerns of *L'Humanité*'s London correspondent, C. David, was to dispel the idea that the British were particularly peaceful and law-abiding.[163]

In addition almost every day *L'Humanité* carried a major editorial statement about the strike and its political implications. Many of these were written by Gabriel Péri, who was respomsible for *L'Humanité*'s foreign coverage. On 2 May Péri pointed out that the strike had to be understood in an international context: 'The English mining industry is being crushed by the modern techniques of its German and American rivals, so that the English coal crisis is only a part of the great world crisis of coal production! ... In these circumstances the victory or defeat of the English miners would be the victory or defeat of the British working class'.

Moreover, he added: 'If a united front is established on the other side of the channel, it would be the signal of renewal for the workers of Europe, the dawn of a victorious workers' offensive'. A defeat would have equally dramatic consequences: 'Weakened, wounded in the heart, the continental workers' movement would experience the most painful period of its post-war history. In these grave hours, the workers of England are the trustees of the destiny of the international working-class movement'.[164]

The CGTU railway workers' organisation launched the slogan 'Not a kilo of coal must be sent to England'. An appeal was directed particularly to miners,

---

onyme: GUILLEAU par Jean-Paul Brunet, version mise en ligne le 25 octobre 2008, dernière modification le 10 mars 2022.

161   See Brunet 1986.
162   See Birchall 2016.
163   David 1926.
164   Péri 1926.

railway workers and dockers.[165] By 6 May transport of perishable goods from Dieppe to Newhaven was suspended, and goods for England were not being loaded at Le Havre.[166] Marseille stevedores refused to load coal for England.[167] Rallies were organised in halls in various parts of Paris and the suburbs on the evening of 14 May, under the slogans 'Support the English strike! Against fascism! Against war!'[168]

In an article written at the start of the strike Alfred Rosmer had stressed the international significance of the dispute: 'To win, the British workers need the assistance of workers from all countries who must not only demonstrate Platonic sympathy, but understand that the present battle is their battle. Everywhere the bourgeoisie is considering attacking workers' living standards, and its victory in England would soon make itself felt throughout Europe'.[169]

The British General Strike showed that a recognition of the need for international solidarity was still powerfully present in the French working-class movement, even if the organisational expression of that recognition did not always come up to the necessary level.

For Communist Parties in Europe the Comintern's Sixth Congress in 1928 was a crucial turning-point. The suicidal Third Period line adopted then, which viewed social democrats as social fascists, made any kind of united front work impossible and seriously weakened any resistance to fascism. In particular it had adverse effects on the party's anti-colonial activity.

Only in the late twenties and thirties did the Comintern begin to take Africa more seriously. The Comintern's intervention came originally in the form of the establishment of the International Trade Union Committee of Negro Workers [ITUCNW Le Comité international des travailleurs nègres.] The ITUCNW was set up under the auspices of the Red International of Labour Unions [RILU], which from the mid-twenties onwards was an increasingly marginalised appendage of the Comintern.[170] To assign the organisation of Black workers to the RILU suggests it was never a major priority for the Comintern's leadership, and the activity of the ITUCNW was always subordinated to the political priorities of the Comintern.

The coming of the Popular Front in 1935 would put an end to such militancy as the Third Period had allowed. The ultimate motivation of the Comin-

---

165   Anon 1926a.
166   Anon 1926b.
167   Anon 1926c.
168   As announced on the front page of *L'Humanité*, 12 May 1926.
169   Rosmer 1926.
170   Tosstorff 2004.

tern leadership was now primarily to encourage anti-imperialist movements in order to weaken the various imperialist powers around the world which had interests contrary to those of the USSR. The priority was fighting fascism, and the demand for colonial independence was dropped because it might endanger the broad alliances that European Communist Parties were trying to create; even references to 'colonial oppression' disappeared. Much of the organisation that had been so painstakingly built up by the courageous militants of the ITUCNW was wound down, and in 1937 it was decided to dissolve the organisation.

Nonetheless anti-imperialist activity in this period should not be written off as unimportant. There was a day-to-day struggle to unionise Black workers [in some countries unions refused Black members and in others Black union members faced serious discrimination], and to fight against exploitation and resist the racism of many employers.

Various publications took up the tradition of *Le Paria* – *La Voix des Nègres*, [The Black Voice] *La Race Nègre* [The Black Race] – launched by Lamine Senghor and aimed at a more popular and less educated audience than *Le Paria* – and later *Le Cri des Nègres* [The Black Cry], promoted by the ITUCNW.[171] The claimed circulation of the latter was 3000, but in reality it may have been smaller, since thanks to colonial repression many copies probably never reached their destination. The work of production and distribution was hazardous, for revolutionary organisations faced constant harassment and infiltration. Sympathetic seafarers played an important role, often being used to smuggle journals into the colonies, sometimes hidden inside other publications.[172] Whatever the limitations, the production of such journals played a valuable role in the circulation of anti-imperialist and anti-racist ideas. *Le Cri des nègres* provided a wide coverage of events in many countries; it won support from striking agricultural workers in Guadeloupe in 1931, and received correspondence from Guinea, Cameroon and Martinique.[173]

However as far as finance was concerned, the whole thing was done on the cheap. The PCF refused to pay Lamine Senghor's fare to an important congress in Chicago and told him to work his passage [he refused].[174] Money alone could not enable the French Communist Party to solve the problems, but the Comintern was more generous with other activities.

---

171   See Adi 2013.
172   Adi 2013, pp. 129, 238.
173   Adi 2013, pp. 233, 245.
174   Adi 2013, p. 209.

By 1928 the PCF had lost many of the key militants who had been involved in founding the party and in some of its most creditable actions, notably the intervention in the Ruhr. The bold and imaginative team that had built up the UIC and *Le Paria* was largely dispersed, and there had been increasing friction between the PCF leadership, seeking to implement the manipulative strategies imposed by Moscow, and some of the best of the colonial activists, such as Hadj-Ali Abdelkader and Lamine Senghor.

9   Lamine Senghor

Yet despite changing views of anti-colonial strategy, the PCF continued to attract a small but significant number of activists from the French colonies. One of the most remarkable was Lamine Senghor.[175]

Senghor was born to a peasant family in Senegal in 1889. He volunteered to fight in 1914, served with the Senegalese infantry at Verdun and the Somme, was wounded and was awarded a medal, the Croix de guerre. Having been gassed at Verdun, he lost a lung and his health declined rapidly. Outrage at his treatment as a soldier, made worse by the fact that his pension was much smaller than those received by his French fellow-soldiers,[176] was a powerful force behind his activism. Radicalised by his experiences in the trenches, he rapidly evolved from being a loyal servant of French colonialism to becoming its intransigent enemy.

At the end of the war he was repatriated to Senegal, but returned to France in 1921, having gained official recognition [probably illegally] as a citizen, and took a job in the post office. He married a French woman whom he had met while in a demobilisation camp. He was briefly a police informer, but seems to have been convinced by the ideas of those he was informing on [always a danger with such activities].[177] He was soon a member of the PCF and was actively involved in the campaign against the Rif war.

He began to write extensively for *Le Paria*. A report by a French government body in 1926 showed that Senghor was in process of becoming what none of his predecessors in the *Paria* group had been, a genuine workers' leader:

> During the few days he spent in Marseille, he displayed prodigious energy ... Despite the few failures which he had to endure, he has shown a dis-

---

175   See Murphy 2020.
176   Goebel 2015, p. 107.
177   Goebel 2015, p. 98.

turbing obstinacy and exerted himself for his goal without counting the cost. Going from boat to boat, from factory to factory, and travelling everywhere that he could find a man of colour, he made such a name for himself that many blacks already consider him as their future liberator. It seems that urgent measures should be considered against this agitator, in order to prevent him from intensifying his pernicious propaganda which could have deplorable consequences.[178]

Senghor's lifestyle was much more proletarian than that of the original *Paria* circle:

> ... his way of life is very much like that of a French worker ... and this Muslim does not hesitate to drink alcohol. If Lamine Senghor is not completely assimilated as are many of his West Indian comrades, he is nonetheless very integrated into metropolitan society.
>
> Unlike most of the black militants who have their headquarters on the left bank of the Seine, Lamine Senghor lives in the rue Myrha, in the 18th *arrondissement*, in the heart of the working-class district of the Goutte d'or.[179]

In 1925 he stood, unsuccessfully, as a candidate in the Paris municipal elections.[180] He seems to have combined a Communist-inspired critique of imperialism with an attempt to forge a sense of black identity. In March 1926, he announced the creation of the Committee for the Defence of the Negro Race [Comité de défense de la race nègre – CDRN] and for much of the following six months embarked on a relatively successful recruitment tour. Now there was constant doubt as to whether he remained a Communist sympathiser or whether he had been won over to black nationalism; he found himself accused by the Communists of having a black nationalist agenda, while within the CDRN he was suspected of being a Communist. Whatever his motivation, Senghor clearly saw the CDRN and its successor the LDRN [Ligue de défense de la race nègre: League for the Defence of the Negro Race] as vehicles that would allow him to reach out to a wider black audience than had been possible under the PCF banner. He believed that most white French Communists simply could not understand colonial racism. His attempt to marry Communism with black internationalism marks him out as a pioneering activist and thinker.

---

178   Dewitte 1985, p. 128.
179   Dewitte 1985, p. 129.
180   *Le Paria* 33, April–May 1925, p. 1.

There is a depiction of Senghor in the posthumous novel, *Romance in Marseille*,[181] by Claude McKay, under the name Étienne St. Dominique. The Jamaican-American writer McKay, a leading figure in the Harlem Renaissance, had attended the Fourth Congress of the Comintern and had known Senghor.

In 1927 Senghor published *La Violation d'un pays* [the rape of a country], produced by the official PCF publisher.[182] This slender pamphlet was a satirical allegory of the history of colonialism, beginning when the first white man – the pale man – arrives in Africa, bringing trade and weapons, plunder and violence. There is a happy ending – successful revolution by the oppressed of all races.

> Everyone was discontented. Anger grew and grew and grew until one day the pale citizens, wishing to revolt against their queen, realised that if they didn't bring the other slaves with them, then the defenders of the 'crown' would enlist them to make them into counter-revolutionaries.
>
> They sent trained representatives into all the lands of slavery to organise their revolt, by showing them how much they had been deceived and robbed.[183]

Senghor represented Africa at the inaugural meeting of the League against Imperialism and Colonial Oppression in Brussels [February 1927], chaired by Albert Einstein. Yet he was acutely aware of his failing health; at one point he requested repatriation to Senegal on health grounds. If he had not wrecked his health by overexertion and died of tuberculosis in 1927 before he was 40, Senghor would undoubtedly have become one of the first great Black working-class leaders in France. He never saw his homeland again. *L'Humanité* published a short obituary which stressed that he 'did not hesitate to sacrifice his severely damaged health in defending his racial brothers', and that he had 'taken on the task of awakening his colonial brothers to class consciousness'.[184]

The significance of Senghor's achievement is shown by the fact that the French authorities seem to have taken him very seriously. The secret police reports revealed a fear that Communism was a contagion that could spread; there was a concern that materials and activities permitted in the metropolis might spread to the colonies.

For a few years France had had a mainstream political party, with representatives in the National Assembly and a leadership role in a trade-union confed-

---

181   McKay 2020.
182   Senghor 1927.
183   Senghor 2012, p. 29.
184   Dérigon 1927.

eration organising half a million workers, which embodied the internationalist principle that workers of all lands had more in common with each other than they did with their own nation states; this party was active in organising subversion in the armed forces and in encouraging demands for equal rights and national independence on the part of colonial subjects.

Yet by the end of the 1920s the PCF was scarcely recognisable as the party founded with such high hopes at Tours. Many of those who had created the party, including those who had defended workers' internationalism during the bitter years of world war, had now departed, voluntarily or as victims of expulsion. A new wave of leaders, too young to have played any significant political role during the war, were taking over; from now on it would be the 'party of Maurice Thorez' as it sometimes styled itself in subsequent years.

The internationalists did not simply vanish. In January 1925 a new monthly magazine appeared, *La Révolution prolétarienne*. The small group which produced it included Rosmer and Monatte as well as Robert Louzon, and other founder-members of the PCF such as Maurice Chambelland, Ferdinand Charbit and Victor Delagarde. Monatte, the driving force in the new journal, envisaged something in the style and spirit of *La Vie ouvrière*, and he explicitly referred to it in his introductory note. It also stood very much on the principles of the early Communist Party. In the first issue Monatte responded to the question of what they intended to do by saying: 'Continue, expelled from the party, what we were doing when we were in the party'. He rejected predictions that they would either join the SFIO or become opponents of the Russian Revolution.[185] The first issue made it clear that the journal would continue on the basis of the early years of the Russian Revolution. A translation of Trotsky's *New Course* was advertised and there was an article by Rosmer commemorating the anniversary of Lenin's death.

10   *Clarté*

Other oppositional currents evolved at a different pace. The journal *Clarté*, founded by Barbusse [see above] originally operated in the orbit of the PCF, though it was not directly controlled by the party. By the mid-1920s it was beginning to develop an independent perspective.

One indication of *Clarté*'s break with the values of the mainstream left came in 1924 when the government proposed to move the ashes of Jean Jaurès to the

---

185   Monatte 1925a, p. 7.

Panthéon, to lie alongside Voltaire, Rousseau, Victor Hugo and Zola. Jaurès was a hero of the left, but *Clarté* argued with some plausibility that had he lived he would certainly have backed the war and would have joined the government alongside his old adversary Guesde. For *Clarté*, Jaurès's view that socialism flowed naturally out of the republican tradition of 1789 was dismissed as naïve idealism. Hence *Clarté* argued that 'between Jaurès and Lenin we must choose, ruthlessly and inexorably'.[186]

A few weeks earlier had come the death of Anatole France. France was one of the country's best-known writers and a representative of the republican tradition; he had supported Dreyfus and was strongly anti-clerical. In his last years he was sympathetic to the Communist Party. *Pravda* in Moscow and *L'Humanité* paid him fulsome tributes. *Clarté* dissented, carrying an article by Marcel Fourrier entitled 'Anatole France, social-democrat, social-chauvinist, social-traitor'.[187] *Clarté* was developing a critical distance from the left republicanism which still influenced many parts of the Communist Party. In 1926 the journal was called to order by the PCF and instructed not to collaborate with the surrealists. At the same time the *Clarté* team were increasingly aware of developments in Russia and of the emergence of the Left Opposition.

The destiny of *Clarté* now became closely linked to that of one individual, Pierre Naville, [1904–1993], who played a significant role on the French left over several decades. Originally a surrealist, he was politicised during his military service and joined the Communist Party. He became joint editor of *Clarté* and under his direction the journal went through the last phases of its short history.

Naville saw himself as a loyal supporter of the Comintern, but in 1927 he was invited by Victor Serge to visit Russia for the tenth anniversary of the October Revolution. While he was there the criticisms he had already begun to develop over the question of the Chinese revolution were confirmed; he met Trotsky and Rakovsky, perceived the reality of Stalinism in Russia, and was convinced of the rightness of the Left Opposition's cause. He became a Trotskyist activist.

On his return to France Naville, together with Francis Gérard [pseudonym of Gérard Rosenthal, with whom he had travelled to Russia], issued a leaflet inside the PCF in support of the Left Opposition. The PCF instructed him to cease supporting the Left Opposition and to abandon the publication of *Clarté*. When he refused he was expelled.

Clarté now became the open voice of the Left Opposition in France. Effectively this meant the end of *Clarté*; it ceased publication early in 1928 and was

---

186   *Clarté* 63, 1924.
187   *Clarté* 68, 1924.

replaced by *La Lutte de classes* [class struggle], the official organ of the French Left Opposition. Naville took with him a number of former *Clarté* collaborators.

French Trotskyism never really took off. By 1934 the membership of the Ligue communiste was no more than 140, and it existed only as a minority current to the left of the PCF; through the big struggles of the decade its membership never rose above 750.[188] It did develop a small cadre which would defend intransigent internationalism during the German occupation and later.

For Alfred Rosmer the wheel had come full circle. Fifteen years earlier he had faced total isolation at the outbreak of World War I. He had gone on to see the early congresses of the Comintern, the Baku Congress, the formation of the French Communist Party, and the founding of the RILU. Now it was back to the politics of tiny groups.

Unhesitatingly Rosmer aligned himself with Trotsky. In 1929 and 1930 he was extremely active in trying to build the Left Opposition, not only in France, but also in Austria, Germany and Belgium. His reports to Trotsky give a vivid picture of the emergence of the Trotskyist current in this period.[189]

The Russian Revolution of 1917 had awakened hopes of a world revolution that might spread within a period of just a few years. This created the context for the growth of an internationalist left in France which reached its peak with the intervention in the Ruhr. As the revolutionary hope began to subside, so the internationalist left had to go onto the defensive. The final blow came with the defeat of the Chinese revolution in 1927. Readers of *Clarté* got their analysis from Victor Serge, who had been a member of a Left Opposition commission studying events in China.[190] He concluded with the vigorous assertion that in the present period there could no longer be a bourgeois revolution in the classic sense of the term in economically developed colonial countries such as China, India and Egypt. The bourgeoisie could no longer carry out its revolution by itself, and while making the bourgeois revolution, the proletarians and peasants would pursue and attain their own aims. The bourgeois revolution would have to be transcended, or it would remain unfulfilled.[191]

For the coming decade, and longer, the internationalist left would face defeat and isolation. A handful, at least, stood by their principles.

---

188 See Dannat 1997.
189 See Trotsky and Rosmer 1982.
190 Serge 2001, p. 678.
191 See Serge 1994.

Midnight in the Century

It was Victor Serge, who had witnessed both the early years of the Russian Revolution and the terrible deformations that followed, who coined the phrase 'Midnight in the Century'.[1] The hopes of the early twenties gave way to a period of disillusion and defeat.

Inspired by the Russian example, European workers made some advances in the period immediately after the world war. Power remained in the hands of their rulers, who were determined to restore their profits, to punish their underlings who had overstepped the mark, and above all to make sure they didn't do it again. The solution adopted took the name of fascism.

By the end of the twenties Mussolini was consolidated in power in Italy. In 1933 Hitler took over in Germany. By the Spring of 1939 Franco had achieved final victory in Spain. France was surrounded on three sides by fascist states.

Though for many Russia still seemed to offer the promise of hope, the revolutionary flame was rapidly being stifled. Some of those politically active in the thirties recall how, in the face of the rising tide of fascism, they looked to Russia as their sole hope, only to be confronted with the reality that Russia too was rotten.

What possibilities were available? For all too many, it was to cling onto whatever justification that seemed halfway plausible, and to continue to defend the Russian regime. Such people had usually first got involved in political activity because they believed in human freedom and the emancipation of the working class. Now they were prepared to go along with what looked like the very negation of their original principles.

A few, but only a few, moved to the far right. Contrary to the lazy assertion that there is an equivalence between extreme left and extreme right, only a small number followed that path, and in each case a particular biographical and political explanation is required. Others simply abandoned political activity altogether.

Only a minority held on to the internationalist principles which had seemed to be gaining ground in 1920 at the time of the formation of the French Communist Party. To do so they had to stand in opposition to the evolving policies of the PCF.

---

1 Serge 2015.

Stalinism was not revolutionary; nor was it reformist. It was a unique historical phenomenon, bred of the peculiar circumstances of a defeated revolution. To become a Communist between the wars required a sharp break with the existing social order and the existing national framework. By becoming a Communist one was aligning oneself with Russia against one's own nation state; as a result one would be constantly attacked as an agent of Moscow. Party loyalty required one to put one's commitment to the party ahead of national allegiance. At various times one would be called upon to take action that put one at personal risk, whether of jail for inciting mutiny within one's own country, or of death fighting as a volunteer in an anti-fascist struggle. To be a Communist in the thirties demanded personal dedication and courage, a willingness to put what was perceived as loyalty to the international working class above any loyalty to state or nation.

Yet the internationalism required of Communists was loyalty to an international organisation – the Comintern – rather than internationalism in the classic sense. As Pierre Broué argued, by 1935 the Comintern – and hence its constituent parties like the PCF – was no more than a 'direct dependency of the political police of the [Soviet] state'.[2]

The Sixth Congress of the Comintern in 1928 had established the strategy of the Third Period, which characterised reformist social democrats as 'social fascists'; to enforce loyalty to Moscow, all other currents in the movement had to be seen as class enemies. For most Communist Parties, including the French, the results were what could be expected from such sectarianism: declining membership and an inability to develop united front activity. By 1930 the PCF claimed, probably exaggeratedly, only 39000 members, little more than a third of what it had had at the time of its foundation.[3] In Germany the consequences were much more serious. The labelling of the Social Democrats as 'social fascists' and the refusal to countenance any sort of united front, enabled Hitler to come to power over a divided left.

1   Popular Front

It was in France that the first moves towards a change of line came. On 6 February 1934 a demonstration in Paris organised by several far-right organisations became violent. Police opened fire and sixteen demonstrators were killed;

---

2   Broué 1997, p. 670.
3   Robrieux 1980, pp. 49, 342.

the prime minister, Daladier, resigned. From the safety of posterity it may be clear that the far right was as yet in no position to take power; just one year after Hitler's victory things did not appear so certain. Some people on the left had the good sense to be frightened. Under pressure from the rank and file the PCF, SFIO, CGT and CGTU came together to call a united demonstration.

This set in motion a dynamic that led, in France and internationally, to the establishment of the Popular Front. In France in 1935 an electoral alliance of the PCF, the SFIO and the Radical Party was formed in preparation for the elections of 1936; this was backed by the CGT [the CGT and CGTU reunited in 1936]. At the Seventh Congress of the Comintern, also in 1935, the strategy of the Popular Front was adopted internationally.

In France the Popular Front fitted perfectly into the national tradition. The idea of republican unity, of defence of the republic, was one that could be traced back to 1789, to Jaurès's insistence that socialism flowed naturally from the republican tradition, to Waldeck-Rousseau's government of republican defence – and to the sacred union of the First World War.

Hence the rapid growth of the Communist Party, the electoral success of 1936, and the rising expectations expressed in the strikes and factory occupations which greeted the Popular Front victory. By 1937 PCF membership was 330,000, a fivefold increase in two years.[4] The fragility of the victory is illustrated by the fact that it was the same National Assembly elected in 1936 which in 1940 handed over power to the pro-Nazi Pétain.

The Popular Front period saw sharp changes in PCF policy, notably on colonial questions. Support for colonial independence, in particular in the case of Algeria, was dropped. Maurice Thorez argued that 'the *right to divorce* did not mean the *obligation* to divorce'[5] – which seemed to imply that the relationship between France and Algeria was comparable to a happy marriage.

The genuinely internationalist current on the French left was small and divided. Some significant tendencies can be identified:

Firstly there was the grouping around *La Révolution prolétarienne*. It was a well-informed journal which contained valuable commentary on the French labour movement and on international questions. Yet it had no organisation and it is hard to establish how much influence it exercised.

Secondly there were the Trotskyists. They were always small in number, and they were based preponderantly in Paris. Trotsky's achievement in defying

---

4 Robrieux 1980, p. 483.
5 Report to the Eighth Congress of the PCF, December 1937, quoted in Moneta 1971, p. 132.

Stalin and in holding together a small but dedicated organisation is undeniable, and the role of the small body of Trotskyists in the Second World War and later during the Algerian War, provide some remarkable examples of internationalism in practice. Yet in his tireless struggle to establish the Fourth International, Trotsky sometimes seemed to fetishise the international organisation at the expense of internationalism itself. In defending what he claimed to be the correct line of the International, he came into conflict with some of the best militants who had previously been his comrades. Among the French-speaking comrades he broke with the Rosmers, with Victor Serge and with Monatte, notably as a result of disagreements about trade-union strategy. Building a Fourth International without such tested militants meant that Trotskyism was depriving itself of some of the most principled activists on the internationalist left.

The most substantial component of the far left was the left-wing current in the Socialist Party, led by Marceau Pivert, and known as the Gauche révolutionnaire [revolutionary left]. Unlike the PCF, the SFIO had a long tradition of internal debate and factional organisation. The bureaucrats who ran the party could ignore the rank and file, but they could not silence them.[6] Formed in 1935 the Gauche révolutionnaire was in effect a party within a party, with its own organisational structure and its own internal democracy.

Pivert swayed between reformist and revolutionary positions. At the time of the strikes and occupations in 1936 he declared exultantly that 'everything is possible', calling for the setting up of 'people's committees' and urging 'the most vigorous anticapitalist offensive'.[7] Caught up by the logic of the Popular Front, he was drawn to the right. One member of the Gauche révolutionnaire, Daniel Guérin, argued there were two distinct popular fronts. On the one hand there was the 'misalliance, on the parliamentary and electoralist level, of bourgeois radicalism and Stalinism, under the banner of national defence'. But there was also a popular front from below, embodied in the factory occupations, 'a genuinely *popular* movement in the sense that it drew behind the working class a not inconsiderable layer of petty bourgeois and poor peasants'.[8]

In 1938 the Gauche révolutionnaire was expelled from the SFIO. Pivert and his followers then formed a new party, the Parti Socialiste Ouvrier et Paysan [Workers' and Peasants' Socialist Party]. A majority of the French Trotskyists,

---

6   See Kergoat 1994.
7   Pivert 1936.
8   Guérin, 1963, p. 93.

following Trotsky's advice, joined this new party; Pivert himself rejected Trotsky's proposal for a fusion of the PSOP and the newly formed Fourth International.[9]

In its early years the Communist International had pursued a course of genuine struggle against imperialism; the results were erratic and the great European empires remained unscathed. Nonetheless the efforts of the early Communists were unquestionably principled and courageous. By the late twenties things were changing; the turning point was the defeat of the Chinese revolution in 1927.

The coming of the Popular Front put an end to even such militancy as the Third Period had allowed. The new line reflected Russian interests rather than the realities of the class struggle. The priority was fighting fascism, and the demand for colonial independence was dropped because it might endanger the broad alliances that European Communist Parties were trying to create.

2   The Colonial Exhibition

The French Empire remained triumphant. To honour its achievements, in 1931 Paris saw the staging of an enormous Colonial Exhibition, which between May and November received some eight million visitors. The aim was to celebrate the economic benefits of empire and France's 'civilising mission'. In his speech at the opening Paul Reynaud, Minister for the Colonies, declared: 'Colonisation is the greatest fact of History. Is it true that at this time when we are assembled together ... we are celebrating an apotheosis which is on the verge of decline? ... Our grip on the world gets tighter every day'.[10]

He could scarcely have imagined that in just over thirty years, and within his own lifetime, there would be nothing left of the French Empire but a few fragments. The Exhibition's critics may have seemed marginal, but history would prove them right.

The PCF took a firm stance. On the day the exhibition opened *L'Humanité* carried a front-page article condemning French imperialism as the work of 'capitalist vultures' and hailing 'the heroic colonial fighters struggling for their independence'.[11] However, when the PCF set up a counter-exhibition under the title 'The truth about the colonies' it attracted only around 5000 visitors, even

---

9   Kergoat 1994, pp. 148–9.
10   Reynaud 1931.
11   Bonte 1931.

though group visits were organised.[12] This would suggest that either PCF membership was at a low ebb, or that the party machine was giving less than total support to the project.

The surrealists, at this time quite close to the PCF, produced a leaflet condemning the Exhibition. They urged boycott, referring to repression in Indochina and the racist recruitment posters for the colonial army. From the time of the Rif war the surrealists had taken a firmly anticolonial position, not only in political campaigning, but also in promoting the value of art from Africa and Oceania.[13]

It was left to the Trotskyists to take direct action. They invaded the notorious Exhibition and smashed various precious exhibits to protest at repression in Indochina, pointing out that the valuable items on display had been stolen from the colonies. They thus got far more publicity for the Indochinese cause than a mere demonstration could achieve.[14]

Meanwhile resistance among the colonial populations intensified. The Étoile Nord-Africaine continued to grow. From it would emerge all the subsequent movements for Algerian independence. Successful meetings were held in various French towns, and by 1934 the circulation of *El-Ouma* [*The Nation –* the ENA's paper] had risen to 40,000.[15] From November 1934 to May 1935 Messali Hadj was in jail, a sign that the government regarded his movement as a serious threat.[16]

In *La Révolution prolétarienne* Busseuil reported the repression against the ENA and explained it by the fact that the government was frightened by the popularity and success of the ENA. 'And you know that when the French bourgeoisie is frightened, it rapidly has recourse to arbitrary power, and when it does so, it is heavy-handed'.

Busseuil regretted that Paris workers did not show the same solidarity to North Africans as they did to the victims of fascism in Germany and Spain. This was a question of self-interest; he warned: 'Be aware that there are 60,000 Arab workers in the Paris region and that it simply depends on you whether they will be for or against you in your struggle against fascism'.[17]

In January 1937 the French Popular Front government, backed by the Communists, took the decision to dissolve the ENA. *L'Humanité* published a long

---

12   Ageron 2006.
13   Coudray and Nadi 2017.
14   Craipeau 1999, pp. 100–101.
15   Simon 2003, p. 161.
16   Simon 2003, pp. 162–4.
17   Busseuil 1934.

article criticising the hostility of the leaders of the Étoile Nord-Africaine to the PCF and to the Popular Front; it did not condemn the dissolution.[18]

As J-P. Finidori pointed out in *La Révolution prolétarienne* the ENA had supported the Popular Front which had now banned it. He commented: 'The Socialists in government seem to have taken on the job of making socialism odious to all colonial peoples'.[19]

On 11 February a meeting was held in Paris to protest against the ban on the ENA, with some 3500 people packed into the hall. Messali himself spoke, and among the other speakers was Hadj-Ali.[20] A month later, on 11 March, at Nanterre in the suburbs of Paris, another meeting was held to launch a new organisation, the Parti du Peuple Algérien [Algerian People's Party – PPA], which effectively would continue the work of the ENA. By now Messali and Hadj-Ali were deeply disillusioned with the PCF; Messali had contacts with other forces to the left of the PCF.[21]

3   Indochina

The Algerian movement was probably the most advanced section of the anti-imperialist opposition within the French Empire. Indochina was much further away and far less familiar to most French people; for that very reason French rule could be more openly brutal, without many people noticing what was going on. Executions were commonplace, and unauthorised violence and killings by police and soldiers were equally frequent. Extremes of wealth and poverty were glaringly visible.

Already by the 1920s an opposition was growing up. An Indochinese Communist Party was founded and took part in many militant actions. Some of the Indochinese students in Paris were drawn to the Trotskyist Left Opposition, notably the young Tạ Thu Thâu, then a student in Paris.[22] While there he met the writer and anti-colonialist activist Félicien Challaye, and Francis Jourdain, a Communist sympathiser. Tạ Thu Thâu wrote a leaflet which ended with the call: 'In our nameless slavery, we appeal to the oppressed of the colonies: Unite against white or red European imperialism if you want to have a firm place under the sun'.[23]

---

18   Moneta 1971, pp. 113–16.
19   Finidori 1937.
20   Simon 2003, p. 221.
21   Simon 2003, p. 308.
22   On Tạ Thu Thâu see Ngo Van Xuyet 1990.
23   Ngô Văn 2000, p. 214.

On 22 May 1930 Vietnamese students in Paris demonstrated on the Champs Élysées against more than fifty death sentences passed on participants in an uprising at Yên Bái; a number of Indochinese activists, including Tạ Thu Thâu, were deported back home.

In 1931 Tạ Thu Thâu and others established the clandestine Trotskyist Ta doi lâp [Left Opposition].[24] Things did not run smoothly; there was severe repression from the French authorities. A small number of French writers and activists reported on the struggles and repression.

As a young man in the 1920s Daniel Guérin had had literary ambitions – he had already published two novels by 1929; politically he had made contact with the grouping around *La Révolution prolétarienne*. He was gay, although he concealed the fact from his political friends, thinking – quite justifiably at that time – that they would not understand.

He wanted to see the world. He travelled, first to the Middle East, then, in 1929, to Indochina. That journey would change the whole course of his life. He saw the French Empire in all its brutality. For the next six decades his pen would be at the service, not of Literature, but of the wretched of the earth. In Indochina he met some of the nationalist leaders [he had already met Tạ Thu Thâu in Paris], and observed the systematic repression exercised by the French authorities, aided by their allies among the mandarin class.[25]

Marcel Martinet had been one of the small group which had opposed the war from its outbreak in 1914. He was a man of high moral principle and a gifted writer. Perhaps under the strain of intense activity, his health broke down. From 1923 until his death in 1944 he was capable of only spasmodic political intervention. When he did return to political writing, his taste for polemic had lost none of its edge.

In 1934 Martinet published a short pamphlet with the ironic title 'French Civilisation in Indochina' [Civilisation Française en Indochine].[26] It was published on behalf of the Committee for Amnesty and Defence of the Indochinese and Colonised Peoples [Comité d'Amnistie et de Défense des Indochinois et des Peuples Colonisés]. The secretary of this was Francis Jourdain, a decorative artist close to but not a member of the Communist Party.

Martinet began with some reflections on nationalism, and the way it was understood in popular consciousness:

---

24   On Vietnamese Trotskyism see articles and documents in *Revolutionary History* 3,2, 1990, and Ngô Văn 2000.

25   Guérin 1964, p. 248.

26   Martinet 1934a.

> Georges de la Fouchardière [a novelist and actor] recently reminded us that there are two sorts of nationalism: ours, which is good, and other peoples', which is particularly loathsome when it stands up against 'our' rule, against the 'civilising' rule of France. Vercingetorix, rebelling against Roman civilisation, is a hero, as the schoolbooks teach French children, whereas if the Vietnamese were to try anything similar against French civilisation, they become criminals in common law who must be treated as such.[27]

He then tried to put Indochinese nationalism into context and to explain the nature of the nationalist revolt against French rule:

> Indochina is, first of all, a *country*: a homogenous country which, before the arrival of the French, was unified and organised; a country which had its own civilisation and which, ethnically, historically and politically, formed a part of China. Obviously that goes some way to explaining the resistances which foreign rule has repeatedly met, as well as the inevitable repercussions on the Indochinese population of the efforts towards liberation that have been made in China for the last ten years.[28]

As a result, Martinet argued, the history of Indochina in recent years revealed two apparently contradictory features, 'the fundamental wretchedness of creatures reduced to despair, and the proud assertion of men whose spirit remains free even when they are in chains'.[29]

He described the events at Yên Bái in 1930; a genuine revolt, partly as a result of the hatred felt by the peasantry for the mandarins, was suppressed within a few days. A criminal commission was then established. Within hours there were 83 death sentences, 22 put into effect immediately. Meanwhile five Europeans, two sergeants and three soldiers from the Foreign Legion, who had tortured and killed Vietnamese, were all acquitted. Since 1930 an official document had recommended the execution without trial of those labelled Communists. Thus

> Not only have the torturers and murderers been acquitted. Their superior officers provided cover for these deeds, and in turn claimed justification on the basis of orders from the civil authorities. So the verdict doesn't only

---

27   Martinet 1934a, p. 3.
28   Martinet 1934a, p. 3.
29   Martinet 1934a, p. 4.

acquit some obscure brutes, it acquits the military and civilian leaders, up to and including Governor General Robin.[30]

Martinet quoted a statement by the legionnaire Billot, who said that 'the orders he had been given were to kill prisoners because there was no room in the prisons'.[31] Meanwhile Captain Doucin admitted that there had been violent acts: 'But what did they shoot? Communists! Well, in my opinion they didn't shoot enough'.[32] Martinet commented acidly in a footnote: 'For the French in Indochina, people aren't arrested because they're Communists, they're "Communists" because they've been arrested'.[33]

In concluding Martinet said that he would leave aside such matters as humanity or the Rights of Man. He would simply address one question to the French government:

> Is it wise, in the present state of the world, is it wise, on the part of a European power which, with a few thousand men, is ruling an Asian empire with several million inhabitants, is it wise to reign and govern only by means of terror?
> *Is it wise to go on killing?*[34]

Though few could have envisaged it, it would be just twenty years to the final French defeat at Dien Bien Phu, and just over forty years to the humiliation of the Americans. The answer to that question would be very plain.

He concluded by referring to the 'heart-breaking' letters from the mothers and wives of those condemned to death or imprisonment: 'these wretched letters make you ashamed to be white'.[35] He added that the members of the government to whom such letters had been addressed 'belong to groups for whom the persecution of Jews by Hitlerites has aroused indignation'.[36] To suggest that the brutality of colonialism was as bad as that of the Nazis was unacceptable in many circles.

Martinet had never been to Indochina, relying for his information on trusted comrades. Someone who had seen for herself was Andrée Viollis, the pen-name of Françoise-Caroline Claudius Jacquet de La Verryère.

---

30   Martinet 1934a, p. 10.
31   Martinet 1934a, p. 10.
32   Martinet 1934a, p. 11.
33   Martinet 1934a, p. 11.
34   Martinet 1934a, p. 13.
35   Martinet 1934a, p. 14.
36   Martinet 1934a, p. 13.

As a reporter she had travelled widely, having reported sympathetically but not uncritically from the USSR, and from India, where she predicted the end of British rule. She did not oppose colonialism in principle, but clearly perceived the reality.[37] In 1931 she had accompanied the colonial minister Paul Reynaud on a visit to Indochina. Her account formed one of her most influential books, *Indochine S.O.S.*, published in 1935 with a preface by André Malraux.

The journey gave Viollis an opportunity for observing Indochinese society. On the one hand she was part of the minister's entourage, was able to hear official opinions and to meet many prominent people in the settler community, who talked freely to her, assuming that she was on their side. She was able to use her status to get access to political prisoners. The result was a devastating account of the sufferings of the Indochinese people and of the wilful ignorance of those responsible for the colony's destiny.

Viollis grasped the contradiction at the heart of French colonialism. The French in Indochina were victims of their own ideology; they perceived the native population only as objects, as workers and the source of wealth. They could not understand the threat to their own rule, because they were unable to recognise the grievances and the aspirations of the indigenous population. Only a genuinely internationalist approach could have avoided the impending disaster – and of that they were incapable.

She identified some of the fundamental causes of the sufferings in the colony – famine, an unjust taxation system and the violent response of the French authorities to peaceful demonstrations. She noted that when she had previously published articles about Indochina she had been accused of underestimating the achievements of French rule; she replied that she observed the achievements, but that railways did not help the starving indigenous population. She added: 'if however people persist in considering that it is harming France to serve truth, then I will willingly take the blame'.[38]

She confined herself to describing the effects of French rule, without explicitly calling for independence. She noted that the nationalists were 'desirous of seeing applied to their country the democratic principles which they have acquired from us'.[39] One of her most shocking experiences was meeting political prisoners and learning of the ways in which they had been maltreated and tortured: 'I shall never forget the sudden start, as of a hunted beast, the look of

---

37   See Jeandel 2006.
38   Viollis 2008, p. 18.
39   Viollis 2008, p. 18.

hatred, of terror, and that awful raucous cry'.[40] She told the horrific story of one prisoner who 'bit off his tongue so as not to talk'.[41]

Viollis pointed to the contradiction between France's 'civilising mission' and the reality of colonial rule. She recalled the Indochinese students she had met in Paris – 'they thought they were free, citizens the same as everyone else'[42] – but on their return they were searched, their newspapers were seized, they couldn't get jobs, and they were subjected to imprisonment, censorship, humiliation and *tutoiement* [use of the familiar form of address reserved for children, animals and servants]. There were many arrests for spurious reasons; those imprisoned were often subjected to torture involving electric shocks and the inflicting of pain on the genitals. She interviewed an employee of the Sûreté politique [political police] who admitted to the use of torture. Viollis had previously visited British-ruled India and noted that she had believed that France 'used more humane and intelligent methods of colonisation than England ... a few days in Indochina would be enough to brutally destroy this illusion'.[43] As she was told: 'All these unfortunate people are illiterate. None of them knows the meaning of the word, communism. They were poor, they were hungry. That's all'.[44]

Apart from political repression Viollis noted many other abuses inherent in French colonialism. The French derived massive profits from the sale of opium and alcohol which had gravely harmful effects on the indigenous population. The mandarins who held positions of power on behalf of the French were 'nothing but bandits'[45] whose conduct made Communist propaganda seem plausible. They lived in luxury and were often appointed to positions on the basis of dubious qualifications. French women in Indochina were able to bully servants that they would not have had at home. Health provision was appallingly inadequate – in one district there was one doctor for 160,000 native inhabitants. Coal miners worked in miserable conditions – nobody even knew what the mortality rate for miners was. Such few reforms as there were could be attributed to the work of progressive journalists like Luc Durtain and Roland Dorgelès.

She heard the minister addressing 'prominent people' from villages where rebels had set up 'embryonic soviets': 'Never has any rising succeeded against our great France, which emerged victorious from the greatest of wars'.[46]

---

40   Viollis 2008, p. 29.
41   Viollis 2008, p. 30.
42   Viollis 2008, p. 35.
43   Viollis 2008, pp. 42–3.
44   Viollis 2008, p. 129.
45   Viollis 2008, p. 52.
46   Viollis 2008, pp. 73–4.

Viollis described the impact of famine and the inadequate measures taken by the French authorities. Paul Reynaud had seen for himself the spectacle of starving people begging for rice – yet as an apologist for colonialism he never spoke of it to the French parliament.

Many Indochinese were calling, not for full independence, but arrangements similar to dominion status in the British Empire. It was becoming clear that if the French believed their own myths and were not prepared to make concessions, all might be lost. As one perceptive member of the French community told her: 'If these wretches or imbeciles make us lose Indochina, then you'll have to admit that we deserved it'.[47]

At one of the luxurious dinners to which she was invited as part of her official role as a reporter, she was told by a planter: 'With this education they've been given, this nonsense about liberty and equality that has been stuffed into their heads, they're becoming intractable. Now it's impossible to get cheap labour'.[48]

Because there was no solution to the contradiction, time was running out. One veteran Indochinese activist told her that he still wanted to see 'honest collaboration with France. But we must make haste, otherwise it will be too late'.[49] In her conclusion she quoted a French civil servant: 'In fifteen years perhaps, we French of Indochina won't be here any more, and it will be our fault!'[50] He was wrong. It would be twenty-three years.

4   The Rise of Fascism

Colonialism and racism were not the only problems facing the internationalist left. The rise of fascism across Europe presented a major challenge, not only in terms of physical repression, but also as a question of political analysis. Fascism was not an incomprehensible phenomenon, but nor was it simply a continuation of other reactionary and ultra-nationalistic movements from the past. It had to be understood in terms of both continuity and change.

By the 1930s there was a greater recognition of the gravity of the problem, despite the fact that the Comintern was trapped in the dead end of the Third Period. Trotsky had argued that fascism in Germany and Italy was 'the most ruthless dictatorship of monopoly capital'[51] and called for a united front of

---

47   Viollis 2008, p. 88.
48   Viollis 2008, p. 96.
49   Viollis 2008, p. 117.
50   Viollis 2008, p. 148.
51   Trotsky 1933.

workers' organisations to resist it. Daniel Guérin had read Trotsky and wrote his book *Fascism and Big Business*.[52] He offered an analysis of the economic factors producing fascism, stressing its originality as against those who saw it merely as continuing earlier forms of reactionary rule, and its durability against those who believed it would not last long. For Guérin fascism emerged directly from the interests of sections of the capitalist class; hence a popular front alliance with an allegedly progressive bourgeoisie was doomed to failure. He also showed that economic factors were not enough to explain fascism, and that ideology, the 'mystique' of fascism, was also essential to an understanding.

The triumph of fascism in Europe was a fearsome phenomenon. Yet its victory was not achieved without resistance. The very brutality which fascism deployed was a tribute to the extent of the resistance to it; only the utmost ruthlessness could enable it to triumph. The working-class movement threw up thousands upon thousands of anti-fascists who fought against the encroaching barbarity.

If some workers turned to fascism, they were only a small proportion of the class as a whole. Behind the rhetoric, the fundamental role of fascism, the reason why its paymasters paid it, was to increase the exploitation of the working class, by smashing those organisations which could defend workers against attack, and by creating an ideology of national and racial unity. The working class were inevitably the victims of fascism, and were equally inevitably thrust into conflict with it.

Although fascism triumphed in three neighbouring countries, it did not succeed in France itself until foreign invasion combined with defeatism and collaboration at home finally led to the collapse of parliamentary democracy. The reasons why France did not succumb to fascism, as Italy, Germany and then Spain did, was partly because of the adoption of the united front strategy as early as 1934 and in advance of the Comintern's instructions, but partly also because the left did not relinquish control of the streets but made the fascists fight every inch of the way. Eventually the adoption of a popular front strategy by the main working-class organisations tended to isolate and marginalise independent working-class action and ultimately prepared the way for the pro-Nazi take-over in 1940. But independent working-class action against fascism did exist and should not be written out of history.

Yvan Craipeau, one of the French Trotskyists, has given us some vivid descriptions of street-fighting. Often the tactics employed were provocative. On one occasion a single frail-looking young man was sent to sell papers in an

---

52   Guérin 1936.

expensive cafe frequented by right-wingers. When a squad of 'patriotic youth' appeared, they were attacked by waiting socialists, and some twenty were hospitalised.[53]

In 1935, after fascists attacked the headquarters of the Seine Federation of the SFIO, Pivert and his followers, together with the Bolshevik-Leninists [as the Trotskyists in the SFIO called themselves], set up the TPPS [Toujours Prêts Pour Servir – Always Ready to Serve]. Craipeau describes what the TPPS were:

> It was not simply a military organisation, but a grouping of activists, ready for any task at any time. Organised in tens, thirties and hundreds, with their leaders elected by the rank and file, the TPPS went out at night to fly-post, paint slogans in red lead, and throw leaflets into factories. The TPPS were likewise mobilised to steward meetings, and when necessary were sent as reinforcements if a fight was expected. They went to defend working-class paper-sellers, and sometimes stopped the fascists selling their papers. There's no need to add that they were very badly armed [usually one revolver among six, the rest having truncheons or improvised weapons]. Sometimes they were routed ... usually the fascists were dealt with. Everywhere they were driven out of the working-class quarters.[54]

Hitler's accession to power in Germany in 1933 was a severe shock for the French left. The triumph of fascism in Italy could be explained by that country's relative backwardness, but Germany was one of the most advanced capitalist economies in the world. It was only fifteen years since France had been engaged in a bitter war with Germany. Hence the error of many in the SFIO and elsewhere, who believed Hitler's rise could be explained in some way by German racial or cultural characteristics. As Daniel Guérin reported, it was not uncommon to hear in SFIO circles the claim: 'All this has happened because they are *boches*'.[55]

Guérin decided to go and look for himself. He had returned from Indochina; he was close to the grouping around *La Révolution prolétarienne* and was briefly a member of the SFIO. In 1932 and again in 1933, he visited Germany, observing the situation before and after Hitler's accession to power. The first visit led to articles in various organs of the left press; the second to a series of articles in the SFIO daily *Le Populaire*, which became a book, *The Brown Plague*, republished

---

53   Craipeau 1999, p. 93.
54   Craipeau 1971, pp. 123–4.
55   Guérin, 1933, p. 61.

several times.[56] Guérin admired Germany; it was a country 'which was dear to me; my testimony contains no chauvinism'.[57]

During his second visit Guérin made contact with what remained of the German opposition, collecting clandestine leaflets which he concealed in his bicycle frame. He did not hesitate to study Nazism at first hand, attending meetings and yelling 'Heil Hitler' so as not to seem conspicuous. As he wrote, he had to 'overcome his repulsion and try to understand'.[58] He showed how the economic crisis had driven peasants, petty-bourgeois and some workers into the arms of fascism; the political failures of Social Democrats and Communists had opened the way for Hitler. He recognised that Hitler enjoyed widespread popularity and saw that the so-called socialist element of National Socialism had a real if distorted meaning; many workers looked to Hitler to achieve what the traditional parties of the left had failed to deliver.[59]

He recounted a conversation he had with a German worker, a carpenter. Initially Guérin imagined he was a Communist:

> His rough proletarian language, his revolutionary arguments deceived me for a moment:
>
> 'You see, us workers, we've been betrayed by both the working-class parties ... There should have been unity of action ... They didn't want it'.
> Then suddenly, this suspect argument:
> 'Now we must look after ourselves ...'
> 'Who do you mean, *ourselves?*'
> 'The German people! We've had enough of being humiliated and treated like slaves. We've had enough of paying taxes for war tributes ...'
>
> And when I object that there is no salvation outside of revolutionary internationalism:
>
> 'Yes ... Yes ... The International, it's all very well ... In 1923 we sent millions of marks in gold to the English miners when they were on strike ... But what did they do for us?'

---

56   Reissued in book form Paris, Éditions L.d.T., 1934, and again in 1945 and 1969. See Guérin 1969, pp. 53–4, 127.
57   Guérin 1933, p. 61.
58   Guérin 1933, p. 4.
59   See Renton 2005.

And, having stuffed his pipe:

> 'We'll have to make our revolution on our own ... While we wait for the
> International to come into existence, we have to think about the
> present ... found a German workers' state!'[60]

The main theme of his reportage was that the first victims of Hitler were the
German working class. When he observed a book-burning he noted that the
publications destroyed were trade-union and socialist leaflets, pamphlets and
newspapers. He met militants who had been imprisoned and physically ill-
treated; he described the way they had been humiliated in jail and the economic hardships they faced even if released; prisoners had the expenses of
imprisonment deducted from future wages.

The dominant message was one of hope. He recounted that when he could
speak in confidence to socialist militants, their response was: 'We remain what
we were',[61] He reported moments of resistance – a socialist who demanded
the right to speak at meetings in Leipzig, workers in Kiel who struck when
their workplace representatives were removed. Former militants kept socialist literature hidden in their cellars and listened to the *Internationale* on Radio
Moscow. Illegal groupings were beginning to circulate publications. News-
vendors slipped copies of Communist papers inside Nazi papers. In the slums
of Hamburg 'Down with Hitler! Long live the Revolution!' was written on the
walls.[62]

The left was beginning to overcome the terrible sectarianism of both Communists and Social Democrats which had allowed Hitler to take power over a
divided working class. One militant told Guérin that they had abandoned the
'democratic illusion' and were now committed to Marx and Lenin's slogan of
the dictatorship of the proletariat.[63] There was a growing recognition of the
importance of internationalism. One comrade told him: 'If you want to understand Hitler's victory, you must never forget this: a Marxist knows that the main
enemy is at home, that we must first of all fight our own capitalism. But we
Germans, even the Communists ... thought our main enemy was foreign capitalism'.[64]

---

60   Guérin 1933, pp. 26–7.
61   Guérin 1933, p. 6.
62   Guérin 1933, p. 51.
63   Guérin 1933, p. 50.
64   Guérin 1933, p. 56.

Guérin's aim was to reveal the 'other Germany'[65] which opposed Hitler and was his first victim. Nazism used the rhetoric of national unity, but it was the product of a class society: 'never has this country been divided into two more irreconcilable camps'.[66]

When Guérin's articles were first published they did not receive immediate approval from the left. The editor of *Le Populaire* told Guérin that he had received many letters of protest. Some wanted to ignore Nazism, imagining it was not a threat. For Guérin the analysis required had to be in terms of class and not of nation:

> Fascism is a system, an ideology, a way out. Certainly it solves nothing, but it endures. It is the response of the bourgeoisie to working-class failure, an attempt to escape from chaos, to achieve, without excessively compromising the privileges of the bourgeoisie, a new disposition of the economy, an *ersatz* socialism.[67]

The central theme of his reportage, that German workers were the victims of fascism and hence objectively – and potentially subjectively – the allies of the French working class, would become ever more important as war loomed.

5   **The Spanish War**

There was little open resistance in Germany and hence people in France were not challenged to take sides. Spain was very different. In the summer of 1936 military forces headed by General Franco attempted to overthrow an elected Popular Front government; the result was a brutal civil war lasting three years before fascist rule triumphed.

The civil war in Spain was widely seen as a trial run for the coming world war: on the one side Franco's fascist forces, assisted by Hitler and Mussolini, on the other the forces of the Republic. For the next two and a half years the question of Spain became central to the political debate, and produced some of the most concrete manifestations of proletarian internationalism.

There were close parallels between the French and Spanish situations. In both countries a Popular Front government was in power. Both had powerful right-wing enemies; there were doubtless numerous people in France who

---

65   Guérin 1933, p. 6.
66   Guérin 1933, p. 39.
67   Guérin 1933, p. 61.

would have liked to emulate Franco if they had been strong enough. Many supporters of the French Popular Front wished France to intervene actively in support of the Spanish Republic. The government of Léon Blum initially wanted to send military supplies to the Spanish Republic, but was persuaded by the British Tory government to adopt a policy of non-intervention [a refusal to export war material to Spain] in order to avoid confrontation with Germany and Italy. This was agreed by the main European powers, including Russia – though it did not prevent Italy and Germany giving massive aid to Franco.

In France the PCF was committed to support for the Popular Front government. When Blum adopted the position of non-intervention and refused to give material support to the Spanish Republic, he was heavily criticised by the PCF, yet they were not prepared to push that criticism as far as open confrontation with the government.

There is some evidence of popular support for the Spanish cause. On 7 September 1936 in the Paris area there was a one-hour strike in support of the Spanish Republic and for economic demands, urging the Popular Front government to end its policy of non-intervention, seen as being effectively a blockade on the Spanish republican government. It was claimed some 300,000 workers struck; in one factory a strike vote was carried by 2000 votes to one.[68] However, the lack of democratic leadership made the strike less effective than it might have been.[69]

French solidarity was affected not only by the political parallels between the situation in the two countries, but also by their close physical proximity. Non-intervention ostensibly meant a ban on volunteer fighters entering Spain. The main means of entry was through the Pyrenees and the PCF had a special role in getting the volunteers into Spain. Movement across France into Spain was made easier by PCF influence.[70]

Robert Louzon had been active in forming some of the first Communist organisations in North Africa [see chapter 7]. In August 1936 he went to Morocco to make contacts in an attempt to prevent Franco from recruiting Arab troops in the Rif. Then in 1937, aged 54, he fought in Spain at the front with the republicans for several months. He also wrote regularly for *La Révolution prolétarienne* on the Spanish struggle, and wrote articles for *Solidaridad Obrera* [Workers' Solidarity], the Barcelona daily of the anarcho-syndicalist CNT, contrasting collectivisation organised by trade unions with state-controlled

---

68   Anon 1936.
69   See Dominget 1936.
70   Durgan 1999, p. 113.

nationalisation as advocated by the Stalinists.[71] Louzon and Victor Serge wrote frequently on Spain for *La Révolution prolétarienne*, in particular showing how Stalinist policies were leading to defeat.

One indication of the enthusiasm for the Spanish Republican cause is the number of international volunteers who went to fight in Spain. Although the organisation of the International Brigades is often described as having been a Communist-controlled manoeuvre, the desire to support the Spanish cause went further than Communist ranks. In general the level of political commitment was extremely high, in what was one of the most politically conscious armies ever assembled. Most of those involved had a clear understanding of fascism, through direct personal experience or through political campaigns. The recognition of the dangers of fascism was far higher among members of the International Brigades than it was among members of most European governments.

The policy of non-intervention meant that it was very difficult for volunteers to cross the frontier. Some rode into Spain clinging to the bottoms of railway carriages. The actual number of international volunteers who went to Spain is a subject of dispute; since many travelled illegally and the whole supporting organisation was clandestine, figures are hard to establish. The probable number is something under 30,000, including medical services and drivers. That nearly 30,000 people from over 50 different countries were willing to face death in Spain is a striking manifestation of working-class internationalism. Many more would have gone had not age, health or family commitments prevented them. They had a high casualty rate and played an important role in the siege of Madrid on 8 November 1936. Of the estimated 53 nations from which volunteers came, the largest contingent was the French, about 9,000, of whom around 60 percent were members of the rapidly growing Communist Party.[72]

The international volunteers were welcomed in Spain, making Spanish workers aware of their place in an international movement.[73] Prior to the establishment of the International Brigades there were already hundreds of foreign volunteers fighting in the workers' militias. These included political refugees living in Spain and individuals who made their way into Spain once the war started.

Heroism and revolutionary internationalism were only half the story. The whole International Brigades operation was closely controlled by the Comin-

---

71   Louzon 1937.
72   Durgan 1999, pp. 112–3.
73   Orwell 1962, pp. 15–16.

tern – and by the Russian state.[74] The strategy was in conformity with the politics of the Popular Front.

Already by 1937 things were turning sour. There was no victory in sight and the conflict between Communists and their left critics had become open. Many of the volunteers fought on to the last bitter stage of the war. On 9 February 1939 International Brigaders were among the last Republican troops to cross the border out of Spain. On 24 February, France recognised the Franco government, and the war was effectively over.

Part of the tragedy of the Spanish war was the fact that the Republican forces were deeply divided, between a Popular Frontist current increasingly under the control of the Comintern, and a revolutionary current which argued that victory against fascism could be achieved only by mobilising the emerging social revolution in support of the war effort. The latter current was represented politically by the POUM [Partido obrero de unificación marxista – Workers Party of Marxist Unity]. The POUM had much in common politically with the Pivertist Gauche Révolutionnaire, and the two organisations had fraternal relations. The Communist Party made the most grotesque accusations of treachery against the POUM and eventually helped to suppress it physically.

The POUM welcomed foreign volunteers. Out of around a total of 10,000 in the POUM militia, up to 700 were foreign, including a group from France. The POUM, as a token of its internationalism, seems to have welcomed supporters of non-Spanish nationality. Another 250 French fought with the syndicalist CNT.[75]

One activist who worked closely with the POUM was Colette Audry [1906–1990]. She was a member of the SFIO and a leading activist in the Gauche révolutionnaire. She visited Spain at the beginning of the war; she was a talented linguist, and during the war she produced a French version of the POUM's journal.

In February 1939, at the time of Franco's final victory, the Popular Front government sent troops to seal off the frontier in the Pyrenees to prevent refugees from Spain making their way into France. A small group of French activists, including Daniel Guérin, Maurice Jacquier [administrative secretary of the PSOP] and Colette Audry took a lorry across the Pyrenees to find the POUM leaders, who risked freezing to death or being murdered by Stalinists. Audry, the daughter of a *préfet* who knew how such things worked, managed to get, from the *préfet* of the Pyrénées-Orientales, a document which would enable them

---

74   Durgan 1999, p. 110.
75   Durgan 1999, pp. 114–5.

to get through the frontier controls. They picked up five POUM leaders, saving them from probable internment[76] in the horrific improvised camps set up on French beaches to accommodate the half million refugees who crossed the Pyrenees at the end of the war. Despite support from political and trade-union organisations, the refugees were left in improvised shelters, without medical assistance or adequate food.[77]

6   Victor Serge

There was an added complexity for internationalists in the age of rising Stalinism. In Spain activists of the left faced a threat not only from the fascist right, but from those whom they might have imagined to be their allies, the Communists. Inside Russia oppositionists faced repression often comparable to that in fascist states. There was a sharp debate on the nature of Russian society under Stalin. About a third of the French Trotskyists came to accept the argument that Russia was now a new type of exploitative society.[78]

One case which posed this issue in concrete form for the French left was the Victor Serge affair. Serge was not French – indeed he was not anything. Born in Belgium of Russian exile parents, he had been politically active in Belgium, France, Spain, Russia and Germany. He was known in France for pamphlets he had written for Marcel Martinet's *Cahiers du Travail* [see chapter 7], for his articles in *Clarté* on Germany [under a pseudonym] and China, and for his book *Year One of the Russian Revolution*;[79] he had also translated some volumes of Lenin's works into French. He had become one of the leading figures in the Russian Left Opposition and had been exiled to a remote area.

The campaign for Serge's release lasted from 1933 to 1936, and involved a large number of prominent literary figures.[80] Serge's supporters included a range of individuals from the fragmented anti-Stalinist left: Boris Souvarine, Pierre Pascal, Maurice Parijanine and Lucien Laurat grouped around *Critique sociale* and the Cercle Communiste Démocratique; the editors of *Combat marxiste*; Maurice Wullens and *Les Humbles*; Magdeleine Paz, writer and pioneer Trotskyist, and her husband, Maurice, lawyer and SFIO member; the editorial group of *La Révolution prolétarienne*, including Pierre Monatte and journalist and art

---

76   Guérin 1963, pp. 255–9.
77   Chauvin 2006, pp. 141–3.
78   Craipeau, 1971, p. 148.
79   Serge 1930.
80   Greeman 1994.

historian Jacques Mesnil; and the radical teachers' group around *L'École éman-cipée*. A Committee for the Repatriation of Victor Serge was formed.

Marcel Martinet gave his support to the Committee by writing a pamphlet 'Where is the Russian Revolution Going? The Victor Serge Affair'.[81] Here he argued, as one who had supported the Russian Revolution from the first day, that the harm done to Russia's reputation by the imprisonment of Serge was much greater than any damage that Serge at liberty could do. Serge had fought to defend all that was best in the Russian Revolution; he had joined the Left Opposition but continued to stand by the same revolutionary values. Martinet regretted the unconditional support to Stalin's Russia given by many intellectuals, including Romain Rolland who had meant so much in 1914. He concluded: 'with Rolland if possible, without Rolland if necessary, against Rolland if we must'.[82]

Things came to a head at the International Writers Congress for the Defence of Culture in June 1935, an event organised in the framework of Popular Front politics. Three supporters of Serge, Charles Plisnier – writer and founder-member of the Belgian Communist Party, expelled in 1928 for supporting the Left Opposition – Magdeleine Paz, and Henry Poulaille, were on the speakers' list. The organisers fiddled the agenda to try to prevent them speaking, and used physical threats to prevent any criticism from the floor. Poulaille and his friends broke into chants, demanding to hear about Serge. Paz did eventually get to speak and made a passionate defence of Serge, arguing that he should be defended against the USSR just as delegates would defend a radical writer anywhere else in the world.[83]

Stalin was anxious to maintain political and military friendship with France at this particular moment, and he realised that the vigorous campaign by Serge's friends could have an influence on the non-Communist left. In April 1936 Serge was released. Four months later the Moscow Trials began; in the changed climate it is highly unlikely that Serge would have survived. While the campaign could not have succeeded without the involvement of many internationalist militants, their intervention came just at the right time.

In the aftermath of the Serge Affair and in the light of developments in Russia and Spain, some of the same activists set up the Committee to Investigate the Moscow Trial and to Defend Freedom of Opinion in the Revolution [Comité pour l'enquête sur le procès de Moscou et pour la défense de la liberté d'opinion

---

81   Martinet 1934b.
82   Martinet 1934b, p. 26.
83   Paz 1935.

dans la Révolution]. Members included the Rosmers, Martinet, Monatte, surrealist poet André Breton, historian Maurice Dommanget and Henri Poulaille. Serge himself became an active member and claimed the Committee's intervention prevented the execution of leaders of the POUM in Spain.[84]

7   In Defence of Immigrants

The rise of fascism across Europe led to refugees seeking asylum in France. The immigrant population was growing and the political heirs of those who had raved against the Jews at the time of the Dreyfus case had fresh targets for their venom. The defence of immigrants and refugees was now a major task for internationalists.

One writer who was particularly sensitive to the situation of immigrant workers was Jean Malaquais. He was born in Warsaw in 1908 in a family of Jewish origin, but his whole life showed a refusal to be trapped in a national identity, as demonstrated by the title of one of his best-known books, *World Without Visa*.[85] He left Poland in 1926 and travelled through various countries from Romania to Palestine. As he told an interviewer many years later, his main aim was to get to Paris, since France was the homeland of the Rights of Man and the Commune. On 14 July he was sleeping rough on the place de la Bastille. He was picked up by two policemen who treated him violently. He realised that despite France's traditions, the French police were particularly brutal. He added that having so often been called a dirty foreigner, he detested xenophobia.[86]

While in France he worked as a labourer and as a mine worker in Provence, and was involved with the anti-Stalinist left; during the Spanish Civil War he fought with the POUM. In 1939 he published *Les Javanais*,[87] which was awarded the Prix Renaudot, was serialised in the CGT newspaper and was praised by Trotsky.[88] He would remain an intransigent leftist and internationalist until his death in 1998.[89]

---

84   Serge 2001, pp. 777, 785.

85   Malaquais 1947.

86   de Massot 1999.

87   Malaquais 1995.

88   Trotsky 1941.

89   Maitron and Pennetier 1964–2023 article 89270, notice MALAQUAIS Jean [MALACKI Vladimir dit] par Philippe Bourrinet, version mise en ligne le 23 septembre 2010, dernière modification le 1er novembre 2011.

Les Javanais is a strange, innovative novel. There is no plot and no central characters, simply a group of workers at a mine in Southern France. Conditions are bad [there is an accident and a strike] and French workers do not wish to be employed there, so it is staffed by a number of migrant workers of different national origins – there are Czechs, Germans, Arabs, Bulgarians, Spaniards, Turks, Armenians and a black American – with one solitary Frenchman. It is written in French slang, interspersed with words from several different languages. There is no explicit political position, but Malaquais shows them one Sunday singing the *Internationale*, and one may imagine he sympathises with the character who says 'If I were king, I would get rid of frontiers and there you are, it's free, no passports or visas or anything ...'[90]

Unlike his fellow-surrealist Louis Aragon, poet André Breton remained staunchly anti-Stalinist. In 1938 he travelled to Mexico where he met Trotsky; together with the Mexican painter Diego Rivera they published a manifesto in defence of independent revolutionary art. This led to the founding of the FIARI [Fédération Internationale de l'Art Révolutionnaire Indépendant: International Federation of Independent Revolutionary Art]. A French branch of the FIARI was set up, which briefly brought together, perhaps under the influence of Trotsky's prestige, the otherwise hostile groupings of the surrealists and the proletarian writers. Its National Committee included Yves Allégret, Jean Giono, Marcel Martinet, André Masson, Henry Poulaille, Gérard Rosenthal and Maurice Wullens, and it had an impressive list of supporters including Roger Blin, André Breton, Claude Cahun, Jean Giono, Benjamin Péret, Marceau Pivert, Victor Serge and Ignazio Silone.[91]

The main organiser was Maurice Nadeau. Later best known as a journalist, literary critic and publisher, Nadeau was born into a poor family; his father died at Verdun, his mother was illiterate. At his primary school, pages from the Larousse encyclopaedia were used as toilet paper. Nadeau grabbed the sheets, and read them in the dormitory. He trained as a teacher and went to the prestigious École Normale Supérieure. He joined the PCF, but after a visit to Germany in 1932 he was shocked by the Third Period policy; he was expelled from the PCF and became a Trotskyist, a protégé of Pierre Naville. He had responsibility for the FIARI publication, *Clé* [Key], of which only two issues ever appeared – the fragile alliance of rival literary schools could not survive any longer.

During its brief life *Clé* manifested an intransigent internationalism. The rise of fascism had led to a growing number of refugees seeking asylum in France,

---

90 Malaquais 1995, p. 20.
91 *Clé*, Bulletin mensuel de la FIARI 1, 1 January 1939.

fleeing anti-Semitism in Germany and Italy, and the Franco regime in Spain. The front page of the first issue of *Clé* carried an editorial statement attacking decrees directed against foreigners residing in France, requiring those entering France to have visas and proof of financial viability. It insisted that 'Art has no country, just as the workers have none'.

> No Homeland!
> The filthy campaigns conducted under the slogans 'France awake' and 'France for the French' are beginning to bear their poisoned fruit. M. Sarraut's May decrees, and certain terms in the appendix of the November statutory orders have brought into force, to the detriment of foreigners resident in France and especially of political refugees, a disgraceful procedure inspired by that of fascist countries. Measures of exclusion already taken, and the preparations for internment which we are currently observing, mark the accentuation of a politics based on panic and force which is tending to establish in France a regime which is 'authoritarian' and will soon become totalitarian ... They bear witness to the rapid contagion affecting 'democratic' countries which are already being dragged, in contempt of the most elementary considerations of humanity, to repudiate the right of asylum, long considered SACRED by them. The FIARI considers it as its prime duty to denounce this new degradation of bourgeois 'conscience', and to expose these xenophobic manoeuvres as one of the main dangers of the present moment ...
>
> In the more specific sphere of our own activity, we will take good care not to forget that if Paris has long been in the artistic vanguard, that is essentially a result of the hospitable welcome which artists coming from all countries have found there: that if some of the great spiritual trends which the world has taken account of have been born in this city, it is because it has constituted a truly international laboratory of ideas. Art has no country, just as the workers have none.[92]

From 1934 onwards, when the new line of the Popular Front began to be introduced, Communist Parties found themselves under the obligation of seeking alliances with the allegedly progressive wings of their native bourgeoisie. Often this progressive bourgeoisie came out of a nationalist tradition – for example the Radical Party in France, which stood very much in the Jacobin tradition. As a result there were concessions to the ideology of this sector of the ruling class.

---

92   Anon 1939.

In France, at the height of the factory occupations in 1936, Communist Party members would lower the red flag and replace it with the tricolour, or insist that the *Marseillaise* be played or sung instead of the *Internationale*. A whole rhetoric of national tradition and national independence was developed, which sat very uneasily with the Marxist language into which it was supposed to be integrated. Indeed, as in 1914, the revolutionary tradition of 1789 now played a conservative rôle.

8   Impending War

Once the flicker of revolutionary hope in June 1936 had passed, it was downhill all the way. Hopes of a defeat for fascism in Spain faded equally quickly. Impending war dominated the political horizon; the question was not whether war would come, merely when and how.

Attitudes to a forthcoming conflict were very different to what they had been in 1914. Fervent patriotism, rooted in *laïcité* and the revolutionary tradition, was much less conspicuous this time round. In its place there was, in the circles of the powerful and privileged, a defeatist sentiment. 'Rather Hitler than Thorez' was a preference quite widely heard in the drawing rooms of the rich. Although Annie Lacroix-Riz's analysis has been challenged, she certainly shows that a significant section of the French ruling class preferred Hitler to the French left.[93]

The response from the leaders of the Popular Front was half-hearted and ambiguous. Léon Blum, SFIO leader and head of the Popular Front government, blended semi-pacifist rhetoric with a firm commitment to national defence. Like all leaders of the moderate left in power, Blum had to demonstrate that he was a reliable defender of the alleged national interest. In a speech in September 1936 he vigorously rejected any 'stirring up of patriotic feeling'. A few days later his government massively increased military expenditure.[94]

The other main party of the working class, the PCF, was a rather different matter. After 1934 the Communists abandoned attempts at direct subversion of the armed forces in favour of a broader appeal for peace. This often involved conferences drawing together distinguished intellectuals and where possible political representatives of the progressive bourgeoisie; friendship with Russia rather than practical means of preventing war became the keynote of the operation. This was integral to the strategy of the Popular Front. In 1935 the

---

93   Lacroix-Riz 2006.
94   Guérin 1963, p. 151.

Communist Party switched its line to approve French rearmament, thus backing up the newly formed military alliance between Russia and France. Both main parties of the left saw military preparation as the main response to the threat of Nazism.

A small authentically internationalist current continued to exist. This was to be found in the Gauche révolutionnaire of the SFIO and in various independent groupings outside of it. One manifestation of this was the creation, in 1935, of the 'Liaison Committee against War and Sacred Union' [Comité de liaison contre la guerre et l'union sacrée]. This involved followers of Pivert such as Daniel Guérin, the Trotskyists, the revolutionary syndicalists around Pierre Monatte, and writers such as Henry Poulaille, Simone Weil, Magdeleine Paz and Jean Giono. It held two conferences in the summer of 1935, on 10–11 August and 28 September.

Guérin explained the Committee's analysis of the international situation:

> The working class was tied down in its struggle against capitalism by the disastrous results of the Franco-Soviet alliance. Under the double pressure of Stalinism and reformism, the proletariat was being urged to abandon all revolutionary action against war. Instead of orienting its unity of action towards a profound social transformation, there was an attempt to make it the foundation of a sacred union for war against Germany in defence of the Treaty of Versailles. Although we felt implacable hatred for Hitler's regime, we didn't hope for it to be overthrown by an imperialist war but by international revolutionary struggle.[95]

Unfortunately divisions within the left meant that little came of this initiative.

Meanwhile the drift towards war continued. In the autumn of 1938 a crisis arose over the question of Czechoslovakia. Germany was demanding the right to intervene in Czechoslovakia in support of the German population in that country. Britain and France came to the brink of war; after negotiations at Munich they accepted the German position, and war was averted. The Munich agreement was popular among people who were glad to see that war had been at least temporarily averted. Yet the agreement could also be perceived as appeasement of Germany. Russia, which had not been involved in the negotiations, felt that it had been betrayed by Britain and France, and the Franco-Soviet agreement seemed doomed, with the possibility of an agreement between Germany and Russia now emerging.

---

95   Guérin 1963, p. 71.

In retrospect the advance towards World War II may seem inevitable; at the time there was considerable evidence of a potential will to resist it. There was widespread anti-war feeling. The mood was very different from that in 1914. There was no enthusiasm for war; memories of World War I were still strong. French people – including peasants who would still make up a substantial proportion of the armed forces – now had a much clearer picture of what war would be like. Photographs in newspapers and cinema newsreels had shown the horrors of war in Spain, and given warnings of what was to be expected from bombing and chemical warfare.[96] Fear of war had been widespread, with a wave of suicides; as war approached there was panic in Paris, as large numbers of people tried to leave the city because of the danger of air-raids.[97]

However there was no effective political leadership which could channel the desire for peace. The working-class movement was left with only two alternatives – either to support the military build-up of the anti-fascist nation states opposed to fascism, or to back the Munich deal as a means of preserving the peace. The PCF paper *L'Humanité* reported trade-union resolutions against Munich, but no direct action.[98] A third way, based on working-class action against war did not have the political support to make it a meaningful option.

Meanwhile the Popular Front was in a state of catastrophic decline. Léon Blum was twice forced to resign as prime minister, and each time was replaced by a Radical. Blum himself was in rapid retreat from the original aims of the Popular Front. The Gauche révolutionnaire became increasingly critical, and by the summer of 1938 it was in open conflict with the main party. It was expelled and immediately declared itself a new party – the Parti socialiste ouvrier et paysan [Workers' and Peasants' Socialist Party – PSOP]. Many though not all of the Trotskyists joined its ranks; it remained too small to have any real influence on the course of events – its national membership was fewer than ten thousand at most. If the PSOP faced organisational repression at the hands of the SFIO bureaucrats, it aroused violent anger from the PCF. *L'Humanité* accused the PSOP of being in the service of Hitler and Franco.[99]

The PSOP did not have a fully articulated analysis of the impending war and how to prevent it; there were a variety of positions within its ranks. One of the members who attempted to fight within the PSOP for a revolutionary strategy against war was Daniel Guérin. He had been wrestling with the problem throughout the decade; recalling his response to Hitler's election results in

---

96   Guérin 1963, p. 236.

97   Guérin, 1963, p. 237.

98   Anon 1938.

99   Kergoat 1994, p. 144.

1930, he described his own position as being: 'We were … anti-fascists for whom it was a mortal error to combat fascism by means of imperialist war'.[100]

In 1938 Guérin prepared a pamphlet, apparently for educational use in the newly founded PSOP, under the title 'Against War and Sacred Union',[101] echoing the name of the committee to which he had belonged three years earlier. He recorded the changing positions of the SFIO and PCF on national defence, accusing the latter of making demagogic use of the traditions of the French Revolution. A war between Britain and France and the fascist powers would not be in the interest of the working class, and sacred union with workers' own exploiters was not the best way of resisting fascism.

Unfortunately Guérin's analysis was not matched by the forces on the ground. The PSOP's organisational structure was quite unfitted for the needs of wartime. Yet the issues raised by Guérin as early as *The Brown Plague* were to be of enormous significance. The beginning of the Second World War was a period of serious confusion for the French left. Some veterans of 1914 ended up collaborating with the Nazis in the name of peace. In August 1939 the Hitler-Stalin Pact compounded the problem. As Guérin noted 'among the "patriots" who, in 1938–9, exhorted us to join the sacred union, quite a few subsequently, following the lead of Moscow or of Vichy [the pro-Nazi government of occupied France], were to come to terms with Hitler'.[102]

As well as the tiny number of would-be Leninists trying to preserve the tradition of revolutionary defeatism there was also a somewhat larger number of pacifists, who from a religious or secular rejection of violence on principle, or from simple disgust at the experience of modern warfare, wished to assert their right to refuse to take part in the forthcoming slaughter.

Louis Lecoin had first been involved in antimilitarist activity before 1914, in the period of the sou du soldat [see chapter 5]. In September 1939 he distributed 100,000 copies of a leaflet 'Paix immédiate' [Immediate Peace] for which he stayed in jail until August 1941, despite the change of regime! This was signed by some thirty individuals from the independent left, individuals who would take different paths when France was occupied, several collaborating with the Germans; signatories included Georges Dumoulin, Maurice Wullens, Henry Poulaille, Marceau Pivert and Robert Louzon.

The leaflet noted that, in contrast to 1914, there was an absence of public enthusiasm for war:

---

100   Guérin 1963, p. 31.
101   Guérin 1938.
102   Guérin 1963, p. 13.

No flowers on the rifles, no heroic songs, no cheers for the departing soldiers. And we are assured it is the same in all the belligerent countries. Thus the war is condemned, from the first day, by the majority of those involved, at the front and at home.[103]

Thus the world drifted to war despite the best efforts of the small minority of internationalists, who were unable to make any impact on the situation. In the Spring of 1939 Guérin argued that the time had come for the PSOP to transform itself into a revolutionary organisation, necessarily small, but prepared to take on the responsibilities demanded by the impending war:

> The time had come to go into illegality, It was urgent to finally liquidate all the pacifist illusions within our ranks. It was high time to prepare our Party to face the storm. If we could show ourselves capable of this effort, then and then alone we should not have failed in our 'historic' mission.[104]

Guérin was unable to convince the majority of his comrades.

In 1939, as in 1914, the left had already failed. In Alfred Rosmer had written of the earlier war 'When war comes, it means the working class is already defeated'.[105] The left, divided and disorented, had not prevented the war; even worse, it was in no condition to face the new challenges that the war would present.

103	Lecoin 1965, pp. 168–75.
104	Guérin 1963, p. 263.
105	Rosmer 1936, p. 9.

World War II

The Second World War was very different from its predecessor twenty-five years earlier. In some ways it was a conflict between rival imperialisms. France and Britain still had the world's two largest empires and they were determined to hold onto them. The intervention of the United States increased that country's economic and political influence in the world. However there was another dimension to the war. Hitler's Germany was a manifestation of fascism which had eradicated democratic freedoms and human rights, and had destroyed working-class organisation. While its plans for racial extermination had not yet fully emerged at the outbreak of war, they were wholly consistent with the ugly ideology it was already promoting.[1]

1914 had seen a confrontation between a tiny internationalist minority and the overwhelming nationalist consensus. World War II saw a more complex interplay of ideologies. Millions fought and died to defend their homelands. Millions more fought because they saw the war as primarily a war against fascism. The dedication demonstrated by men and women from many nations was inspired by a range of causes and ideals – nationalism was not always the primary motivating force. Despite the tangled web of ideology the grip of nationalism was weaker not stronger in World War II than it had been in World War I, but the space for intervention by internationalists was somewhat larger.

There was a second factor complicating the situation in France. In 1914 there had a been a 'sacred union' right across the political spectrum; with very small exceptions all social classes and all political forces had supported the war. In 1939 there was no such unity. A significant section of France's upper and middle classes had been severely frightened by the strikes of 1936 and were prepared to welcome the sort of discipline a fascist regime could provide. While some who actively collaborated with the German occupiers between 1940 and 1944 were merely accepting superior force, a considerable number were enthusiastic in their support and had undoubtedly been willing to smooth the way for a Nazi victory.

Many of the policies pursued by the French government at the outbreak of the war show that even when preparing to resist German invasion, the French state was happy to use methods remarkably similar to those of the Nazis. The

---

1 See Gluckstein 2012.

internment camps set up in France *before* the German invasion have largely been written out of history. The first camps were set up at the end of the Spanish Civil War for the half million refugees who came over the Pyrenees, and who were less than welcome to the French government. They were simply herded onto the beaches, where some died of hunger and exhaustion; then they were redistributed to a number of camps in Southern France. Even before the outbreak of war, the government rounded up Germans, making the xenophobic assumption that all Germans [even anti-Nazi refugees] were on the side of Hitler.[2]

If France had had a coherent, well-organised internationalist left then it might have been able to take advantage of the contradictions in the situation. However the left was in considerable disarray. The major working-class parties were a consistently reformist Socialist Party and a Communist Party which combined left nationalism with obedience to the Kremlin.

The smaller currents on the left may have been more principled, but they lacked the ability to intervene effectively. *La Révolution prolétarienne* suspended publication at the outbreak of war. Its final issue contained a brief piece by Robert Louzon commenting on the Hitler-Stalin Pact of August 1939. The world situation, he argued, was now clear: 'on the one side, all the totalitarian powers: Russia, Germany, Italy; on the other our poor old capitalist "democracies" whose impotence and incapacity become clearer every day'. It was unclear whether there would be a war, but in any case there had been a major historical turning-point: this was 'the collapse of the West'. Europe would no longer dominate the world as it had done for the last four centuries.[3] Prophetic as this was in the long term, in the short term Monatte and friends had no alternative strategy or organisation to offer.

As for the assorted anarchist groupings, their historian David Berry recounts that they 'were not practically prepared for dealing with war or occupation and simply disappeared, as did their newspapers'.[4]

The formation of the PSOP had raised high hopes, but they soon faded. The PSOP lacked either the organisational coherence or the political clarity to make any decisive intervention in the face of impending war. By the summer of 1940 the PSOP had, in the words of Maurice Jaquier, 'vanished into thin air'.[5]

The followers of Trotsky found themselves operating with a mistaken perspective. Leon Trotsky had a powerful political brain, but he did not have a

---

2 Chauvin 2006, pp. 141–7.
3 Louzon 1939.
4 Berry 2002, p. 256.
5 Quoted by Kergoat, 1994, p. 166.

supernatural ability to predict the future, something his followers sometimes failed to recognise. In the last two years of his life he gave his supporters a fundamentally false perspective which would mislead them during and after the war.

Trotsky's position was resolutely internationalist. He rejected national defence in favour of 'the Socialist United States of Europe as a stage on the road to the Socialist United States of the World'. He rejected any notion of taking sides in the war. 'The victory of the imperialists of Great Britain and France would not be less frightful for the ultimate fate of mankind than that of Hitler and Mussolini'.[6] Before dismissing this as obvious ultra-leftism, we should balance the victims of Nazism during its short life against the victims of imperialism in the half-century after 1945. However this was combined with a false appraisal of the world situation. Like so many Marxists before and after him, Trotsky underestimated the resilience of capitalism. In his *Manifesto of the Fourth International on the Imperialist War and the Proletarian World Revolution* of May 1940 he gave a gloomy prognosis for the outcome of the war:

> All countries will come out of the war so ruined that the standard of living for the workers will be thrown back a hundred years. Reformist unions are possible only under the regime of bourgeois democracy. But the first to be vanquished in the war will be the thoroughly rotten democracy. In its definitive downfall it will drag with it all the workers' organisations which serve as its support. Capitalist reaction will destroy them ruthlessly.[7]

In short, reformism was dead. Its leading protagonists would be buried alongside it:

> Attlee and Pollitt, Blum and Thorez work in the same harness. In case of war the last remaining distinctions between them will vanish. All of them together with bourgeois society as a whole will be crushed under the wheel of history.[8]

In fact at the end of the war Attlee and Blum both achieved prime ministerial office, while Thorez and Pollitt saw their parties grow to a greater size than ever previously. Trotsky failed to offer any real indication of a strategy which would enable the tiny Trotskyist current to relate to the broad anti-fascist movement

---

6   Trotsky 1973, p. 221.
7   Trotsky 1973, p. 213.
8   Trotsky 1973, p. 43.

that would emerge in occupied Europe. The movement entered the war with no real base, and ended it little better off.

As for the Communist Party, it had its own problems. Just before the outbreak of war Stalin's Russia and Hitler's Germany had signed a non-aggression pact. It is now difficult to imagine just what a shock the pact was for everyone on the left, inside or outside the PCF. From the point of view of the Russian state there was a certain justification for the pact; France and Britain were appeasing Nazi Germany and Stalin believed that the West wanted to encourage German aggression against Russia. For workers and anti-fascist activists in France things looked very different. For nearly five years the PCF's strategy had been centred on the idea of the Popular Front; it had argued tirelessly that the struggle against fascism must take priority over everything else, including the struggle for socialism, which could be postponed until later. It had presented itself as a party of republican nationalism, of the tradition of 1789, of *laïcité*, and on that basis it had increased its membership considerably, attracting recruits as the most consistent fighter against fascism.

Now party members were told that their loyalty must be, not to the political traditions of their own nation, but to an international affiliation. It was a paradoxical kind of internationalism, commitment not to the international working class – whose interests were barely served by a diplomatic boost for Hitler's Germany – but to the foreign policy of the Russian state.

This provoked a terrible internal crisis. 25 out of 72 PCF deputies resigned from the party. Once war was declared, prime minister Daladier took the opportunity to make the PCF illegal. [Just three years earlier Daladier had been a member of the Popular Front government backed by the PCF.] Many PCF members left the party, no longer seeing it as leading the opposition to fascism; others were victims of state repression or isolated from contact with the party after being called up into the armed forces. The party, which a couple of years earlier had seemed to be at its strongest yet, was now in serious disarray.[9]

The first few months of war were relatively uneventful; this period became known as the 'phoney war'. Many socialist activists were conscripted. France had a long tradition – going back to the *sou du soldat* – of socialist agitation inside the armed forces, and there were various attempts at such activity. In the confused atmosphere of the period it was often unclear what form such activity should take. If the general mood in the army was relatively favourable to subversive propaganda, it was not at all clear what demands it was appropriate to raise. Jean-René Chauvin was conscripted into the army and was immedi-

---

9 Robrieux 1980, p. 504.

ately warned that his political record as a Trotskyist was known and that if he made any propaganda he would be sent to a court martial. Although his fellow-soldiers knew his reputation, he was unable to go beyond minor gestures of revolt like failing to salute an officer.[10] One Trotskyist, the poet Benjamin Péret, was given a post in military intelligence, where he managed to create chaos by switching files.[11] He was later imprisoned.

1   Nazi Occupation

When the German offensive came, in May 1940, it was quick and effective. For the third time in a single human lifespan [1870, 1914, 1940] German forces were threatening Paris. The spread of rumours and press censorship which suppressed news of the actual military situation led to confusion and panic. To many people the simplest solution seemed to be flight. By the summer of 1940 there were some 8 million refugees on the roads of France. During the phoney war the left, and especially the organised labour movement, had been in disarray; the CGT effectively split again when Communists were excluded after the Hitler-Stalin pact. Now the whole country was plunged into chaos.[12]

It was not clear what was going on; whatever it was, it was not a united nation facing an invader. French society was deeply divided, socially, politically and ideologically. A small but not insignificant minority was preparing to give the invader an enthusiastic welcome, believing that a bit of Hitlerite discipline was what the working class – and the Jews – were in need of. Others, while not politically committed to Nazism, were prepared to give it a positive response. Many more, seeing their own national leaders divided and ambivalent, were confused. Those who did not understand what was going on were justifiably frightened. Those who did know what was going on were even more frightened.

This was a society deeply divided by race and class. France had an ethnically diverse population. There were migrant workers of many origins, and refugees fleeing the rise of fascism in Italy, Germany and Spain. There were workers from Indochina, brought to France as cheap labour. Students from North Africa and Indochina were concerned with human rights in their native lands. All, knowing Nazi beliefs on racial purity, had cause for alarm. Jews had every reason to believe that they were in serious danger.

---

10   Chauvin 2006, pp. 69–71.
11   Craipeau 1999, p. 155.
12   See Risser 2012.

The most important dividing line was class, or even more crudely, wealth. To have money – and perhaps a friend in the right place – could make those terrible days a bit easier. Car owners – a smaller privileged group than in later decades – could flee more rapidly than those on foot, at least if they could get hold of some petrol.

Amid the chaos it would take months before the French population could grasp what occupation meant. The National Assembly surrendered its powers into the hands of Marshal Pétain. France was divided into two main zones, an Occupied Zone in the North, and a Southern zone, governed from the spa town of Vichy, normally a resort for the privileged élite. In November 1942 the Southern zone was also occupied by German forces.

Hatred of Jews had been intrinsic to Hitler's doctrine from the very beginning. As soon as the occupation of France began, the Germans started to impose their racial policies. They required strict control of the Demarcation Line between the two zones, in order to enforce the exclusion of Jews from the Occupied Zone. German border guards sent back entire trains if they were carrying a single Jewish person.

There were some 300,000 Jews in France. This Jewish population was divided by class and origin; some were well integrated into French society, while others were recent Yiddish-speaking immigrants, some of them naturalised French citizens.[13] But the racist nationalism of Vichy defined them as other, so the defence of all Jews became a priority for any French internationalist.

To grasp the complexities of this horrific situation it is necessary to make certain qualifications. There was not, in 1940, a clear and coherent plan leading directly to the Holocaust. The German functionaries who were now occupying France were corrupt and divided, with factions and individuals jostling for power. There was open hostility between the army and the secret police. The exact details of policy towards the French Jews remained to be elaborated.

Above all, it was not a question of anti-Semitic Germans imposing their policies on reluctant French underlings. Quite the contrary. The Nazis worked closely with French anti-Semites who were sometimes more enthusiastic and took the initiative. As early as October 1940 Vichy authorised prefects to intern Jews and foreigners in special camps when the Nazis had not yet demanded any such thing.[14]

The anti-dreyfusards had been defeated, but they had not gone away. They had maintained their organisations – the Action Française produced a daily

13   Drake 2015, pp. 128 ff.
14   Chauvin 2006, p. 149.

paper and sold it in public throughout the twenties and thirties. They had suffered the indignities of living under not only a left-wing government, but a Jewish prime minister; now they sensed that the tide was turning.

There were two conflicts: a struggle for French national independence against the conquering foreign invader, and an internationalist struggle against fascism and in defence of Jews against persecution, internment and deportation. There was an overlap, but they were not identical. The divisions between different sections of the French population were at least as important as those between the invaders and the native population; this remained true as the occupation continued.

As German troops overran France in 1940 there was widespread panic. While many women feared rape by Germans, they were often coerced into sex with members of the French army. It gave an ironic twist to Liebknecht's warning that the main enemy is at home.[15]

When the German occupation and Vichy rule were established, it became clear that anti-Semitism was being vigorously promoted by native French Jew-haters. Vichy's first anti-Semitic laws, which stripped some Jews of French citizenship and barred them from various professions, were introduced without any pressure from the Germans. The French police rounded up Jews and staffed the camps they were detained in.

Anti-Semitism was deeply ingrained in sections of the French population, and Nazi policies enjoyed considerable popularity. David Drake, who has researched the German occupation, has found a number of letters sent by Parisians to the authorities, denouncing their neighbours as Jews and for being in breach of the anti-Semitic regulations. Such letters show the depths to which so-called respectable people could sink.[16]

As opposition to the occupiers began to grow it became clear that Resistance fighters in France were fighting against occupying German troops, but also against their own compatriots – the pro-Nazi collaborators occupying parts of the state machine of their native land. Anyone who joined the Resistance came up against the Vichy state. Often it was French police and militiamen who handed over Resisters to the Gestapo [German secret police], or tortured them themselves. The Resistance had a considerable element of civil war about it.

One of the worst atrocities of the Nazi occupation was the massacre at Oradour-sur-Glane in June 1944, when 642 civilians were murdered, many

---

15   Risser 2012, pp. 128–9.
16   Drake 2015, p. 276.

burned alive. When some of those responsible were put on trial in 1953, 14 out of 21 were from Alsace, which had been incorporated into Germany in 1940, but was restored to France at the end of the war. They had thus grown up as French citizens and were French again when they were on trial. This is just one example among many of how problematic it is to see the Occupation and Resistance in terms of national identities.

Initially there was no political force able to lead resistance. The PCF was entangled by the Hitler-Stalin Pact. According to the Comintern analysis, the war between Britain and Germany, from which France had now withdrawn, was an imperialist war in which Britain was the main aggressor.[17] Thus the PCF had no particular quarrel with the Germans. It had been banned by the government of the Third Republic and it stayed banned.

The PCF now made approaches to the German occupying powers, asking for it to be allowed to publish its press, in particular *L'Humanité*, legally. This got nowhere, but it was not wholly unrealistic; Communist publications did appear legally in Belgium and elsewhere.[18] This approach was not publicly admitted until 1967.[19]

The Comintern line made some headway in the initial period of the war. Only a tiny minority were prepared to take the full consequences of the view that it was an imperialist war, like those PCF members who were executed for sabotaging their own country's military equipment. For many more the argument had a certain plausibility. The rapid collapse of the French armed forces in face of Hitler, and the absence of resistance when the Germans entered Paris, indicates that the PCF line corresponded to a certain aspect of the consciousness of the population. In July 1940 the clandestine *L'Humanité* noted with satisfaction that 'many Parisian workers could be seen conversing amiably with the German soldiers'.[20] Certainly there was a widespread bourgeois defeatism, which preferred firm government under the Nazis to any further threat from the left of the sort that had erupted in 1936; there was also a feeling among some workers that the present society was not worth defending, and that things would be no worse under the Germans. They learned that this was not the case when the occupying Germans banned strikes and froze wages.

Much of the SFIO had endorsed Pétain [90 SFIO deputies and senators voted for Pétain, while only 36 voted against]; the smaller groups of the left were in disarray. Such resistance as did emerge was often spontaneous. The first acts

---

17   See Degras 1971, Volume III, pp. 462–5.
18   Robrieux 1980, p. 510.
19   Institut Maurice Thorez 1967, p. 73.
20   Thourel 1980, p. 244.

came from isolated individuals and the fightback often started around economic rather than political issues. The coal strike of May 1941 in North-Eastern
France, the first major struggle against the occupiers involving 100,000 miners,
began with demands for money, bread and soup. Strikes continued during the
occupation, and although employers got support from the German authorities,
some struggles were won, for example against the imposition of Sunday working in the mines.[21]

In the aftermath of the occupation it was often claimed, by both Communists and Gaullists, that the vast mass of the French population had backed the
Resistance. Later an opposing myth gained ground, that the majority had actively collaborated. Both views are misleading. David Drake has concluded from
his study of the realities of life in occupied Paris that there was a small minority of heroic resisters, and an equally small minority of active collaborators.
The majority of the population just aimed to 'survive increasing hardship and
deprivation while making as few compromises as they could'.[22]

While French anti-Semites actively encouraged Nazi policies, there were
also courageous French internationalists who defended persecuted Jews. From
May 1942 all Jews, including children, were required to wear yellow stars when
they went out in public; there was widespread sympathy from the Parisian population, resisting attempts to exclude Jews from shops. Some non-Jews decided
to wear stars too in solidarity – often with facetious labels like 'Auvergnat' [nat-
ive of the Auvergne, a rural region in central France], thus implying that Jews
were just as French as those originating from a French province. Some protest-
ers were sent to the camps where Jews were held. Those interned came from a
range of backgrounds: 'a respectable, middle-class lady in her late fifties, who
had worn a yellow star with a crucifix on it; a post-office employee engaged to
a Jew; a couple of office-workers; a secretary; and a female newspaper-seller,
who had tied a yellow star to her dog's tail'.[23] There were a number of illegal
demonstrations.

One of the most remarkable aspects of internationalist solidarity with persecuted Jews was the protection of the so-called 'hidden children', Jewish children whose parents had disappeared into the camps and who were adopted in
French rural villages. A million and a half children, mainly Jewish, died at the
hands of the Nazis.

Suzanne Weiss, now resident in Canada, has attempted to find out something of how she was protected as a two-year-old. Her mother, a Jew from

---

21   See Cushion 2006.
21   See Cushion 2006.
22   Drake 2015, p. 427.
23   Drake 2015, p. 260.

Poland, was sent to Auschwitz, where she died. Suzanne was taken to the Auvergne and was sheltered by a peasant family; individuals and whole communities played a part in protecting refugees and especially children.

Historian Floriane Barbier explains that the entire community helped in different ways to protect the fugitive children. 'Hidden children took part in community life, going to school, celebrating Christmas, and in other activities'. Support, at least passive, was remarkably widespread. Local police often turned a blind eye. Sometimes when the Vichy authorities were planning a raid, sympathisers within the administration would leak information. 'There was a group of German soldiers in Le Chambon being treated for wounds. They told local people that they knew there were Jews here, but they did not tell their officers'. Most of the Jews in Auvergne survived. Le Chambon became a village in which a quarter of the children were Jewish.[24]

Although some Muslims sympathised with the Nazis as their enemy's enemy, others recognised that Jews were the victims of Nazism just as Muslims were victims of colonialism, and showed them solidarity. While the details remain contested, it seems clear that the rector of the Grande Mosquée in Paris, Si Kaddour Benghrabit, used his position to shelter Jews in the building.[25]

2 Resistance

As resistance to the occupation began to emerge, it initially took the form of small groupings, generally made up largely of intellectuals. One of these was *Socialisme et Liberté* [Socialism and Freedom], in which the most prominent figure was philosopher Jean-Paul Sartre. After the French defeat Sartre was a prisoner of war, but early in 1941 he returned to Paris. He made contact with a group called *Sous la botte* [Under the Jackboot] set up by Maurice Merleau-Ponty. The group initially brought together Sartre's friends and associates.

By June 1941 the group had some fifty members, mostly students and teachers, divided into cells of five. It was oriented towards discussion rather than mass propaganda or armed struggle. This must be put in the context of the disarray of the French left; it was necessary to start rebuilding from scratch. It looked quite probable that Germany would win the war, and that the occupation would last for a generation or more.

---

24 Weiss 2015. See also Weiss 2019.
25 Katz 2012.

Though the group had little in the way of activity, it did consider the important question of what attitude to take towards rank-and-file German soldiers. At a presentation in 2008 three former members of Socialisme et Liberté recounted their memories of the organisation, and Dominique Desanti recalled that she had given out leaflets to German soldiers on the métro [during the Occupation first-class compartments were reserved for German soldiers].[26] This must have been one of the earliest attempts to distribute propaganda to German workers in uniform.

Quite a few former revolutionary syndicalists, including some who had played a prominent and creditable role in the antimilitarist struggle before and during the First World War, ended up engaging in collaboration in one form or another with the Nazi occupiers.

This requires careful explanation. The various instances of syndicalists becoming collaborators should be examined on a case-by-case basis rather than as examples of some generalised phenomenon. They can be understood only in the context of the specific historical circumstances in which they took place.

One of the saddest yet most reprehensible instances was that of Maurice Wullens. In World War I Wullens had fought in the trenches and had become a prisoner-of-war, of which he wrote a moving account, describing how he had come to see his German captors as workers like himself [see chapter 6].

In the interwar period he produced a journal, *Les Humbles*, which was of the left but firmly anti-Stalinist; he campaigned in defence of Victor Serge, and Trotsky contributed an article to the issue on Marcel Martinet.[27] He became a member of the Parti d'unité prolétarienne, which brought together various ex-members of the PCF and which joined the SFIO in 1937. He remained haunted by memories of the First World War, and for him the avoidance of war overrode all other political questions. In the late thirties he remained on the far left – he was a member of the FIARI and he signed the leaflet 'Paix immédiate' [Immediate Peace], but his concern to avoid war led him to be less critical of Nazi Germany; in 1938 Victor Serge considered that some of the things he had published were too sympathetic towards Nazi Germany and broke with him.[28] Despite his pacifism he turned up for the call-up in 1939, aged 45, and criticised Jean Giono for encouraging conscientious objection.[29]

---

26   Birchall 2008b.

27   Trotsky 1936.

28   Serge 2001, p. 792.

29   Maitron and Pennetier 1964–2023 article135428, notice WULLENS Maurice par Jean Prugnot, version mise en ligne le 30 novembre 2010, dernière modification le 30 novembre 2010.

Under the Occupation he advocated *rapprochement* with the Nazi Third Reich and contributed articles to the collaborationist and openly anti-Semitic press, for example *Je suis partout* or Drieu La Rochelle's *Révolution nationale* – notably an article on the death of Marcel Martinet to the latter journal. He was denounced by the Resistance but by the time of the Liberation he was in poor health and bed-ridden, and was not prosecuted; he died in February 1945.

Wullens' conduct cannot be explained by cowardice or corruption nor yet by a change of heart. Rather he allowed his profound anti-war feelings to override his judgement on other matters. While he was scarcely innocent he was in some sense a victim of a historical period whose contradictions were too much for him.

Georges Yvetôt was a leading actitivist in the CGT before 1914, and a prominent representative of French syndicalism in the international movement. He was particularly involved in antimilitarist activity, for which he was repeatedly arrested and more than once imprisoned. In 1942 he became president of the *Comité ouvrier de secours immédiat* [workers' committee for immediate aid], which helped working families affected by allied bombing and was generally regarded as a collaborationist organisation. He was now old and in poor health, and died shortly afterwards.[30]

There was one other possibility for those unwilling to collaborate and unwilling or unable to engage in Resistance, namely emigration. There was not much scope left in Europe – even Britain's future hung in the balance, but Hitler was unlikely to invade North America. Southern France was not yet occupied by the Germans, and in 1941 various anti-fascists gathered in Marseille in the hope of getting a boat to the American continent.

Americans Dwight and Nancy Macdonald set up an Emergency Rescue Committee to enable refugee intellectuals to make their way to North America – those who could not enter the USA for political reasons went to Mexico or the Caribbean. They were represented in Marseille by Varian Fry, a heroic individual who did much to enable European intellectuals to escape death at the hands of the Nazis, together with Daniel Bénédite, a former member of the Gauche révolutionnaire who helped hundreds of refugees to escape from occupied Europe.[31] Victor Serge, surrealist poet André Breton and anthropologist Claude Lévi-Strauss all crossed the Atlantic on the same boat.[32]

---

30   Maitron and Pennetier 1964–2023 article135463, notice YVETOT Georges, Louis, François par Henri Dubief, version mise en ligne le 30 novembre 2010, dernière modification le 6 février 2020.

31   Maitron and Pennetier 1964–2023 article16229, notice BÉNÉDITE Daniel [UNGEMACH, Daniel, Pierre dit]. Pseudonyme dans la Résistance: CORBLET, Marcel par Laurent Jean-pierre, version mise en ligne le 20 octobre 2008, dernière modification le 19 juin 2019.

32   Serge, 2012, pp. 57–87.

On 22 June 1941 everything changed. Stalin's erstwhile German allies cast the pact aside as a worthless piece of paper. German troops made their way into Russian territory. For French Communists it was immediately obvious that the nature of the war had been transformed and that Germany was the main enemy. Emotions were mixed. There must have been a considerable degree of apprehension. Hitler was evil but not stupid; he would not have undertaken the invasion without some reasonable belief in the possibility of success. Other French Communists may have had a sense of relief. The divided loyalty experienced by many Communists – class struggle versus allegiance to Moscow – was now a thing of the past.

The entry into the war of Russia – and of the USA a few months later after Pearl Harbour – made it clear that this was a world war and that it would be fought to a finish. Those under Nazi occupation who had had illusions that the Germans might not be that bad were beginning to learn the truth. In the occupied countries resistance movements, hitherto fairly small groupings, received a massive input of energy from the Communists and their supporters. A layer of workers extending far beyond the ranks of organised Stalinism looked to Russia as a source of salvation, and were inspired by the heroic resistance put up by the Russian armed forces and civilians against the German invasion.

3   The Communist Party

Now the French Communist Party threw its full weight into opposing the occupation. It faced a situation where the Germans took hostages and executed them in retaliation for acts of violence. Resisters were not recognised as prisoners of war. The PCF mobilised its members for direct action against the occupying forces. Initially this involved mainly its youth organisation, which had received no serious training, and some very young men were executed.[33]

The Communist slogan 'Chacun son boche' [Let everybody kill a Kraut] invited the assassination of individual German soldiers. On some occasions Resisters would ask a German soldier in the street for a light, then shoot him. The Germans responded with savage reprisals – ten or twenty Resisters were executed for each soldier killed.

The Communists provoked Nazi repression, because this made it easier to encourage supporters to engage in armed struggle. They needed martyrs. The German authorities responded by denouncing Resistance fighters as terrorists

---

33   Drake 2015, pp. 204–5, 215–7. 227.

and common-law criminals who did not deserve to be treated as prisoners of war – just as the French had treated those who opposed their rule in Indochina and other colonies.

The strategy was initially introduced at Russian instigation. Many PCF members were unhappy, feeling individual attacks to be alien to French socialist traditions. According to historian Philippe Robrieux 'it took several months to convince Communist militants to take action ... It was difficult to persuade Communist militants to agree to kill Germans at random'.[34] Some were happy to assassinate officers, but were against random killing of rank-and-file soldiers. Internationalist traditions clearly survived within the PCF's membership.

PCF tactics ignored the fact that most German soldiers were working-class conscripts, and that the German working class had been Hitler's first victim. It was only twenty years since the great revolutionary wave of 1918–23 in Germany. Many soldiers remembered these events, or knew of them through their families.

There were other forms of resistance more in keeping with the PCF's working-class traditions, especially in the form of economic sabotage. Workers brought their skills to the movement. Miners experienced in working with explosives stole dynamite from their pits and used it, for example to blow up electricity pylons. Engine-drivers developed a method of derailing trains that did maximum damage to the carriages while giving the driver and fireman a good chance of surviving.[35]

One example of internationalism in the PCF was the Paris engineering worker Jean-Pierre Timbaud. Timbaud had joined the Communist Youth in 1922, and during his military service campaigned against the war in Morocco. In 1933 he led a 35- day strike at the Citroën factory, with a massive growth in union membership. In 1937 he was part of a metalworkers' delegation to Spain, taking money collected in the factories. In 1940 he left the army illegally, and was interned on his return to Paris. In October 1941 he was executed along with other prisoners in retaliation for the killing of a German officer by the Resistance.

His final letter combined the PCF line with commitment to his internationalist roots: 'Long live France! Long live the international proletariat!' As he prepared to die he shouted 'Long Live the German Communist Party' – a remarkable internationalist gesture.[36]

---

34   Robrieux 1980, pp. 529–30.
35   Cushion 2006.
36   Monjauvis, 1971, pp. 110, 157.

The politics of the PCF leadership were completely aligned with Stalin's régime in Russia. Russia wanted the opening of a second front in the West to reduce the military pressure, and in the meantime any activity which tied down German troops in the West was welcome. While terror tactics by the Resistance in France and other occupied countries would lead to increased repression hopefully they would win more support for the Resistance.

If specific tactics can be attributed to the PCF's Stalinism, its overall strategy in the Resistance – which enabled it to achieve political hegemony and to recruit rapidly during and after the war – derived from the Popular Front. This coincided with the current line of the Communist International and the Communist movement after its dissolution – but it had much deeper roots in the traditions of the French left. The Popular Front was the direct continuation of Jacobin nationalism, and France was the homeland of the Popular Front [see chapter 8]. The PCF was able to convince its supporters that the Resistance was essentially a national liberation struggle against foreign invaders, often encouraging the crudest nationalist rhetoric. The war was seen as a re-enactment of the conflicts of 1870 and 1914–18.

French Communists who, twenty years earlier, had listened enthusiastically to Clara Zetkin and Rosi Wolfstein and waited eagerly for news from Germany of a rising which would begin a new phase of the European revolution, now dismissed their German sisters and brothers as 'boches'.

Yet in reality anyone who joined the Resistance came up against the Vichy state, staffed by French collaborators who rounded up Jews and handed over Resisters to the Gestapo, or tortured them. As Daniel Guérin had shown, it was Germans – especially Communists, trade unionists and assorted leftists, who were Hitler's first victims. The German soldiers shot down by the Resistance were often unwilling conscripts.

The PCF did not entirely neglect this dimension of the struggle. It recognised the need for propaganda directed towards rank-and-file German soldiers; it offered safe-conduct passes to soldiers who were transferred to the Eastern Front and might then desert. This was conceived in terms of a military strategy to weaken the enemy forces rather than as an attempt to see workers in uniform as a potential ally against the French and German ruling classes. The PCF distributed far more propaganda aimed at German troops than the small groupings of the revolutionary left; yet what they produced fell within the normal framework of military propaganda aimed at demoralising enemy forces.

4   International Resistance

If the French Resistance was a civil war, it was also an international struggle. At the Liberation both Communists and the followers of General de Gaulle did what they could to define the Resistance as a French national movement. The fact that tens of thousands of foreigners of various nationalities had fought against the occupiers was largely forgotten and written out of history; only many years later the hidden history of international participation in the Resistance began to be rediscovered.[37] Out of a population of 42 million in France at the start of the war, there were some two million foreigners, above all Spanish, Italian and Polish;[38] many became involved in the Resistance.

Firstly there were a significant number of Germans fighting against the occupiers. Many Germans, especially Communists and Jews, had left Germany when Hitler came to power; some had come to France, others had gone to fight in Spain and, after the defeat of the Republic, had escaped to France. Facing the prospect of being rounded up by the Nazis, they had gone to join the groups of Resisters, the only refuge for those on the run. There were some 30,000 German-speaking refugees in France.

They were integrated into the Resistance, occupying positions of trust. If German refugees fighting with the Resistance were captured by the Gestapo they could expect brutal treatment. French Resisters would often put themselves at considerable risk to defend German comrades.

Within the MOI [Main d'Oeuvre Immigrée: Immigrant Labour Force, formed in the 1920s: see chapter 7] the PCF established what became known as the 'Travail allemand' [German work]. This consisted of the organisation of German speakers from central Europe – many Austrian, many Jewish. The aim was to penetrate the German armed forces, to obtain information, and beyond that to challenge Nazi ideology and encourage support for peace among German soliders; the ultimate object was to sabotage the German army from within. German-language papers were produced, aimed at occupying troops.

As anti-Nazi campaigning this was positive and sometimes successful. Yet there was frequently a contradiction within the ranks of the Resisters. For the PCF the overriding aim was the national struggle and the liberation of France from foreign occupation. But as it became clear that Hitler was headed for defeat, the Germans and other refugees from central Europe became more focussed on the perspective of establishing new regimes in the post-war period.[39]

---

37   See for example Peschanski 2002, Moos and Cushion 2020.
38   Peschanski 2002, p. 17.
39   Collin 2008.

Many Spanish veterans of the Civil War had escaped at the time of Franco's victory. If they crossed the Pyrenees into France they were interned by the French government; when the French Republic collapsed, they had little alternative but to join the Resistance.

Africans and others from the French Empire, though lacking the rights of French citizenship, took part in the armed struggle against fascism. At the beginning of the war in 1939 Indochinese workers had been brought to France, as a source of cheap labour at a time when French workers were being called up into the army. Some were forced to do excavation work at starvation wages. When fighting ended in 1940 they were put into internment camps. Here they often made contact with the French working-class movement; in particular the Trotskyists were involved in establishing contacts with the Indochinese camps. Some made their way to the Resistance.

One of the national groups in the Resistance, which helped give it its internationalist texture, was that of the Armenians. There have been books,[40] films, poems and songs about the exploits and tragic end of the group led by Missak Manouchian.

Manouchian survived the Armenian genocide of 1915 in the Ottoman Empire, in which his parents perished. He came to France in 1925 and got a job as a lathe operator in a Citroën factory. He became involved in trade-union activity as a CGT member, and in 1934 joined the French Communist Party. He rapidly became active in one of the organisations which the PCF set up for immigrant workers. A talented organiser and writer, between 1935 and 1937 he edited an Armenian-language weekly paper called *Zangou* [named after an Armenian river]; this was closely aligned on Communist Party policies, being anti-fascist, pro-Russian and strongly committed to the Republican cause in Spain.

During the German occupation he became the political chief of the Armenian section of the MOI. In February 1943 he was transferred to the FTP-MOI [Francs-tireurs et partisans – irregulars and partisans], a Resistance group of gunfighters and saboteurs consisting of foreign Communists under the direct discipline of the Comintern. By the summer of 1943 he was leader of the FTP-MOI, commanding three detachments, a total of about 50 fighters, Eastern European Jews and anti-fascists from Spain and Italy.

In military terms they proved very effective. In September 1943 they assassinated General Julius Ritter, a leading organiser of the deportation of workers under the Compulsory Work Service whereby over 600,000 French workers were sent to work in Germany. They carried out nearly 30 successful attacks,

---

40   See Robrieux 1986, especially bibliographical survey pp. 353–429.

while maintaining a certain degree of political independence. On one occasion they refused to plant a bomb in a brothel used by German soldiers because they did not want to kill innocent civilians.[41]

In November 1943 the French police arrested members of the Manouchian group. They were tortured by the French, and handed over to the Germans. Following a show trial Manouchian and 21 others were executed in February 1944.

The Manouchian group acquired a legendary status, and efforts were made to co-opt them for the myth of the French Resistance. The PCF poet Louis Aragon wrote a tribute to them which claimed 'twenty-three shouted France as they fell'.[42] This seems unlikely. The last letters of sixteen of the group, written just hours before their deaths, have been preserved.[43] They are a powerful testimony to the courage of their authors, but very few mention France. Manouchian and his comrades died for freedom and the fight against fascism. As immigrant workers who had undoubtedly experienced oppression in France and at the hands of French people, before and during the war, their commitment was to internationalist social ideals, not to a national struggle. The role of the FTP-MOI was certainly an important internationalist element of the anti-fascist struggle, but it was only a small strand in the predominantly nationalist politics of the PCF in the Resistance.

One of the members of the group was Arben Tavitian [or Davidian], who had served with the Red Army in the Caucasus. He had become a member of the Left Opposition and was expelled from the party and imprisoned, but managed to escape and find his way to France, where he made contact with Leon Sedov, Trotsky's son, and with *La Révolution prolétarienne*. He became a member of Manouchian's group and took part in its military activities. Manouchian knew of his anti-Stalinist past, but was keen to involve him – perhaps an indication of Manouchian's own political independence. Tavitian was shot alongside his comrades in February 1944.[44]

5   Trotskyism

To the left of the Communist Party there were a variety of groupings and tendencies which opposed fascism from an internationalist position. Generally they

---

41   According to Robert Guédiguian's film Army of Crime [2009].

42   Aragon 1955.

43   Manouchian Group 1944.

44   Maitron and Pennetier 1964–2023 article73527, notice MANOUKIAN Armenak [DAV'TIAN Arben, Abramovitch, dit TAVITIAN (Holban), dit DAVIDIAN (SGE), dit ANDRE] par Rodolphe Prager, version mise en ligne le 25 août 2009, dernière modification le 12 mars 2020.

were very hostile to Stalinism and the USSR, and opposed all manifestations of nationalism, insisting that the main enemy was at home and that the primary task was to fight their own ruling class. Generally they were isolated and lacking in resources, so the existence of such groupings was often ephemeral.[45]

One example was the group around Pavel and Clara Thalmann. Of Swiss origin, they had supported the anarchist Durrutti Column in Spain before moving to Paris for the period of the German occupation. They had a large house in which they sheltered Jews and others persecuted by the authorities, and they produced and distributed leaflets and a journal called *Le Réveil prolétarien* [proletarian awakening]. They gave material support to Martin Monath and *Arbeiter und Soldat* [see below], but refused to join the Trotskyists. The fundamental points of their position were that the USSR was a new imperialist state, that the workers' movement needed to be rebuilt, independently of Bolshevism, and that 'the present war is an imperialist war in which revolutionaries cannot take part on either side'.[46]

The main current which defended internationalist ideas in this period was Trotskyism. Alongside the mass organisation of the Resistance in which the Communist Party played a central role the French Trotskyists may seem insignificant. They were numbered in hundreds rather than thousands and had no military achievements to their credit. Yet their story deserves a hearing. A number of individuals showed remarkable courage and capacity for self-sacrifice. From the Bolsheviks they had inherited an intransigent internationalism. From repeated attacks at the hands of their Stalinist adversaries they had learned to defend proletarian democracy.

At the outbreak of war the Trotskyists were weak and disorientated; in conditions of defeat, illegality and political isolation they had to rebuild their organisations almost from scratch. Yet despite their small numbers they had some significant achievements. Certainly the Gestapo took them seriously enough. At least a hundred were arrested, and a number died, mainly after being deported to concentration camps. Yvan Craipeau narrowly escaped the French plainclothes police by hitting one of them on the chin with the *Complete Works* of Oscar Wilde, then running away despite getting a bullet in the buttock.[47]

Slowly the fragments of the Trotskyist movement began to move towards establishing a unified organisation. The pre-war Parti Ouvrier Internationaliste [POI], which had been deeply divided by entry into the PSOP, regrouped by the end of 1942. Its membership was only about 300 to 400, almost all under the

---

45   See Rayner 1989.
46   Thalmann 1997, pp. 230 etc.
47   Craipeau 1999, p. 169.

age of 25. It had a clandestine printing press in the cellar of a suburban villa near Paris, and its paper *La Vérité* [truth] appeared regularly.

Militants of the pre-war Parti Communiste Internationaliste came together to form the Comité Communiste Internationaliste pour la Construction de la IVe Internationale [CCI], which published the paper *La Seule Voie* [the only road]. The Octobre group, which had evolved out of the pre-war Abondanciste movement [the followers of Jacques Duboin who argued that technology made abundance for all a practical possibility] developed towards Trotskyist positions. The Lutte de Classes group had broken from the rest of the French Trotskyist movement in 1940, over its insistence on tighter organisational forms and what it saw as the nationalist deviations of other Trotskyists.

Early in 1944 the POI, CCI and Octobre groups united into a single organisation, the Parti Communiste Internationaliste [PCI], which became the French section of the Fourth International. Only the Lutte de Classes group stood aside from the unification. International contacts were difficult to maintain in wartime conditions. The International Secretariat ceased to function. Its tasks were taken on by the European Secretariat set up by Marcel Hic during the war, and led by Michel Pablo after Hic's death in a Nazi concentration camp.

Even when the Nazis appeared triumphant there were signs of resistance in various parts of Europe. From the February 1941 general strike in Amsterdam to the Warsaw Ghetto uprising, the French and Belgian workers' strikes against deportations to Germany and the strike movements in northern Italy which brought down Mussolini, hundreds of thousands of people took action in face of extreme repression.

These struggles lent some credibility to the Trotskyists' hopes that the conclusion of the Second World War would coincide with a revolutionary upheaval as great as that which had followed the end of the 1914–18 conflict. Civil war seemed to be rapidly approaching. In retrospect much that was written by the Trotskyists appears over-optimistic, projecting the hope that the war's end would lead to a re-enactment of 1917. In the short term the central question was the orientation to the German working class.

The Trotskyists hoped a German defeat could lead to a workers' uprising. In contrast to the PCF vilification of Germans as 'boches', the illegal Trotskyist press adopted as a basic principle 'We are the friends of the German people, that is why we fight Hitlerism'.[48] The aim was not to physically attack or demoralise German workers in uniform, but rather to try to make them aware of their potential strength and of their common interests with French workers. The

---

48   *La Vérité*, 15 October 1940, quoted by Horn 1989, p. 57.

Trotskyists saw the German working class as the victims of Nazism, and recalled in their propaganda that only twenty years earlier Germany had seemed to be on the brink of socialist revolution. While for the PCF German soldiers were seen simply as agents of fascism, to the Trotskyists German workers, often unwillingly in uniform, were potential allies. The Nazi authorities regarded the potential for fraternisation as a serious threat and a number of executions ensued.

The French Trotskyists always put the possibility of a German revolution at the centre of their perspective. As *La Vérité* argued, terrorism created a barrier between French workers and German soldiers, whereas victory required unity between them.[49] They succeeded in producing illegal publications throughout the period of the occupation. Historian Jacqueline Pluet-Despatin has identified over thirty publications that can be identified as Trotskyist from this period, though of necessity some were short-lived.[50]

If the attitude to German workers in uniform was a central question, and one which differentiated the Trotskyists from the PCF on a matter of principle, it was not the only strategic issue. The belief that the USSR was a workers' state, albeit degenerated, led to some serious illusions about the potential role of the Red Army; *La Vérité* in 1944 told its readers that 'the flags of the Red Army will join our red flags'[51] – a serious misunderstanding of what would be the role of Russian forces in the post-war carve-up of Europe.

Although some tentative links were made with Resistance leader Jean Moulin in early 1943, the POI never actually entered the Resistance movement; as Yvan Craipeau, who was centrally involved, recorded, the Trotskyist military organisations were 'derisory'.[52]

The question of the national struggle remained central. Early in the occupation one grouping of Trotskyists argued that in a situation of foreign occupation, as in a colonial territory, the working class should become part of a national resistance. Another current opposed this, arguing that national demands meant 'importing bourgeois ideology into the proletariat in order to demoralise it'.[53]

The argument was developed by Marc Loris [Jean van Heijenoort] in an article dated September 1942 and published in the clandestine *La Vérité*. As he put it: 'National independence remains a democratic demand. As such, we struggle

---

49   *La Vérité*, 15 March 1942.
50   Pluet-Despatin 1978, pp. 71–106.
51   *La Vérité*, 10 February 1944.
52   Craipeau 1999, p. 165.
53   Broué 1985, p. 52.

to achieve it, but with our own methods and we integrate it into our programme for socialist revolution'.

As a result. he argued 'the slogan of national liberation has played until now and will continue for some time to play an important role in regrouping the masses, overcoming their atomisation and leading them to political struggle. That is sufficient for it to appear on our flag'.[54]

In short, the position of the French Trotskyists, endorsed by the European Secretariat of the Fourth International, was that revolutionaries could not simply ignore the upsurge of opposition to the German occupation, however nationalist it might be. The question of progressive nationalism remained a difficult and contentious one, and there were different currents of opinion within the Trotskyist ranks.[55]

Though there were a number of limited achievements the Trotskyists never managed to break out of their isolation. The grip of Stalinism and social democracy on the working class was too strong for them to break through.

The Lutte de Classes grouping – a small nucleus around David Korner [Barta] – had broken with the rest of the French Trotskyist movement at the beginning of the war. It claimed to be the most intransigently internationalist of the Trotskyist currents; it gave priority to factory organisation and produced a duplicated bulletin during the occupation. Its activities must have caused some problems for the PCF, for at the Liberation one of its members, Mathieu Bucholz [known as Pamp] was accused of being a Nazi and killed by PCF members.[56] During the Occupation he had worked with members of the PCF youth, notably in organising forged papers.[57]

Other activists not directly linked to the Trotskyist organisations also became involved in opposition to the Nazi occupation. Raymond Molinier had been a founder member of the PCF at the age of sixteen and by the end of the 1920s had become a Trotskyist, though later Trotsky broke with him. During World War II Molinier ran a circus based in Lisbon; it seems to have provided a means for Trotskyists in occupied Europe to escape, using the cover of its tours. Unfortunately there is not much information about this operation or how it worked.

Claude Cahun and her partner Suzanne Malherbe became associated with the surrealists in the 1930s. As well as opposing racism and imperialism they set

---

54   Loris 1985, pp. 95, 108–9.

55   C.E.I. de la IVe. Internationale 1985.

56   Barcia, 2003, pp. 79–80.

57   Maitron and Pennetier 1964–2023 article18137, notice BUCHOLZ Mathieu. Pseudonyme: Pamp, version mise en ligne le 20 octobre 2008, dernière modification le 25 août 2019.

out to challenge traditional gender roles. Cahun was a signatory of the FIARI Manifesto. In 1937 they moved to Jersey; when the Channel Islands were occupied by the Germans they began to try to encourage a spirit of mutiny and to undermine authority among the soldiers. They produced anti-German fliers, often based on German translations of BBC reports, which were sometimes turned into poems; they also painted anti-Hitler slogans on coins. The couple attended German military events and placed leaflets in soldiers' pockets, on their chairs, or through their car windows. In 1944 Cahun was arrested and sentenced to death, though the sentence was never carried out; but jail damaged her health and she died in 1954.

Some Trotskyists attempted the hazardous task of making contact with German soldiers, confronting them with revolutionary arguments and trying to involve them in activity. Yvan Craipeau was a leading figure in the French Trotskyist organisation before the war, and had served as a bodyguard to Trotsky during his brief residence in France. When war came, he was unfit for military service, which left him at liberty to play an important role in the organisation of the POI, together with Marcel Hic. Pursued by the Gestapo, he went into illegality with false papers and a moustache.[58]

Ernest Mandel, later prominent as a leader of the Fourth International, was only sixteen at the outbreak of war, but as the son of a Trotskyist activist in Belgium he was already involved in the revolutionary movement. He was an internationalist through and through; born in Germany with a Polish father, he obtained Belgian citizenship only in 1956. He worked closely with Abram Leon, author of *The Jewish Question*, who was murdered by the Nazis in the Auschwitz camp. He was involved in producing a pamphlet in German, which told soldiers that they were being sacrificed as cannon fodder while their masters negotiated to save their possessions. He worked with the French comrades in fraternising with German soldiers.[59]

Michel Pablo was the pseudonym of Michalis N. Raptis. Born in Egypt, he became involved in politics in Greece; he was imprisoned and exiled and eventually made his way to France. He represented Greece at the founding conference of the Fourth International; he was involved with the production and distribution of *Arbeiter und Soldat* [Worker and Soldier: see below]. He played a key role in the unification of the various Trotskyist groupings.[60]

---

58   Craipeau 1999, pp. 166–71.

59   Stutje 2009, pp. 24–37.

60   Maitron and Pennetier 1964–2023 article151998, notice RAPTIS Mikhalis dit PABLO Michel et autres pseudonymes [Dictionnaire Algérie], version mise en ligne le 6 janvier 2014, dernière modification le 21 mars 2015.

6   Martin Monath

Martin Monat or Monath, later known by various pseudonyms, notably Paul Widelin, was litle known until some seventy years after his death, when Nathaniel Flakin finally wrote a reasonably full biography[61] [there are still some open questions]. He was born in Berlin in 1912 and first became involved in politics in Hashomer Hatzair, a socialist Zionist youth organisation; Zionist organisations were tolerated by the Nazis until 1937, and he was even able to read an article by Trotsky in Hebrew. Unlike a number of his comrades he did not go to Palestine.

He left Germany in 1938 to escape the Gestapo and went to Belgium, where he was active with the Trotskyists there and worked alongside Ernest Mandel. Subsequently he came to France, where he played a key role in the fraternisation work, becoming editor of *Arbeiter und Soldat*. Until March 1944 he was accommodated in the home of Swiss militants Paul and Clara Thalmann, who had a clandestine printing press. The paper was produced and distributed in Paris, and 150 copies were sent to Brest, where there was a sympathetic group of German soldiers at the military base. The basic strategy was explained by the American Trotskyist George Breitman: 'It was far easier to stick a knife between the ribs of a German soldier on a dark night, than to meet that same German in the daytime, win his confidence and enlist him in the ranks of the revolutionary fighters against fascism. But difficult though this work was, Widelin [Monath] carried it out with growing success'.[62]

He undertook the risky journey from Paris to Brest once or twice a week, and held discussions by night with German soldiers. There was a group of between 15 and 27 soldiers and sailors, many from Hamburg. The paper was circulated elsewhere in France – Toulon, La Rochelle, etc. – but claims that it reached Germany are dubious.[63] In his spare time he attended classical music concerts in Paris, and sat, as an unrecognised Jew, amid Nazi officers.

In July 1944 he was arrested by the French police; they handed him over to the Gestapo who tortured him. He was then shot in the head and chest, allegedly while trying to escape. He survived and was taken to hospital; by now the Nazis, facing defeat, were determined not to let him survive and seized him from his hospital bed and murdered him.

Monath's biographer concludes that while, in a sense, he achieved nothing, he nonetheless

---

61   Flakin 2019.
62   Quoted by Flakin 2019, p. 63.
63   Flakin 2019, p. 73.

... created an example for future generations that survived long after his own destruction. In the face of capitalisms's greatest slaughter (until now), Viktor [Monath] presented an alternative to chauvinism. Had there been 1,000 or 10,000 Viktors in France – or more precisely had there been 1,000 or 10,000 Bolshevik cadres – the whole world war might have turned out differently. Like Karl Liebknecht, Viktor kept the flame of proletarian internationalism alive during the darkest hours.[64]

Robert Cruau was a postal worker in Nantes who encountered Trotskyist members of the PSOP through the Youth Hostel Movement. As a member of the POI from the beginning of the war he produced the clandestine duplicated paper *Front ouvrier* [Workers' Front] for the Nantes region. In 1943 he moved to Brest to avoid compulsory labour service in Germany; there he organised cells of some 27 German soldiers and distributed *Arbeiter und Soldat*. In October 1943 he was betrayed and died, either under torture or while trying to escape.

Arbeiter und Soldat, a German-language paper, was the main tool of a tiny minority of people who, sometimes at the price of their lives, tried to organise fraternisation with German workers in uniform. Six issues appeared from July 1943 to July 1944, a remarkable achievement for a small group with no more than a few hundred members across the country. The paper's six issues are testimony to a powerful internationalism embodied in the determination of exceptional individuals.[65]

The paper insisted that, like the 1914–18 war, this was an imperialist war:

> ... in the first days of August 1914 the first imperialist world war began ... On our side they said: fight the Tsar. On the other: fight the Kaiser. In reality both sides were interested in capitalist war profits, capitalist markets and redivision of colonial territories among imperialist slave-owners. This time only the slogans have changed. The content and the real aims of the war are exactly the same again. Colonial profits, not democracy or national socialism.[66]

Arbeiter und Soldat followed Lenin in calling for 'revolutionary defeatism':

---

64   Flakin 2019, p. 92.
65   All translations from the German are taken from Flakin 2019. The original German can be found in Flakin 2018. There is a different English version at https://www.marxists.org/history/etol/newspape/soldat/.
66   *Arbeiter und Soldat* 2, August 1943; Flakin 2019, p. 145.

We want the defeat of our capitalist class in this war. Let all the knights of industry and the bank barons, all the Nazi bosses and the generals, and all those who are still blinded and deceived by them clamor against the 'betrayal of the fatherland' and shout 'agents of the enemy'. We will hold firm. We want the defeat of our capitalists; we prefer that to their victory.

...

Moreover. We do not only damn the victory of our own robbers against the brigands on the other side. We want their defeat. Defeat in revolutionary [probably an error for reactionary] wars led to the first uprisings of the revolutionary class: 1871 in France, 1905 and 1917 in Russia, 1918 in Germany. Therefore Lenin coined the principle for workers of all countries: 'In a reactionary war, the revolutionary class must wish for the defeat of its own government'.[67]

Hence the call to transform the war into an international class struggle; the August 1943 issue urged: 'we must march hand in hand with the London proletarians against the common enemy, German and English capital'.[68] Nazi leader Goebbels was said to be trying to 'dispel his fear of the revolution which has now become inevitable'.[69]

The consciousness of German workers was rapidly changing in the light of events:

So it is wrong to think that the German workers have learned nothing since 1918. It is wrong to believe that the tragedy must be repeated. It is superficial to say that after ten years of fascist rule we must start all over again. ...

The experiences of the German worker in uniform in Russia are still causing more confusion than clarity, more doubt than hope. Already, however, groups are forming everywhere to give answers. Old cells which survived the years of terror by keeping to themselves are again putting out feelers. New groups are being organized. New information is spreading, mouth to mouth and in print, in newspapers and leaflets. On the first day of open struggle the best of these groups will unite to form the new revolutionary Communist Party.[70]

67   *Arbeiter und Soldat* 3, September 1943; Flakin 2019, pp. 147–8.
68   *Arbeiter und Soldat* 2, August 1943; Flakin 2019, p. 144.
69   *Arbeiter und Soldat* 1, July 1943; Flakin 2019, p. 122.
70   *Arbeiter und Soldat* 1, July 1943; Flakin 2019, pp. 125–6.

This meant that German workers would have to follow Karl Liebknecht's reminder that the main enemy was at home; in 1916 he had told German workers that *'This war is not our war. It has to be transformed into a proletarian revolution. The main enemy is at home'*.[71]

Hence Germany would be central to the coming European revolution:

> The pioneering struggle of the German working class for socialist revolution will be the catalyst for the proletarian revolution across Europe. The victorious advance of the German revolution will sweep away the counter-revolutionary, chauvinist influence of the Stalinist clique everywhere, first of all in Russia itself. It was the defeat of the German working class in 1923 which definitively demoralized the Russian proletariat and placed the bureaucracy in the saddle.[72]

So German workers should adopt as their basic slogans:

> REVOLUTIONARY FRATERNIZATION WITH THE ENGLISH AND AMERICAN SOLDIERS AGAINST THE GERMAN, AMERICAN AND ENGLISH GENERALS AND THEIR CAPITALIST BACKERS!
>
> REVOLUTIONARY FRATERNIZATION WITH ALL EUROPEAN WORKERS FOR A COMMON STRUGGLE
>
> PROLETARIAN REVOLUTION IN GERMANY, EUROPE AND THE WORLD![73]

Though this perspective was immeasurably superior in terms of internationalism to that put forward by the PCF with its crude anti-Germanism, there was sometimes a tendency to overestimate the immediate revolutionary potential in the situation. For example it was claimed that the Stalinists

> ... only embitter the German soldier, obscuring the revolutionary solution for him and throwing him defenseless back into the arms of the Göbbels propaganda, thus prolonging the war. One German worker, upon receiving revolutionary material from a comrade, said: If these writings were distributed throughout Germany for only a few days the war would be over and the revolution would be here. This worker had a more 'realistic'

---

71   *Arbeiter und Soldat* 4, April–May 1944; Flakin 2019, p. 154.
72   *Arbeiter und Soldat* 4, April–May 1944; Flakin 2019, p. 157.
73   *Arbeiter und Soldat* 5, June 1944; Flakin 2019, p. 170.

political outlook than all the Russian bureaucrats have ever shown in the 25 years of their corrupt rule.[74]

Arbeiter und Soldat was keen to remind German workers of their national traditions. Each issue carried the slogan 'The German Revolution is the World Revolution. K. Liebknecht', and issue No. 6 carried a long quotation from Liebknecht's speech on May Day 1916. It was important to encourage German soldiers to connect with the internationalist traditions of the German working class.

While there were some lapses into a cataclysmic view of impending revolution, other articles offered a much more sober view of the tasks of building a revolutionary current. One article advised:

> You want to win over your colleagues in the factory, your fellow soldiers at the front or in the barracks. You don't always succeed. Some are still Stalinists, others even hope for a resurrection of the S.P.D. [Social Democratic Party], a third wants to see the 'good times' from before 33 again and a fourth doesn't want to hear anything about politics. But you cannot let this prevent you from standing together with all of them when there are resistance actions against a factory manager, a tyrannical foreman, an officer who is mistreating people or against new reprisals by the Nazi clique. On the contrary.[75]

Another writer recognised the difficulties ahead and the need to start from small-scale activity:

> But revolutions do not appear out of thin air. They are prepared by many partial struggles in which the revolutionary class closes its ranks. But today such struggles almost never break out anywhere in Germany. The struggle for the most minimal demands, for food, wages, for the most basic rights and freedoms, protests, strikes and demonstrations are crushed by the Hitler reaction with the bloodiest terror.[76]

There was detailed concrete advice on how to organise:

> Illegal proletarian groups of four must be formed in every factory and in every military unit! In these groups, the most active and class-conscious

---

74   *Arbeiter und Soldat* 1, July 1943; Flakin 2019, p. 128.
75   *Arbeiter und Soldat* 1, July 1943; Flakin 2019, p. 129.
76   *Arbeiter und Soldat* 5, June 1944; Flakin 2019, p. 168.

militants must band together. They must follow political developments with the greatest diligence. Wherever proletarians begin to resist the repressive machine, action groups must take the lead of the struggle.[77]

...

Form secret cells of three or four! Admit all workers into these groups who understand the need for proletarian struggle and want to campaign for it!

Soldiers who have the confidence of your units, form committees of revolutionary struggle!

ON EVERY SHIP, IN EVERY BARRACKS, IN EVERY TRENCH, THERE MUST BE REVOLUTIONARY CELLS AND A COMMITTEE OF STRUGGLE![78]

Arbeiter und Soldat was clear about the British and American regimes and their links with the French ruling class. By 1944 it was arguing that the 'Allies' were allowing the war to drag on too long:

The 'Allies' could have finished long ago if they had wanted to. But the English and American capitalists – JUST LIKE THE GERMANS – want to prolong the war as long as possible.

The longer the tide of arms deals and billions in profits lasts and the ebb of the post-war sales crisis can be delayed, the better! The more Germany and Russia weaken each other – the finer! The worse the German and Russian proletariat bleed, the nicer![79]

So German workers in uniform ought to look for alliance with British and American workers:

Arms alone will not be enough to fight against the European revolution. The people carrying the weapons on the Anglo-Saxon side are themselves workers and peasants. They could still be mobilized against a fascist Germany. Will they let themselves be misled into fighting against a proletarian Europe? Didn't the bourgeoisie already have quite unpleasant experiences in 1918–19 when it tried to strangle the victorious October Revolution of workers and peasants in Russia?[80]

---

77   *Arbeiter und Soldat* 4, April–May 1944; Flakin 2019, p. 158.
78   *Arbeiter und Soldat* 5, June 1944; Flakin 2019, p. 169.
79   *Arbeiter und Soldat* 5, June 1944; Flakin 2019, p. 164.
80   *Arbeiter und Soldat* 2, August 1943; Flakin 2019, p. 137.

It pointed to the fact that in Britain the class struggle was continuing even in wartime [these figures may be approximations, but reflect the fact of a very high level of strike action in Britain in 1944]:

> In the first three months of 1943 the English workers celebrated two hundred thousand strike days. In the same period this year it was almost 2 ½ million. … Hear these numbers! Understand what they mean! They are a greeting from our fighting class comrades on the other side of the Channel.[81]

Although communication must have been extremely risky, *Arbeiter und Soldat* did make contact with German soldiers and from time to time published letters from German soldiers who, as Germany faced defeat, were feeling extremely bitter. One soldier wrote from the front:

> My brother had lost several fingers to frostbite. He also had frost wounds on his feet. Which didn't stop the dogs from sending him out again. He stayed in the East …

while another reported from Hamburg after the bombing [the allied bombing of Hamburg in July 1943 – Operation Gomorrah – left some 37,000 dead, about 2.4 % of the total population of the city]:

> The dead were piled up and burned with flamethrowers. I can only tell you: don't come back here. You won't recognize the city any more …

and another declared:

> I have lost everything. And for whom? Just because the capitalist dog, just because the capitalist dog wants to live better and swim in his fat.[82]

Another letter from a serving soldier explained that it was necessary to understand why the ss [paramilitary organization] always got everything first, and why the ordinary private soldier was sent to the front without weapons:

> It is obvious: first of all the Hitler regime is on its last legs, and Hitler and co are only waiting for a great miracle that will strengthen their rule again …

---

81   *Arbeiter und Soldat* 5, June 1944; Flakin 2019, p. 167.
82   *Arbeiter und Soldat* 3, September 1943; Flakin 2019, pp. 152–3.

But they can only give weapons to the Landser [private] at the front, where there is no going back for him, where he is forced to shoot forward, and there is no danger that a stray bullet will endanger a Nazi boss, since he only shoots at his peers: the fellow soldier, the comrade from the other side.[83]

Arbeiter und Soldat attempted to report on actions where French and German workers had come together. There were several mutinies by German troops on French soil. At Palinges in Eastern France the population fraternised with German soldiers who had been jailed for indiscipline.[84] There was one particularly striking case of solidarity between French and German workers:

A train full of ss men coming from Russia derails. Terrorism or an accident? That hardly mattered to the ss officer. He needed revenge, so he had the French railway workers who came running up put against the wall, and had all the men who would be found in the village snatched and mowed down. What did a few human lives matter to this professional killer who was accustomed to thousands of workers' corpses?

But he had not counted on the fact that the German worker, despite five years of war, has not lost his good sense and solidarity still lives on within him. The German railway workers helped many French people escape, thus saving their lives.

When an investigation later revealed that the accident was not caused by sabotage but rather by the poor condition of the rolling stock, the outrage among the French and German railway workers grew. They resolved to strike for one hour in protest against this murder of innocent workers.

The trains stopped for one hour on this line, with the German railway workers standing by the French workers and in no way obstructing the protest strike.

With their courageous behaviour the German railway workers showed that workers do not know national hatred and their solidarity knows no national borders.[85]

With the murder of Widelin the project collapsed. The German soldiers recruited by Cruau were arrested; some were executed, others sent to the Eastern

---

83   *Arbeiter und Soldat* 6, July 1944; Flakin 2019, pp. 179–80.
84   *La Vérité* 28, 20 January, 1942.
85   *Arbeiter und Soldat* 4, April–May 1944; Flakin 2019, pp. 159–60.

front. The Trotskyist organisation in Brest was dismantled and the Paris organisation also destroyed.

Arguably some of those involved had not taken security seriously enough; on one occasion 10 soldiers met together in the home of a newly recruited comrade. The German authorities were determined that subversion of their troops should not succeed. Eventually a German soldier betrayed both the French activists and his fellow soldiers. Yet the smashing of the Trotskyist organisation came only after the Normandy landings when the German forces were in retreat; if it had survived a few months more it might have evaded capture. In any case *Arbeiter und Soldat* did prove that there was a potential for such work if the political will had existed in any section of the French Resistance.

The promised revolution did not come, but there were mutinies in the occupying army, though often by soldiers not of German nationality. As Germany was invaded and occupied, Anti-Fascist Committees were set up across the country; there were over 500 of these, involving thousands of members, overwhelmingly working class, but independent of the Communist and Social Democratic organisations. They called strikes and replaced Nazi functionaries with their own nominees. They were rapidly suppressed by the occupying forces, but their brief existence shows that *Arbeiter und Soldat*'s perspective was not wholly unrealistic.[86]

7　　　　Nazi Camps

Some of the small band of French Trotskyists died at the hands of the Nazis; others were sent to one of the German camps, which served both as a source of cheap labour and as a means of extermination. Much has been written about the Nazi camps, and it would be foolish to suggest that there was anything uniquely terrible about the fate of the Trotskyists. Yet there were particular problems for Trotskyists who found themselves in a Nazi camp. Significant numbers of the camps' inmates were Communists of various nationalities, for the crushing of Communism was always a major priority for the Nazis, one that was given equal weight to the elimination of the Jews. The Communists were well organised, maintaining a remarkable degree of political coherence and discipline; loyal Communists had been conditioned to hate Trotskyists, to regard them, not as a different political current in the labour movement, but

---

86　　Gluckstein, 1999, pp. 219–20.

as open enemies, as bad as fascists. So a Trotskyist in a Nazi camp faced two dangers, from the camp authorities and from Communist fellow inmates.

In the period immediately after the end of the war, when the truth about the camps was first becoming known and some of the survivors were beginning to tell their stories, there were controversies in France about the camps and how they should be understood. David Rousset's two books on the concentration camp experience were generally disparaged by the PCF. This was partly because Rousset was a Trotskyist, but also because he argued that the camps had a certain rationality, that they embodied to the most intense degree features inherent in all class society. He showed how the society inside Buchenwald was divided into various classes and controlled by a bureaucracy; the Communists were able to organise and operate effectively within these structures.[87]

Hence his account challenged the logic of the Popular Front, namely that fascism was something distinct from capitalism against which it was possible to unite with the so-called progressive bourgeoisie.[88]

Rousset had been a leading Trotskyist activist in the 1930s. During the occupation he was involved with the reorganisation of the POI and was active in making contact with members of the Wehrmacht. In October 1943 he was arrested by a French police officer and two Germans, working closely together. He was sent to a jail at Fresnes to the south of Paris. In order to communicate with comrades outside, messages were written on cigarette paper and inserted into the crotch of dirty underpants being sent home for washing; the underpants were encrusted with damp bread to discourage close investigation by guards.

Then he was sent to Buchenwald, and later other Nazi camps. He survived, but only just. Before his arrest he had weighed nearly fifteen stone; on his return he weighed just over eight, and looked like a skeleton. He had now broken with the Trotskyist organisation and became a contributor to the *Revue internationale*, a Marxist journal not aligned to any organisation. For this he wrote his first accounts of life in the camp, later expanded into two books, *L'Univers concentrationnaire* [the universe of concentration camps] and the 800-page novel *Les Jours de notre mort* [the days of our death], based on his experiences but also drawing on other accounts of the Nazi camps.

Jean-René Chauvin was another remarkable survivor. He had become a Trotskyist by 1937 and built a small branch of the organisation in Bordeaux. At the outbreak of war there were about a dozen of them, and they produced 3000

---

87   Rousset 1946.
88   See Surya 2004, pp. 211–13.

copies of a leaflet distributed in the shipyards in Bordeaux; this stated that all workers in Europe would be victims of the coming war.[89] After a spell in the army he moved to Paris, where he was less well-known and able to work clandestinely. He was a member of the POI and distributed its paper *La Vérité*.

In 1942 he took on an even more dangerous job. He set out to contact German refugees in Southern France, not yet occupied by the Nazis, with the perspective of publishing leaflets and a paper aimed at German soldiers. He travelled across the country, memorising the necessary details so that he could not be caught in possession of incriminating documents.

In 1943 the French police picked him up during a raid. They handed him over to the Gestapo, who tortured him. He then spent two years in various camps – an account he wrote many years later contains the extraordinary description of Buchenwald: 'after having been in Mauthausen and Auschwitz, the atmosphere there seemed to me much more relaxed'.[90]

If he had to deal with the Nazi guards, he also faced a threat from his fellow-prisoners. On one occasion he was attacked by two Stalinists, who screamed at him that he was a 'Hitlero-Trotskyist' and beat him. Fortunately he was rescued when two other Communist Party members came to his rescue. The Communists in the camp were by no means a monolithic body – for some the Moscow line predominated, for others their sense of class solidarity. As he noted, in other cases Trotskyists were put to death by Stalinists in the camps.[91]

As an internationalist, he was able to establish relations of solidarity with fellow-prisoners of many nationalities, and even to form some sort of human relationships with those supervising him; he managed to engage a German foreman in a political discussion.[92] He attributed his survival to the fact that he was fit and agile, having been a boxer and rugby player.

In 2006 he published *Un Trotskiste dans l'enfer nazi* [A Trotskyist in the Nazi Hell], both a personal account of his experiences in the camps and a more general historical study of concentration camps.

8   Liberation

The Liberation did not bring the promised revolution, but there was an upsurge of struggle in France and around the world, which offered possibilities for inter-

---

89   Chauvin 2006, p. 65.
90   Chauvin 2006, p. 109.
91   Chauvin 2006, p. 217.
92   Chauvin 2006, pp. 195–6, 213.

vention to the internationalist left, but also faced it with a whole set of new problems. Indeed the very notion of liberation was turning out to be problematic. At various conferences and meetings the leaders of the USA, Britain and the USSR [with de Gaulle doing his best to get a share for France] agreed a division of the world between them. In return for a free hand in Eastern Europe, Stalin would ensure that his followers in France and Italy would not try to take power and would cooperate with right-wing forces in post-war reconstruction. Above all there was to be no question of working people taking control of things into their own hands.

What this meant became clear in May 1944, just weeks before the Normandy landings marked the beginning of the end for Nazi rule. Terrible food shortages provoked a general strike in Marseille; mass involvement was so great that the Nazis hesitated to try and break the strike by armed force. If the strike had spread then the French population, and especially the working class, could have begun to become the agent of its own liberation. This is not to say that revolution was an immediate prospect, but a dynamic might have developed that would have shifted the balance of forces in favour of working people.

The strike was no more welcome to the Allies than it was to the Nazis. American bomber planes made their contribution by flattening 10,000 working-class homes and killing 1700 people. The strike's potential was destroyed.[93]

It was in this context that, at the time of the Normandy landings, *La Vérité* headlined 'They're no different'. The following article quite reasonably urged workers not to trust Eisenhower for their liberation, but to organise militias on a class basis in the factories.[94]

It was true that the major imperialist powers – Britain, which still had the largest empire in the world, and the United States which aspired to replace it with a rather different model of imperialism – were aiming to eliminate Germany in order to consolidate their own grip on the world. If necessary they were quite prepared to be murderously ruthless about it, as the Marseille bombing showed. They were preparing to hold power for a whole historical epoch. So it is possible to justify *La Vérité*'s analysis.

In tactical terms the position was seriously misguided. There is a real difference between liberal democracy and fascism. The restoration of free speech and a free press – even if the PCF tried to prevent those rights being extended to Trotskyists – offered new possibilities to the left at a time when there was a fer-

---

93   Tasca and Peschanski 1986, p. 591.
94   Quoted by Nick 2002, pp. 314–5.

ment of ideas. The daily paper *Combat*'s slogan 'from Resistance to Revolution' had real resonance in the aftermath of the war.

The Allies did demolish fascism – except in Spain and Portugal – and in France and other countries their victory restored the rights of political and trade-union organisation. They did so at the price of – and in practice in order to achieve – the strangling of a potential revolution. The strategy of fraternisation which a small minority of the left had advocated offered an alternative way out of the war, one that could potentially have led to a very different post-war world. The ruling blocs in both the USA and the USSR were determined that this alternative should be crushed. Stalin's primary concern was to establish his control over Eastern Europe, and until the Cold War began in 1947 he was prepared to cooperate with the West. On the left Russia was highly regarded for its major role in defeating Hitler. Many also believed the growth of Moscow's empire was an extension of socialism, and even many anti-Stalinists called the new People's Democracies in Eastern Europe workers' states.

1945, like 1848 and 1917, could have become a year of international revolution. From Vietnam to Italy there were risings as working people tried to take society into their own hands. In France workers' councils were set up in a number of places, though they did not last long. Meanwhile American GIs in France were marching to demand the abolition of officer privilege.[95]

But the forces opposed to revolution at this point proved all too strong. The PCF joined de Gaulle's government and used its powerful organisation to crush opposition. The revolutionary left did not have the forces on the ground to intervene in the struggles and develop a real challenge to the existing order.

World War II was a composite of several wars. In France it was, in part at least, a civil war against the most racist elements in French society. It saw the emergence of an internationalist current that offered an alternative future for French society. In the short term this current could not prevail against its enemies, but it would reappear in new forms.

---

95   Cortright 1975, pp. 150–51.

War in Indochina

By the autumn of 1944 most of France was liberated; though the war continued till May 1945, the government in Paris was already laying the foundations of the new Fourth Republic. The government was headed by General Charles de Gaulle, an autocratic conservative nationalist, who had led opposition to Vichy from London. Of necessity his government was based on left and left of centre parties: Communists, Socialists and Christian Democrats [MRP]. Other political forces from the pre-war Third Republic had been discredited by their support for the Nazi occupiers. De Gaulle was forced into an alliance with the political representatives of the left; without their backing he could not control a society with thousands of armed resistance fighters, and persuade workers to rebuild the French economy.

As the Germans and Japanese were defeated, France regained control of its overseas territories in Africa and the Middle and Far East. France still had the second largest colonial empire in the world, covering nearly one tenth of the world's land area, and 5 percent of the world's population; France seemed unlikely to abandon it in the near future. De Gaulle was undoubtedly being honest in his broadcast of September 1945 announcing the founding of the Fourth Republic, when he declared with pride that France was recovering its empire and taking back its place in the world.[1]

In the course of the Second World War the Atlantic Charter, agreed by Churchill and US President Roosevelt, promised to 'respect the right of all peoples to choose the form of government under which they will live'; this created considerable interest throughout the colonial world. In Washington in September 1945 de Gaulle assured Roosevelt's successor Truman that steps would be taken towards the early independence of Indochina.[2] He was lying.

Over the next twenty years the French colonial empire would disappear, leaving behind little more than a few islands. Those twenty years were marked by two major wars, in Indochina and Algeria. These tore into the very heart of French political life, destroying the Republic established in the aftermath of World War II, and confronting many French people with painful choices and fundamental questions about their identity.

---

1 *Le Monde*, 6 September 1945.
2 Smith 2007, p. 41.

The course followed by France is illuminated by a contrast with France's main imperial rival, Britain. Britain too disposed of its empire in the two decades following World War II. India gained independence in the 1940s, and most of the rest of the empire followed fairly rapidly. Britain did not surrender all its territories voluntarily, and there was considerable brutality, notably in Kenya and Malaya.[3] Unlike in France, the decolonisation process had relatively little impact on British political life and colonial questions were not a major issue in any post-war British general election. By contrast in the French election campaign of 1955, a poll asked voters to name the most important issue facing the incoming government: 25 percent named North Africa as against 15 percent for wages and the cost of living.[4]

The French left's failure to oppose the re-establishment of the French Empire was the result above all of the republican tradition which dominated French political thinking. This encouraged the notion that France's role in the world was a progressive one, bringing enlightenment to more benighted territories, the so-called 'civilising mission'.

France's determination to hang on to its colonial territories cannot be explained in strictly economic terms. There is no evidence that France suffered economically from the loss of its colonial empire. On the contrary, the period of decolonisation coincided with the 'trente glorieuses', the thirty glorious years of the post-war boom which saw full employment and rising living standards. In a changing world France did not need direct political rule over its colonial territories in order to guarantee raw materials, markets or cheap labour.[5] Many sections of big capital were quite sanguine about the loss of empire. Various centre-left intellectuals, notably Raymond Aron, argued for French withdrawal from its colonial empire. In terms of a simple balance-sheet the continuation of empire offered nothing to justify the horrendous expenditure, of money and lives, involved in two long colonial wars.

In political terms things were more complex. France had a very large petty-bourgeoisie. This had a powerful electoral weight, and tended to identify with, and often to have personal links with, the European settlers in North Africa. If big capital could cheerfully contemplate the end of empire, for the settlers of Algeria it meant an end to their property and their livelihoods. Politicians of the mainstream parties, trapped in the logic of electoral politics, tended to have little understanding of the realities of colonial society. Often leftists, who

---

3   Newsinger 2006, pp. 189–92, 209–10.
4   *L'Express*, 16 December 1955.
5   See Kidron 1962.

had developed links with the movements of the colonised, had a better grasp of the way things were actually developing.

The SFIO was committed to the preservation of empire. While advocating reforms in education, health, working conditions etc., the SFIO's fundamental aim was to assimilate Algeria to France.[6] Veteran leader Léon Blum favoured the formula of recognising Vietnam as a free state within the French Union [the State of Vietnam, under former Emperor Bâo Dai, was proclaimed in 1949 within Indochina], but he justified it with a rhetoric that was very much that of imperialism, arguing that this was the best way to preserve France's political and spiritual influence, as well as its material interests.[7] He belived that colonialism should end 'when the colonised people has been made fully capable of living in an emancipated fashion and governing itself'.[8] In other words, the colonised populations could only learn to run their own societies if they were taught to do so by their colonial rulers.

As for the Communist Party, the central factor determining its policy was total loyalty to Russia, which at that point did not wish to rock the boat by challenging Western imperialism. The Communists expressed no opposition to the recolonisation of Indochina. An Indochinese delegate who visited France in 1946 reported a meeting with Communist leader Maurice Thorez, at which the latter declared that his party did not intend to liquidate France's position in Indochina and that he wished to see the French flag flying in all corners of the French Union.[9] Although the PCF position was primarily determined by its loyalty to Moscow [which meant it would change its line dramatically with the onset of the Cold War], its exposition of the line would often borrow the rhetoric of republican nationalism, something which would take on growing importance as the party evolved to a greater independence from Moscow over the following decades.

1   Sétif

Tuesday, 8 May 1945 was VE [Victory in Europe] Day. Celebrations were held throughout France, including Algeria. Algerians had been hoping that liberation might mean something for them, but proposals for reform were decidedly modest: a few thousand Algerians would get full rights of citizenship, while the

---

6   Vétillard 2008, p. 444.
7   Lacouture 1977, pp. 536–7.
8   Léon Blum, speech to Assemblée Nationale, 23 December 1946, quoted by Quilliot 1972, p. 194.
9   Devillers 1952, p. 268.

rest would be represented through an electoral system rigged in favour of the Europeans. The previous week many activists had been jailed.

A victory parade was held in Sétif, a market town in Kabylia in Northern Algeria. Many Muslims assembled, including members of the Muslim Scouts, a legal organisation set up by the main nationalist organisation, the Algerian People's Party [PPA]. The nationalists wanted a large demonstration, but had no plans for violence. They brought banners calling for national independence and the release of their leader Messali Hadj. The local chief official, Butterlin, ruled all banners and Algerian national flags illegal.

There are competing reports of what exactly happened, but apparently one of the police opened fire, killing a boy carrying a flag. This enraged the crowd which sought revenge. Some Muslims were armed; many were not, but they used knives, bottles, clubs and railings. After a hundred years of accumulated bitterness, all Europeans were seen as the enemy; they were killed and their bodies mutilated.

Around a hundred Europeans died. The rising spread to the whole region. About 50,000 people, one twentieth of the Muslim population in the area, took part. Violence continued for four or five days until troops ended it. Now the settlers wanted to reassert their power. Large numbers of troops were brought in, including Senegalese soldiers, who unfortunately did not make common cause with the local population. There were executions and widespread arrests. Villages were bombed from the air and a town was shelled from a cruiser at sea. Attacks were more or less random. The point was not so much to punish the original rioters as to teach the whole Muslim population to know their place. Settlers set up death squads and killed hundreds of Muslims. German and Italian prisoners of war were released to take part in the massacre; torture was widespread. Muslims were not allowed to travel around unless they wore white armbands; those not wearing them were liable to be shot on the spot. At least 15,000 died, though there are some claims it was as many as 50,000. Even on the lowest estimate, the Europeans killed 50 Muslims for every European life lost.[10]

The massive military retaliation could not have been carried out without the full approval of the French government. The repression was a clear signal to the rest of the French Empire, in Africa and Indochina, that French colonialism would carry on where it had left off in 1939. For many Algerians Sétif marked a vital turning-point. Any hope of peaceful progress towards independence had been lost.

---

10   Lacouture 1977, pp. 536–7.

L'Humanité, the Communist Party's daily paper, put the blame on the Algerian nationalists, from whom it had taken its distance before the war. Shortly after Sétif *L'Humanité* blamed the events on a 'handful of big landowners who are responsible for starvation' and demanded the dismissal of pro-Vichy officials.[11] A few days later the paper called explicitly for the punishment of 'the Hitlerite killers who took part in the events of 8 May and the pseudonationalist leaders who have deliberately tried to deceive the Muslim masses'.[12] The finger was pointed at the PPA, the organisation led by Messali Hadj which had taken over from the Étoile Nord Africaine when it was banned by the Popular Front government in 1937.

Communist François Billoux, who was a member of de Gaulle's government throughout 1945, subsequently claimed that Communist ministers did not know the extent of the repression until much later, since many things were settled directly by de Gaulle with the ministers concerned.[13] This may well be true – de Gaulle certainly had an authoritarian style. However the PCF was a mass organisation, with over half a million members, [544,989 according to the party's own figures[14]], and the Algerian Communist Party in 1945 had 6000 to 7000 members, of whom a third were Muslims.[15] It could hardly claim it did not know what was going on. In his own book about the experience of governmental participation Billoux stresses the PCF's anticolonialism, making no specific mention of either Sétif or the reoccupation of Indochina.[16] Charles Tillon, a long-standing PCF member and participant in the Black Sea mutinies of 1919, was Air Minister, though he had no responsibility for military aircraft.[17] Tillon's own account, published after his final break with the PCF, blames the repression on pro-Vichy elements in Algeria [and notes that some former Resistance fighters sent to Algeria refused to participate in the repression].[18]

The SFIO was equally complicit in the repression.[19] SFIO members Adrien Tixier,[20] Minister of the Interior in de Gaulle's government, and Yves

---

11   Anon 1945a.

12   Anon 1945b.

13   Amrani 2010, p. 95.

14   Fauvet 1965, p. 364.

15   Planche 2006, p. 92.

16   Billoux 1972.

17   Vétillard 2008, p. 217.

18   Tillon 1977, pp. 430–33. See also the recollections of Pierre Daix, who worked in Tillon's ministry: Daix 1976, pp. 166–170. [Thanks to Steve Cushion for these two references.]

19   Gallissot 2006, pp. 157–8.

20   Maitron and Pennetier 1964–2023 article132760, notice TIXIER Adrien, Pierre par Gilles Morin, version mise en ligne le 23 septembre 2013, dernière modification le 29 août 2015.

Chataigneau[21] actively supported the massacre, being hostile to anything that could encourage the development of Algerian nationalism.

The mainstream left had no criticisms of Sétif. These would come only from the small and fragmented far left. In 1945 a paper called *Ohé Partisans* was published briefly by a Trotskyist, André Calvès, who had fought in the Communist-led Francs-Tireurs et Partisans, but refused to be integrated into the regular army.[22] In August it carried an article under the headline 'Oradour-sur-Glane in Algeria'. [For the Oradour massacre see Chapter 9.] Over the next few years comparisons between the rule of the Nazis in France and French rule in its colonial territories were to become increasingly common; this was one of the first, and to make such a parallel just three months after the end of the war took a certain degree of courage.

The article was quite clear in attributing the blame for the events in Sétif and beyond to the French government and the parties of the mainstream left participating in it:

> With their policy of supporting the government, the French workers' parties have lost a great deal of their influence. The Algerians clearly recognise that when the SFIO and the PCF criticise the big colonists, it is only demagogy. It is obvious that the colonists could not exploit the Algerian people for long if they didn't have the support of the bayonets of the 'democratic' government to which the SFIO and the PCF belong.

It described the repression in Sétif:

> Natives are forbidden to leave home unless they are wearing special arm-bands to show that they are going to work. Any Muslim seen without an armband is killed without notice. In a public garden in the middle of Sétif a child picking flowers was killed by a sergeant. In the Sétif region, repression is carried out by the Foreign Legion and Senegalese troops who massacre, rape, and loot and burn the homes of natives.

And it concluded:

> We feel great shame thinking about this. We struggled for four years against oppression. No! Algerian comrades, we refuse to be the accom-

---

21   Maitron and Pennetier 1964–2023 article19589, notice CHATAIGNEAU Yves, Jean-Joseph [Dictionnaire Algérie] par René Gallissot, Jean-Louis Planche, version mise en ligne le 25 octobre 2008, dernière modification le 1er février 2014.

22   Pluet-Despatin 1978, p. 114.

plices of the bourgeois government and its killers! Long live the struggle
of the Algerian people for its independence! Workers of the world unite![23]

Sétif was not the only massacre as France set about restoring its empire at the
end of the World War. In November 1944 a large number of black African soldiers, perhaps as many as 300, were gunned down near the Senegalese capital
Dakar. They were former prisoners of war and were demanding equal pay with
white soldiers; as a result they were accused of mutiny. Only recently has the
French government so much as admitted what happened in Senegal.[24]

One area in which France managed to preserve its colonial rule – at least
temporarily – was Madagascar. On the evening of 29 March 1947, nationalists, most armed only with spears, launched coordinated surprise attacks on
military bases and French-owned plantations. Smouldering discontent at continuing French rule and the failures of reform proposals meant that the revolt
spread very rapidly, and it was estimated that the nationalist rising drew in as
many as a million peasants. At its peak the insurgency controlled one third of
the island.

The French state adopted terror tactics deliberately designed to demoralise
the population. The uprising was effectively put down by December 1948; total
deaths may have been as high as 100,000. Just 12 years later, in the context of
wars in Indochina and then Algeria, Madagascar got its independence. French
action had been savage but futile.

Opposition to French imperialism came largely from the Communist Party
which had now left the government and was pursuing militant left policies. It
was Communist campaigning which ensured that death sentences passed on
two leaders of the uprising were commuted to imprisonment.[25]

The main task facing French internationalists in the immediate post-war
years related to Indochina. In the interwar years there had been a number
of Indochinese, workers and students, in France, where they had developed
their political positions. During the Occupation some 500 Indochinese workers
were interned in a camp at Montauban. In October 1946 the camp had a strike,
followed by a hunger strike; leading activists were arrested.[26] The French Trotskyists in the Parti communiste internationaliste had given what support they
could to the strikes organised by the Indochinese workers.

<hr>

23   Anon 1945c.
24   Moshiri 2013.
25   Clayton 1994, p. 86.
26   Thourel 1980, p. 298.

Meanwhile in Indochina there were new developments. With the defeat of France in 1940 a pro-Vichy regime had been established in Indochina, which in 1945 gave way to direct rule by Vichy's allies, the Japanese. The war against Japan ended in August 1945 after the use of atomic weapons on Hiroshima and Nagasaki. Such a sudden end had not been expected by the Allies, who had not made full political preparations for the postwar situation. Ho Chi Minh remained loyal to the Russian Communist leadership through its various twists and turns, and conceived the fight for independence as a predominantly national struggle which could unite the various classes in Vietnam.

2   Vietnamese Independence

On 2 September 1945 in Hanoi, the Viet Minh [League for the Independence of Vietnam, a broad coalition including Communists], led by Ho Chi Minh, issued the Declaration of Independence of the Democratic Republic of Vietnam.[27] At the Potsdam conference in July–August it had been decided that Chinese forces would occupy the northern part of Indochina, and that British troops would take over the southern half.[28] France was still recovering from four years of occupation, and needed time to reorganise its armed forces; it was the British Labour government which bailed out French rule in Indochina. French troops started leaving for Indochina only in October.

France was ruled by left-wing parties – Communists, Socialists and Christian Democrats – but parties which were committed to preserving the French Empire. If they had not insisted on clinging onto the imperial territory, the long French war and the even longer American war need never have happened. 3 million or more deaths might have been avoided.

There was a further complication, namely the deep divisions within the Indochinese left. Indochina was one of the few countries where the Trotskyist Left Opposition had won substantial support. One of the most prominent Trotskyist leaders was Tạ Thu Thâu [see chapter 8].

In the 1930s there had been cooperation as well as conflict between Communists and Trotskyists, for example they worked together on the journal *La Lutte*. In 1945 the stakes were much higher. Independence was not just a distant aspiration but a very real possibility. Ho Chi Minh depended on political guidance and practical support from the USSR; he believed in the feasibility of

27   Saville 1993, pp. 176–204; see also Smith 2007, Neville 2007.
28   Neville 2007, pp. 101, 104.

cooperation with his old comrades from the PCF now in the French government. For Tạ Thu Thâu and the Trotskyists there was considerable scepticism about the role of the USSR and the PCF; they believed that if anything was to be achieved from the apparently favourable situation, the Indochinese workers would have to rely on their own strength and organisation. On 21 August there was a mass demonstration in Saigon; the Trotskyists brought banners calling for the arming of the people and workers' control of the factories. In the following days, as Ngô Văn, one of the Trotskyist activists, recalled: 'numerous people's committees ... arose spontaneously, as organisations of local management'.[29]

For the Communists this was a serious challenge to their control of the movement which could endanger their whole carefully elaborated strategy. The most extreme ruthlessness seemed justified. The Trotskyist organisation was crushed and its leadership eliminated; Tạ Thu Thâu himself was murdered.

One individual who attempted to show internationalist solidarity in this situation was Daniel Guérin, who had been in Indochina in the 1930s [see chapter 8]. When Ho Chi Minh came to Paris in 1946 for negotiations, Guérin had a long discussion with him and confronted him about the murder of Tạ Thu Thâu by Ho's supporters. Ho responded that he had been a 'great patriot', insisting however: 'but all who fail to follow the line we have laid down will be broken'.[30]

During 1945 and 1946 negotiations were held between the leaders of the Viet Minh [the national independence movement founded in 1941] and the French government. None of the parties in the governmental coalition supported independence for Indochina. If the French left, and especially the Communists, had been less committed to republican imperialism, and had been willing to defend the fundamental principle of Indochina's right to independence, even at the cost of threatening the unity of the post-war coalition, things might have turned out differently.

In November 1946, the French fleet bombarded Haiphong, a provocation aiming to crush the independence movement; full-scale war broke out. Both major parties of the working class, the Communists and the Socialists, were in the government. The Communists found themselves in an ambiguous position – their comrades in Indochina were heading the fight for independence, yet they were committed to remaining a party of government. For the first few crucial months the task of opposing the war was left to individuals and small groupings on the left.

---

29   Ngô Văn 2000, pp. 168, 173.
30   Guérin 1973, pp. 19–20.

There was some evidence of anti-imperialist feeling in France at this time. One account tells how troops waiting to leave Marseilles for Indochina in the autumn of 1945 found the walls of the city covered with slogans demanding the independence of Indochina.[31] This was at a time when the PCF's daily *L'Humanité* was barely mentioning Indochina. If this account is accurate, this must have been the work of some grouping outside the PCF-SFIO mainstream.

One of the first voices raised against colonialism was that of Joseph Rovan in the monthly *Esprit*. In November 1945 he insisted that one day France would have to yield freedom to Indochina, but that this was being delayed by the inhumane positions of colonialism. Rovan, who had been in a Nazi concentration camp, made a comparison which was to become increasingly common among anti-colonialists over the next two decades. Commenting on the claim by French General Leclerc that the Viet Minh were bandits and extremists, he noted that it was not long since French Resisters had been described as terrorists and common-law criminals.[32]

On 22 December 1945 the independent left daily paper *Franc-Tireur* [with a circulation over half that of the PCF's *L'Humanité*[33]] published a vigorous attack on French policy in Indochina, citing a letter from a French soldier which again compared French actions in Indochina to the massacre at Oradour.

The journal which put forward the most vigorous opposition to the war was *Les Temps modernes*, an independent left magazine edited by Jean-Paul Sartre and philosopher Maurice Merleau-Ponty. In an editorial dated 24 December 1946, only a few weeks after the bombardment of Haiphong, *Les Temps modernes* not only called openly for the withdrawal of French troops, but made a direct comparison between French rule in Indochina and the German occupation of France.[34]

Over the next few months *Les Temps modernes* published a number of articles on Indochina. The aim was not merely to denounce but to understand, and there were descriptions of the Indochinese experience by soldiers who had served there, and first-hand accounts of the brutality of French colonial rule.

---

31   See Kilian 1948.
32   *Esprit* 116, 1 November 1945.
33   Bellanger, Godechot, Guiral and Terrou 1975, p. 300.
34   *Les Temps modernes* December 1946. For a full analysis of the role of *Les Temps modernes* see Drake 1998.

3   Claude Lefort

One of the most interesting contributions to the discussion of the situation in Indochina in *Les Temps modernes* was an article published in March 1947 by Claude Lefort [1924–2010]. Lefort had first become politically active as a school student during the German occupation. One of his teachers was Merleau-Ponty, who told him that if he read Trotsky, he would become a Trotskyist. Lefort joined the Comité Communiste Internationaliste and organised a clandestine Trotskyist group in his *lycée*. Merleau-Ponty then brought him into the *Les Temps modernes* circle and encouraged him to write for the journal. He was a critical thinker who, a couple of years later, broke with what he considered the sterile dogmatism of orthodox Trotskyism and became one of the founders of the Socialisme ou barbarie group [SouB: Socialism or Barbarism], a small split from the French Trotskyist movement.

The article was entitled 'The Colonial Countries: Structural Analysis and Revolutionary Strategy'.[35] It drew on both Trotsky's theory of permanent revolution and the philosophical work of Merleau-Ponty. From the former Lefort took the idea of the world as a socio-economic totality, within which any specific struggle had to be evaluated in the context of the whole. From the latter he took a critique of Stalinist Marxism which rejected the notion that human history could be understood as a series of predetermined stages.

Lefort began by clearly demarcating himself from the mainstream of the French left on the question of the war in Indochina. He insisted that the responsibility of revolutionaries was to give *unconditional* support to struggles against their own imperialism. This was not simply a moral stance; for workers in the imperialist countries those fighting for national liberation were fighting the same ruling class, and thus the same enemy: 'The struggle of the colonial peoples against imperialism is the very same struggle as is being carried on by the proletariat of the metropolitan countries against this imperialism. It weakens it economically and militarily, it deepens its contradictions and makes it more vulnerable to an internal revolution'.[36]

Lefort went on to develop an analysis based on Trotsky's *Permanent Revolution*, especially the concept of combined and uneven development. In Indochina – as in pre-1917 Russia, China or Japan – archaic and modern economic and social forms existed side by side. In countries such as Indochina the bourgeois and socialist revolutions were not separate stages but were closely intertwined.

---

35   Lefort 1947.
36   Lefort 1947, p, 1070.

In Lefort's analysis, the Indochinese struggle was part of the same history which working people in France were living. Internationalism required seeing the whole political process as a single totality.

Lefort argued that since colonialism favoured the large landowners in Indochina, there was a tendency towards fusion between the landowning class and the embryonic bourgeoisie; this bourgeoisie remained subordinate, since such major industry as existed was in French hands. The bourgeoisie could not carry through a democratic revolution, since it preferred the preservation of feudal land ownership. Once the struggle for independence began, 'the masses caught up in the revolutionary process could not fail to come into conflict with their own exploiters'.

Over 90 percent of the Indochinese population were peasants, driven by poverty to revolt against their exploiters, who were 'in the first instance, foreign imperialism, but also and equally the indigenous feudal bourgeoisie which, under the protection of imperialism, was keeping them in poverty'.

The working class proper made up only 2 percent of the population, but since they were often drawn from the countryside and returned there on the expiry of their contracts, workers and peasants were 'closely linked'.[37] The Indochinese bourgeoisie was incapable of leading a revolution and saw the greatest danger as an internal revolution. It could not lead a genuine fight for national independence but merely manipulated the popular movement 'as a means of pressure on imperialism'.[38]

The very concept of an Indochinese nation was called into question; the mere demand for national independence became simplistic. The struggle for independence would lead to conflict within Indochinese society. Class divisions were more fundamental than national divisions.

Lefort went on to make a devastating critique of the politics of the Indochinese Communist movement and its leader Ho Chi Minh. Ho stood for 'revolution by stages'; the Viet Minh had been dissolved in the name of 'national unity'; this was 'political suicide' and a 'symbolic counter-revolutionary gesture'. The compromises of the Indochinese Communists had paved the way for a new imperialist offensive.[39]

In analysing the role of the Indochinese Communists Lefort was making another point. His support for national independence was unconditional; but there was no obligation on the French left to confine its role to that of cheerleader for nationalist movements. Precisely because the French left were

---

37   Lefort 1947, pp, 1080–81.
38   Lefort 1947, p. 1082.
39   Lefort 1947, p. 1088.

involved in a struggle of which they themselves were an integral part, their duty of support was inextricably linked to a duty to criticise the leadership of the independence struggle.

In the final section of his article Lefort reasserted the internationalist premises of his article:

> There cannot be a victorious revolution in a single country. We have put too much stress on the internationalist basis of Marxism for us in turn to fall victim to national illusions. Even if the Indochinese revolution were led by the most competent party it could not in the last resort avoid failure if it remained isolated.[40]

This, he insisted, must not be understood fatalistically: there were no guarantees of success; there was no predetermined end to the historical process. Even if it ended in defeat, a real struggle could be an experience from which the future movement could learn, whereas a failure to take the risk would lead simply to demoralisation.

Lefort's analysis might have helped arm the French left for the difficult years ahead. Yet the PCF did not even deign to debate with him; that would have been to grant legitimacy to his argument. Only *Les Temps modernes* published a reply, from the pen of another of Merleau-Ponty's students, the Indochinese philosopher Tran-Duc-Thao in an article called 'On the Trotskyist Interpretation of the Indochinese Events'.[41]

Tran disputed Lefort's economic analysis, saying that feudalism no longer existed in Indochina, and that Ho had shown correct leadership in the difficult post-war situation. Most seriously he accused Lefort of assisting French imperialism, albeit against his will. By calling the policies of the Viet Minh 'counter-revolutionary' Lefort was giving French imperialism 'magnificent weapons which enable it to undermine "from within" the real solidarity between the Vietnamese proletariat and the French proletariat'.[42]

Tran returned to Indochina in 1951, but was sacked from Hanoi University in 1958; in his self-criticism, he admitted links with *Les Temps modernes*, described as being a Trotskyist group.

---

40   Lefort 1947, p. 1090.
41   Tran-Duc-Thao 1947.
42   Tran-Duc-Thao 1947, p. 1705.

4   SFIO Youth

For the first six months of the war PCF ministers remained in the government. When it came to a vote on war credits in the National Assembly, the PCF adopted a compromise position – their ministers voted in favour, but the other Communist deputies abstained.

Although the SFIO was also in government, many of its members, especially in its youth organisation, were strongly opposed to the war. Unlike the PCF, the SFIO had a long tradition of internal debate and factional organisation. From January 1947 it was an SFIO member, Paul Ramadier, who headed the tripartite government, so the party clearly took responsibility for France's colonial policy.

The Parti communiste internationaliste [PCI] had a cadre hardened by their role in the Resistance. Early in 1946 the PCI paper *La Vérité* had published an article by an Indochinese militant who declared that Indochina's freedom and independence 'would be the work of the Indochinese workers themselves, struggling alongside French workers and the world proletariat against oppression wherever it may come from'. An editorial note predicted that the United States was already trying to get Indochina in its grasp in order to replace one capitalist exploiter by another. The paper called for a 'free, independent soviet Indochina'.[43]

The PCI decided to call a meeting at the Mutualité, a large hall in Paris often used for public meetings. This was banned by the Minister of the Interior, Édouard Depreux of the SFIO. Over a thousand people, French and Algerian, with the Algerian leader Messali Hadj at their head, marched to the locked hall, and held a street meeting. PCI leader Yvan Craipeau addressed the crowd, perched on his comrades' shoulders, until the police arrested him.[44]

Opposition also came from the SFIO youth, the Jeunesses Socialistes [JS]. After the bombardment of Haiphong tensions between the JS and the party machine rapidly intensified. The JS paper *Drapeau Rouge* [red flag] called for a negotiated peace, condemning the 'exploitation of men of colour by colonial capitalism'.[45]

The bureaucracy tried to silence the JS. Colonial minister Marius Moutet assured them he was working for peace. Party leader Guy Mollet told them the youth organisation was not there to discuss politics; André Essel of the JS responded that the war was very much a question for the youth, since if the war continued conscripts would be sent.

---

43   *La Vérité*, 29 March 1946, quoted by Craipeau 1978, pp. 156–7.

44   Craipeau 1999, p. 191.

45   Ayme 1983, p. 88.

Drapeau Rouge ran a series of headlines calling for opposition to colonial war and for immediate peace. The JS organised a campaign of leaflets, fly-posting and meetings. Leaflets stated: 'People think they're dying for their homeland, but they're dying for the rubber planters ... Not a halfpenny, not a man for Indochina'.[46]

In April the JS held their national congress. On Sunday, 6 April, the delegates joined a demonstration in Paris, ostensibly in honour of the dead of the Commune; in fact it was an opportunity to display their opposition to the war. Some 1000 congress delegates were joined by another 1000 Young Socialists from Paris. Among their banners was one demanding 'Immediate Peace with Vietnam'.[47]

The demonstration was noisy and vigorous, and terminated with a rally. When he spoke, André Essel, a Trotskyist active in the JS, drew the internationalist conclusion of the JS position, arguing that the Commune showed that the struggle between capitalism and the proletariat allowed no compromise. That was why they refused to sing the militaristic and chauvinist song called the *Marseillaise*, and honoured only one flag – the red flag of the *communards*.[48]

One of accusations thrown at the JS by the SFIO bureaucracy was that they were being manipulated by Trotskyists who had infiltrated the party. The PCI had done entry work in the SFIO under the leadership of Essel, a Trotskyist who had joined the JS under the name Dunoyer. However in 1946 the SFIO Youth had over 30,000 members. The membership of the Parti communiste internationaliste [PCI] was less than 600, and the number of comrades involved in entry work was very small, though some Trotskyists were elected to key positions, because they were experienced militants with a coherent position. The attempt by Pierre Mauroy and others to blame all opposition on the Trotskyists[49] did not reflect reality.

Although they would never have admitted it, when the PCF later launched a major campaign against the war they were building on foundations laid by Trotskyists and Young Socialists when the PCF were still in government.

5   **Cold War**

Everything changed in the summer of 1947. The post-war honeymoon between the victorious powers of the Second World War came to an end with the Tru-

---

46   Ayme 1983, p. 89.

47   Essel 1985, p. 217.

48   Essel 1985, pp. 217–18.

49   Ayme 1983.

man doctrine, the commitment that the USA would intervene against any revolution it believed to be Communist. This was followed by the Marshall Plan – economic aid to Europe in return for political subordination to US policy. Stalin responded with the formation of the Cominform [Communist Information Bureau], a body consisting of the ruling Communist Parties of the USSR and Eastern Europe [minus Albania], plus the Communist Parties of France and Italy. 1948 was the year when Communists took power in Czechoslovakia and the year of the Berlin blockade and airlift; 1949 saw the formation of the North Atlantic Treaty Organization [NATO].

The international situation transformed the political line-up inside France. From the Liberation to 1947 France was governed by a series of coalitions, in almost all of which the PCF had participated alongside the SFIO. In May 1947, under pressure from Washington and in the context of a Trotskyist-led strike at Renault, the SFIO Prime Minister Ramadier dismissed Communist ministers from his government. The PCF, which had opposed strikes, now encouraged a wave of industrial militancy. The SFIO took an increasingly pro-American stance, while a new militantly right-wing organisation, de Gaulle's Rassemblement du peuple français [RPF: Alliance of the French People], emerged.

The USA was opposed to colonialism and to the re-establishment of the European empires. Despite the rhetoric, this did not result from compassion for the 'poor ... huddled masses' of the world, but rather from a recognition that if the European empires were to withdraw it would make it easier to spread US political and economic influence. Nonetheless the fight against the spread of Communism was paramount, and the USA supported France economically in the later stages of its war to retain control of Indochina, while preparing alternatives for the eventuality of a French defeat.

Only in 1947, after the departure of both de Gaulle and the PCF, was a French government, headed by the SFIO, able to take an openly pro-American position in the emerging Cold War. For a while the PCF seemed to think it could get back into government, perhaps forcing its way back by a display of industrial militancy.[50] The PCF could now launch a vigorous campaign against the war in Indochina, using militant methods.

For the next decade and more the world would be polarised between the two power blocs. If a nuclear balance of terror prevented all-out confrontation, there were proxy wars between East and West, notably in Korea. Before French political life became completely entrapped in the logic of the Cold War, the authentically internationalist current on the French left made one more appearance.

---

50   Barjonet 1968, p. 49.

The launching of the Rassemblement Démocratique Révolutionnaire [RDR: Revolutionary Democratic Alliance] came in the spring of 1948. The main initiators were former Trotskyist David Rousset, Jean-Paul Sartre, and Georges Altman, editor of *Franc-Tireur*, a daily newspaper of the independent left. This developed from a statement published in November 1947 under the title 'First appeal to international opinion'. This argued that war could and must be avoided, but this would require European unity on a socialist basis. It went on to take a third camp position – neither Washington nor Moscow – in relation to the Cold War: 'Between the rottenness of capitalist democracy, the weaknesses and defects of a certain social democracy and the limitation of communism to its Stalinist form, we believe an assembly of free men for revolutionary democracy is capable of giving new life to the principles of freedom and human dignity by binding them to the struggle for social revolution'.[51]

Briefly this struck a chord with a section of the French population. As applications for membership flooded in, the RDR's leaders anticipated rapid growth. At the opening press conference Rousset declared 'we need 50,000 members in three months'. Not to be outdone, the following week Léon Boutbien set targets of '50,000 members in a month, 200,000 in three months'.[52] When Rousset went to the USA to seek money from American trade unions – and ended up getting a subsidy from the state – the whole thing began to fall apart; by the end of 1949 it had effectively disappeared.[53]

The RDR defended internationalist principles, not only independence from the two power blocs, but also opposition to French imperialism. On 18 November 1948 Sartre and other speakers addressed a largely Muslim audience on the question of Morocco. Sartre stressed the links between the class struggle in France and colonial oppression.[54]

Having been expelled from government, the Communist Party was able to start campaigning against the war in Indochina. It could call up significant support, from its own base and its periphery.

From now on it would be the big battalions of the PCF and the CGT which would lead opposition to the war in Indochina. The PCF swung sharply to the left and launched a series of militant actions. Ultimately the party's work was governed by a popular frontist logic and the action tended to be intensified or played down in order to fit the party's other political priorities. In particular the PCF often gave an anti-American tone to the anti-war campaign.

---

51   Comité pour le RDR 1948.
52   Ronsac, 1988, p. 234; J.F. 1948; R.S. 1948.
53   Birchall 1999.
54   Lamouchi, 1996, pp. 56–7. See *La Gauche RDR* 8, November 1948, pp. 1, 3.

Nonetheless some very effective work was done which helped to make the French war effort less efficient and popular. Many individual episodes of the PCF's campaign against the war were impressive, and could be seen as exemplary in the mobilisation of mass working-class action against an imperialist war.

PCF propaganda identified the war as an American war. There was a deal of truth in this. The French were fighting in Indochina as proxies for the Americans, and in the interests of its efforts to contain the spread of Communism. From 1950 onwards almost three quarters of the total cost of the French war was paid by the US government. Yet to identify the war in this way let the French government off the hook. The argument that the war was against French national interests, and that the whole nation should unite against it, prevented any serious analysis of who was responsible for the war.

The war was far from popular, though declining support for the war probably reflected the military fortunes of the French forces rather than the impact of Communist propaganda:

Opinion Poll figures 1947–54[55]

	July 1947	July 1949	October 1950	May 1953	February 1954
Send more troops:	37%	19%	27%	15%	7%
Negotiate:	15%	–	24%	35%	42%
Bring troops home:	22%	49%	18%	15%	18%

6　　Anti-War Action

In the tense atmosphere of the late forties, and in a situation where US arms and supplies were being shipped to Indochina via France, demonstrations against the war were vigorous. In Marseille:

> In the city itself, the la Joliette district, from where the 'official' demonstration was due to start, was surrounded by the police. It was forbidden to enter the district or to park in the streets. But the organisers of the demon-

---

55　　Ruscio 1985, p. 200.

stration had planned their response in advance; the CGT drivers of trams and trolley-buses suddenly stopped work, leaving their vehicles where they were. Immediately, Marseille was completely blocked off. This had the advantage of preventing the police from getting around. At the same time, the demonstration announced for la Joliette began on the famous Canebière. Strikers from various factories in the city arrived. Rapidly the whole centre of Marseille was swarming with people. The few police – on bicycles – who managed to reach the fringes of the demonstration were jostled by the crowd. Many of them had to abandon their peaked caps and bicycles, to the cheers of the crowd.[56]

In Nice two thousand anti-war demonstrators broke through police lines and threw what they believed to be a rocket-launcher into the sea.

Industrial action against the war reached its high point in the years 1949–50. This centred on dock-workers, who systematically refused to load or unload ships conveying supplies for Indochina. Such action began with dockers in Algeria but spread rapidly to Marseille and ports throughout France [only Cherbourg, where the pro-US breakaway union Force ouvrière was dominant, was an exception].

> Dunkirk: dockers refuse to load the *Auray* [1 February 1950], the *Boulogne* [31 March], the *Monkay* [12 May] ... These ships have to be loaded by troops.
>
> Castres: Railway workers delay on two occasions [23 January, 21 February] the departure of trains carrying military material.
>
> Caen: 60 people attack the last wagon of a train carrying munitions and armaments and throw an armoured caterpillar-tractor onto the track [17 February].
>
> Grenoble: four large guns are thrown onto the tracks by demonstrators [22 February].
>
> Paris [gare de Vaugirard] a military vehicle is damaged by demonstrators [24 April].
>
> Brive: demonstrators unload the contents of 38 barrels of explosives onto the tracks [9 March].
>
> Algiers: nearly 100 actions by dockers recorded from summer 1949 onwards.[57] [These were Algerian dockers, encouraged by the Com-

---

56   Ruscio 1985, p. 253.
57   Ruscio 1985, pp. 257–8.

munist Party; Algerian women, family members of the dockers, were heavily involved, sometimes stoning police.[58]]

The dockers showed exceptional determination and self-sacrifice. For many, refusal to work on US ships meant a severe cut in an already small wage-packet. The employers and authorities tried to discipline the ringleaders; there were numerous sackings. In 1950 parliament introduced a new law limiting the right to strike, and the militant action subsided.

Whether all the credit for such industrial action goes to the PCF remains unclear. A tradition of militancy existed among dockers. There was a powerful anarcho-syndicalist heritage, and union discipline was very strong – members could be fined for not attending union meetings.

Pierre Codet, a CGT official, described events:

> In the morning, I arrived at the port. The delegates went onto all the boats: 'Comrades, we're on strike. There's a meeting'. No need for explanations; they stopped work first. Then everyone gathered together ... and in the name of the *Union départementale* I proposed striking against the presence in the port of a ship loaded with arms. When the decision was taken, discipline was total. No question of any docker trying to work.[59]

The PCF certainly capitalised on the dockers' militancy, yet Charles Tillon later argued that the PCF had failed to demand equally militant action from railway-workers, who were just as central as dockers to the transport of military goods.[60]

There were widespread accusations of sabotage of military supplies. In 1949 French General Revers, after an inspection tour of Indochina, made a top-secret report [which rapidly passed into Viet Minh hands and was broadcast by them] showing that 40 percent of French equipment arriving in Indochina had been sabotaged. Obviously no formal instructions were issued about such activity, and it is hard to establish to what extent sabotage had direct political motives.[61]

In February 1950 a young woman, Raymonde Dien, lay down on railway lines in front of a train carrying military supplies, challenging the driver to run over

---

58   Drew 2014, p. 166.
59   Ruscio 1985, p. 243.
60   Tillon 1977, p. 483.
61   Fall 1955, p. 505.

her. She was subsequently arrested and imprisoned for 10 months. Much was made in the subsequent campaign of her youthfulness, femininity and courage. While her courage is undisputed, she was 20 years old and the secretary of a PCF official. This was an effective stunt, but nonetheless a stunt. Direct action alone could never defeat the state, since it always depended on the *political* limitations constraining the state's use of force in response. It would have been easy enough to run over Dien, but the effect on public opinion would have been catastrophic, perhaps even leading to the fall of the government. But in the last resort the state had a monopoly of physical force and would not allow itself to be diverted from its plans.

7   **Henri Martin**

One area where the PCF's campaigning made a particularly strong impact was in the affair of a young sailor called Henri Martin. Martin had been a Resistance fighter who joined the PCF in 1944. He had been recruited as a result of the Party's stress on the national liberation of France, its anti-fascism, and the undoubted courage of its members in the Resistance struggle. It is unlikely that anti-colonialism or the liquidation of the French Empire were much spoken of in the PCF at this time. Martin remained in the armed forces, and was happy to be sent to Indochina, where, he was told, he would be fighting against the remnants of Japanese fascism and so-called bandits who were disrupting the reconstruction of the country.

Martin's actual experience in Indochina was very different. His parents preserved a set of 31 letters which he sent home from the Far East. These depict his progressive disillusion as he came to understand the reality of Indochina. He observed the arrogance of the French rich and the terrible poverty of the Indochinese poor. He realised that he and his fellow-soldiers had been sent to suppress people who wanted to fight for their own freedom. Time and again the parallel with the Resistance came up in his letters, as Martin recognised that the French in Indochina were playing exactly the same role that the *boches* had played in France. Although his point of reference was the French nationalism he had learnt from the PCF during the Occupation, his own nationalism was progressively undermined by this very fact.

> [21 April]: Meanwhile, behind targeted machine-guns, under a leaden sun, we mount guard *against men who want to be free.* ...
>
> [18 May 1946]: In Indochina the French army is behaving as the *boches* did in France. I am completely disgusted to see that. Why do our planes

machine-gun (every day) defenceless fishermen? Why do our soldiers pillage, burn and kill? In order to bring civilisation?[62]

Martin seems to have taken no action while in Indochina. After two years in the Far East he applied for release from the armed forces; this was refused. He was sent to work in a fuel testing centre at Toulon [much more akin to an industrial environment], where he was known as a conscientious worker. In 1949 and 1950 he distributed, clandestinely, some sixteen leaflets – mainly bearing the signature 'a group of sailors' – which expressed direct opposition to the war and urged his fellow-workers to oppose it, calling on troops to refuse to embark for Indochina. The leaflets presented clear opposition to the war:

[August 1949]: Enough is enough, we didn't join up to go and die in Indochina, in order to increase the profits of French and American bankers and rubber-merchants, nor to waste our youth in an unjust war against a people which, as ours did from 1940 to 1944 against the *boches*, is also fighting for its freedom and independence ... *Enough dead, enough blood. All together let us refuse to go next December.*

[February 1950]: Like the dockers, railwaymen and other workers who refuse to load, transport or produce supplies for war, and who demand the return home of the French expeditionary force, *French sailors, following the example of the soldiers at Fréjus who, on 9 January, refused to board ship, we shall also struggle against the dirty war by refusing to leave for Indochina on 4 February on the* Île d'Oléron.

[March 1950, addressed to striking dockers]: Comrade dockers, we hail your magnificent struggle against the war. At the head of the working class you are showing us the road to victory. We, sons of workers at present in uniform, assure you of our solidarity. We shall never agree to play the role of scabs and break your strike. We know your struggle is ours, and that it is also for us that you are fighting. We, as sailors in the Navy, are part of the French people, and we shall never betray the working class.[63]

After one leaflet was issued in the name of the PCF, Martin was arrested and put on trial. He was sentenced to imprisonment and was kept in jail for three years before being released early as a result of a vigorous public campaign.

---

62   Quoted in Sartre 1953, pp. 39, 41.
63   Sartre 1953, pp. 87–90.

At his trial in July 1951 Martin stated that the war was for capitalist profits and of no value to the people of France. ... 'If I had remained inactive, I should not have done my duty as a Frenchman'. He added 'At school ... I was always told that France did not conquer, but liberated. When I arrived in Vietnam, I saw that this was definitely not the case'.[64]

Although the PCF put extensive resources into defending Martin, the fact of Martin's PCF membership was played down, and even the hostile press was unsure whether he was a party member. Only after his release did Martin publicly acknowledge having been a PCF member for ten years. He remained a Communist and was later a party full-timer. It therefore remains unclear whether Martin was acting on party instructions in distributing the leaflets.

The campaign which the PCF waged in support of Martin was impressive. Large numbers of non-party activists were involved, in particular well-known intellectuals. Sartre edited a book with contributions from several other well-known writers. A pamphlet was published with an original drawing by Picasso on the cover. A play based on Martin's trial was performed some three hundred times, and was seen by some 100,000 people, despite police repression. So-called 'acrobats of freedom' hung banners and painted slogans on high build-ings.[65]

While the style of the campaign was within the traditions of the Popular Front, it was in general effective, and had an impact on the authorities. However the campaign was primarily organised around a civil liberties issue – the ques-tion of free speech for a member of the armed forces – and in that sense, although Martin was opposing the war, the campaign can still be seen as a retreat from the central issue of ending it.

An interesting perspective on the PCF's struggle against the war can be found in the novel by André Stil, editor of *L'Humanité, Au château d'eau* [The Water Tower], published in 1951; it was the first volume in a trilogy entitled *Le Premier choc* [The First Clash].[66] It was based on events that took place at the port of La Rochelle on the Atlantic coast and described a community of dockworkers living in poverty in a shanty-town. The dockers, many of them Communists, struck in opposition to the use of French ports as American bases and refused to receive American ships in their ports. Stil showed the workings of the local Communist branch, depicting heated meetings where problems and tactics were debated, and showed the tensions that sometimes

---

64   Sartre 1953, pp. 143–4.
65   Freeman, Martin and Delmas 1998, pp. xvii–xviii.
66   Stil 1951.

arose when the Communists tried to combine struggle around immediate economic issues with campaigning on international questions. One comrade complained that meetings were becoming like geography lessons, while another pointed out that unloading arms for the Americans was preparing death for other people.

Already by 1950 there was a major switch in the PCF's orientation, away from a campaign to end the war and towards a more generalised opposition to US imperialism. The Mouvement de la paix [Peace movement] was founded in 1948 and concentrated on issues such as Korea, NATO, German rearmament and various peace conferences involving prominent intellectuals from around the world. Maurice Thorez argued that the Peace movement should be supported by *all* French people – that is, class issues were to be dropped, and the abstraction of peace pursued rather than focusing on specific questions like Indochina.

In 1952 the PCF's main activity was organising a major demonstration against the arrival in Paris of the American General Ridgway, who had commanded in Korea and had allegedly used biological warfare. In the course of the demonstration, two workers were killed while others received savage injuries from bullets and tear-gas. The result was to isolate the PCF from its own periphery and to produce a decline in support.

Then the PCF was flung, as part of the international Communist movement, into the campaign for a Five Power Peace Pact. An international petition – the Stockholm Appeal, calling for a ban on nuclear weapons – was launched by the World Peace Council, and Communist Parties throughout the world were mobilised into collecting signatures. This led to the erosion of the CGT's factory base, since the union was perceived as not devoting enough time and energy to the pursuit of workers' economic interests. The sharpest decline in the CGT's membership came, not after the split with Force Ouvrière in the late forties, but rather during the period of the stress on peace activities. The relative improvement in workers' living standards during the *trente glorieuses* also tended to reduce combativity.

In the later years of the war, as the PCF moved to the right with its quest for a renewal of the Popular Front – an alliance with the SFIO and other parties of the left centre – the level of activity was reduced. The tactics adopted by the Communist-led peace movement were very much in the traditions of the Popular Front: large peace congresses, addressed by distinguished intellectuals from outside the ranks of the Communist Parties and petitions urging arms limitation by international agreement.

8   André Marty

For the first few years of the Indochina war the PCF's military work was under
the leadership of André Marty. Marty was effectively number three in the party
hierarchy; he had been one of the leaders of the Black Sea mutiny in 1919,
and Political Commissar of the International Brigades in the Spanish Civil War.
Whereas the two top leaders, Thorez and Duclos, had made their careers inside
the Party apparatus, Marty had credentials as a leader of mass working-class
struggle, and this may have been a source of tension. Nonetheless he had been
a loyal Stalinist over more than two decades and showed the respect for legality which characterised the PCF's strategy even in its most radical phases.
When told of a group of Communist soldiers in Indochina who were supplying
arms to the Viet Minh, he flew into a rage. 'Marty listened to him, and suddenly,
bursting into a fit of anger, he hurled his fountain pen at the wall: "You are pro-
vocateurs!", he yelled. "The Party cannot tolerate such provocations: dismantle
this network.!" '[67]

Then in the late summer of 1952, when the PCF should have been concen-
trating all its efforts on opposing the war in Indochina, the Marty-Tillon affair
erupted. [Charles Tillon had been head of the Francs-Tireurs et Partisans Français, a Resistance organisation controlled by the PCF.]

In 1952 both men were stripped of their party positions; Marty was subsequently expelled, while Tillon was reduced to rank-and-file status. The affair
was probably linked to a series of show trials in Eastern Europe at the time,
designed to weed out any leaders with nationalist deviations which might
make them less than totally loyal to Moscow. Such accusations of nationalism
revealed the extent to which the idea of internationalism had become totally
perverted; it had come to mean simply the total subordination of international
Communism to Moscow.

After his expulsion Marty wrote a book, *L'Affaire Marty* [The Marty Affair].
It presented an interesting critique of the PCF's activity over Indochina, in particular the turn away from direct action against the war in Indochina towards
more propagandist campaigning for peace.

> In fact, from 1946 to 1949, our propagandists, journalists and deputies,
> when they spoke of atrocities committed in Indochina, blamed them all
> on former SS men and members of Pétain's militia who had joined the

---

67   Doyon 1973, p. 316.

Foreign Legion. It is true that these fascists were abhorrent murderers. But by speaking only of their responsibilities, we missed those of the French troops.[68]

Marty's book showed a three-way tension within the Party apparatus, between unconditional loyalty to Moscow, a Jacobin orientation to the French national interest and an authentic internationalism. While no policy could be promoted that diverged from Moscow's wishes, not all members were motivated purely by Stalinist principles. An internationalist tradition continued to inspire many of the rank and file in their actions against the war in Indochina.

In the fraught situation of the 1940s and 1950s, with a mass Communist Party that seemed to sympathise with the enemy, no French government would have dared to send conscripts to fight in Indochina. Given that in 1951 over 26 percent of the electorate voted Communist, the possibility of an army that was one quarter Communist in sympathies was an alarming one. [In fact the PCF was very cautious about advocating insubordination in the military; however, the government could not rely on this remaining the case.] The absence of conscript soldiers was one factor that made the war seem more remote to the French public.

9 French Troops

The war to keep Indochina French was fought by the *Corps Expéditionnaire Français en Extrême-Orient* [French Far East Expeditionary Corps]. This consisted of French professional soildiers, troops from French colonies in Africa, and the Foreign Legion. It fought alongside the Vietnamese National Army, trained by French officers.

When the French armed forces were reorganised at the Liberation the PCF obtained the integration of the Resistance militias [the *Forces françaises de l'intérieur* which included the PCF-controlled *Francs-Tireurs et Partisans*] into the framework of the regular army. Resistance fighters were encouraged to stay in the army, ostensibly to finish off the war against Japan, but in reality to preserve the French Empire.

Many of the troops who had gone to fight in Indochina had just emerged from a struggle against fascism in France. Frequently they were surprised to find that the situation in Indochina was remarkably similar to that in occu-

---

68   Marty 1955, p. 37.

pied France. The Viet Minh were not recognised as an army, but described as criminal elements – just as the Resisters had been in occupied France – so the Geneva Conventions did not apply. There was widespread torture and random killing of civilians.

The French Foreign Legion was a particularly brutal outfit. In the immediate aftermath of World War II it attracted many former combatants, especially Germans, who wanted to be well away from investigations into war crimes. Among the Germans there were some anti-fascists, but many more who had participated in the occupation of France, including some who continued to be Nazis.

European soldiers were far from their native terrain, and had problems with climate, food and disease. Guerrilla warfare put additional demands on them. Louis Dalmas in *Les Temps modernes* showed that the actual experience and attitudes of the French fighting in Vietnam were very different from what was expected by the politicians in Paris who had sent them there. He described French troops standing up to their necks in water, wearing condoms to protect them from leeches. French soldiers faced 'partisans who know everything about a region, who control its inhabitants, who appear and disappear as they please'. As a result French soldiers had come to respect the 'courage, skill and organisation' of their opponents and to feel 'a sort of reluctant admiration for people who are giving them such a hard time'.[69]

It was an unpopular war – the troops were well aware of the demonstrations and strikes in France. Morover, the political instability of the Fourth Republic meant that no government could develop a long-term strategy. While there was a widespread recognition that sooner or later the war would end with a negotiated peace, how this would happen was impossible to predict. The feeling by soldiers that they were fighting for nothing led to demoralisation; among senior officers there developed an impatience with parliamentary democracy that would manifest itself during the Algerian War. Even if a soldier had been determined to devote himself to the French national interest, he would have had great difficulty establishing what that interest was.

There was a significant level of desertion during the war. Of the 30,000 or more deserters the vast majority were Indochinese troops. Of the 200 or 300 French soldiers who went over to the Viet Minh, most did so primarily for personal reasons, such as the desire to marry a Vietnamese woman, or to escape responsibility for a crime. Initially the Viet Minh had urged French soldiers to desert. Then in 1950 the PCF and the Viet Minh agreed on the slogan: 'Demand

---

69   Dalmas 1953, pp. 199–200.

individual and immediate repatriation!'[70] However, a small number of French soldiers [and also some Germans from the French Foreign Legion] went over to the Viet Minh on the basis of political conviction. There is a detailed account in Jacques Doyon, *Les Soldats blancs de Ho Chi Minh* [Ho Chi Minh's white soldiers].

An unpopular war, an army with low morale and a mass Communist Party with hundreds of thousands of members seemed to offer the potential for effective revolutionary agitation within the army. In practice the PCF was very cautious about organising within the armed forces.

The PCF was committed to having members in the army. Its Resistance activists remained in the regular army, and Communists were firmly admonished against draft-dodging, desertion or conscientious objection. All this was justified in the name of 'Leninism'. Whether there is in fact such a clear-cut Leninist doctrine is open to question – there is for example a letter from Lenin to Radek in the summer of 1915 advising him very strongly against joining the army: 'I advise you *not* to enlist. It's stupid to help the enemy. You will be doing a service to the Scheidemanns. Better emigrate'.[71]

However if the PCF was insistent that its members should be in the armed forces, it was less clear about what they should do there. In practice PCF members were simply told to act as Communists and to do 'mass work'.[72] The Party's inhibitions about organising in the army derived from its political strategy. When it was ousted from government in May 1947 the PCF took a sharp turn to the left. Yet the recreation of the Popular Front of 1936 remained a central aspiration, and by the 1950s it was again an explicit aim. Crossing the boundaries of legality in the armed forces could have endangered that strategy.

There were various possible courses of action for Communist soldiers in Indochina. They could decide:

– to try and ensure that the war was fought reasonably humanely and attempt to prevent atrocities, oppose torture and killing of prisoners, etc.;
– to argue against the war with their fellow soldiers;
– to take positive action to sabotage the war effort;
– to provide information – or even supplies – to the Viet Minh.

The practical possibilities of all these were limited, and they were mutually contradictory. A soldier claiming to represent the interests of his fellows would hardly enhance his credibility if he were seen to be responsible for sending them into battle with defective weapons. Anyone giving material assistance

---

70   Doyon 1973, pp. 148, 409.
71   Lenin 1966, p. 335.
72   Doyon 1973, pp. 271–2.

to the enemy would have to assume a pose of political orthodoxy to divert suspicion from himself. In one case a French Communist who was providing information to the enemy allowed himself to accuse French troops of atrocities in an argument with other soldiers. He was told by the Viet Minh that he had blown his cover and must desert.

The conditions of warfare in Indochina made it very difficult to organise effectively. Communist soldiers were isolated, dispersed and frequently transferred, and generally found themselves surrounded by men with Vichyite sympathies. Known Communists sometimes fell victim to a 'stray' bullet from their own side.[73]

A small number of French soldiers went over to the Viet Minh on the basis of political conviction. The Vietnamese used these defectors for their propaganda work, in broadcasting and as political education officers in prisoner of war camps. Two notable examples were Albert Clavier and Georges Boudarel.

Albert Clavier, born in 1927, was too young for any serious involvement in the Resistance; his elder brother was a Communist who had survived Buchenwald. At the Liberation, hoping to see something of the world, he enrolled in the Colonial Artillery – though, as he recalled, 'I didn't know much about what the colonies were'.[74] He was sent to Indochina. On the boat there were a number of Foreign Legion soldiers, some of them former Nazis. A stop at Djibouti, part of French Somaliland, revealed to him the enormous contrast between wealth and poverty in a colonial territory.

On arrival in Indochina he made friends with a Vietnamese family who were probably Viet Minh sympathisers. He also observed a fellow-soldier being beaten to death by members of the Foreign Legion for being a Communist. He saw other French atrocities and made friends with a Vietnamese teacher who was a Viet Minh supporter. He decided to defect, though he made it clear he was not prepared to bear arms against his compatriots. A fake kidnapping was arranged and he went over – subsequently he was condemned to death.

He was employed on propaganda work, addressing French troops with a loud-speaker and urging them to lay down their arms, making parallels between the Vietnamese struggle and the French Resistance. Later he worked with the French-language service of the Viet Minh radio station. He shared the living standards of his Vietnamese hosts, and ate nothing but two bowls of rice per day. He married a Vietnamese woman, and after a divorce married another. In 1964 he moved to Hungary, but was not allowed to return to France until 1967.

---

73   Doyon 1973, pp. 291, 297.
74   Collin 2011, p. 151.

10   **Boudarel**

Georges Boudarel, born in 1926, had been brought up in a Catholic family; he became a Communist under the influence of a fellow-worker while employed as a supervisor in a *lycée* in the post-war period. He does not seem to have been a particularly active member, and when, in the late 1940s, he applied for a teaching post in Indochina, his PCF contacts told him to drop his party membership since the party did not organise abroad, and only reluctantly gave him a contact address in Vietnam.

> I asked for advice from the PCF colonial bureau in the rue Saint-Georges. I was advised to leave my membership card in France and not to present myself as a party member. This was a question of principle, for the party had no branches outside of the national territory. However, a comrade who worked as a full-timer for the CGT in the rue de Solférino gave me a recommendation to someone called Canac, who lived in Saigon where he had formed a Marxist Cultural Group, banned by the authorities. Prudence, silence and circumspection were, in short, the instructions.[75]

The Marxist Cultural Group [Groupe Culturel Marxiste] had been formed in 1945 by a few dozen French Communists and sympathisers in Indochina who supported national independence. Briefly it produced a weekly publication with a circulation of 5000, and later maintained a library, but faced repeated repression, and ceased to exist by 1950.[76]

Boudarel spent some time teaching in Vietnam and Laos, and became sympathetic to the indigenous population. In 1950 he defected to the Viet Minh; had he not done so he would have been called up for military service in France. He was aware that he was acting against the explicit advice of the PCF.

Boudarel was accepted by the Viet Minh, who used him for various jobs; like Clavier, he did not take arms against his compatriots. He had to adapt to a tough lifestyle, travelling long distances through the Vietnamese jungle. He worked for some time on a Viet Minh radio station, then became political education officer in camp 113, a prisoner of war camp for French troops. There are differing accounts of his activity here. He denies having given long lectures and says he attempted to organise discussions. He was obliged to keep a considerable distance from the prisoners, many of whom regarded him with distrust. The

---

75   Boudarel 1991, pp. 31–2.
76   Ruscio 1985, pp. 320–31.

very high death rate in the Viet Minh prisoner of war camps was not a result of Viet Minh cruelty; it was caused by the shortage of food and medicine and the climatic conditions.

One prisoner recalled:

> We talked about politics in general, reasons for the war, what was wrong with it, what was going on in France, the opposition to the war in France, the slogans: 'Peace in Vietnam by bringing home the expeditionary force', etc. There was absolutely no question of indoctrination ... We never had *L'Humanité* in the camp.[77]

After the amnesty in the 1960s Boudarel returned to France and, using his knowledge of the language and culture of Vietnam, pursued an academic career. He wrote a biography of Vietnamese General Vô Nguyên Giap which was largely favourable to the liberation struggle, although he developed various criticisms of the Communist regime.[78] In 1991 – the time of the collapse of the Eastern bloc, when the political right were on the offensive – he was giving a paper at an academic conference at the Senate when he was challenged by Jean-Jacques Beucler, a former right-wing junior minister, who had been a prisoner in camp 113. The subsequent furore showed that France's colonial past was still a live issue, with some on the right demanding that he be executed for treason or stripped of French citizenship.[79]

11   Dien Bien Phu

In 1954 the pointless slaughter came to an end. The French had constructed an allegedly impregnable fortress at Dien Bien Phu. The Vietnamese succeeded in surrounding and capturing it. Racial arrogance and racist ignorance meant that the heirs of Napoleon could not conceive that they would be defeated by the superior generalship of Vô Nguyên Giap. It was a stunning military victory – it also revealed that France lacked the economic and political will and means to continue the war. It was the end of French rule in Indochina. The French had lost 20,000 soldiers; total casualties were at least 400,000.[80]

---

77   Einaudi 2001, p. 206.
78   Boudarel 1977.
79   Charuel 1991.
80   Dalloz, 1987, p. 251.

During the siege of Dien Bien Phu the Vietnamese played the famous Resistance song *Le Chant des partisans* [partisan song] over loudspeakers to the besieged French forces.[81] The obvious parallel between the French anti-fascist struggle and the Indochinese fight against French colonialism may have helped to demoralise the French troops.

After the fall of Dien Bien Phu Radical Pierre Mendès-France became prime minister. The Geneva agreements were rapidly concluded, with the support of Russia and the USA. Laos and Cambodia had already become independent states. Vietnam was now partitioned in two; the seeds of a new conflict had been sown.

For those around the world fighting for national independence, Dien Bien Phu was a moment of enormous encouragement. It showed that advanced industrial nations like France, even when backed by the USA, were not invincible but could be defeated. After Indian independence and the Chinese Revolution, it showed that European rule in Asia was coming to an end. In particular it was significant for the Algerian nationalists who would found the FLN later that year.

Unfortunately the French left had learned relatively little from its experiences. Despite the fact that its policies in Indochina had led to humiliating defeat, the SFIO maintained its attachment to the 'civilising mission' of French colonialism; it became the main architect of the war in Algeria and in the process came close to destroying itself. Meanwhile the PCF had also learned little; it remained committed to the strategy of the Popular Front, and failed to develop an approach to organising within the armed forces.

However, a new current began to grow on the French left. In 1952, in an article in *L'Observateur* entitled 'Three Worlds, One Planet',[82] Alfred Sauvy coined the term *tiers monde* [third world], which became central to the discourse of the European left by the 1960s. Sauvy implied a parallel with the Third Estate of the French Revolution; for the French republican tradition the term acquired connotations of a struggle for liberty, equality and fraternity. A growing awareness of Third World poverty called into question the myth of France's 'civilising mission' in its colonial territories. It was, however, in Algeria that France's colonial heritage would be challenged in a way that undermined the Fourth Republic.

---

81   Doyon 1973, p. 400.
82   Sauvy 1952.

Carrying Suitcases for Algeria

In 1953 *Les Temps modernes* published Daniel Guérin's article 'Pity for the Maghreb'.[1] In the late 1940s Guérin had spent two years in the United States and, before the eruption of the civil rights movement, had written powerfully about the deep-lying racism of US society and the emergence of Black revolt. He recounted how, when extracts from his book had appeared in the *Pittsburgh Courier*, he had received a letter from Atlanta, Georgia, urging him to keep his own French doorstep clean instead of concerning himself with the Southern USA. Guérin noted the obvious response, that as an internationalist he was entitled to criticise abuses in any country. He went on to say that, after a three-month journey through North Africa, he had decided his American critic was right.

In 'Pity for the Maghreb', Guérin gave a vivid picture of the human suffering he had observed in Morocco, Algeria and Tunisia, stressing in the Algerian case both the wretchedness of urban overcrowding and unemployment, and the way the authorities had 'tried to kill the soul of this country' by suppressing indigenous culture, especially the Arabic language and Islam. He ended by stating that North Africa was the last bastion of French capitalism and predicting that the owners of the great plantations would let the Maghreb be covered by fire and blood rather than surrender their power. This would be a challenge for the French left. Guérin was sceptical as to whether that left, in which the Communist Party played such an influential role, would be able to rise to the challenge.

It was a prophetic piece. For twenty-five years Guérin had written about colonialism in its various manifestations. He had listened to the victims of the system, and put his pen at the service of the oppressed. He had a much better understanding of the situation than the professional politicians who insisted unanimously that Algeria could never become independent.

It is doubtful whether the so-called political realists who made up the French government, preoccupied with parliamentary arithmetic and public opinion, even glanced at Guérin's article. If his warning had been heeded there might have been many fewer corpses.

---

1   Guérin 1953.

The movement for Algerian independence, founded by Hadj-Ali Abdelkader and Messali Hadj in the 1920s, had survived repression and bans. Messali himself spent much of his time in jail or under house arrest. The Sétif massacre of 1945 left a legacy of deep bitterness. Some modest reform proposals were partly sabotaged by the settler population. Massive impoverishment and unemployment in the indigenous population made French rule increasingly unpopular.

The independence movement, now under the name of Movement for the Triumph of Democratic Liberties [MTLD: Mouvement pour le Triomphe des Libertés Démocratiques] was still led by Messali Hadj. Messali was widely respected as a veteran of decades of struggle, but a new generation entering the movement was becoming impatient with his leadership.

Messali had spent relatively little time in Algeria since he came to Paris in 1923. He had a rather authoritarian style; even when under house arrest in France, he tried to keep control, telephoning orders every day. When there were divisions in the organisation he demanded full powers to rectify the party.[2] He had always advocated political rather than military action,[3] and had what seemed to many of the younger militants an excessive respect for constitutional action. After Sétif many of the younger activists came to believe that only armed struggle would get results. In 1954 Dien Bien Phu confirmed them in that view.

The deep divisions within the MTLD were getting out of Messali's control. A secret grouping developed which became the Revolutionary Committee of Unity and Action [CRUA: Comité Révolutionnaire d'Unité et d'Action] and then the National Liberation Front [FLN – Front de Libération Nationale].

A typical representative of the new generation was Ahmed Ben Bella. He joined the MTLD and became a councillor in Maghnia where he had responsibility for rationing and food supplies. He moved to clandestine work, becoming involved in the Special Organisation [Organisation spéciale], the underground military wing of the MTLD. In 1950 he was jailed for his part in planning a hold-up of the Oran post office. He escaped and moved to Cairo, where he became a leader of what would become the FLN.

1   The FLN

On 1 November 1954 the FLN launched a wave of synchronised attacks across Algeria, leaving nine dead and a large amount of damage to property. The

---

2 Harbi 2001, pp. 113, 118.
3 Stora, 1991, p. 140.

French government considered the FLN to be criminals rather than a political movement, but the National Liberation Army [ALN: Armée de Libération
Nationale], with initially a strength of 1000 at most,[4] continued to grow, sometimes using intimidation to extend its influence. Rapidly the revolt became
a major problem for the French government – it was one of the major issues
in the January 1956 election. Yet the French government did not recognise the
events in Algeria as a war, defining FLN activity as criminal. The refusal to admit
that there was a war going on continued despite mass escalation. The criminal-
isation of the FLN and the refusal to treat its fighters as legitimate combatants
had an exact parallel – not missed by many of those involved – with the way
the German occupiers had responded to the French Resistance.

Initially neither Messali's followers nor the French state took the actions
of 1 November 1954 very seriously. It was only individuals like Guérin and
small marginal groupings like the Trotskyists and anarchists who understood
that this was the beginning of a major struggle. The FLN's rapid growth after
1 November 1954 reflected the fact that there was still deep anger after the massacres in 1945, and increasing impatience at the French government's failure to
introduce significant reforms.

The relations between the FLN and Messali's organisation – renamed the
Algerian National Movement [MNA: Mouvement national algérien] became
deeply problematic. While there was no significant programmatic difference
between the two nationalist organisations, the FLN insisted on being the only
organisation representing the Algerian people; it demanded that other organisations, including the MNA, should dissolve and their members join the FLN as
individuals. Though Messali was critical of the tactics adopted by the FLN, he
could not condemn what was obviously a very popular action. But he refused
an invitation to move to Cairo and join the FLN.[5]

Soon there was armed conflict between the two organisations, a vicious war
within a war, with shootings, assassinations and massacres across Algeria and
mainland France that left several thousand dead. By late 1955 the FLN was
already the majority movement in Algeria, with MNA members flocking to join
the rival organisation.[6] This made things difficult for those French people who
supported Algerian independence; which of the rival organisations were they
to support? Even when it became clear that only the FLN could win a victory,
its image as a lethal bully made it rather less attractive.

---

4 Evans 2012, p. 123.
5 Stora 1982, p. 232.
6 Evans 2012, p. 141.

For seven and a half years the war raged on, until the eventual conclusion, independence for Algeria, although at the outset all but a tiny handful of marginal critics had refused to admit even the possibility. The war tore through the institutions of French society. Almost every family in France had a member who had been conscripted to fight in Algeria, or knew someone who had fought there.

From the beginning the leading figures of the non-Communist left and centre left – Guy Mollet of the SFIO, François Mitterrand of the UDSR [Union Démocratique et Socialiste de la Résistance: Democratic and Socialist Union of the Resistance] and Radical Pierre Mendès-France – made it clear there could be no question of independence for Algeria. A left formed by the traditions of the 'civilising mission' and *laïcité* was not prepared to compromise with a nationalist movement led by Muslims who wanted to destroy the territorial integrity of the Republic. The obstinacy of the mainstream French left merely encouraged the most intransigent elements in the FLN, which grew steadily in the course of 1955. The response of the French government was to treat it as a question of law and order and send in more troops.

It had been Mendès-France who had produced a solution to the question of Indochina. Some hoped the feat could be repeated in Algeria. Mendès-France's government had fallen by February 1955 and he was replaced by Radical Edgar Faure, who tried to resolve the Algerian situation by giving the army new powers and recalling reservists. In late 1955 an early general election was called.

During the election campaign the Algerian question achieved considerable importance. How that concern could be translated into a party vote was more of a problem. The biggest slice of left-wing votes would go to the Communists. In the Cold War climate no other party was willing to cooperate with the Communists in any circumstances. Any government would have to be cobbled together from the remaining non-Communist deputies.

2   Guy Mollet

So the non-Communist parties of the centre left formed the Republican Front [Front républicain]. The election results showed a shift to the left, with the Communists and the Republican Front doing well. When asked, a week before the election, who they hoped to see as Prime Minister, 27 percent of a sample of voters named Mendès-France, while only 2 percent named Guy Mollet, leader of the Socialist Party. This had no influence on the parliamentary manoeuvring which led to Mollet becoming prime minister. Mendès-France was his second in command, but it was Mollet and the SFIO who determined government policy.

Mollet came to power because of a widespread wish for a peaceful settlement in Algeria. He had no sympathy with the demand for Algerian independence. The myth of the 'civilising mission' was deeply rooted in the SFIO. When he visited Algiers in February he was met by a mob of angry settlers, furious at any threat to their privileges. This confirmed him on the path he would now follow. He determined to crush the rebellion. More troops were sent and the first executions of Algerian prisoners were ordered. The hard-liner Robert Lacoste became Minister-Resident and governor general of Algeria.

The role of the Communist Party was a complicating factor. It had done well in the elections, with over 5,5 million voters out of over 21 million votes cast [25.7 percent], and had 144 deputies out of 596. The Party had long-standing anti-imperialist traditions and many of its members were undoubtedly committed to a revolutionary internationalist position. Nonetheless over the years of the war the PCF often took positions that were surprisingly cautious; it scrupulously avoided any declaration of support for the FLN. There were a number of reasons for this.

Firstly, the PCF remained loyal to Moscow. The Russians understood that the USA's hostility to European colonialism sprang from a desire to supplant European influence, and were concerned that a French withdrawal from Algeria could lead to a stronger US influence in North Africa. In 1956 a senior Russian official told Jean-Paul Sartre that any attempt to push the question of Algeria within the Communist-led Peace Movement would be inopportune.[7]

Secondly, the PCF some years earlier had made a turn towards putting the demand for peace at the centre of all its propaganda and agitation. Thirdly, PCF strategy centred on the call for the renewal of the 'Popular Front', the electoral alliance of Communists, Socialists and Radicals formed in the 1930s.

Finally, the PCF was careful not to move too far ahead of its mass base. It knew that the Algerian settlers had millions of relatives, friends and supporters in mainland France, and it could not afford too sharp a confrontation with them.

Clara Benoits, a dissident PCF member who worked at Renault Billancourt, described her experience of working in an anti-war committee which contained Communists but was not under PCF control.

> To the PCF, we seemed to be in competition with the Mouvement de la paix ... On the demonstrations for peace in Algeria, we were criticised for linking the demand for peace to that for independence. During one of our

---

7   de Beauvoir 1963, p. 361.

meetings to which we had invited a leading figure from the Mouvement de la paix, he, horrified by our calls for independence, left the meeting in a rage: 'You're talking about something quite different from peace in Algeria. You're not dealing with French interests'. To which we replied: 'If our interests coincide, all the better, but our struggle isn't for "French interests", but for justice! And that inevitably means independence'.[8]

The Mollet government stepped up the war. More troops were sent to confront the rapidly growing FLN. Those troops increasingly used illegal methods, in particular torture and the killing of prisoners. While the Mollet government did not directly order such atrocities, it would be naïve to think they did not know what was going on. Ministers kept in close touch with Algiers by telephone, and the Minister-Resident, Robert Lacoste, was generally seen as very close to the most right-wing settlers and army officers.

Prisoners were a particular problem. Since the resistance had been criminalised, there could be no prisoners of war, and if all prisoners had been tried, even with an accelerated procedure, the court system would have collapsed under the sheer numbers. So a great many were simply murdered. One well-known device was the *corvée de bois* [wood duty] – prisoners were sent to collect wood for a fire, then shot down while allegedly trying to escape. Neither the army nor the government wanted to put FLN leaders on trial; that would have given a platform to the enemy.

A particular part was played by François Mitterrand. He held the position of Garde des Sceaux [Keeper of the Seals] or Minister of Justice. This made him number three in the government hierarchy. Mitterrand was just thirty-nine, and very ambitious; it was suggested he might succeed Mollet as prime minister quite soon. At the outbreak of the insurrection in 1954 he had insisted that negotiation with the rebels was inconceivable. He was totally committed to keeping Algeria French.

Mitterrand played a particularly significant role on the question of executions.[9] He established himself as a hard-liner; of the 45 executions during his period in office, he opposed clemency in at least 32 cases. After the first executions the FLN issued orders to its supporters to shoot down any European male aged between 18 and 54. This provoked settlers into forming racist lynch mobs, thus further polarising the situation. Then the FLN launched a wave of bombings in Algiers.

8　Benoits 2014, p. 89.
9　Malye and Stora 2010.

3   **Special Powers**

In March 1956 the Mollet government persuaded the National Assembly to vote
for 'special powers' to deal with the situation in Algeria. These gave Lacoste, the
Minister-Resident, the right to rule by decree, and transferred police powers to
the army, giving it the authority to detain and interrogate suspects, replacing
civilian courts by military courts. This made it easier for the authorities to use
torture and kidnapping.

The special powers were supported right across the political spectrum. To
the consternation of many of their own supporters, the Communist deputies
voted in favour. Their main concern was to try to renew a Popular Front and
they hoped – somewhat implausibly – that if they did not oppose the SFIO on
this question it might make an alliance more likely.

The new measures confirmed the Algerian population in their perception
of the whole French nation as hostile, and strengthened the influence of the
FLN. Algerians living in France felt threatened. At Renault Billancourt, where a
number of Algerian militants were active in the CGT, Algerian Communists tore
up their party cards, and helped to organise the FLN in the factory by bringing
together different political currents.

In the autumn of 1956 came the joint French and British invasion of Egypt.
The attack was seen by the Mollet government, which took the initiative in
drawing in Britain, as a means of breaking the Algerian revolt. It was true that
Nasser was giving support to the FLN, but foolish to believe the revolt could be
destroyed by cutting off its alleged head in Egypt.

Within nine days Britain and France were called to order by the United
States. It was the final gasp by the old European empires, now doomed to
decline and disintegration. The French Empire would take some years before it
realised it was dead.

There was little opposition to Suez in France. The invasion was seen quite
clearly as an integral part of the Algerian War. The potential movement to stop
the war in Algeria had collapsed earlier in 1956 and it was difficult to arouse
interest in Suez as a separate issue. Guy Mollet later told his party congress that
the Suez invasion had been a manifestation of proletarian internationalism.[10]
This showed how the very name of internationalism had been corrupted into
meaninglessness.

The contrast between different conceptions of internationalism was high-
lighted by events in Hungary in autumn 1956. A popular rising, in which work-

---

10   Reported in *Le Monde*, 2 July 1957.

ers' councils spread rapidly across the country, was crushed by Russian tanks. In Communist Parties around the globe there were sharp divisions between those who backed the Russian intervention and those who identified with the Hungarian workers. For some, internationalism still meant identifying with the international network built around the heirs of the October Revolution. For others it meant recognising a fundamental similarity with workers in other countries, in their creativity and their victimhood – and hence solidarity.

A fully internationalist response to the Hungarian events was to be found among the smaller organisations of the far left, notably Socialisme ou barbarie. SouB's perspective enabled it to perceive aspects of the Hungarian rising largely ignored by other commentators. Its stress was overwhelmingly on the capacity of Hungarian workers to organise themselves, with the creation of workers' councils. Hungarian workers were not perceived simply as the victims of Stalinist barbarity; rather they were the protagonists of their own struggle.

> Our task today is first of all and above all to propagate the programme of the Hungarian revolution, to help the French proletariat in its struggle against its own bureaucracy, which is inseparable from its struggle against capitalist exploitation. It is also to work for the regroupment, in all forms, of the workers and militants who recognise in the struggle and the programme of the Hungarian workers their own struggle and their own programme.[11]

In 1957 the French army set out to crush, by the most brutal means, the FLN's organisation in the capital. This was the so-called 'Battle of Algiers', depicted in Pontecorvo's movie *The Battle of Algiers* [1966]. In military terms this was a major setback for the FLN, but the war continued in the mountains and rural areas, and the Muslim population felt even greater hatred for the French. By now 400,000 French troops were deployed in Algeria.

Algeria would dominate the development of the left for the next few years. The mainstream left – the PCF, SFIO and figures like Mitterrand and Mendès-France – had been complicit in the escalation of the Algerian war. If an internationalist opposition to the war was to be found, it was among the activists of the far left, outside the political mainstream.

This was not a wholly negligible current. There was still an audience for radical internationalist politics, non-aligned in the Cold War, and hostile to racism

---

11   Chaulieu 1956–7, p. 171.

and imperialism in all their manifestations. It was in this fragmented milieu that the first activists prepared to oppose the war would be found.

The first organisation to oppose the war was the Committee of Struggle against Colonialist Repression [Comité de lutte contre la répression colonialiste], set up by the anarchist Fédération Communiste Libertaire [FCL: Libertarian Communist Federation] and the Trotskyist Parti Communiste Internationaliste [PCI], together with Daniel Guérin in December 1954.[12] The first public meeting against the war in Paris would have been on 21 December 1954, but it was banned by François Mitterrand.[13] One of the first anti-war meetings was held in 1955, when 50 stewards armed with iron bars, assisted by Algerians attending the meeting, fought off 300 far-right activists who came to disrupt the event.[14]

On 27 January 1956 a meeting was held at the salle Wagram, organised by the Comité d'action des intellectuels contre la poursuite de la guerre en Afrique du Nord [Intellectuals' Action Committee against the Continuation of the War in North Africa]. The speakers came from various sections of the independent left, and included Guérin, Michel Leiris [a former surrealist and contributor to *Les Temps modernes*], Aimé Césaire, Pierre Stibbe [former Pivertiste], and Jean Rous [ex-Trotskyist and leading figure in the RDR].[15]

One publication which consistently opposed the war and expressed solidarity with those fighting for national independence was *Les Temps modernes*, the journal founded and edited by Jean-Paul Sartre. Though Sartre himself would later have some impact on the movement against the war, it was probably not he who initiated the policy on Algeria, but Francis Jeanson, the managing editor [see below].

In October 1955 an editorial statement appeared under the title 'Refusal to Obey'. This described Algeria as a 'colony' [rejecting the official fiction that it was an integral part of France] subject to 'the most obvious exploitation'. It went on: 'A war is starting in North Africa; it is up to the government whether to stop it, or, on the contrary, to make it inevitable ... To this war, we say no'.[16]

The following month's issue went further. Under the title 'Algeria Is Not France' [a slogan which also appeared on the cover], it came very close to urging soldiers to fraternise with the enemy: 'Yesterday, Robert Barrat [a left

---

12   Gottraux 1997, p. 114.
13   Guérin 1979, p. 62.
14   Pattieu 2002, p. 137.
15   Contat and Rybalka 1970, p. 297; see also *Le Monde*, 29–30 January 1956; *Le Libertaire*, 2 February 1956.
16   Les Temps modernes 1955a.

Catholic journalist] was arrested for having held a meeting with the "rebels". Tomorrow, on the trails of the Aurès mountains, perhaps the conscript soldiers will come to recognise them as brothers'.[17] Perhaps the best tribute to the effectiveness of *Les Temps modernes* in its campaigning against the war is the fact that it was seized by the authorities in Algeria no less than four times in 1957.

Another current of the left which was to acquire greater significance in the course of the Algerian war was what came to be known as the 'Nouvelle gauche' [new left]. This drew on various sources and brought together former Trotskyists, disaffected members of the SFIO and left Catholics. The Nouvelle gauche had no formal structure, but it did reflect a significant minority of public opinion which would have some importance as opposition to the war grew. It included prominent editors and journalists like Claude Bourdet and Gilles Martinet of *France-Observateur*, and lawyers like Yves Dechezelles, who defended members of the far left who were victims of repression.

In 1955 the Nouvelle gauche took on a more structured form with the foundation of the Mouvement Uni de la Nouvelle Gauche [United Movement of the New Left]. Among its leading figures were former Trotskyists such as Yvan Craipeau and Pierre Naville. In 1956 a journal, *Nouvelle gauche*, was launched, edited by Colette Audry. In 1957 the Union de la Gauche Socialiste [UGS: Union of the Socialist Left], was set up. It had some 6000 members,[18] and aspired to recruit former PCF members disillusioned by the special powers vote and by PCF support for Russian action in Hungary. As Craipeau put it, it welcomed 'all Communists who have ceased to be Stalinists, but not Stalinists who have ceased to be communists'.[19]

Beyond the Nouvelle gauche was the far left fringe. When the war began this was a very small milieu. In practice it consisted of small groups of anarchists and Trotskyists, who counted their members in hundreds. While they might seem numerically insignificant, it was from these groups that some remarkable activists emerged. They described themselves as revolutionaries; because they did not recognise the legitimacy of the existing political institutions, they were prepared for illegality and clandestinity. Some of their activists put their heads on the line in a way that nobody else on the French left was prepared to do. They became the pioneers of the solidarity movement.

---

17   Les Temps modernes 1955b.
18   Craipeau 1999, pp. 264, 266.
19   Quoted by Pattieu 2002, p. 138.

4   Anarchists

In the first year of the war it was the anarchists who took the initiative. In the immediate post-war period the Fédération anarchiste [FA Anarchist Federation] had a paper, *Le Libertaire*, which sold between 20,000 and 30,000 copies.[20] In 1953 the FA changed its name to Fédération communiste libertaire [FCL Libertarian Communist Federation]; it had between 200 and 300 members, largely workers and teachers.

The FCLwas active on the Algerian question before the war broke out. In June 1954 the FCL paper *Le Libertaire* was confiscated as well as a poster 'Free Algeria'. Two FCL militants were charged and held in custody for some days.[21] On 4 November 1954, three days after the rising, *Le Libertaire* declared its support for the Algerian Revolution, claiming that the population was behind the insurgents.[22] In December 1954 and January 1955, two issues of the paper were prosecuted for endangering the external security of the state; five FCL members were questioned by the criminal police.

In the summer of 1955 Pierre Morain, a building worker and an FCL member from Roubaix, became the first French citizen in mainland France to be jailed for activity in support of the Algerian revolution. On 22 June 1955 he was accused of distributing leaflets for the Mouvement de lutte anticolonialiste [Movement of Anticolonialist Struggle, a committee set up by the FCL]. He was questioned for a whole day, then charged with endangering the internal security of the state.[23] He was defended by Yves Dechezelles, the MNA's lawyer, when he was tried alongside nineteen Algerian militants and sentenced to five months in jail.[24] When the judge expressed surprise that he was French, he responded: 'No, I am not French, I am a worker'.[25] He was subsequently sentenced to a year in prison for having 'defended actions by Algerians on 1 May, actions with the intention of reconstituting the MTLD', and for 'antinational activity'. The authorities were determined to deter activists from showing solidarity with the Algerians.[26]

---

20   Pattieu 2002, p. 46.

21   *Le Libertaire*, 19 May 1955; Fontenis 2000, p. 119.

22   Fontenis 2000, p. 118.

23   *Le Libertaire*, 30 June 1955.

24   *Le Libertaire*, 3 August 1955.

25   Maitron and Pennetier 1964–2023 article154642, notice MORAIN Pierre, Louis, Robert [Dictionnaire des anarchistes] par Daniel Goude, version mise en ligne le 27 avril 2014, dernière modification le 11 août 2020.

26   Pattieu 2002, p. 78.

Morain was confronting not only the French state, but the CGT bureaucracy. *Le Libertaire* of 19 May 1955 carried his article 'Bonzes, Draw Your Own Conclusions!' [the term 'bonze' – a Buddhist monk – was used in far-left terminology to refer to bureaucratic leaders]. He attacked the CGT which had refused to allow Algerian workers to address the May Day march. While the mainstream French left was still in confusion, trying to work out what was happening in Algeria, Morain demonstrated the integrity of a true internationalist.

The FCL understood that the state machine was the weapon of the enemy class; however the tiny organisation was not equipped to confront the French state. Confiscations, arrests, interrogations and financial penalties brought it into deep crisis. A meeting of the National Council on 5 July 1955 decided to suspend publication of *Le Libertaire*; it did not appear again. The very existence of the FCL was in question.

There was now an internal debate, with some comrades advocating suspension of publication of the paper and going into clandestinity.[27] The problem was that they had no experience of clandestine work. It was the end of the road for the FCL.

It should be added that if the anarchist organisation was too fragile for the tasks it faced, the individuals who made it up were extremely tough. Many of the FCL militants remained active in difficult circumstances. Georges Fontenis [1920–2010] in particular stayed active throughout the war, and remained an anarchist for the rest of his life. After the FCL was dissolved, he and others left their jobs and homes to become clandestine and tried to maintain a network, Action communiste [communist action], with former FCL members, though this was short-lived.[28] This was followed by a spell in Fresnes prison. He was not discouraged and along with other members of Action communiste later joined the *Voie communiste* team [see below]. Morain remained active till his death in 2013, for a time as a Maoist and later in the anti-globalisation movement, and in solidarity with New Caledonia and Palestine.[29]

Mohamed Harbi had, during the early years of the war, been responsible for making contacts between the FLN and the French left and trying to organise solidarity. He wrote of this period: 'On the far left only the libertarians and the Trotskyists recognised the events of 1 November as the start of a war and

---

27   Fontenis 2000, pp. 134–7.

28   Fontenis 2000, p. 144.

29   Maitron and Pennetier 1964–2023 article154642, notice MORAIN Pierre, Louis, Robert [Dictionnaire des anarchistes] par Daniel Goude, version mise en ligne le 27 avril 2014, dernière modification le 11 août 2020.

showed themselves to be ready to respond to it in the name of the principles of universal socialism, in the name of internationalism'.[30]

5 Trotskyists

At the outbreak of the war the combined forces of the Trotskyist movement amounted to little more than a hundred activists throughout France. Small in number and marginal to the labour movement, they were often pretentious in their claims to vanguard status and, after splits, vehement in their denunciations of those closest to them.

Yet from their depleted ranks came some of the most imaginative activists who put themselves at the service of the anti-imperialist struggle. They defended the best traditions of internationalism, carrying forward the principles of the Bolshevik Revolution and socialism from below. Organisationally they had the experience of clandestine work during the German occupation. More recently they had faced attacks from both fascists and Stalinists, and had learned how to defend their meetings. Some were doing entry work in the PCF which required a high level of clandestine organisation.

The various Trotskyist groups had had personal contacts with Algerian nationalists before 1954. The first approaches by the FLN were made through Yvan Craipeau. Craipeau had played a leading role in the Trotskyist movement during the German occupation, but had later broken with the Trotskyists, and was now active in the Nouvelle gauche. He recognised that the Nouvelle gauche did not have the sort of organisation able to deliver the solidarity required.[31]

There were three main Trotskyist groups in France after 1954. The group which became Voix ouvrière [VO: Workers' Voice] played little part in solidarity activity, but did produce regular propaganda on the Algerian question, distributed to workers, including Algerian workers, through paper sales and regular factory bulletins.[32]

In 1952 the international Trotskyist movement suffered a deep split. Michel Raptis [known as Pablo], who would play a central role in support for Algeria, argued that Trotskyists should enter Communist Parties; their opponents opposed this as liquidation. Pablo's opponents in France were led by Pierre Lambert [pseudonym of Pierre Boussel], and were often known as Lambertists.

---

30   Mohamed Harbi. 'Préface' in Pattieu 2002, p. 7.
31   Pattieu 2002, p. 73.
32   Barcia 2003, pp. 188, 192.

Lambert had known Messali Hadj for some time and had helped to shelter him when he made a clandestine visit to mainland France.[33] Lambert's organisation, the PCI, was regularly in contact with Messali when he was under house arrest at Niort and elsewhere from 1952 to 1959. The PCI ran a campaign for his release and took part in the demonstrations organised in mainland France by the MTLD.

Lambert allowed this valuable solidarity action to spill over into political support for the MNA. On one occasion he compared the MNA to the Bolshevik party and Messali himself to Lenin.[34] By 1958–9 Lambert was coming to realise that he had made a mistake, and the MNA was dropped.[35]

In the early phase of the war the Lambertist PCI, despite its small size, mounted some quite impressive united front solidarity actions. The Committee for the Release of Messali Hadj and the Victims of Repression [Comité pour la Libération de Messali Hadj et des Victimes de la Répression] was formed in 1954, when Messali Hadj was put under house arrest. Between 1954 and 1957 it produced eleven issues of an information bulletin, with news of repression in Algeria, including executions and death sentences. There were reports of meetings held and of support from trade-union organisations. If the attendance figures claimed were more or less accurate, the Committee clearly made an impact. The FCL was also active in this Committee. Supporters included Marceau Pivert, Jean Rous, Daniel Guérin and André Breton.

On 21 April 1955 the Committee for the Release of Messali Hadj and the Victims of Repression held a meeting attended by over 400 workers in the public hall at Lourches, a mining centre in the Nord. On 13 May 500 workers in Clermont-Ferrand heard an extensive report by Pierre Stibbe on the situation in Algeria.

In November 1954 a delegation led by Hébert, general secretary of the Force Ouvrière departmental union for the Loire Inférieure, and including members of the CGT, FO and the autonomous teachers' union, went to Sables d'Olonne to meet Messali Hadj who was under house arrest. On orders from Mitterrand the police refused to allow the delegation to make contact with the imprisoned leader. PCI members were arrested and detained.[36]

---

33   Pattieu 2002, p. 55.
34   *La Vérité*, 16 December 1955.
35   Birchall 2012.
36   *Bulletin d'Information du Comité pour la Libération de Messali Hadj et des Victimes de la Répression*, June 1955, November 1954.

6   Lyotard

The ex-Trotskyist grouping Socialisme ou barbarie's membership was minute, but it was one of the few tendencies on the left to attempt new analyses of a changing world. Its contribution to an understanding of the Algerian situation was largely the work of a single individual, Jean-François Lyotard, later to become known as a post-modernist philosopher.

From 1950 to 1952 Lyotard was a lycée teacher in Algeria and was influenced by another teacher, Pierre Souyri; in 1954 he and Souyri joined SouB. Since he was geographically isolated from the organisation in North-West France, he was given the job of becoming SouB's expert on Algeria.[37] He wrote a series of twelve articles between 1956 and 1963, initially under the pseudonym François Laborde, and later in his own name, in which he recognised the potential of the liberation struggle but also its limits.[38]

Many years later Lyotard revealed that he had been actively involved in the Henri Curiel support network [see below], something of which his organisation was unaware at the time.[39] Such a combination of practical solidarity and lucid analysis was rare on the French far left.

The Trotskyist groupings had attempted to understand Algeria in terms of Trotsky's theory of permanent revolution, developed for Russia before 1917. Lyotard believed the theory was inapplicable to Algeria; hence a different theoretical framework was needed. He set out to analyse the nature of the FLN, which he saw as giving the peasant masses a leadership originating in the petty-bourgeoisie.

> The present cadres of the FLN are for the most part elements from the middle classes, which means that the resistance is the point of convergence between the Jacobin bourgeoisie and the peasants.[40]
>
> The process going on within a revolutionary situation that is five years old is that of the formation of a new class, and all the factors which make up this situation mean that this class will necessarily be a bureaucracy.[41]
>
> The FLN is now already preparing itself for the role of being the managing stratum in Algerian society and ... is working objectively to blur the lines between present organisation and the future state.[42]

---

37   Gottraux 1997, pp. 72–3.

38   See Lyotard 1989.

39   Lyotard and Vidal-Naquet 1989.

40   Lyotard 1959–60, p. 26.

41   Lyotard 1959–60, p. 36.

42   Laborde 1957, p. 168.

Lyotard's view of the perspectives for the Algerian revolution was pessimistic:

> By strengthening the apparatus, [the Algerian leaders] are seeking (even if they are not aware of it) to channel the living forces of the future society for as long as the liberation struggle enables them to demand and to get almost unconditional support; this will undoubtedly be less easy when the next stage comes. Thus even before imperialism has relaxed its grip, the class struggle in independent Algeria is being prefigured.[43]

Lyotard rejected the view current among many supporters of Algerian independence that the struggle could lead directly to a transition to socialism. The only alternatives were the continuation of colonialism or an independent regime based on a new form of exploitation. Yet the latter would open up new possibilities; if today internationalism meant support for independence, tomorrow it might mean solidarity with the oppressed seeking a new social order:

> In reality; there is no alternative to exploitation other than socialism; in reality the national-democratic struggle of the North African people contains within itself the premises of a new form of exploitation. But for all that we should not underestimate the subjective and objective content of its aim. Subjectively, it expresses the maximum potential consciousness of a proletariat crushed by material and moral terror; it crystallises the meaning of a rediscovered dignity. Objectively, the winning of national 'independence' will force the settlers to step back, to abandon the terrorist apparatus which was necessary for superexploitation; it thus creates a revolutionary situation characterised by the sharing of power, economic to the settlers, political to the 'nationalists'; and within this situation the question of property will eventually have to be posed. ...
>
> To recognise the potential revolutionary scope of a struggle for independence is necessary. But we must also be able to denounce the objectives of the nationalist leaderships which, under the cover of this struggle, are tending to impose the dominant indigenous strata as new exploiters who, in order to achieve this position, will inevitably join one of the imperialist blocs, the American or the Russian. Finally we must understand and explain that the only solutions, which none of the forces in

---

43   Lyotard, 1961–2, p. 16.

struggle are prepared to put into practice, are class solutions – the very first of these being the direct take-over of the land by the peasants.[44]

The questions posed by Lyotard were important ones. Many of those who gave practical support to the FLN would have described themselves as socialists, and their commitment to the Algerian struggle flowed from the internationalism that was integral to the socialist tradition. But support for the FLN was not conditional on seeing its struggle as potentially socialist. Solidarity began with a rejection of France's right to rule over Algeria, and of the repressive methods used to preserve that rule.

7 PCI

The group which gave most practical support to the FLN was the PCI led by Pierre Frank. [Confusingly, for a while both halves of the split called themselves the PCI.] This group followed the positions argued within the Fourth International by Pablo, namely that with world war between East and West looming, there was no time to build independent organisations, and that Trotskyists should enter mass Communist Parties. Entrist militants should try to form an internal opposition in the PCF by supporting the Algerian struggle as well as by raising questions about inner-party democracy and about events in the Eastern bloc after the death of Stalin.

The PCI rapidly became involved in practical solidarity work. They became pioneers of what was known as 'carrying suitcases'. Formal contacts were established between the PCI and the FLN, and the PCI began to take on a variety of tasks. These were generally of a mundane and non-violent nature, although any action in support of the FLN was of its nature illegal. The FLN wanted to win support from Algerian workers living in France and asked the Trotskyists to assist with the distribution of propaganda. Initially this meant printing and distributing a leaflet and also the first FLN newspaper.[45]

Then there was the typing and duplicating of leaflets for the FLN and the pro-FLN trade-union body AGTA [Amicale générale des travailleurs algériens: General Association of Algerian Workers]. These leaflets and appeals were handed over to Algerian-run shops and businesses, which distributed them to their customers. This simply meant leaving packets like a delivery to shops and bars controlled by the FLN.

---

44   Laborde 1956, p. 94.
45   Pattieu 2002, p. 75.

The Trotskyists also provided forged papers to enable Algerian militants to evade police persecution. These forged papers were often printed abroad through Fourth International contacts.[46] The comrades delivered FLN communiqués to the press, and to embassies, parties and unions. On one occasion members received eleven large suitcases containing pages of *El Moudjahid*, the FLN newspaper. They had to sit up all night collating these – then go to work the next morning.[47]

It became necessary for the Trotskyist network to set up its own printshop; the FLN gave them money to rent premises. The equipment had to be easily transportable, so duplicators were preferred. Several premises were rented under the names of figureheads.[48] One of these was Dr Raphaël Zakine, who had been born in Algeria where he lived till 1925. A founder-member of the Communist Party, he was jailed for six months in 1932 after a false accusation of having carried out an abortion when this was illegal under repressive legislation. After a visit to the USSR he became a Trotskyist. He was active in support of the FLN.[49]

The PCI was a tiny organisation, but from its ranks came a number of remarkable individuals, who showed initiative, organisational skills and great courage. Pierre Avot-Meyers was a metal-worker and CGT militant, and a member of the PCI leadership. His special concern was with organising printing on behalf of the FLN. Initially he found various small printers who didn't take too much notice of what they printed, providing they got paid. By 1956, as repression was stepped up, this became too risky, and Avot-Meyers was put in charge of setting up a printshop. A major problem was repairs. Maintenance workers could not be invited into the clandestine premises, and Avot-Meyers himself had to find spare parts. When manufacturers asked for addresses to send the bills to, he sometimes claimed to be working for a travelling circus whose printing machine had broken down. This dangerous existence continued until 1960, when the police discovered the clandestine press. Avot-Meyers escaped to Italy.[50]

---

46   Pattieu 2002, p. 77.

47   Benoits 2014, pp. 93–4.

48   Pattieu 2002, p. 89.

49   Maitron and Pennetier 1964–2023 article135492, notice ZAKINE Raphaël [Dictionnaire Algérie] par Rodolphe Prager, version mise en ligne le 30 novembre 2010, dernière modification le 20 janvier 2021.

50   Maitron and Pennetier 1964–2023 article194392, notice AVOT-MEYERS Pierre dit Julien, Serge par Robert Kosmann, version mise en ligne le 7 août 2017, dernière modification le 7 août 2017.

Simonne Minguet became a Trotskyist as a student during the German occupation. From 1944 to 1948 she worked at the Caudron-Renault aircraft factory in the Paris suburbs, where she was involved in the 1947 strike wave. The factory was the site of one of the first experiments in workers' management.[51] In the 1950s she was one of the Fourth International's few women leaders. She was actively involved in soldarity work for the FLN and jailed for two months in 1956.

Through the Fourth International the PCI was able to call on the support of militants from a number of different countries. When getting printing done in France was too risky, it was Belgian Trotskyists who took on the job. Printed copies were sent in packets to post-office boxes in the names of various militants or publications.[52] In Germany, Belgium and the Netherlands, Trotskyists were involved in broad organisations to assist prisoners and refugees in Tunisia. In 1958 Georg Jungclas, a German Trotskyist militant, and his friends obtained a garage in Cologne for the FLN to serve as a store for weapons.[53]

Another German Trotskyist, Jakob Moneta, had gone to Palestine before the Second World War, and had been expelled from a kibbutz for being an anti-Zionist; he was later imprisoned by the British. On returning to Germany he became a trade-union activist and from 1953 was attaché for social affairs at the West German Embassy in Paris – where he used the 'diplomatic bag' to transport FLN documents.[54]

Working with the PCI militants in France was an American poet and journalist, Sherry Mangan. His nationality, and his respectable appearance – he was a Harvard graduate – made him well suited for clandestine work, while his employment as a journalist gave him a cover. He duplicated FLN publications in an isolated country house but died too soon to see the Algerian independence he had made such sacrifices for.[55]

The fact that the Trotskyist activity was having some impact was shown by state repression, although the penalties suffered by French activists were relatively mild compared with those imposed on Algerians. While FLN militants faced torture and execution without trial, 'suitcase carriers' often merely got imprisonment – though this could be an unpleasant enough experience. Pierre Frank, Simonne Minguet, Janine Weil and Raymond Bouvet were imprisoned. After *La Vérité des travailleurs* had been seized several times, Pierre Frank and

---

51   Minguet 1997.
52   Pattieu 2002, p. 76.
53   Pattieu 2002, p. 121.
54   Pattieu 2002, p. 121.
55   Wald 1983.

Jacques Privas were prosecuted for endangering the external security of the state and got a suspended sentence of six months' jail.

In the earlier years of the war prosecution of activists was mainly under the press laws. There were many confiscations of publications by the police. 60 newspapers were confiscated in metropolitan France between November 1954 and May 1958, and 179 between June 1958 and June 1962.[56]

The Ministry of the Interior could initiate action against any article defined as threatening state security. The journal could be confiscated at the printers, the distributors or the newsagents; the publisher then had to produce a second issue without the incriminated article. Even if there were no further penalty, this was a serious financial burden for a small publication. It was not only revolutionary publications that were affected, but also journals from the mainstream left which dared to criticise the war. In 1956, Claude Bourdet – a long-standing anti-imperialist activist – was prosecuted for an article in *France-Observateur* where he had stated:

> a hundred thousand young French men face being thrown into the dirty war in Algeria, to waste the best years of their lives, perhaps to be wounded and even killed, for a cause which few of them support, in a type of struggle which outrages most of them.[57]

The PCI responded to repression by using it to make propaganda. In April 1956 the PCI organised a meeting at the Sociétés savantes hall in Paris which linked Trotskyist militants being prosecuted to Claude Bourdet and the Catholic historian Henri-Irénée Marrou.[58] A petition in support of those jailed was signed by CGT and Force ouvrière militants, and personalities including Francis Jeanson, Jean-Paul Sartre, Claude Bourdet and Gilles Martinet. The aim was to challenge SFIO militants to dissociate themselves from the actions of their government.

Repression entailed clandestinity. This required considerable skill, avoiding the dangers of carelessness and the romanticisation of illegality. The PCI still had comrades who had been active under the Nazi occupation a decade or so earlier. They were currently engaged in attempting entry work into the PCF.

Entry into the PCF was a difficult strategy – very different from work in a looser and more open social-democratic party like the SFIO – and with the

---

56   Gervereau, Rioux and Stora 1992, p. 122.
57   *France-Observateur*, 29 March 1956, quoted by Hamon and Rotman 1979, p. 47.
58   Pattieu 2002, p. 81.

limited resources of the PCI the results were initially meagre. André Fichaut, a shipyard worker in Brittany, became a successful entrist. He had to spend three years dissociating himself from his former comrades and insisting that he had renounced Trotskyism. In 1953, as a CGT branch secretary, he was required to convey condolences on the death of Stalin – since he was following a long-term strategy he had to comply.[59]

The PCI's combination of clandestine organisation with an open press and the ability to pursue united front activity, especially with the Nouvelle gauche, meant it was well prepared to work closely with the FLN and give support.

Both the possibilities and difficulties of the PCI's entry work are illustrated by the case of Alain Krivine, later well-known as an activist in 1968 and subsequently as a Trotskyist leader. In 1957 Krivine was just 16 years old; he enthusiastically joined the PCF and was active in its youth organisation. As a successful seller of the PCF youth paper, L'Avant-garde, he was chosen to attend the Sixth World Festival of Democratic Youth in Russia in the summer of 1957. It attracted thousands of young people from many countries.[60] The young Krivine was in for a shock. When he set up a meeting with an FLN youth delegation, he was taken aback to find the Algerians were highly critical of the PCF line on the war. Then he was sharply reprimanded by the PCF for having made contact with the FLN.

He came back to France disillusioned with the PCF and determined to get more involved in support work for the FLN. He didn't know that his two brothers – the older Jean-Michel and his twin Hubert – were already clandestine Trotskyist militants.

Hubert belonged to an FLN support network, and offered to put him in touch with it. Alain agreed on condition that he was assured that this network was not Trotskyist. Hubert gave him the assurance – and introduced him to Michel Fiant, a member of the PCI leadership.[61] It was a couple of years before Alain's reservations about the PCF became so strong that he accepted Hubert's invitation to join the PCI.[62]

In 1959 he joined the Jeune Résistance network, in which the Trotskyists were active. This brought him into various forms of illegal activity quite alien to the PCF. Though he remained in the PCF until his expulsion in 1966, the party did not know of his involvement in solidarity activity. He helped army deserters escape to Switzerland, and distributed leaflets to soldiers on trains bound for

---

59   Fichaut 2003, p. 66.
60   Hamon and Rotman 1987, pp. 13–39; Pattieu 2002, p. 107.
61   Pattieu 2002, p. 107.
62   Hamon and Rotman 1979, pp. 88–9, 140–42.

Algeria, as well as sabotaging railway signals to disrupt the transport of conscripts to Algeria. He was involved in planning jailbreaks of Algerians from the Fresnes prison, and helped to build a mass student organisation to keep defenders of French rule in Algeria out of the Latin Quarter in Paris. He considered that the experience of activity in support of the Algerian cause gave those involved a practical experience of internationalism.[63]

PCI members working in the PCF had been involved in the ferment in 1956 caused by Khrushchev's 'secret speech' denouncing Stalin and the Hungarian rising; they set up a publication aimed at dissident PCF members, *Tribune de discussion* [discussion platform]. In order to establish dialogue with PCF members they denied any Trotskyist connections. When attempts were made to draw in PCF members, there were real problems about revealing the personnel involved. *Tribune de discussion* merged in 1957 with *L'Étincelle* [Spark], a journal produced by dissident PCF members.

8   *La Voie communiste*

The merged journal collapsed; a new venture replaced it. January 1958 saw the launch of *La Voie communiste* [The Communist Path], financed by the psychotherapist Félix Guattari who used profits from his clinic to pay for it.[64] *La Voie communiste* appeared publicly, and was sold on newsstands. It was addressed to PCF members but also to non-members; its Draft Manifesto stated that it aimed to reach 'all Communists, including those who are no longer in the party or who find themselves expelled as a result of the leadership's policy'.[65] In addition there were new layers of activists radicalised by the Algerian war. The new journal began with a circulation of 5000; by the end of the war it was 30,000.[66] It became an organisation outside the control of the PCI; the PCI members central to it were expelled or left the organisation. In addition to former PCI members it also brought together expelled Communists like Simon Blumenthal or Gérard Spitzer, and anarchists like Daniel Guérin and ex-members of the FCL.

Although *La Voie communiste* did not concern itself exclusively with Algeria, the context of the war was essential to its success. For the remaining years of the war it offered an example of a non-sectarian regroupment which made possible

------

63   Krivine 2004. See also Krivine 2011.
64   Pattieu 2002, p. 112.
65   Pattieu 2002, p. 269.
66   Pattieu 2002, pp. 112–14; Evans 1997, p. 182.

dialogue between revolutionaries from different traditions. Algeria provided the vital focus, and the journal did not survive long once the war was over.

One notable activist with *La Voie communiste* was Gérard Spitzer [1927–1996]. Spitzer was the child of Jewish refugees from Miklós Horthy's anti-Semitic regime in Hungary [1920–44]; he joined the PCF during the German Occupation and became a resister at the age of fifteen. Since he knew something of Hungarian fascism, he was appalled by the PCF line on the Hungarian uprising; he was expelled for an article on Hungary he contributed to *Les Temps modernes*. He was arrested and accused of being an FLN agent, and jailed for 18 months; a solidarity campaign was launched, while Spitzer went on hunger strike to demand political status. The trial of Gérard Spitzer and then those of various members of the Jeanson network [see below] made it possible to popularise the activities of the suitcase carriers.[67]

The *Voie communiste* team developed various forms of practical support for the FLN far removed from the normal activities of the intellectual milieu. They succeeded in winning the confidence of the FLN so that they were entrusted with dangerous tasks, in particular the organisation of jailbreaks.

After 1958 the FLN were concerned that a right-wing takeover in France might lead to the execution without trial of the FLN leaders. They approached activists linked to the *Voie communiste*, which had already achieved some successful jailbreaks, notably the escape of other FLN leaders, and of five young women belonging to the Jeanson network from the La Roquette prison.[68] They were now asked to develop a plan to enable the FLN leaders to escape. The *Voie communiste* activists got support from local Communists who disagreed with their party's policy of refusing practical support to the FLN and developed two escape plans – one using underground tunnels from the cellars of the château where the prisoners were held, the other requiring cars with capacious boots in which the leaders could be concealed. Ben Bella seems to have been unenthusiastic about the plans; perhaps as a result of his indiscretions additional riot police were brought in, meaning that no escape would have been possible without a shoot-out. The FLN leaders remained in jail till released in March 1962 at the time of the Évian agreements which ended the war.

Denis Berger was one of the central figures in *La Voie communiste*, especially in the jailbreak activity. He had become a Trotskyist in 1950 as a student; it was not an easy time. Paper sellers faced physical attacks from Stalinists, while at

---

67   Maitron and Pennetier 1964–2023 article152157, notice SPITZER Gérard [Dictionnaire Algérie] par René Gallissot, version mise en ligne le 9 janvier 2014, dernière modification le 9 septembre 2015; Evans 1997, pp. 162–6.

68   Hamon and Rotman 1979, pp. 340–51, 362–4.

a meeting in 1953 Berger was attacked by cudgel-bearing right-wingers including the young Jean-Marie Le Pen. In 1952 he sided with Pablo and Frank against Lambert; he joined a student cell of the PCF in 1953, though he had to confess his past as a Trotskyist. He took part in the founding of *La Voie communiste*; this brought him into conflict with the PCI leadership, and he was excluded in 1958. Now Algeria became the central issue. Berger used to meet Moussa Khebaïli, a leader of the French Federation of the FLN, and began to do jobs for the Algerians.[69] Later in 1958 he was held for ten days in the cellars of the DST [Home Security Police], though unlike his Algerian comrades he was not tortured.

The collaboration between the Fourth International and the FLN extended to two further ambitious projects. Pablo proposed to the FLN the setting up of an arms factory in Morocco to make weapons which the FLN was having difficulty in obtaining. This was functioning from 1959, disguised as a marmalade factory, with equipment from Eastern Europe; it was staffed by skilled workers. While the majority of these were Algerians, it was an international enterprise; there were also French workers and others from several countries including Britain.[70] Some of those involved in running the printshop for the FLN had had to leave France to avoid arrest, so they went to Morocco, and Louis Fontaine, formerly of the Vernon factory, [see below] also went to work in the arms factory.

It doubtless made its small contribution to the FLN's military campaign. It also posed certain problems. Politically it went further than other forms of solidarity, since the weapons being made would be used to kill French soldiers; for some that was a step too far. Secondly it meant transferring industrial militants to perform a technical function, taking them away from trade-union activity and from arguing the Algerian cause with their fellow-workers. Such were the choices of priorities for a tiny organisation like that of the French Trotskyists.

Pablo was central to another project in solidarity with the Algerian revolution. The FLN proposed that he should set up an illegal printshop to produce forged French currency for the FLN. The primary aim was to finance the FLN, by supplementing the income received from Algerians working in France. However, it was also suggested that enough forged currency might be produced to destabilise the French economy; this was pure fantasy.

Pablo joined forces with Salomon Santen, a leader of the Fourth International in the Netherlands; they approached a libertarian printer, Albertus

---

69   Pattieu 2002, p. 114.
70   Plant 2012, p. 197.

Oeldrich, who had a long record of left-wing activity. The equipment was functioning by November 1959, and paper was obtained early the following year; but one of the two workers taken on by Oeldrich was a police informer. In June 1960 the police raided the secret printshop and Pablo and Santen were questioned. Under interrogation Oeldrich confessed everything.

Pablo and Santen were put on trial in June 1961. The Fourth International decided to wage a major international campaign in support of Pablo and Santen, who admitted being in solidarity with the Algerian revolution; they denied forgery – in fact no forged notes had yet been produced.

The accused got support from Jean-Paul Sartre, André Breton, Claude Bourdet and many others on the French left, and internationally from Salvador Allende, Michael Foot and Isaac Deutscher. Two British MPs, John Baird and Konni Zilliacus, appeared as character witnesses.

Pablo and Santen were probably treated more leniently in the Netherlands than they would have been in France. They were sentenced to 15 months imprisonment. Since they had already been detained for 14 months up to the trial, this was a very short sentence. Politically the trial was a success, since the defendants turned it into a means of attacking French rule in Algeria.

9   Francis Jeanson

One individual who played an important part in solidarity activity with Algeria was Francis Jeanson. He had first visited Algeria as a young resister during World War II, and spent another six months there in 1948 when he met nationalist activists. At the same time he was intellectually involved with the circle around Jean-Paul Sartre and became managing editor of *Les Temps modernes*.

In December 1955 Jeanson and his wife Colette published *L'Algérie hors la loi* [Outlaw Algeria].[71] This was firmly partisan for the FLN – indeed some reviewers, notably Daniel Guérin, had reservations, believing it to be too uncritical. It also showed much greater knowledge of Algeria than most French politicians had. Francis had spent six months working in Algeria and had taken the opportunity to get to know Algerian society. Colette visited Algeria three times in 1955, travelling clandestinely, meeting activists in a shanty town and interviewing an FLN leader.[72] The book made some strikingly accurate predictions – that there would be a war lasting some eight years, that Algeria would get its independ-

---

71   Jeanson 1955.
72   Ulloa 2001, p. 135.

ence [something then almost universally regarded as unfeasible] and that the struggle would produce a political crisis leading to de Gaulle's return to power.

In 1957 Jeanson abandoned his other activities to devote himself to building a solidarity network; by April 1958, just before de Gaulle's return, he had to become clandestine. His was one of the four main networks, together with the Fourth International, *La Voie communiste* and Henri Curiel's organisation.

Jeanson maintained his political independence; he worked with the FLN but never became a member. He argued against the FLN bombing campaign in mainland France in 1958, which he considered would be politically damaging. Encouraged by the FLN's French Federation, Jeanson organised a network that was clandestine and divided into separate cells. Its main task was, naturally, carrying suitcases – that is collecting, counting and taking abroad the money raised by the FLN from migrant workers in metropolitan France. The FLN levied a monthly tax on Algerians living in France – 500 old francs for students, 3000 for workers and 50,000 for shopkeepers [a thousand francs was roughly equivalent to a pound sterling of the time].[73] This was an essential source of finance for the armed struggle.

The network also helped to organise the visits of FLN leaders from one country to another by diverting the attention of the authorities, provided hiding places in safe accommodation and produced forged documentation. Jeanson aimed to use the activity as a means of reinvigorating the French left and urging it to support the anti-colonialist cause.[74] He was critical of the PCF's position and hoped the Algerian war would transform the French left. Jeanson showed a positive delight in taunting the French state. In April 1960 he organised a clandestine press conference in Paris; he denied government claims that the network had been dismantled and replied to his various critics.[75]

In September 1960 the network was put on trial – without Jeanson who was at liberty in Switzerland. The trial of six Algerians and 18 French people linked to the network gave an opportunity to the accused and their lawyers to use the court as a platform to denounce the role of France in Algeria. Long prison terms were imposed on several defendants; the trial raised the profile of the suitcase-carriers. The Commander in Chief in Algeria, General Crépin, was briefly concerned that the morale of the army might be affected.[76]

---

73 Evans 2012, p. 278.

74 Letter from Francis Jeanson to Jean-Paul Sartre published in *Les Temps modernes* May 1960, reproduced in Hamon and Rotman 1979, p. 59.

75 Hamon and Rotman 1979, pp. 208–13.

76 Ulloa 2001, pp. 189–97.

As well as carrying out practical tasks for the FLN, the Jeanson network produced a clandestine publication entitled *Vérités pour* [truths for], launched in September 1958. Those involved came from a range of ideological positions, including the left Catholic Robert Barrat, the first French journalist to interview FLN leaders. The papers were sent to sympathisers, to left-wing personalities, and to trade unionists and journalists. Up to 5000 copies were distributed. Intellectuals like Sartre and Vercors [Jean Bruller, a Resistance veteran and one of the founders of the clandestine publishing-house Éditions de minuit under the German Occupation], were interviewed in *Vérités pour* and supported assistance to the FLN.[77]

Following the trial Jeanson was sentenced to ten years in jail – in his absence. He was being too closely watched to continue his role of directing the network; with the support of the FLN Henri Curiel took over. Curiel was an Egyptian Communist who had been living in France since 1950; he was repudiated by the PCF because of his connections with André Marty. He was put in contact with Francis Jeanson in the autumn of 1957,[78] and organised a support group for the FLN consisting of his followers, Jewish Communists exiled from Egypt. While Jeanson disagreed with Curiel's orthodox Communist politics, he recognised him as an efficient organiser; the two networks were complementary in their activity.

There was a certain distrust of Curiel on the part of the FLN. When he was jailed for 20 months in 1960 for his solidarity activity, the FLN was very concerned that the classes he was running for the Algerians imprisoned together with him touched on Marxism and agrarian reform, and kept him under close surveillance. In 1978 Curiel was murdered – very probably as an act of revenge for his work in solidarity with the Algerian struggle.[79]

10   Suitcase-Carriers

The suitcase-carriers were the most committed supporters of the Algerian independence struggle. It was risky work and could lead to arrest, imprisonment and rough handling by the police. While it is often thought that such activities were limited to intellectuals, in fact significant numbers of workers took part, while most of those involved had some background in the working-

---

77   Hamon and Rotman 1979, pp. 155–9; Jeanson's interview with Vercors was published in *Vérités pour* 8, May 1959; that with Sartre in Vérités pour 9, June 1959.

78   Hamon and Rotman 1979, p. 94.

79   See Perrault 1984.

class movement or in socialist politics. The number of suitcase carriers was small, probably between 500 and 1000.[80]

They were the active minority; many thousands more attended meetings, took part in demonstrations, argued with their friends and workmates. Some of the most prominent opponents of the war – figures like Sartre and Bourdet – could not carry suitcases because they were too conspicuous. Those who carried suitcases could not be too vocal in publicly defending the cause of Algerian independence. Some activists had to negotiate an uneasy balance between clandestinity and public campaigning.

The suitcase-carriers came from a variety of political positions, and their internationalism had many different roots. The Trotskyists had their own history, going back to the defeat of the Russian Revolution and their attempts to organise during the German occupation. For Jeanson and others from the *Temps modernes* circle the dominant influence was an existentialist Marxism derived from the work of Sartre. The Communist Party instructed its members not to carry suitcases, but some dissident members of the PCF, like Étienne and Paule Bolo or Jean-Louis Hurst did so. The Bolo couple were leading activists in the Jeanson organisation, assisting with publications and organising illegal frontier crossings. Etienne Bolo was jailed in 1960, which seriously damaged his health.[81] Hurst [Maurienne], after trying to agitate inside the army, deserted and was active supporting other deserters.[82] Many from the French left were attracted to the FLN by its adoption of Marxist language, though the implications of this did not go very deep. Others came from a Christian background, like the worker priests Robert Davezies and Jacques Berthelet.[83]

For many their internationalism consisted in the insistence that they were not simply supporting Algerian nationalism, but were also concerned with the liberation of the French people. For Sartre the task of the French left was to struggle alongside the Algerian people in order to liberate both Algerians and French from colonial tyranny.[84] Jérôme Lindon, who published several books

---

80   Evans 1997, p. 5.

81   Maitron and Pennetier 1964–2023 article151648, notice BOLO Etienne [Dictionnaire Algérie] par René Gallissot, version mise en ligne le 29 décembre 2013, dernière modification le 29 décembre 2013.

82   Maitron and Pennetier 1964–2023 article152731, notice HURST Jean-Louis, pseudonyme MAURIENNE [Dictionnaire Algérie] par Tramor Quemeneur, version mise en ligne le 25 janvier 2014, dernière modification le 20 mai 2014.

83   Evans 1997, pp. 101–5, 125–9.

84   Sartre 1964, pp. 25–48.

on French torture, insisted that what he had done, he did for France, not for Algeria[85] – many others involved would have said something similar.

There are various fictionalised accounts of the period which draw out the motivations of the individuals involved. François Maspero's *Le Figuier* [the fig tree],[86] is a mixture of autobiography and fiction, drawing heavily on Maspero's own experiences as a left-wing publisher and bookshop owner. It vividly recreates the atmosphere and events of the period. The narrator's bookshop begins to promote the Algerian struggle, leading to police raids and attacks. When the shop is attacked by the far right, left-wing activists stay overnight to defend it. They publish pro-FLN material, some of which is seized by police. The FLN is not romanticised; some material is published under threats from the FLN. The group around the narrator are also involved with the Manifesto of 121 in support of the Algerian struggle and the October 1961 police massacre of Algerian demonstrators [see below]. The fortunes of various characters link the Algerian struggle back to the Spanish Civil War and forward to revolutionary struggles in Latin America in the late sixties.

One common theme among suitcase-carriers from various points on the political spectrum was the drawing of parallels with the German occupation. When the Algerian war began, it was only ten years since France's liberation from Nazi rule. There were many activists who had been involved in the Resistance, and who saw clear parallels between the activities of the French armed forces in Algeria and the way the German occupiers had behaved in France, including their use of torture. They had seen themselves as victims of oppression; now they began to realise they were part of an oppressor nation.

Since the end of the Second World War the various mainstream political parties had created the myth of a democratic France whose citizens enjoyed equal rights, set up as a model in face of the Nazi totalitarianism which had just been defeated or the Stalinist totalitarianism which remained a threat. Now colonial policy was demonstrating the limits of French democracy. The colonial peoples were largely excluded from these rights; even in metropolitan France the consensus about liberal democracy revealed its limitations. The government did not hesitate to infringe freedom of expression by censoring newspapers, jailing French militants and torturing Algerians with methods worthy of a dictatorship.

Racist attitudes were deeply ingrained in French society, and the working class was certainly not immune. Yet at the same time French workers were

---

85   Evans 1997, p. 43.
86   Maspero 1988.

increasingly finding themselves working alongside Algerians. The period of the war was a time of full employment, in which there was increasing immigration of Algerian workers into France. At the outbreak of the war there were over 200,000 Algerian workers in mainland France, often doing unpleasant, unhealthy, low-paid jobs. By 1962 the figure had more than doubled, with Algerians often replacing French workers who had been conscripted to fight in North Africa. The experience of working alongside Algerians, sharing the daily life of the workplace and participating with them in trade-union activities, helped to counteract the racist prejudices that existed.

11 Renault

One notable example was the huge Renault factory at Billancourt in Paris. Renault had been nationalised at the Liberation and had well-organised unions. In the 1950s Billancourt had around 40,000 workers, of whom over 10 percent were North African. These were mainly concentrated in the foundries and on the assembly lines. Many were active in the CGT, and some were in the Communist Party, though most left after the vote for special powers in 1956 [see above]. There were powerful pressures towards unity between French and Algerian workers. These were described in the joint autobiography of two left-wing activists from the factory, Henri and Clara Benoits, *L'Algérie au coeur* [Algeria in our hearts]. As Henri pointed out, police checks were conducted on a racial basis:

> Somebody walking along with a packet, if they had an Algerian face, would be stopped. It was easy to ask a mate from your shop to look after the packet. This was probably the sort of 'little job' which French people, more numerous than is often thought, carried out. ... Kaddour Ladlani, the coordinator of the FLN French Federation at the time, told us in October 1991 that if anyone had tried to make a serious calculation of the number of acts of solidarity by French people with their Algerian workmates, there would probably be several thousands. In short, racism was not as widespread as has been claimed.[87]

Henri described one incident which showed the potential for French solidarity with the Algerian struggle:

---

87   Benoits 2014, p. 97.

... when Algerians alleged to be FLN members were asked to leave their work and go to the factory gate, supposedly for personal reasons, but in fact to be handed over to the police, there was concrete solidarity to protect them.

Early in 1958, a representative from the foundries, Abdelghani Ben Nacef, a CGT representative, found himself in this situation. Security staff came into the workshop, together with his foreman, and asked him to go to the office. He refused to follow them. He thought 'they're trying to arrest me'. He went into the next workshop (the forge), where the CGT representative was Arezki Ziani and his deputy Raymond Husse. The workers in the forge stopped work, booed the security staff: 'clear out of the factory, no security in our workshop'. At this time most forge workers were French, skilled workers, sometimes ranked as management (paying into Agirc, the management pension scheme) because their pay was sometimes more than double that of other workers. This 'labour aristocracy' had a pronounced sense of class. More than 90 percent of them voted for the CGT. The Algerian workers from the foundries and the French workers, mainly from the forges, united to drive out the security and Ziani hid Ben Nacef in the factory. When we were informed of the attempted arrest, we decided to act. It was payday and we had to get his clothes – he was in overalls. This was done by Michel Eloy, the CGT representative in the foundries, helped by Claude Poperen, the secretary of the union, and the clothes were left at the factory committee office.

We took advantage of the large number of workers going out at the noon lunch-break to leave the factory discreetly and hide him in Billancourt. I handed over to him his pay which had been collected by another Algerian who had borrowed his identity as well as his clothes. He then became clandestine and in February 1963 became the UGTA representative in France. This example enables us to measure the enormous potential for solidarity which existed, and which, spontaneous to begin with, offered the possibility for a much greater solidarity in support of the Algerian people ... if the French labour movement had been willing.[88]

The Benoits couple provide a remarkable example of what internationalist activists could achieve in a workplace. Henri, a draughtsman, became a lifelong Trotskyist at the age of 18. He recalled how he became an internationalist at the time of the revolts by Vietnamese, who had been called up into the army in

---

88   Benoits 2014, p. 96.

1939, and who in 1945 were demanding the right to go home. He demonstrated with them on May Day 1945, demanding independence for Indochina.[89] Asked years later what motivated his actions during the Algerian war, he wrote:

> Class feeling must have precedence over national feeling. This war of Algerians against the colonial system, and not against French people, was therefore profoundly in tune with such aims. It fitted more generally with the struggle of all oppressed peoples who, since the end of the Second World War, had risen up against the domination of imperialisms in general, and mine in particular, which was committed to defending the remnants of the colonial empire. Since the class struggle has a universal content it seemed to me that the natural application of consistent internationalism was to support this struggle ... Finally, since the practice of unity is the basis of common action, it seemed to me that any blow against my enemy, French capitalism, could only help to weaken it and encourage the struggle of the working class against its exploiters.[90]

At the outbreak of the war Benoits was already an established trade unionist in the Renault factory and worked closely with Algerian activists. He gave practical support to the AGTA. He set up training courses in the CFTC [Catholic union] premises in which he was asked to emphasise the idea of class, and the struggle for independence. He had precise instructions to talk not only about trade unionism and the primacy of the working class, but in addition to say that they were fighting not only for a flag but also for the content of independence with a social character. He helped to produce leaflets for the AGTA. A prisoners' aid committee was set up at Renault. This drew in people who were willing to be involved in humanitarian assistance such as helping prisoners, but who would have been reluctant to take part in something more explicitly political.

His activities brought him into conflict with the CGT leadership, which was in the hands of the PCF. An attempt was made to force those giving individual assistance to the FLN to resign their union positions. The Algerians then threatened to leave the union if any disciplinary measures were taken against them. Later he was advised by the PCI to join the newly formed Parti Socialiste Unifié [PSU: see below] since this contained many well-known journalists and politicians, and it was more difficult for the authorities to victimise its members than isolated Trotskyists. He succeeded in winning over the PSU branch

---

89   Pattieu 2002, p. 55.
90   Quoted by Pattieu 2002, p. 260.

at Renault to back Algerian independence and to give practical support to the
FLN, policies which the PSU majority rejected.

Clara Benoits, originally a shorthand-typist, derived her internationalism
from her family. She had Hungarian parents, immigrants to France – her grandmother had taken part in the Hungarian Soviet Republic in 1919; her great-uncle
was murdereded in Auschwitz, and her uncle died fighting in Spain. She was a
member of the Communist Party, and remained one, though highly critical, till
1970. She described her activity at Renault as follows:

> In building A, where the offices are, we had formed early in 1956 a com-
> mittee for peace in Algeria which had some support. Several issues of a
> duplicated bulletin were produced by this committee, composed of about
> fifty employees, draughtspersons, technicians and engineers. It distrib-
> uted in a non-sectarian fashion publications and literature opposed to
> the war, such as *Vérité Liberté*, or *Témoignages et Documents*, *La Question*
> by Henri Alleg, *La Gangrène by* Bachir Boumaza, as well as various doc-
> uments that were more or less clandestine and were often seized. This
> committee held regular meetings of a good 20 people including half a
> dozen from the PCF, even if the party was not involved as an organisa-
> tion. This initiative was not welcomed by the Renault PCF branch, which
> nonetheless tolerated its existence. But could it have opposed it?
>
> This committee never took anti-Communist positions. At our meetings
> we invited all the organisations which existed at Renault without distinc-
> tion (from the Socialist Party to the far left groupings). What distinguished
> it was its position in favour of peace by the recognition of independence
> and negotiation with the FLN.[91]

Another revolutionary socialist activist at Renault was Daniel Mothé, a milling-
machine operator. As a member of Socialisme ou barbarie he did not work
through the trade-union organisations, simply engaged in arguing and campaigning with his fellow-workers. Mothé wrote regular reports on the situation
at Renault for *Socialisme ou barbarie*. Here he described how he attempted to
organise against the war, meeting opposition from both employers and the PCF-
dominated trade union.

Mothé drew up a statement in conjunction with some others; he then tried
to get other workers to sign it. The statement was a direct attack on the strategy
of the PCF; nonetheless some PCF members signed, while others refused:

---

91   Benoits 2014, pp. 89–90.

Without condemning small exemplary actions, we believe that to stop the war in Algeria we must launch general coordinated actions. Ending the war in Algeria cannot be left in the hands of the government. It must be forced to act. That is why we condemn the method of action which consists of sending petitions to these very traitors, of continuing to trust them, of bursting into tears because they are taking away young men to get them massacred. It is not by tearful petitions but by forceful actions that we shall say to the government:

No, you don't have the confidence of the workers!

No, we don't believe you any longer.

You have betrayed us … Well! We shall fight against you because you are the henchmen of the colonialists and the gravediggers of youth!

We must address all workers throughout France for an appeal and propose to them a general stoppage of work against the war, against the recall of the reservists. Strikes of struggle, not petitions of confidence.[92]

When Mothé and his friends attended a meeting about the war, the Communists spread rumours that they had behaved disruptively. Later the CGT issued a leaflet saying that they had had to admit 'Trotskyist elements' into the Committee for a Cease-Fire in Algeria [Comité d'Entente pour le cessez-le-feu en Algérie] because the other unions [FO and CFTC – French trade unions are divided along political and religious lines, so there are several confederations] had insisted on it, but warning workers that the Trotskyists 'by launching adventurist slogans, always contribute to the weakening of the struggle and the divisions among workers'. When there was a demonstration outside the factory, the Communists chanted 'negotiate' and 'Peace in Algeria', while Mothé and his friends shouted 'No soldiers for Algeria'.

They also had a critical position with regard to the Algerian nationalist struggle:

Whether it is the FLN and the MNA on the one side, or the French unions and 'left' parties on the other, nobody is trying to give this struggle a proletarian character. ...

The French proletariat, which does not believe in its own government and which is somewhat distrustful of its political and trade-union leaders, carries over this distrust and opposition onto the political and military

---

92 Un ouvrier de chez Renault 1956, p. 78.

leaders of the Algerian movement. In general it does not believe that the North African proletariat will be emancipated by national independence.[93]

Mothé described what happened at Renault when a strike of Algerian workers was called. Attitudes among indigenous French workers ranged from hostility or total indifference to mild sympathy which did not lead to any positive solidarity. An electrician reported that in his workshop 'a proposal to hold a collection in support of the North African workers on strike in the workshop was met with an outcry of indignation'. Mothé noted that support was greater in parts of the factory where significant numbers of Europeans and North Africans worked alongside each other: 'Where there is no contact chauvinism has a greater grip'. In one workshop 17 workers were asked to do the work of striking North Africans. They refused and were promptly sacked.[94]

In 1956, at the time of the events in Suez and Hungary, Mothé and a few friends gave out a leaflet on the Place Nationale, opposing the war in Algeria, the invasion of Egypt and Communist dictatorship:

> We declare our opposition to all wars, whether they be:
> The Russians who are crushing the will to struggle of the Hungarian workers and peasants.
> The Algerian war which has lasted over two years without offering any solution, and which each day brings more victims and thus more wretchedness.
> The war in Egypt whose aim is to defend the shareholders of the Suez Canal Company.[95]

Mothé reported that:

> The tone was violent, but workers took it sympathetically. It expressed what many of them felt. Small groups of workers were prepared to protect the leafletters; few among them were over 30. The situation was tense, but it didn't come to blows; we were stronger, and that naturally strengthened the sympathy we were given.[96]

---

93   Mothé 1957.
94   Mothé 1957, pp. 146–7.
95   Mothé 1956–7, p. 126.
96   Mothé 1956–7, p. 128.

Another factory, less prominent than Renault since it was isolated in the Vernon forest in Normandy, was the Vernon LRBA factory [Laboratoire de recherches balistiques et aérodynamiques Laboratory for Ballistic and Aerodynamic Research]. This had military management, but the workers were civilians, not under army discipline. It became the scene of some intense political activity.

A leading activist in the Vernon factory was Camille Januel. He had been a Trotskyist since before the Second World War. In 1940 he had agitated in the army when the officers were deserting; when he was sent to Germany to do forced labour he set up a clandestine Trotskyist cell. Working as a draughtsman, he moved to Vernon in around 1952 and rapidly established himself as a CGT delegate, leading strikes, and eventually became general secretary of the union in the factory, despite the opposition of the PCF which had previously controlled the CGT branch. He set up a PCI cell in the factory. Leaflets were distributed, *La Vérité des travailleurs* was sold and calls for desertion from the army were posted on the factory walls. By 1957 there were eight PCI members in the factory – as well as Januel there were four fitters, two milling-machine operators and a radio technician.

One of Januel's recruits was Louis Fontaine. Initially he had not been very political despite having spent a few months in the PCF. He was transformed by his year as a reservist in Algeria. He was appalled by the terrible poverty of the indigenous population and outraged by French colonial policy. He developed contacts with the Algerians he met, including *harkis* [Muslim Algerians who served as auxiliaries in the French Army], some of whom were FLN activists who had infiltrated the French forces. On his return to France he joined the PCI.

Another of Januel's recruits was Roland Vacher, a radio technician. The son of a PCF member of the Resistance, he had originally been active in the Catholic union, the CFTC, but under Januel's influence he joined the PCI and was active in the CGT. He became a member of the political bureau of the PCI and in particular was active in Jeune Résistance [young resistance], an organisation that encouraged desertion from the armed forces and set up networks to assist deserters. Working with a deserter from the armed forces he set up clandestine meetings of Jeune Résistance and took on the job of recruiting draft refusers.

Another PCI member who had some success in organising in his workplace was Gilbert Marquis at the Nord-Aviation factory at Bourges in central France. He formed a PCI 'youth committee', and distributed leaflets against the special powers and the sending of conscripts to Algeria. He established an active cell with seven or eight members, which engaged in such activity as forging identity cards and producing leaflets.[97]

---

97   Pattieu 2002, pp. 102–5, 256.

These examples show that where there was an internationalist activist giving a lead, it was possible to swim against the tide and get a response. Unfortunately in the vast majority of workplaces the political leadership was, at best, in the hands of the PCF. The French trade-union movement played a relatively subdued role in the opposition to the Algerian war.

Yet public opinion was swinging, under the pressure of events, towards support for independence. In September 1957 only 23 percent backed independence for Algeria, but by March 1959 71 percent favoured ceasefire negotiations with the FLN.[98]

Working-class attitudes to the war were undoubtedly contradictory, with a significant element of racism. Nonetheless there was a clear potential for opposition to the war on the part of at least a section of workers, and a more effective internationalist lead might have mobilised this opposition and shortened the war. When a worker from the Berliet vehicle factory in Lyon was killed in Algeria in 1959, his shop downed tools and a message was sent to the President calling for negotiations with the FLN. CGT officials recognised that they had underestimated the possibilities for campaigning against the war in the factory.[99]

12   Conscript Revolt

The small group of suitcase-carriers, and activists in a few workplaces; these were two crucial areas in which internationalism began to develop. There was a third area – the armed forces. The role of the French army in Algeria will mainly be remembered for its brutality – torture and the illegal killing of prisoners. Yet there were currents of internationalist opposition within the army, and under different circumstances they could have been more effective.

The Algerian war was fought with conscripts. All young men were required to do military service and having done it, they became part of the reserve and for the next three years could be recalled immediately if required. In September 1955 the government called up reservists. Then in April 1956 conscripts from 1951–4 were recalled and military service was extended from 18 to 27 months. By the end of 1956 there were 450,000 French troops in Algeria. This was scarcely popular. Many thousands of young men were torn away from their loved ones, their families, their jobs or their studies to be sent to fight a savage and dangerous war.

---

98   Evans 2012, pp. 223, 257.
99   *La Voie communiste* 5, March–April 1959.

Resentment boiled over into open rebellion. From 1955 to 1957 there were a number of revolts and riots by conscripts being sent to Algeria.[100] When reservists were recalled to fight in Algeria, they often resisted. On a number of occasions reservists and conscripts refused to board the trains, and in some cases when they were put on the train they systematically pulled the communication cord in order to reduce speed to a minimum. In some cases they made a point of visiting cafes frequented by North African workers.[101] Soldiers destined for Morocco chanted 'Morocco for the Moroccans!'[102] On 11 September 1955, soldiers refused to board trains bound for Algeria in the Gare de Lyon in Paris; civilians joined in, including wives, families and friends of the reservists; the station was cordoned off. When they were finally forced to board the train, the rebels set off the alarm bells every three hundred metres to stop it. They were finally sent to Algeria by plane.

A Trotskyist paper carried various first-hand reports by conscripts involved in the revolts. At the Gare de Lyon in Paris several hundred conscripts were due to leave for Marseille. They got out of the train and demonstrated on the platform, demanding to go home. They were taken in police vans to barracks; later they were put onto aeroplanes for Algeria with riot police to guard them.

Other reservists vandalised the vans taking them to a naval troop-ship, or entered the Brest arsenal singing the *Internationale*. Some ransacked their living quarters and put in hospital a naval policeman who was making them board a plane. As one participant pointed out, they were ready to fight, but not against North African workers.[103]

When, on 12 April 1956, the government decided to call up reservists and to send conscripts to Algeria, the demonstrations of opposition by the reservists and those who supported them resumed, and trains were again obstructed; on 3 May at Lézignan, on 10 May at Saint-Aignan-des-Noyers in Loir-et-Cher, on 17 May at Le Mans, on 18 May at Grenoble. There were also actions in the ports, on 23 May at Antibes, on 24 May at Le Havre, on 28 May at Saint-Nazaire. Often there were violent confrontations, and local inhabitants, dockers and railway workers, gave their support to actions in which were involved the New Left, the far left and also the PCF, despite the reluctance of its leadership faced with these so-called provocations.[104]

---

100   Evans 2006.
101   Reported in *Le Parisien libéré*, 12 September 1955.
102   Vittori 1977, p. 28.
103   *La Vérité des travailleurs*, October 1955.
104   Hamon and Rotman 1979, pp. 48–49.

In a shipyard in Brittany, Trotskyist André Fichaut, working with a PCF member who was somewhat more militant than his party, got his CGT branch to agree that if any worker in the shipyard were recalled as a reservist, the workers would go to the station to support him. The policy was put into practice, and there was a small demonstration which significantly delayed the departure of the train. Some demonstrators were arrested and taken to the police station, where the PCF member taunted the police for not having volunteered to fight in Algeria. There was a potential for resistance where a militant lead was offered.[105]

Other attempts were made to organise action in workplaces when conscripts were due to be sent to Algeria. Daniel Mothé described the situation in 1956 in his workshop at Renault the first time one of their workmates was called up as a reservist for Algeria. There was a widespread desire for action, to prevent the worker being forced to go or at least to show solidarity. Faced with management intimidation and the reluctance of the unions to take action, there was only a half-hour work stoppage. This showed the potential, but was totally ineffective, despite being in one of the best organised factories in France.[106]

There was vigorous opposition to the use of conscripts and reservists, though obviously self-interest was a predominant factor, and solidarity with the Algerian struggle secondary. Yet the young men involved, and their friends, families and workmates, were being thrust into opposition to the state machine, and with effective political leadership the opposition to conscription could have developed, for some at least, into an internationalist opposition to the war.

Such leadership was absent. The Socialist Party was in government, and spearheading the escalation of the war. The PCF's demands went no further than peace, stressing the French national interest. There were only the meagre forces of the far left to try to give a political focus to the rebellious conscripts. There were demands that soldiers' support committees be set up in every workplace, and that a fund on the model of the 'sou du soldat' be established.[107] Unfortunately the far left did not have the resources to put these demands, excellent in principle, into practice.

In early October 1955 an attempt had been made to set up a Committee against Sending Conscripts to Algeria. [Comité contre l'envoi du contingent en Algérie]. This brought together the SFIO Youth, the UJRF [French union of

---

105   Fichaut 2003, pp. 79–81.
106   Un ouvrier de chez Renault 1956, pp. 73–5.
107   *La Vérité des travailleurs*, October 1955.

republican youth, a PCF-controlled organisation], the libertarian and Trotsky-ist youth, the Youth Hostels, the New Left, the SFIO Students and the secular boy scouts.[108] Mollet forced the withdrawal of the SFIO Youth,[109] and the UJRF soon followed, denouncing the presence of 'Trotskyist and libertarian police elements'.[110] The Committee called a meeting on 13 October at the Mutual-ité, but this was banned; there were clashes with the police.[111] The Committee could not survive these setbacks and disappeared.

The conscripts were subject to military discipline and could be physically forced to go to Algeria, with only a few minor delays. What was needed was a substantial expression of support from other sections of the population. Poten-tially this was there – the soldiers had families, friends, lovers and workmates. Often these joined in the demonstrations, though only on a random and per-sonal basis.

The most significant conscript revolt had come in Rouen in September 1955 when there were violent clashes between security police and the soldiers, with significant involvement by sections of the population, in particular local work-ers. If this potential had been developed it is just possible it could have forced the government to shift its policy. The PCF was cautious about direct action, and while it held a demonstration of support for the rebel soldiers on 8 October,[112] it steered clear of any more militant action. These events coincided with consid-erable trade-union militancy on the part of the French working class, notably big strikes at Saint-Nazaire and Nantes, and it might have been possible to bring the struggles together. The vote in the elections at the end of 1955, and opinion polls taken at the time, showed that the war was not popular.[113]

Except in the case of a small number of individuals, opposition to conscrip-tion or recall did not lead on to a critique of the war as such. Indeed the frustra-tion and anger felt by many conscripts was often redirected, once they found themselves in Algeria, against the Muslim population, and made the soldiers all the more likely to support torture and brutality. Nonetheless, for a brief period, there was a glimpse of an internationalist alternative.

The volatile consciousness within the French armed forces, which could move rapidly from radical antimilitarism to overt racism, was well described by Olivier Todd [who had served with the French army in Morocco]:

---

108   Hamon and Rotman 1979, p. 41.
109   Hamon and Rotman 1979, p. 41.
110   Pattieu 2002, p. 101.
111   Hamon and Rotman 1979, p. 41.
112   Hamon and Rotman 1979, pp. 19–22.
113   See *L'Express*, 16 December 1955.

We all know too many of our mates in the army who demonstrated violently when they had to leave, and who, on their return, can't stand the sight of a North African without wanting, as they say, to smash his face in. It isn't, as the right would have us believe, 'because they have understood and appreciated France's task in Algeria'. This contamination, this transition to repressive and colonialist positions, whether in the case of young men objectively on the left, workers for example, or those subjectively on the left, such as humanist students, often springs from the desire not to have fought in vain and above all not to have fought against oneself, against what gives one's life a meaning. To the extent that you can't observe a satisfactory transformation of the overall political situation, you transform yourself. By adapting to circumstances, you take responsibility for them. It isn't always the beginning of becoming fascist. Often it's the beginning of political apathy.[114]

In 1957 Daniel Mothé at Renault reported some interesting observations about the young workers who returned to the factory after having done military service as reservists in Algeria. Few had changed their attitudes as a result of what they had experienced:

> The reservist's resentment tends to be directed against the army. Often the reservist joked bitterly that he was forbidden to shoot, or that he had to account for the number of bullets allocated to him. He would conclude: 'we didn't have the right to defend ourselves'. ...
>
> Except for a few Communist militants, there was never any sign of proletarian solidarity between the reservists and the North Africans. However, it would be wrong to think that because a worker has put on a uniform, he has lost all the reactions which characterised him in the factory. The reservist behaved like a soldier towards the North Africans, but he often behaved like a worker towards his officers. ...
>
> At Renault a substantial number of workers were prepared to struggle to prevent workmates from their shop being called up ... the possibilities which undoubtedly existed at that time were undermined, sabotaged and finally crushed by the attitude of the 'left' organisations.[115]

Mothé's observations were often pessimistic, yet he was always alive to the potential for internationalism among his fellow-workers.

---

114   *Esprit*, May 1958; quoted by Maschino 1961, p. 61.
115   Mothé 1957, pp. 151, 152, 154.

There were some signs of low morale in the French forces. These were most obvious in the Foreign Legion, which had a very high casualty rate. The ALN developed a repatriation organisation aimed at members of the Foreign Legion, based on a similar strategy adopted by the Viet Minh in Indochina. Wherever off-duty legionnaires in Morocco went, street traders and shoe-shine boys would give them leaflets urging them to desert. After a significant number of desertions the Legion moved out of Morocco. The rifles of the sentries outside the barracks were fastened by chains in case they were taken away by deserters, and even at the farewell parades some legionnaires disappeared, seizing their last chance to desert. The response was brutal. In some Legion bases executions were carried out in front of the assembled troops as a deterrent, although such a procedure was forbidden by French military law, since the legionnaires had not sworn an oath to the flag. There were collective punishments like the cancellation of leave for the whole unit. Algerian civilians who assisted deserters and were betrayed by French agents posing as deserting legionnaires were tortured and killed. Nonetheless there were a substantial number of desertions from the Legion, some three or four thousand in the course of the war.

Desertion and draft-dodging among French forces was less substantial, but not wholly insignificant, and as with the Foreign Legion, it was not spontaneous, but encouraged by opponents of the war. Networks were set up to enable young Frenchmen to leave the country, in particular to go to Switzerland. There may have been no more than 400 deserters and draft refusers – though higher figures, up to 3000, were claimed – but the debate about the refusal to serve was high profile, and influenced many thousands of young people.[116] Militants, often deserters themselves, like Jean-Louis Hurst or Louis Orhant, who belonged to the Jeanson network, helped to run these systems and encouraged desertion by distributing leaflets at demonstrations. Hurst had gone into the army as a Communist, but rapidly came to believe that it was impossible to organise within the army. He went to Switzerland and became involved in organising deserters.[117]

There was no organised opposition within the army. The fight for internationalist principle came only in the form of individual actions, often showing great courage and principle, yet limited in their effect because they did not inspire more generalised opposition.

Georges Mattéi was called up as a reservist in 1956 and sent to Algeria. He was soon confronted with the reality of brutality and torture, and faced

---

116   Hamon and Rotman 1979, pp. 216–7.
117   Evans 1997, pp. 129–35.

disciplinary measures. He wrote about his experiences in *Les Temps modernes* – the issue was seized. After leaving the army he became involved in solidarity work in the Curiel network and was later involved with founding the journal *Partisans*. He became disillusioned with the French working class and spent many years in Latin America supporting revolutionary movements there.[118]

In 1982 he published a novel, *La Guerre des gusses*, which drew heavily on his experiences of the Algerian war. The 'gusses' of the novel's title are the conscripts and reservists sent to fight in Algeria. The book begins with an attempted revolt by conscripts; one of them, Nonosse, has exaggerated hopes of working-class action against the war, but is bitterly disillusioned and tears up his party and union cards. He becomes violently anti-French: 'I hate my country! A people of cops and pigs'. Mattéi traces how the majority of the conscripts take out their anger on the FLN, but a small minority are radicalised. There are vivid descriptions of the brutality of the war, and savagely satirical portrayals of the army officers. Nonosse deserts and goes over to the FLN, for whom he makes bombs, working with Algerians and with other European supporters. While the book unambiguously supports the Algerian cause, there are criticisms of both the political ambitions of some FLN leaders and the tactics of bombing civilian targets. A final section describes the police massacre of North Africans in Paris on 17 October 1961 [see below], which Mattéi himself had witnessed as an FLN observer. In the conclusion the narrator meets Algerians in Paris 20 years later: 'Was the Algerian war finished? I wasn't convinced ...'[119]

Alban Liechti, a gardener and PCF member, was called up to fight in Algeria. However, he went far beyond the recommendations of his party, and refused to participate in any military activity. He was imprisoned for two years, and then physically obliged to participate in the war. He continued to take a position of total non co-operation and refused to put bullets in his gun.

Henri Maillot was a childhood friend of Fernand Iveton [see below] and grew up in Algeria. He became involved with a Muslim woman, Baya. She had been forced into an arranged marriage at the age of 14; at 20 she demanded separation from her husband and stopped wearing the *hijab*. Their relationship caused antagonism in both communities; only in the Communist milieu could they hope for some understanding. In the spring of 1956 Maillot, who had been called up into the army, stole a lorry-load of weapons and handed them over to the FLN. He was later captured and killed without trial.

---

118   Evans 1997, pp. 105–8; see also Einaudi 2004.
119   Mattéi, 1982, pp. 30, 235.

The Communist Party did not support such individual acts and was sometimes slow to take up the defence of militants, even when its own members were involved. The Algerian Communist Party's endorsement of Maillot's desertion marked a divergence from the positions of the PCF.[120] The PCF's position was largely negative. It insisted vigorously that Communists should not refuse or evade military service, but should join the army. However as Alain Krivine pointed out, it did nothing to organise the conscripts or propose what they should do inside the army.[121] Some Communist conscripts did distribute *La Voix du soldat* [Soldier's Voice], a monthly duplicated bulletin produced by the Algerian Communist Party.[122]

After the failure of the conscript riots there was little hope of collective resistance within the French army. The one time when there was collective action by soldiers was towards the end of the war when right-wing army leaders tried to organise a coup in Algiers and rank-and-file soldiers refused to obey orders. This went no further than supporting de Gaulle's peace negotiations.

The Leninist tradition did oppose individual desertion and conscientious objection; mass revolt against war was a different matter. As long ago as Eugène Pottier's *Internationale* – 'Appliquons la grève aux armées' ['the soldiers too will take strike action'] – revolutionaries had called for mass disobedience in the armed forces.

Many conscripts opposed to the war decided that they would not be able to achieve anything in the army. Maurice Lemaître, a young Communist called up early in the war, wrote: 'How could I take effective action in Algeria? The Party had not yet pronounced on the role that we could play in this war'.[123]

They deserted or evaded the draft, leaving the army to those who had fewer scruples. Those around the Jeanson network were scornful of the PCF's attitude. An article in the network's clandestine paper, *Vérités Pour*, savagely dismantled the PCF's interpretation of Leninism which argued that soldiers should not refuse conscription or desert. It was pointed out that Lenin had written that 'a revolutionary class cannot but wish for the defeat of its government in a reactionary war'[124] and that 'wartime revolutionary action against one's own government indubitably means, not only desiring its defeat, but really facilitating such a defeat'.[125]

---

120   Drew 2014, p. 203.
121   See Krivine 2004.
122   Drew 2014, p. 199.
123   Lemaître 1961.
124   Lenin 1970, p. 315.
125   Lenin 1974, p. 275.

Jeanson and his supporters argued that in the case of the Algerian war the refusal of the call-up in 1955 by reservists and conscripts had the potential to become a popular demand involving the mass of soldiers, and supported by workers and peasants. By refusing to support this movement the French Communist Party had abandoned revolutionary action.[126]

If the antimilitarists of the Jeanson network had the better of the argument, they remained in a tiny minority. There was nothing comparable to the vast networks of draft-dodgers and support for dissident soldiers that grew up during the American war in Vietnam.[127]

13   Settlers

If internationalist initiatives were rare in the French armed forces, they were also very much in hostile territory among the European settlers in Algeria. The settlers enjoyed privileges which, while meagre by the standards of mainland France, gave them enormous advantages over the mass of the Muslim population. Their culture was profoundly racist, sometimes combined with the rhetoric of the 'civilising mission'. In April 1961 a putsch organised by retired generals attempted to prevent de Gaulle pursuing negotations for Algerian independence. After the failure of this the supporters of French Algeria formed the Organisation Armée Secrète [OAS – secret army organisation] which adopted terror tactics in Algeria. This got the backing of most settlers.

As far as workers were concerned there was a contradiction at the heart of their situation; they were undoubtedly exploited, although far less than their Muslim fellow-workers. As Albert Camus pointed out in 1955, 80 percent of the French in Algeria were wage-earners or tradespeople. The standard of living of wage-earners, though higher than that of Arabs, was lower than that in metropolitan France.[128] There was a potential for appealing to class-consciousness.

There had been a Communist Party in Algeria [PCA] since the 1920s. Originally overwhelmingly a European settler party, it became the only ethnically mixed political party in Algeria; by the 1940s it was having some success in recruiting young Algerian workers, notably dockers and miners. By 1954 only around one third of the membership was European.[129]

---

126   See *Vérités Pour* 17, 26 July 1960.
127   See Neale 2001.
128   Camus 1955.
129   Drew 2014, pp. 128, 159, 181.

The internationalist traditions of the party had not disappeared. Some individuals and groups within the party pushed for a position of support for the FLN, not only because they believed its demands were justified, but because they saw the growing estrangement between the Muslim and settler populations, and wanted to do something to restore the possibility of Muslim trust in European socialists. When the FLN launched armed struggle in 1954 the PCA was divided.

In 1956 it was agreed that groups of Communists would fight under the discipline of the FLN and break contact with their party for the duration of the war. However the PCA refused to dissolve its organisation, and faced continuing suspicion from the FLN, which was intolerant of any political rivals. By the end of the war the party was much weakened.[130] But the collaboration with the FLN did provide significant evidence of an internationalist current on the Algerian left, and showed that the positions of the PCF were not imposed on its Algerian comrades.

A small but significant minority of the European population did adopt an internationalist position, putting their heads on the line. A European Communist, Raymonde Peschard, had joined the armed struggle as a nurse and social worker. She was captured and executed by the French forces in November 1957, the only European woman to die in this way.[131]

A leading FLN representative, Frantz Fanon,[132] paid generous tribute to the substantial numbers of Europeans who took frequently dangerous action in support of the FLN:

> We should perhaps add that often a European would say that they did not want to know the details of the matter for which their assistance was being sought. But the leadership would make no compromise. The FLN wanted responsible people, not people who at the slightest difficulty would break down and claim that they had been misled.
>
> The European women and men who have been arrested and tortured by the police and by French parachutists, in their behaviour under abuse, have shown how right was this position taken by the FLN. In fact not a single French person has revealed to the colonialist police information vital to the Revolution. On the contrary, the arrested Europeans held out long enough to let the other members of the network disappear. The tor-

---

130   Drew 2014, pp. 190, 204–5, 209, 269.
131   Drew 2014, p. 227.
132   See Zeilig 2016.

tured European behaved like a genuine militant in the national struggle for independence.[133]

14   Fernand Iveton

Two Europeans in Algeria who took courageous internationalist positions were Fernand Iveton and Henri Alleg.

Fernand Iveton[134] was born in Algiers in 1926, of a French father and a Spanish mother. As a poor settler he grew up living in a Muslim quarter; there were close contacts between his family and their Muslim neighbours. In 1940 his father was sacked by the Vichy government for having taken strike action and he had to leave school and get a job to help the family finances. He worked as a turner and at the age of 16 became a Communist like his father.

In 1954 Iveton was a CGT delegate in a gasworks. He regarded it as his duty to represent workers from both communities, saying to Muslim workers: 'I'm a European, you're Muslims. There is no reason why you shouldn't have the same pay as me for doing the same work. You eat just as I do, and you pay the same price for goods'.[135]

In September 1955 the FLN exploded two bombs in cafes in Algiers. Iveton opposed such acts because they implied that all Europeans were the enemy, and that the two communities were being driven apart. He was also concerned that some European chemistry students had helped the FLN manufacture the bombs.

He therefore resolved to take a different form of action; he seems to have done this on his own initiative and without the approval of his party. He planted a small bomb in his workplace, the Algiers gasworks. It was timed to explode at a time when it would have damaged property, but when no people would have been injured; it was a symbolic gesture. In fact the bomb was discovered before it exploded.

Iveton was arrested and tortured. His trial took place within weeks of his arrest. The Communist Party did not provide a lawyer, so he had a rather ineffective legal defence. The Communist Parties in both France and Algeria were somewhat half-hearted in campaigning in his defence. He was sentenced to death. On 6 February 1957 an appeal for mercy was heard and rejected. The Justice Minister, François Mitterrand, voted against the appeal.

---

133   Fanon 1972, p. 124.
134   This account is based on a remarkable study of Iveton in Einaudi 1986.
135   Einaudi 1986, p. 38.

The prospect of settlers siding with the FLN was an alarming one and the government felt it necessary to make Iveton an example. The fact that he was a Communist made it easier to denounce Communist influence on the FLN; this was important because the United States was unsympathetic to French colonialism, but if it were argued that the fight against the FLN was a fight against Communism, this might win American support. On 11 February 1957 Iveton was executed.

15   Henri Alleg

Henri Alleg, of Polish Jewish origin, was a member of the PCA and a journalist on *Alger Républicain*, a paper sympathetic to Algerian nationalism. Alleg's friend Maurice Audin, who had been a Communist since 1951, active in campaigns for peace and against the war in Indochina, was arrested by parachutists during the Battle of Algiers and was killed, after torture, on the orders of General Massu, a leading French general in Algeria and later an opponent of de Gaulle. [Only in 2018 did the French state accept responsibility for his death.[136]] Alleg decided to go into hiding.

In June 1957 he was arrested by paratroops who kept him, without trial, in a building in the El-Biar district of Algiers for a whole month, while he was repeatedly tortured. Electric shocks were administered to his ears, hands and genitals. A rubber tube was attached to a tap and running water was forced into his mouth until he felt he was drowning; he was repeatedly punched in the stomach [what later became known as 'waterboarding']. Burning paper was applied to his legs, penis and nipples. The charges against him were extremely vague – 'endangering national security' and 'reconstituting a banned organisation' [the Algerian Communist Party]. Despite constant searches in the prison, Alleg wrote an account of his experiences. Sections were clandestinely passed under the table to his defence lawyers and smuggled out of the prison. He remained in jail for three years until he succeeded in escaping. In February 1958 his account was published as a short book called *The Question*. [In French *La Question* means both question and torture.] The book was confiscated by the police, the first time this had been done for political reasons in France since the eighteenth century. It had sold 66,000 copies before being banned, after which

---

136   Maitron and Pennetier 1964–2023 article153671, notice AUDIN Maurice [Dictionnaire Algérie] par René Gallissot, version mise en ligne le 19 février 2014, dernière modification le 21 juin 2020.

a further 90,000 were sold clandestinely.[137] A Swiss publisher produced a new edition within a month, and copies were smuggled into France.

There had been many previous protests about the use of torture in Algeria, but Alleg's book raised discussion to a new level. Alleg was white, of European descent. Most victims of torture were Muslims. Alleg's story gave a voice to them all.

In March 1958 Jean-Paul Sartre wrote an article – 'Une Victoire' [A Victory] – about the book for the weekly *L'Express*.[138] Within hours the police went round the newsstands and seized every copy. Sartre had the last laugh. The satirical magazine *Le Canard Enchaîné* printed a reduced photograph of the article with large crosses through it; this was not seized and could be read easily with a magnifying glass.[139]

Sartre's article drew out the political logic of torture. Less than fifteen years earlier torture had been widely practised on French soil – by the Nazis who were torturing French Resisters. For Sartre torture was inherent in the whole logic of colonial warfare, just as terrorism was the only option available to the weaker side. The FLN did not choose these forms of action; it was simply doing what was possible for it. 'The balance of forces between them and us obliges them to attack by surprise; invisible, uncatchable, unexpected, they have to strike and disappear, or else they will be exterminated ... for the regular army and the civil authorities, the whole throng of the wretched become the permanent, uncountable enemy'. Sartre concluded that the war could not be humanised; torture was an inextricable part of it. There was no point simply opposing torture; it was necessary to oppose the war as such.

In strictly military terms the FLN was not progressing. After 1957 it had little influence in the cities, and there were serious divisions within the leadership. By 1959 the French army was having considerable success; the National Liberation Army suffered heavy losses and defections, and morale was low. However, by 1958 the war was imposing intolerable strains on French political institutions. The Fourth Republic was fragile; the constitution encouraged a multiparty system in which each successive government was based on a coalition cobbled together. In eleven years the Republic had twenty-one prime ministers. In principle this could have continued indefinitely – a similar constitution in Italy has survived over eighty years, but Italy had no colonies.

---

137   Evans 2012, p. 224; see also Birchall 2008a.
138   Sartre 1958.
139   *Le Canard enchaîné*, 12 March 1958.

16   De Gaulle's Return

It was not the activities of the internationalist minority which threatened the regime; they were only a minor irritant. Economically France was thriving – it was the middle of the post-war boom. The challenge to the regime came from the far right, impatient that the governments of the Fourth Republic were pursuing the war with insufficient energy. In May 1958 a military-settler rising in Algeria called for a de Gaulle government. The Fourth Republic collapsed amidst threats of civil war. De Gaulle called a referendum which established a Fifth Republic with a new constitution, under which he was elected as President.

De Gaulle's return came as a surprise to most of the left, and their reactions often showed signs of confusion. Despite his rather old-fashioned style, de Gaulle was a shrewd political operator. In 1958 he was hailed by the military leaders as one of theirs and a supporter of French Algeria. Within four years he had negotiated a settlement giving complete independence to Algeria. Whether he had worked out his strategy in advance is impossible to know, but he kept his nerve and his freedom of manoeuvre.

Although sections of the left, above all the PCF, tried to organise a defence of the Fourth Republic, it was quite clear that most of their base felt there was nothing worth defending. Attempts to mobilise industrial action were largely ineffective. Daniel Mothé wrote an article describing the response in a number of Parisian workplaces, showing the limited and half-hearted involvement in the stoppages called by the unions.[140] In the parliamentary elections the PCF lost over a million votes and most of its deputies [the number fell from 150 to 10].

The left was effectively marginalised. The far left, which ever since 1954 had made the argument that Algeria should, could and would become independent, was to be proved right, yet its forces were too small to make any impact on the political process. The initiative passed to the right. Once a nationalist consensus was accepted across the political spectrum, the right had greater freedom of manoeuvre than the left, since their patriotism was not in question. De Gaulle, a figure of the political right, was able to accept Algerian independence, while a 'Socialist' like Guy Mollet was afraid of losing votes and supported barbarous measures to maintain French rule in Algeria.

Some sections of the bourgeoisie, with a direct interest in the colonies, opposed decolonisation, while the rest of the bourgeoisie was quite happy to

---

140   Mothé 1958.

see them become independent. It was the small settlers who had everything to lose from a French withdrawal, while big capital was quite well aware that it could make any kind of deal it wanted with an independent Algeria. At Renault, as Henri Benoits reported, Dreyfus, the Chief Executive, arranged a meeting with FLN militants in the factory even before the end of the war. He clearly believed that independence was inevitable and that the company would have to find a place in a potential market![141]

In 1957 the Mouvement de Libération du Peuple [MLP: People's Liberation Movement], an organisation of Christian workers, joined the New Left to form the Union de la Gauche Socialiste [UGS]. Mollet's backing for de Gaulle in 1958 led to a section of the SFIO splitting away to form the Parti Socialiste Autonome [PSA: Autonomous Socialist Party]. In April 1960 a fusion of the UGS and the PSA led to the formation of the PSU [Parti Socialiste Unifié: United Socialist Party]. This was a broad organisation which included even the followers of Mendès-France, who had now come to oppose the war he had initially supported. The new party had some 30,000 members.

In the fraught atmosphere of the last years of the war the PSU was necessarily caught up in direct action and played a positive role in opposing the war. On 27 October 1960 the UNEF [Union nationale des étudiants de France: French national students' union] called an anti-war demonstration. The PSU played an active part; when demonstrators were attacked by the police, a former minister, Tanguy-Prigent, was seriously injured, and Mitterrand [whose careerist instincts had now brought him into opposition to the war] was slightly hurt. The PCF refused to support this action, causing some discontent among its members. The demonstration mobilised some 15,000 people, marking a new stage in public opposition to the war. A left current began to develop within the UEC [Union des étudiants communistes: Union of Communist Students]. This was encouraged by Trotskyists like Alain Krivine, still doing entry work inside the PCF.

There had been a major expansion of higher education. Students belonged to the age group most affected by conscription to fight in Algeria. So a process of radicalisation was taking place in UNEF, the French students' union, which had been campaigning against student conscription.

The result was the formation of the Front Universitaire Antifasciste [FUA: University Antifascist Front]. Its main activity was organising self-defence groups to defend the university area in Paris against the OAS, who were distributing literature and attacking left-wing militants. The FUA attacked right-wing

---

141   Benoits 2014, p. 99.

paper sellers, defended left-wing bookshops and prevented a public meeting in defence of 'Algérie française' [Algeria must remain French] from being held.

The FUA involved Trotskyists, members of the PSU, Young Communists, Christians and others on the student left. According to Alain Krivine, the front could regularly mobilise large numbers in Paris; as he recounted, several hundred students would meet in the courtyard of the Sorbonne to discuss what to do; there were people riding round town on scooters, and as soon as they heard that pro-OAS or similar leaflets were being given out, they went and put a stop to it.[142] This led to a regroupment among the student left which continued after the end of the war.

17   The Manifesto of 121

Another action which raised the profile of the internationalist opposition to the war was the publication in the autumn of 1960 of the Manifesto of 121. The manifesto was a direct challenge to legality, openly supporting suitcase-carriers and deserters who acted in solidarity with the Algerian revolution:

> We respect and consider justified the refusal to take arms against the Algerian people.
>
> We respect and consider justified the actions of those French people who regard it as their duty to offer assistance and protection to Algerians oppressed in the name of the French people.

Though known as the Manifesto of the 121, it had at least 172 signatories, all of them well-known figures. They included a number of activists from the internationalist left – Alfred Rosmer, Robert Louzon and Daniel Guérin in particular. From the surrealists there were André Breton, Michel Leiris and André Masson, and a number of former Communists such as Henri Lefebvre and the novelist Marguerite Duras. The most famous was Sartre. Very few signatories came from the PCF, which disapproved of the action. Hélène Parmelin and Édouard Pignon were called before the Central Committee to explain why they had signed.[143]

The authorities responded immediately. One of the two journals in which it was due to appear was seized, and *Les Temps Modernes* appeared with two

---

142   Quoted in McGrogan 2012.
143   For a full list of signatories see https://www.marxists.org/history/france/algerian-war/1960/manifesto-121.htm.

blank pages as a result of government censorship. State employees who signed the Manifesto were penalised and dismissed; artists and journalists were sacked from French radio and television, and actors did not get jobs in state theatres. However there were no judicial proceedings; the authorities feared the publicity a trial would bring.

Obviously those actively engaged in illegal activity did not sign, since that would have drawn attention to them. But there were signatories from the Trotskyist left, for example Simonne Minguet and Michel Lequenne. The PCI distributed the text of the Manifesto, in particular at factory gates, which sometimes led to violent clashes with PCF militants.

The Manifesto was originally drafted by novelist and philosopher Maurice Blanchot and Maurice Nadeau on the basis of a project initiated by Dionys Mascolo.[144] Nadeau's office at *Les Lettres nouvelles* [a literary review he had founded in 1953] was used to organise the Manifesto; it was searched by police and Nadeau was taken in for questioning. Nadeau was the chief recruiter of signatories; he also organised the printing of the illegal document.

Nadeau had a long political history. He had been a Trotskyist in the 1930s and 1940s and had been centrally involved in the FIARI [see chapter 8]. By the time of the Liberation he had broken with organised Trotskyism, though he had not abandoned his revolutionary commitment and was active in getting Trotsky's works back in print in France. His involvement with the Manifesto was the continuation of his activity as a revolutionary internationalist.

The right-wing military leaders in Algiers who had originally brought de Gaulle to power moved into open opposition. The OAS began a bombing campaign in mainland France. Among many others Pierre Frank's flat was bombed. Some leading military figures, notably General Salan, went underground.

Now that de Gaulle was clearly moving towards a French withdrawal from Algeria, there was a danger that the left, which had failed to hegemonise the demand for Algerian independence earlier in the war, would find itself effectively backing up de Gaulle's policies rather than offering an alternative.

18   The October Massacre

The road to independence was not a smooth one. The state machine was staffed by people who had little sympathy with de Gaulle's strategy. In 1961 the head of the Paris police imposed a curfew on Algerians, forbidding them

---

144   See Lévy 1991, p. 15.

to go out between 8.30 p.m. and 5.30 a.m., seriously interfering with their working and family lives. This despite the fact that the 1947 Statute of Algeria granted Algerian men full citizenship in mainland France – though they were officially called French-Algerian Muslims, a widely resented ethnic designation.

In protest the FLN called out its supporters in Paris for a peaceful demonstration in breach of the curfew on the evening of 17 October. Demonstrators were instructed that they must be completely unarmed; they must not even carry a pin or a knife. The FLN leadership were aware that things could turn nasty. It is unlikely they had any idea just how nasty. The head of the Paris police was Maurice Papon. Many years later he was imprisoned for having ordered the arrest and deportation of 1,560 Jews, including children, during the German occupation. He openly encouraged a murderous response.

The peaceful demonstrators were attacked by the police. Exact figures for the number who died are difficult to establish, since many of the bodies were simply thrown into the river, but the total was probably as high as two hundred.[145] Efforts were then made to suppress reporting of the events.

The fact that French comrades who had been involved in suitcase-carrying had established a relation of trust with the FLN was shown by the fact that a number were asked to act as observers during the demonstration. Henri and Clara Benoits, together with other sympathetic workers from Renault and individuals like Georges Mattéi, were among those who took part. They were instructed to observe, but not, under any circumstances, to intervene. They observed police violence; only later did they become aware of the full scale of the horror.[146]

An issue of *Témoignages et documents* was published dealing with the events, and the next week in *L'Express*, Oumar Ouadj, a leading figure in the AGTA, made a series of revelations about the atrocities. Claude Bourdet, a veteran anti-imperialist and now a member of the PSU, made a speech at the Paris Municipal Council. A demonstration was called outside the town hall at Billancourt but was not well attended. On 1 November a demonstration called by the PSU attracted only a few hundred, doubtless because it was impossible to announce the place in advance.[147]

The PCF and CGT were cautious in their protests. There was a sharp contrast with the response to the police attack on demonstrators at the Charonne tube station early in 1962, when nine demonstrators [eight of them Communists]

---

145   Einaudi 1991, pp. 318–9.
146   Benoits 2014, pp. 106–11.
147   Benoits 2014, p. 109.

were killed. At least half a million attended the funeral and there were strikes in Paris and elsewhere. It seemed European lives were more highly valued than North African.

The far left appealed for more decisive action, but were too small to give any effective leadership. When a demonstration called for 1 November 1961 was banned, the PSU went ahead with the action. Their members assembled in cinema queues, then formed a march, laid a wreath where two Algerians had been killed by police, and dispersed before the police could intervene. Such actions were limited. *Socialisme ou Barbarie* commented sourly on the lack of action:

> No question of active solidarity in the streets. Demonstrations were organised a fortnight or a month later; they only involved young people. The CGT 'asks workers to support this demonstration', but Communists at the Chausson factory at Gennevilliers [in the northern suburbs of Paris] confronted supporters of *Pouvoir ouvrier* [workers' power: the paper of the Socialisme ou barbarie group] and called them provocateurs when they gave out a leaflet calling for support for this demonstration.[148]

Despite the government cover-up some courageous journalists attempted to reveal the truth. Paulette Péju was a radical journalist and broadcaster who had been involved in practical support for the FLN.[149] Within weeks she wrote a short book, *Ratonnades à Paris* [racist attacks in Paris], published by Maspero before the end of 1961; based on such documentation as was immediately available, it vividly evoked the brutality and violence of the Paris police. The book never reached its audience for it was confiscated by police at the publishers before it could be distributed. Again there was no prosecution – obviously the authorities did not want the publicity of a trial. Only in 2000 was it finally made available.[150]

Following negotiations at Évian on the Swiss border, an agreement was reached between France and the FLN for an immediate cease-fire and independence within a few months. The OAS, having failed to keep Algeria French, pursued a scorched earth policy of death and destruction. De Gaulle decided to legitimate his policy by one of his favourite methods, calling a referendum.

---

148   Anon 1961–2.

149   Maitron and Pennetier 1964–2023 article145748, notice PÉJU Paulette [née FLACHAT Paulette] par Gilles Manceron, version mise en ligne le 24 mars 2013, dernière modification le 17 octobre 2017.

150   Péju 2000.

The text of the referendum endorsed independence for Algeria, but also gave extensive powers to de Gaulle. This put the left in a difficult position, showing how it had been marginalised by de Gaulle. To vote 'No' would be impossible; that would mean lining up with the die-hard supporters of French Algeria. The PCF called for a 'Yes' vote, but the PSU called for abstention. So that their votes would not be hidden among those too apathetic to vote, they told their supporters to go to the polling-stations and spoil their papers. There were a million spoilt papers, just over 5 per cent of the turnout. De Gaulle had a massive success, with over 90 percent voting 'Yes'.

19   Independent Algeria

By July Algeria was independent. Ben Bella moved from a French jail to become head of the new regime. The internationalist left had saved the honour of the French people during one of the most brutal episodes of its history. It had little impact on the outcome of the war.

In strictly military terms the FLN did not win a victory. The war had to end because most of the French capitalist class did not need to hang on to Algeria – and because the war was becoming intolerable to more and more sections of the French population. Yet the internationalist left had been unable to take the lead in promoting this discontent and defining its direction.

Thousands of Algerians, who had come to mainland France when Algeria was said to be an integral part of the French nation state, remained in France. They, their descendants and their memories, would continue to play a part in French political life in the twenty-first century.

For the small minority of internationalists the end of the war posed new problems. Many of them [actively encouraged by the FLN] believed that the struggle had been, not simply for national independence, but for social transformation. The initial years of independent Algeria seemed to encourage their belief; various measures were introduced which were described, rather optimistically, as 'workers' control'. Some of the suitcase-carrier generation, seeing little hope in Gaullist France, decided to move to Algeria, when large numbers of European settlers were fleeing in the opposite direction. This involved a degree of risk and sacrifice on their part; they were putting into practice the internationalist commitment which they had developed during the years of the war. With ironic reference to the term 'pieds noirs' [black feet] applied to the settlers, they became known as 'pieds rouges' [red feet].

For a little while it seemed that French leftists were having some influence on the new regime. Ben Bella surrounded himself with advisers, some of whom came from the revolutionary left, including Michel Raptis [Pablo], formerly Secretary of the Fourth International. The impact should not be overstated. The influence of the far left waned quite quickly, as they discovered that the process of decolonisation was turning out to be more contradictory and ambiguous than they had expected. In 1965 Ben Bella was overthrown by his former comrade Boumediène in a bloodless coup where Algerian workers showed little interest in defending the 'workers' control' now being snatched from them. The coup led to the arrest and expulsion from Algeria of Pablo's supporters. Some were even tortured in a manner similar to that used by the French army against FLN militants; it must have been a disheartening experience for those who had sacrificed so much for the Algerian cause. Yet at least some were not disillusioned; Pablo, Simonne Minguet and others remained committed revolutionaries until their deaths.

It was some of the most intransigent of the French internationalists who made the shrewdest analyses of how independent Algeria developed. Jean-François Lyotard of Socialisme ou barbarie had already analysed, while the war was in progress, the way in which the FLN was developing into a potentially bureaucratic ruling group. Now he looked at independent Algeria from the point of view of peasants and workers, and showed that the new regime did not represent their interests. For Lyotard socialism was not on the agenda: the 'inability of the workers to create their own political organisation and ideology ... shows that the problem confronting colonial Algeria was not that of socialism'.[151]

Some of the most acute comments on Ben Bella's rule came from Daniel Guérin, who spent a month travelling in Algeria in November 1963, and submitted a report to Ben Bella personally. He was initially enthusiastic about the new regime, describing the first flowering of *autogestion* [self-management] as a mixture of authoritarian conservatism and libertarian socialism. He also noted the authoritarian intrusion of the governmental bureaucracy which stifled initiative from below. When Ben Bella's rule came to an end, Guérin analysed his fall; Ben Bella had tried to play a balancing game between his left and his right. Like Robespierre on the eve of 9 Thermidor, he had sawn off the branch on which he was perched. The left, which was the only force that could have defended him, no longer had enough confidence in him to save him.[152]

Denis Berger, who had organised jailbreaks for the FLN, now took a sober view of what had been achieved. He argued that the French left had overestimated the socialist potential of the Algerian revolution, and he backed Boudiaf

---

151   Lyotard 1963, p. 11.
152   Guérin, 1973, pp. 346, 170, 175.

against Ben Bella. He admitted: 'We let ourselves be deluded by the Marxist-sounding demagogy of the FLN's French Federation'.

Berger believed that French militants had failed to correctly evaluate the adoption of a discourse with some Marxist overtones by numerous leaders of the FLN. This was in the context of the Cold War, when the Algerians knew that in Europe they could count only on the camp of the left; it did not mean endorsement of the project of social and political revolution, but was rather a product of the immediate strategic imperatives of the struggle against French colonialism. Berger also pointed to what he saw as 'excessive trust in the automatic nature of the way in which a national democratic revolution would grow over into a socialist revolution'.[153]

There was no happy ending for the internationalists, just a recognition that the road ahead would be hard. Within six years that road would take an unexpected turning.

------

153   Pattieu 2002, p. 215.

The Struggle Goes On

From the Paris Commune to the end of the Algerian war there was an internationalist current in French political life. Often this current was small and marginalised, notably at the outbreak of the First World War and during the German occupation. Only once, in the aftermath of the Russian Revolution, was it briefly embodied in a major political organisation, the newly formed French Communist Party.

At times the internationalists had the chance of a wider audience. The mutineers of 1917 or the recalcitrant conscripts of 1955–56 were not principled internationalists; their motivation was generally a narrower self-interest. They were thrust into opposition to the state machine; if more effective political leadership had existed, they might have developed an internationalist consciousness. Such changes can take place very rapidly, as the history of revolutions shows.

The internationalist current had to face many different enemies. Often the most insidious opponents have been nationalists of the left, imbued with the principles of *laïcité*. *Laïcité* has served as an alibi for those willing to attack religion in order to cover up for the fact that they aren't prepared to fight real social grievances. The left nationalists have helped to make possible the most reactionary policies pursued by the French state. It was the myth of republicanism that enabled the regime to send millions of workers and peasants into the trenches in 1914, and the so-called Socialists Mollet and Lacoste spearheaded the war against the Algerian people. More recently, *laïcité* has been invoked by the right as well as the left, and used in support of Islamophobic racism.[1]

1962 marked an important turning-point in French history. France's colonial empire was effectively gone. While eyes were focussed on Algeria, de Gaulle negotiated independence for the African colonies. Algeria had aroused murderous passions, but there were few strong feelings about the rest of Africa.

Internationalism was not dead. On the contrary the drive to war and, above all, racism were still very much alive in French society and an internationalist opposition continued to make itself felt. There was no single focus for it; with the slow decline of the PCF and the rapid rise, and then fall, of the Socialist Party, the French left was more dispersed and fragmented than ever. Over the

---

1 See Wolfreys 2018.

six decades since 1962 individuals and groupings have emerged to defend internationalist principles.

Many of the older generation continued to be active after 1962. Jean-René Chauvin had tried to organise fraternisation with German soldiers, and paid the price in Auschwitz, Buchenwald and Mauthausen; later he supported the Algerian struggle in La Voie communiste. Till the end of his life he was visiting schools to talk about his experiences and the dangers of fascism. He kept his concentration camp number tattooed on his forearm.

He and many others passed on the principles to a new generation. Younger activists were appearing, radicalised by the Algerian experience. Born during, or just after, the German occupation, they had a sense of belonging to a single world system, of being aware of the interconnections between struggles in various parts of the world. They were distrustful of both major power blocs, equally outraged by the American bombing of Vietnam and the Russian invasion of Czechoslovakia.

The world economy was now more integrated than at any time in the past. Population movement was more extensive. At the time of the Russian Revolution radio and air travel were in their infancy; by the 1960s they were fully developed, with transistors and mass tourism, and in addition there was television. Vietnam was the first war to be watched, day by day, in millions of homes. The broadcasters controlled the agenda, but American setbacks in Vietnam were transmitted around the planet. The French and other Europeans perceived themselves as part of a global community.

The left too has changed radically since 1962. The SFIO was increasingly discredited as a result of its support for the Algerian war and its capitulation to de Gaulle in 1958. By the sixties it had lost most of its members who made any claim to socialist politics – many of whom had gone to the PSU – and quite a lot of those who did not. In the 1969 presidential elections its candidate Gaston Defferre got a derisory vote of around 5 percent. The PCF, after the destalinisation of the USSR and with the changing culture and rising living standards of the working class, was slowly shifting away from its Stalinist past. The Sino-Soviet split of 1963 saw some of the more radical elements – especially in the student milieu – turn to Maoism.

The struggle for Algerian independence had aroused considerable international support. Soon the attention of the world was captured by the escalating American war in Vietnam; demonstrations spread from Europe to Latin America and Australia. France was affected by this international movement. There were marches, Vietnam Committees were set up, there was assistance to draft-evaders and deserters, based on experience acquired during the Algerian war. By 1968 there was a well-developed movement. Vietnam, alongside the more domestic issues of university overcrowding and discipline, was a major factor in the rise of France's student movement. The left had to clearly distinguish itself from de Gaulle, who also opposed the US intervention in Vietnam, as part of his strategy to reassert France's role as a world power.

Campaigning about Vietnam created a milieu in which internationalist ideas could develop. This process was accelerated by the Tet offensive in early 1968. Although this was not a military success, for a time it appeared that the liberation forces were winning; the Vietnamese were no longer victims, but heroes. Their achievement encouraged other struggles, extending what Sartre called the 'field of the possible'.[2]

Support for the Vietnamese struggle was one element in the emergence of a new current on the French left, what is often referred to as 'Third Worldism'. The term *tiers monde* became central to the discourse of the European left in the 1960s. While there was a major miners' strike in France in 1963, in general the *trente glorieuses* had left the working class fairly dormant. In the aftermath of the Algerian war, the action seemed to be elsewhere. In 1958 the Cuban revolution established an anti-imperialist beacon in the United States' sphere of influence, and Vietnam saw the USA pushed onto the defensive.

A new wave of thinkers were supplanting the Marxist classics. The bookshop and publishing house of François Maspero, deeply involved in solidarity with Algeria, made the work of Régis Debray, Frantz Fanon, Che Guevara, etc. available to activists. Leading intellectuals encouraged Third Worldism. Writer Jean Genet, once a social outcast, had become rich and famous, but devoted himself to support for the Black Panthers and the Palestinians; in 1982 he was the first European to enter the Shatila refugee camp near Beirut after the Zionist-inspired massacre, and wrote a powerful account of what he saw.[3]

There was much positive in Third Worldism. A younger generation was trying to think the world in global terms rather than starting from the nation state. This led to practical solidarity ranging from humanitarian assistance to support for armed struggle. It could encourage action in one's native country. When an Italian Communist delegation to North Vietnam asked Ho Chi Minh how they could help the Vietnamese fight, Ho responded 'make the revolution in your own country'. It was not bad advice.[4]

Then came May 1968, a crucial turning-point in the history of the French left. Ten million workers struck, many of them occupying their workplaces, the biggest general strike in human history. Internationalism was at the heart of

---

2 Sartre 1972, p. 273.
3 Genet 2012.
4 Vitale 1967–8, p. 36.

1968. From Vietnam to Czechoslovakia to the United States, it was a year of international revolt, comparable to 1848 and 1917.

Prophecies that the French May was a dress rehearsal for revolution in France and worldwide seem over-optimistic in retrospect, but the French events sparked off a wave of revolt in Western Europe that lasted almost a decade. May was followed by the Italian 'hot autumn' of 1969, and the Portuguese revolution of 1974–75. In Spain the Franco regime was dismantled; in Britain industrial action by miners overturned a Conservative government. Reaction held the line, but the potential was there, and the hopes it aroused should not be written out of history.

Internationalist consciousness was most marked among student activists. On demonstrations the *Internationale* replaced the *Marseillaise* beloved of the PCF. Only six years after Algerian independence there were many echoes of the war.[5] In particular the students were well aware of the role of the police during the war. When they found themselves confronting the police, they had no illusions about its neutrality; they had a clear grasp of the class nature of the state. That is why they built barricades. When student leader Cohn-Bendit was attacked as a 'German Jew' the students adopted the slogan 'We are all German Jews'.

Before 1968 Third Worldism had been a response to the apparent passivity of the working class; 1968 offered the possibility of giving the working class a central place in an internationalist perspective. Most of the 1968 activists were born during, or just after, the Second World War, and knew what their parents had gone through; France had scarcely been at peace between 1939 and 1962. Now a new generation began to redraw the map of the French left.

The biographies of various student militants show how a generation formed by the Algerian war turned to revolutionary politics. Alain Krivine had come into conflict with the PCF leadership in the student movement; he had carried suitcases and helped to organise anti-fascist demonstrations. In 1968 he became one of the most prominent student leaders and in 1969 he was a candidate for the presidency after de Gaulle's resignation.[6]

There were many students like the Maoist Jean-Paul Dollé, who had been shocked to read of torture in mainstream papers such as *L'Express*, *France Observateur* and *Témoignage Chrétien*. From 1960 onwards he read *Les Temps modernes*, and was impressed by the Manifesto of 121. Later he took part in a

---

5   Ross 2002, pp. 36–64.
6   Krivine 2011.

support network for the FLN. This meant an identification with the far left. He was active, above all as a journalist, in 1968 and the years following.[7]

It was not only student leaders who had roots in the Algerian war. Arlette Laguiller originally became politicised by seeing parallels between the French Resistance and the resistance of the Algerian people. As she put it: 'It was in the name of the very values which I had been told were French that I very quickly came to feel in solidarity with the Algerian people'.[8] In 1968 she led a strike of bank clerks at the headquarters of the Crédit Lyonnais, independently of the union bureaucracy. Later she became the public face of the Trotskyist Lutte ouvrière organisation and was several time a presidential candidate.

Perhaps the most remarkable story was that of Yvon Rocton, a name often unknown even to those familiar with the events of 1968, but whose role was at least as significant as that of the student leaders. At the age of 16 he became an engineering worker at the Sud-Aviation aircraft factory near Nantes; he joined the PCF. Called up for military service he was sent to Algeria, where he was shocked to observe torture, spoke up against it and was sent to a punishment battalion. On leaving the army he joined a Trotskyist organisation, the Parti Ouvrier Internationaliste.[9] He returned to Sud-Aviation, where he campaigned for the withdrawal of troops from Algeria. He was expelled from the CGT and joined Force ouvrière. In 1968 he played a leading part in initiating the occupation of Sud-Aviation, where workers took over the factory and held the manager prisoner. This was the first factory occupation, on 14 May, the spark which ignited the strike movement which spread across France in the following days.[10]

An important aspect of the 1968 events was the role played by immigrant workers. There were over 2 million Algerians, Spaniards, Italians and Portuguese in France. Most immigrant workers lived in poverty; over 50,000 lived in *bidonvilles* [shanty towns] around the large cities, in rough shacks without gas, electricity or sanitation. They were used as cheap labour, and intimidated by threats of deportation.

Before 1968 the left had taken relatively little interest in immigrant workers. By the 1960s there were some signs of a fightback, and of effective solidarity between French and immigrant workers. A notable example had come in March 1967 when an official strike of chemical workers in the Lyon area was called by both the CGT and the CFDT. The Cellophane factory at Saint-Maurice-

---

7   McGrogan 2012.
8   Laguiller 1996, p. 34.
9   Gildea, Mark and Warring 2013, pp. 41, 110; Zappi 2008.
10   See Le Madec 1988.

de-Beynost joined the strike. The factory was situated in a village with about 3000 inhabitants, of whom around 1000 were foreign. 20 per cent of the factory's labour force were foreign; 19 nationalities were represented. The majority of the foreign workers were Portuguese – recruited by the management at the reception centre for Portuguese immigrants in Paris. During the 23- day stoppage, the employers made great efforts to get the Portuguese workers to act as strike-breakers. Portuguese embassy officials were called in and a meeting was held at the town hall to persuade the Portuguese to go back to work, but they maintained solidarity throughout the dispute.[11] Six months after the strike the three leading Portuguese militants were sacked.

In May 1968, with ten million workers on strike and occupying their factories, immigrant workers could not be outside the struggle. Large numbers of Portuguese and North African workers, as well as immigrants from many other countries, were involved in demonstrations, strikes and occupations. They came closer to indigenous workers than they would have done during ordinary working. Committees were established to pursue the specific problems of immigrant workers.

The famous poster produced by students from the École des Beaux-Arts that declared 'French and Immigrant Workers United' was in some ways overoptimistic. Students from relatively privileged backgrounds had little understanding of the realities of immigrant poverty. Immigrants feared – sometimes with some justice – that political activists wanted to manipulate their struggles.

Nonetheless Daniel Gordon is right to argue that 'bonds were ... forged between French and immigrant workers where they had previously been absent'.[12] In the short term there was serious repression. Some 250 foreign workers were expelled for their part in the events of 1968.[13] Yet the response of the authorities in deporting immigrant militants showed the alarm created by such unity between foreign and indigenous workers.

A significant event was the launching in 1969–70 of a short-lived paper called *Le Paria*, which took its name from the paper edited by the young Ho Chi Minh in the 1920s[14] [see chapter 7]. Many of those involved were Maoists, but the managing editor was Daniel Guérin, who had been involved with internationalist campaigns since the 1930s. As a well-known intellectual he took legal responsibility, and gave financial support, while the immigrants who actually ran the paper would have been at risk of deportation. While the first issue sold

---

11   Castles and Kosack 1973, p. 165.
12   Gordon 2012, p. 65.
13   Fysh and Wolfreys 1998, p. 33.
14   McGrogan 2012, p. 226.

only 600 copies, *Le Paria* produced 150,000 supplements in January 1970 in response to the deaths from a faulty heating system of five African workers in a migrant workers' hostel at Aubervilliers in the Paris suburbs, and the ensuing occupation of the headquarters of the French employers' federation in Paris. It used the slogan 'No to capitalist murder', to stress its approval of direct action, and saw antiracism and anticolonialism as forming a single struggle, with the slogan 'Imperialism kills in Aubervilliers and in Chad' – a reference to French intervention in its former colony.[15]

In 1972 a Maoist worker at Renault, Pierre Overney, was handing out leaflets protesting at the sacking of three colleagues, including a Tunisian and a Portuguese, when he was murdered by a security guard. This reawakened the spirit of internationalist solidarity that had characterised 1968, with a funeral attended by some 200,000, including many workers from Renault, despite the lack of support from the CGT organisation.[16]

Support for immigrant workers was a major challenge for the French left in the 1970s and after. Attitudes within the labour movement were ambiguous. The PCF and the CGT often made concessions to nationalism, but the PCF and CGT also contained many militant antiracists. This was shown by the notorious incident at Vitry-sur-Seine in 1981, where the Communist municipality ordered the bulldozing of an immigrant hostel, claiming that immigrants were being dumped in Communist municipalities. However a CGT member refused to drive the bulldozer, as was reported by Marius Apostolo, head of the CGT immigrant organisation, who himself tried to oppose the bulldozing.[17]

Another campaign which expressed antimilitarist and internationalist positions was the movement against the extension of the Larzac military base in the southern Massif Central, which involved the expropriation of local farmers. The movement began as a campaign of non-violent civil disobedience by local farmers, but soon acquired national support, notably because of the base's links to the French nuclear weapons programme. Large numbers of left-wing activists adopted the campaign in opposition to what they saw as the militarism of the Pompidou government.

In August 1973 a mass rally was held, illegally, within the military base, attended by between 60,000 and 100,000 people. The organisers stressed the international significance of the event; there were speakers from revolutionary currents in Chile, Italy and Greece, as well as two members of the Irish Republican Army.

---

15   Gordon 2007, pp. 206–10.
16   Benoits 2014, p. 146.
17   Gordon 2012, p. 206.

The campaign continued until 1981, when it achieved success; one of the first acts of the Mitterrand presidency was to cancel the plans for the base. The activity developed into what would later become the antiglobalisation movement; José Bové [see below] first came to prominence in the Larzac campaign.

France's place in the world was changing, and this required the internationalist opposition to change too. While the brutality of direct colonial rule, the 'Native Code' and associated atrocities, were gone, French imperialism was not dead; there were plenty of reasons for internationalists to challenge the French state. In the West Indian colonies of Guadeloupe and Martinique repression of nationalist movements has continued, while France has clung on to its territory of New Caledonia. France's former colonies in Africa got formal independence, but France maintained close political and economic links with its former territories, a substantial part of Western Africa which was often referred to as 'Françafrique' [France-Africa].[18] There were repeated military interventions in support of regimes friendly to France. Sometimes the troops involved were badly treated, discontented and demoralised.[19] But the interventions were generally on a small scale, and often involved regular soldiers; conscription was finally ended in 2001. As a result the military action had little impact on French political life; there was nothing comparable to the wars in Indochina and Algeria.

Eventually opposition began to emerge. When French President Macron held an Africa-France Summit in Montpellier in October 2021, there was widespread support for a 'counter-summit'.

> The counter-summit of a hundred organisations and supported by several political parties and unions succeeded in organising itself around a message which clearly showed what the meaning of 'putting an end to the coloniality of France-Africa' had to involve. The meetings, debates and events they organised on the side-lines of the official summit showed a great mistrust towards Macron, based on their deep knowledge of existing contradictions between France's discourse and its actions in Africa.

The basic demands showed a fundamental opposition to France's continuing imperial role in Africa, advocating
(a)   ending [France's] military presence in Africa,
(b)   ending the neo-liberal trade policy of France and the EU in Africa,

---

18   Chafer 2005.
19   See Bergot 1982, p. 233.

(c)   stopping support to presidents who remain in power in an undemocratic manner and French interference in the internal political and economic affairs of African countries,

(d)   cancelling the odious and illegitimate debts of African countries,

(e)   cancelling the freedom of movement and settlement of people as well as putting an end to expulsions of asylum seekers from France in accordance with international treaties.[20]

France had lost its empire, but the historical legacy remained. Liquidating that legacy could have serious ideological consequences. French President Macron has acknowledged that French troops in Algeria were guilty of torture and murder,[21] but much more remains to be said.

One of the most remarkable literary depictions of France's imperial past is Alexis Jenni's *L'Art français de la guerre* [The French Art of War],[22] which won the Goncourt Prize in 2011. This epic narrative traces the life of the soldier Victorien Salagnon through twenty years of warfare, from the Resistance and the war in Indochina to Algeria. Jenni, who disclaims any overt political intention, depicts starkly the brutality of French colonialism, though its opponents are not romanticised. The episodes of Salagnon's military life alternate with another narrative, set in the 1990s, in which Salagnon teaches a young man to paint. The alternation between past and present allows Jenni to link France's colonial past to modern-day racism.

He shows that riots in Lyon have short-term causes, often trivial, which relate to a long-term historical context. Observing a police operation in a quarter inhabited by people of North African descent Salagnon comments:

> They are as beautiful as we were ... they have as much force as we had, and it won't do them any good either. They are as few in number as we were, and those they are pursuing will always get away, into the jungle of staircases and cellars, for there is an endless supply of them, they produce as many as they catch, for catching them produces more. They'll experience failure, just as we experienced failure, the same bitter, heartbreaking failure, for we had force too.[23]

In face of the advance of so-called globalisation, internationalism was more necessary then ever; it had to take new forms. One manifestation was the

---

20   Bisoka, Mwambari and Ndlovu-Gatsheni 2021.

21   Willsher 2021.

22   Jenni 2011.

23   Jenni 2011, p. 620.

founding of ATTAC in 1998. 'Action for a Tobin Tax to Assist the Citizen', [ATTAC: Association pour la Taxation des Transactions financières et pour l'Action Citoyenne] was originally a single-issue movement demanding the introduction of the so-called Tobin tax on currency speculation, but it later took up a range of issues related to globalisation.

ATTAC's politics were clearly directed against the neoliberal, aggressively free-market capitalism which characterised the post-1989 world. One of its slogans was 'Our world is not for sale', denouncing the 'commodification' of society. A second was 'Another world is possible' pointing to an alternative globalisation where people and not profit would be primary. The term 'altermondialisme' [anti-globalisation] came into use. Such a radical critique of international capitalism caught the imagination of a wide audience and invited them to develop an opposition to the world system. Its influence was undoubtedly positive.

ATTAC was clear that the enemy was international and that only an international movement could challenge it. Though originally a French organisation it spread to at least forty countries. Among questions it took up were democratic control of the World Trade Organisation and other international financial institutions, defence of public social services, opposition to tax evasion, cancellation of the debt of developing countries, and fighting against climate change. How this was to be done, what was the agency of transformation, were more difficult questions. From the outset there were profound ambiguities. Whether these aims could be achieved by lobbying existing governments or by mass campaigning remained uncertain.[24]

One of the founders of ATTAC was José Bové, born in 1953. Involved in the campaign against the Vietnam war as a teenager, he refused to do his military service, and being denied the right to become a conscientious objector, he was classed as a deserter. A pacifist and supporter of non-violent direct action, he had connections with progressive Christian movements and was involved in the Larzac campaign [see above].

Bové took part in Greenpeace protests at French nuclear tests in the Pacific, supported campaigns for independence in New Caledonia and Tahiti, visited Palestinian peasants – until he was expelled by Israel – and took part in the demonstrations against the World Trade Organisation in Seattle in 1999. He also took up the cause of undocumented immigrants [*sans papiers*]. Whatever criticisms could be made on specific issues, Bové was undoubtedly a principled campaigner on international questions, and a model for other activists.

---

24   See Harman 2000.

But the central question for internationalists in France over the last four decades has been racism, attacks on migrants and in particular Islamophobia. In 1981 François Mitterrand was elected the first Socialist President of the Fifth Republic. Little more than a year later his government made a sharp turn; austerity and cuts replaced social reform. Mitterrand's evolution offered challenges and opportunities to the radical left. A particular test came with the rapid rise of the Front National [FN], led by Jean-Marie Le Pen, a force which, forty years on, under its new label of Rassemblement National [National Alliance], remains central to French politics. Le Pen's rise was a direct consequence of Mitterrand's retreat. By 1984, with Mitterrand's economic strategy in ruins, and cuts in health care and unemployment pay on the agenda, Le Pen's followers got over two million votes in the European elections. Le Pen could play on the experience of the Algerian War, which had bred racist hatred, especially towards North Africans, among many French citizens. Former Algerian settlers living in France were fertile ground for Le Pen's recruiters. Le Pen's rise was accompanied by a number of violent attacks against immigrants.

The first significant response came in late 1983 with the Marche pour l'égalité et contre le racisme [March for Equality and Against Racism], also known as the Marche des beurs [beur is a slang term for French-born descendants of North African immigrants]. Beginning with a group of children of immigrants in Lyon, a small march began in Marseille, independent of any political organisation; after 50 days, the march ended with a demonstration of more than 100,000 people in Paris. The success of the march showed that there was nothing inherent in the French situation that made the triumph of racism inevitable.

Then in 1984 a small group of anti-racists, including Harlem Désir, decided to take action against Le Pen. They produced a badge showing an open hand and a simple message of racial solidarity – 'Touche pas mon pote' (Don't touch my mate). The badge caught the imagination of the potential mass of anti-racists, On 1 December 1984 there was a second march of *beurs* in Paris. 5000 badges were sold in an hour and a half.[25]

The new organisation took the name SOS-Racisme. By Spring 1985 one million badges had been sold; all who wore one to work were letting themselves in for arguments about racism. Meetings were held in protest at racist murders encouraged by the political success of the FN, and token stoppages of a minute's silence were organised in workplaces. On 15 June 1985, half a year after the group had been launched, a massive festival with music – modelled on the Brit-

---

25   Désir 1985, p. 37.

ish Rock Against Racism carnivals – was held in the Place de la Concorde in Paris; a turn-out of between 300,000 and 400,000 was claimed.

sos-Racisme showed that racism could be fought and that there was a huge potential of people to be mobilised. The sheer speed with which the badges spread on the streets within a matter of weeks was proof of that potential. The advent of sos-Racisme interrupted Le Pen's rise; his popularity fell for a while rather than growing in the alarming progression which it had shown hitherto.

Yet Le Pen was not stopped and went on to get 35 deputies in 1986 and to achieve a score of four million votes, over 14 percent, in the 1988 presidential elections. Here a good part of the blame lies with sos-Racisme. From the outset much of the initiative had come from supporters of the Socialist Party. The campaign defined racism as essentially a humanitarian issue and so did not link the question of racism to the failures of the Mitterrand government. On the contrary, the Socialist Party found sos-Racisme useful and gave it direct support, and sos-Racisme made no effort to assert its political independence. Many of its critics saw it as a vehicle for Socialist Party interests that was used to marginalise autonomous anti-racist activism.

As a result sos-Racisme never developed as a mass organisation with grass-roots involvement; it was a stage army to be mobilised by its celebrity leaders when they wanted a show of strength. The great festival in 1985 was financed partly by subsidies from the Socialist government's Ministry of Culture, and partly by private sponsors such as the Philip Morris tobacco company.

A more grass-roots anti-fascism was embodied in the various Sections Carrément Anti-Le Pen [Solidly anti-Le Pen sections], with the acronym SCALP. The first SCALP was set up in Toulouse in June 1984 – before the formation of sos-Racisme – on the occasion of a demonstration against Le Pen's visit to the city. Groups with the same name were then set up in some dozen French towns. SCALP was considerably less respectable than sos-Racisme, advocating violent confrontation with the fascists, and based in the autonomist and libertarian milieus. If sos-Racisme had been too top-down, the opposite was the case with the SCALP groups. Another anti-fascist group was Motivé-e-s [motivated], based on the multiracial band Zebda, which got over 12 percent of the votes in the 2001 municipal elections in Toulouse.

The attack on the World Trade Centre in New York on 11 September 2001 was a turning-point in the history of the whole world. The old Cold War divisions were gone for good; instead there was an alleged 'clash of civilisations', with Western liberal democracy claiming to face a threat from the Muslim world. In France this new Islamophobia merged with an older racist tradition, stemming from the Algerian war, promoted by Le Pen, and infecting much of the political left.

Le Pen continued to increase his influence. This led to a shocking result in the 2002 presidential election. A few weeks before the election, polls were showing that over half the voters could see no difference between the two main candidates, the incumbent right-winger Chirac and Jospin of the Socialist Party. Le Pen came ahead of Jospin and the second round was to be between Chirac and Le Pen. Three Trotskyist candidates had got 10 percent of the vote between them, showing that there was an audience for an internationalist alternative as well as a rightist one.

The left reacted quickly. Thousands of demonstrators took to the streets that very night in Paris and other cities. Although they were predominantly young, one of the most popular slogans was 'We are all children of immigrants'[26] – a direct echo of the 1968 students' slogan 'We are all German Jews' [see above]. Further mass demonstrations were called. The left had shifted the emphasis towards mass action on the streets and away from the tactical question of whether to vote for Chirac to stop Le Pen.

Many thousands of anti-fascists reluctantly decided to vote for Chirac. However there was a real problem. After the election was over Chirac would be in power for five years to come. If left activists had called for a vote for Chirac, then when he attacked workers' conditions and living standards, they would have faced the response: 'You told us to vote for him'. Rather than centring their campaign on an election two weeks away, the left took the initiative immediately. The dynamic of the demonstrations moved support away from Le Pen so that he was on the retreat well before the second round vote. Voting became a secondary question, and those who opposed voting for Chirac did not make the question an obstacle to working with anyone who wanted to fight Le Pen.

While the far right ranted about immigrants, mainstream politicians passed a new law in 2004 which prohibited the wearing of conspicuous religious symbols, including the *hijab*, in state schools. The justification for this was that mainstay of 'republican values', *laïcité*, but the introduction of new measures seemed to imply that existing legislation was inadequate and needed strengthening. A statement by intellectuals – including Régis Debray, erstwhile admirer of Che Guevara – saw the admission of young Muslim women with *hijabs* to schools as a threat to the very existence of the Republic: 'the Munich of republican education'.[27]

Worse was to come. In 2003 two Muslim sisters were excluded from school at Aubervilliers for wearing the *hijab*. It was teachers who were members of the

---

26   See *Le Monde*, 23 April 2002.

27   *Le Nouvel Observateur*, 2 November 1989.

Trotskyist Lutte ouvrière who took the initiative in calling for the exclusion, in the name of *laïcité*.[28]

The French state's claim to be independent of all religions meant that there was no distinction between Christianity, which despite ostensible secularism still held great prestige in society, and Islam, which in France was the religion of an oppressed minority. Many Muslims saw this as a survival of a colonial mentality. David Drake summed up the colonialist assumptions which underlay both sides of the debate:

> What both camps have in common is a refusal to accept that Muslims have a right to attend school without denying their attachment to their culture and/or faith. For the hard-liners, they should leave their cultural identity at the school gates; for those defending a more 'liberal' interpretation of *laïcité*, they should be allowed into school in order to be weaned away from Islam.[29]

In 2005 came a wave of riots in the suburbs of French cities, a response by youth of immigrant origin to systematic police harassment against a background of high unemployment. Although most of those involved were French citizens, they were attacked and denounced in racist terms. Unfortunately they got little support from the established French left. But the following years saw the emergence of new organisations opposed to racism, for example Mamans toutes égales [Mums all equal] in opposition to the exclusion of *hijab*-wearing mothers from school activities.

There was also action by, and in support of, undocumented immigrants. There are said to be between 200,000 and 400,000 such 'illegal' immigrants in France. Government attempts to round them up and expel them have provoked occupations, and occasional strikes. There has been substantial support, with some French people hiding the children of illegal immigrants in their homes [recalling the way Jewish children were sheltered during the Nazi occupation].[30]

However in 2010, when a local section of the Nouveau Parti Anticapitaliste [NPA – an attempt at a broad far-left regroupment based on the Trotskyist Ligue Communiste Révolutionnaire] selected a *hijab*-wearing woman, Ilhem Moussaïd, as an election candidate, many members demanded her withdrawal; others defended her in the most half-hearted fashion. Eventually the woman, a

---

28   Boulangé 2004a.
29   Drake 2000, p. 55.
30   Chrisafis 2010.

well-known local activist, left the NPA to continue her activity independently.[31] If the left had been trying to drive Muslims away it could hardly have been more successful. Again the justification was *laïcité*.

Things got worse after the appalling massacre of the staff of *Charlie Hebdo*, followed by mass killings in the streets of Paris. The vast majority of French Muslims deplored this terrorism. The political mainstream responded with clichés about 'republican values'.

Faced with the challenge of Islamophobia, the left seemed to have lost its way. One exception was the emergence in 2005 of the Indigènes de la République.[32] The name – Natives of the Republic – was a play on words; – it referred to those born in France, and therefore native citizens, but also descendants of the 'natives' who had been subjected to the 'Native Code'. The founder of the organisation, which subsequently became a political party, was Sadri Khiari, and its principal spokesperson Houria Bouteldja. They declared themselves to be the heirs of those French people who resisted the Nazis and of all who took the side of the oppressed. They were anti-imperialist and anti-Zionist, and opposed all discrimination on the basis of race, sex, religion or origin, believing that in France racial discrimination is omnipresent since it is linked to the colonial past. In their founding statement they stressed that 'France was a colonial state ... France remains a colonial state!'[33] For Bouteldja the logic of this position was a total rejection of nations and nationalism:

> Frontiers bug me, space belongs to everyone, we're at home everywhere ... The national state bugs me, for me it's what produces racism ... it creates frontiers, it homogenises populations, on racial, ethnic or religious foundations, and so, for France, those who aren't Catholic and white are not really French.[34]

In terms of actual members the Indigènes are very small, but although – and perhaps because – they have attracted some violent and often unjustified criticism, they have had a certain influence and have contributed to the critique of racism, colonialism and Islamophobia in contemporary France.

Others have stood up against the prevailing hostility to immigrants. Cédric Herrou, a farmer from South-Eastern France, was arrested on several occasions for bringing African refugees across the frontier from Italy into France.

---

31   Tevanian 2013.
32   See Robine 2006.
33   Quoted by Robine 2006.
34   Quoted by Robine 2006.

This raised a certain amount of public sympathy, and he was able to exploit contradictions within the ideology of the French state when the French Constitutional Council ruled that Herrou's actions to help migrants were legal.

What of the future? Racist nationalism persists in various forms; there have been vicious attacks on Roma people by leading politicians. Anti-Semitism persists, but in France today the main enemy for any internationalist is Islamophobia. Over the last two decades Muslims have been the victims of repeated violent attacks. Mosques have been vandalised and attacked, Muslim graves have been desecrated, halal butchers' shops have been shot at. Women wearing the *hijab* have been physically attacked in the streets. The rhetoric of Islamophobia resembles and often seems to echo the anti-Semitism of the Dreyfus case or the Vichy regime. Yet all too many who would be horrified to associate themselves with anti-Semitism deny the very existence of Islamophobia, or even join in the attacks on Muslims in the name of 'republican values'.

In the 2022 presidential election there was the appalling spectacle of two far-right candidates competing for the racist vote. The danger was not that one might win [though such a posssibility should never be ruled out] but rather that effectively they had both already won. By laying down the themes of the election, they exerted enormous pressure on the candidates of the centre and even the left, and drew the whole debate onto their – racist – ground. The two currents which had dominated the French left in the twentieth century, Communism and social democracy, were both reduced to derisory votes and marginal status. The only current on the left which continued to have some electoral impact and to offer hope of an alternative was La France Insoumise [insubordinate France], led by Jean-Luc Mélenchon. Mélenchon has opposed racism and Islamophobia; despite earlier negative comments on the *hijab*, he took part in the 2019 demonstration against Islamophobia, which brought together different currents of the left. He has denounced attempts, notably by Nicolas Sarkozy, to give the Christian church a more active role in public life, while defending 'republican *laïcité*'.[35] Despite the dismal choice offered in the second round of the presidential election, there is now the potential for the emergence of a different kind of left. Only a positive alternative to the reactionary policies of Macron, and not mere denunciations of racism, will be able to push back the Rassemblement National. Unless it puts internationalism at the very centre of its strategy it will not be able to confront France's changing place in the world, the liquidation of France's colonial heritage and the deep-lying racism in French society.

---

35   Mélenchon 2008, pp. 7, 45.

The left, in France as elsewhere in the world, is weak and on the defensive. Nationalism is on the rise, but is riven by a deep contradiction. Capitalism has created the nation state, and its defenders are constantly required to try to revive nationalism, in order to ensure that the subordinate classes have something to express their loyalty to. At the same time capitalism is an international system. Multinational companies have cheerfully leapt across frontiers in pursuit of raw materials, cheap labour and larger markets. Yet they have clung to national states in their need for finance, links with arms production and legal and political protection. The logic of capitalism will not lead to the withering away of the state – it is more likely to lead to intensifying international competition and its logical consequence, war.

The threat from the far right cannot be resisted by moralising clichés. The only way to oppose it is by a vigorous assertion of internationalism. What is needed is ideological struggle – 'culture war' as it is termed in the current jargon. In France, increasingly anyone with even mildly internationalist and anti-racist sympathies is accused of *islamogauchisme* [Islamoleftism] and 'le wokisme' – the latter has no more definable meaning in French than in the English original. The only effective response is a clear and coherent exposition of what internationalist principles really entail. That means a head-on confrontation with 'republican values', with *laïcité*, with the Jacobin tradition, and with the whole complex of values associated with racism, colonialism and the nation state. The widespread demonstrations against racism and the far right before and during the 2022 election show the potential that exists. As this book has tried to show, there is an alternative tradition on the French left, a tradition of uncompromising internationalism. It is that tradition that can be mobilised to fight the values of nationalism and Islamophobia that dominate French political life today.

Yet if the present situation seems bleak, there is also hope. In a world in which ever more people cross frontiers, at best to enrich their experience, at worst to flee war and famine, and when technology puts international communication into the hands of everyone, national solutions look less and less plausible. Internationalism increasingly corresponds to lived experience.

In France the internationalist current has continued to re-emerge over the last half century, for example:
- in May 1968;
- in opposition to the far right;
- in anti-globalisation movements;
- in opposition to Islamophobia.

Often it was only individuals, isolated and sometimes persecuted, who gave expression to internationalist principles. Yet there is always a complex relationship between individuals and the collective; individuals are inspired by subterranean tendencies in the collective, and sometimes the statements or acts of individuals achieve a resonance in the collective.

What its new manifestations will be we do not know, but we can be sure that the tradition that ran from the Commune and Dreyfus to the Algerian war and beyond is not exhausted, and that the actions of French internationalists will have parallels in every country around the globe.

The greatest threat facing humanity in the twenty-first century is climate change. This will produce a migration crisis many times worse than the one we are currently experiencing. A far right – whether or not fascist in the classic sense – demanding closed borders will get stronger. Increasing tensions between nations will make nuclear war ever more likely.

There are no national solutions. A global crisis requires a global solution. There is no solution to be hoped for from an economic and political system geared to this year's profits and next year's election. Rosa Luxemburg was quite right to see the choice of socialism or barbarism, though barbarism has now taken on potential forms which she could not have envisaged in her gloomiest hours.

Throughout the period covered by this book the internationalists have been proved right. Dreyfus was innocent. The First World War was a massive and unnecessary waste of life. Fascism was a deadly threat not to be temporised with. France was part of Europe and killing Germans was not an end in itself. Indochina and Algeria needed their independence. Each time the internationalists were right – but it was only recognised too late.

This time the choice will be – internationalism or barbarism.

Bibliography

Abidor, Mitchell and Miguel Lago 2022, 'France's Old Bigotry Finds a New Face', *New York Times*, 2 December, available at: https://www.nytimes.com/2021/12/02/opinion/eric-zemmour-france-jews.html.

Adam, Rémi 2007, 1917, La Révolte des soldats russes en France: Pantin: Bons caractères.

Adi, Hakim 2013, *Pan-Africanism and Communism*, Trenton, New Jersey: Africa World Press.

Agence France-Presse 2019, 'French couple can keep tilde in son's name after court battle', *Guardian*, 17 October, available at: https://www.theguardian.com/world/2019/oct/17/french-couple-can-keep-tilde-in-sons-name-after-court-battle.

Ageron, Charles-Robert 2006, 'L'exposition coloniale de 1931', *Études coloniales*, 25 August, available at: http://etudescoloniales.canalblog.com/archives/2006/08/25/2840733.html.

Agulhon, Maurice 1975, *Les Quarante-huitards*, Paris: Gallimard/Juillard.

Alexandre-Debray, Janine, 1983, *Victor Schoelcher*, Paris: Perrin.

Alexandre-Debray, Janine 2006 *Victor Schoelcher*, nouvelle édition, Paris: Perrin.

Alexis, Paul 1882, *Émile Zola, notes d'un ami*, Paris: Charpentier.

Ali, Tariq 2022, *Winston Churchill*, London: Verso.

Allen, Barbara C. 2016, *Alexander Shlyapnikov 1885–1937: Life of an Old Bolshevik*, Chicago: Haymarket Books.

Amoré, Henri 1909, 'Les Organisations patronales allemandes', *La Vie ouvrière*, 20 December, 375–9.

Amrani, Mehana 2010, *Le 8 mai 1945 en Algérie*, Paris: L'Harmattan.

Andler, Charles 1932, *Vie de Lucien Herr (1864–1926)*, Paris: Rieder.

Anon 1923a, 'A Essen Monmousseau arrêté', *L'Humanité*, 10 January: 1, available at: https://gallica.bnf.fr/ark:/12148/bpt6k400638q/f1.item.zoom.

Anon 1923b, 'Mais les mobilisés, à la gare de l'Est, chantent l'*Internationale*', *L'Humanité*, 26 January: 3, available at: https://gallica.bnf.fr/ark:/12148/bpt6k400654w/f3.item.zoom.

Anon 1923c, 'Des soldats français se mutinent', *L'Humanité*, 27 February: 1, available at: https://gallica.bnf.fr/ark:/12148/bpt6k400686p/f1.item.zoom.

Anon 1923d, 'Dans la Ruhr', *La Caserne* 3, 1 August: 3, available at: https://gallica.bnf.fr/ark:/12148/bpt6k6643558m/f3.item.zoom.

Anon 1923e, 'Une mutinerie?', *L'Humanité*, 9 February: 3, available at: https://gallica.bnf.fr/ark:/12148/bpt6k400668r/f3.item.zoom.

Anon 1924a, 'Une visite du camarade Mahmoud ben Le Khal', *L'Humanité*, 24 August: 1, available at: https://gallica.bnf.fr/ark:/12148/bpt6k4014412/f1.item.zoom.

Anon 1924b, 'En Rhénanie et dans la Ruhr', *Le Temps*, 7 June: 1, available at: https://gallica.bnf.fr/ark:/12148/bpt6k245494k/f1.item.zoom.

Anon 1924c, 'Un travailleur colonial candidat communiste', *L'Humanité*, 28 April: 2, available at: https://gallica.bnf.fr/ark:/12148/bpt6k401313g/f2.item.zoom.

Anon 1924d, 'Une belle réunion intercoloniale', *L'Humanité, 13 September: 2, available at*: https://gallica.bnf.fr/ark:/12148/bpt6k401461r/f2.item.zoom.

Anon 1925a, 'L'offensive riffaine sans Riffains', *L'Humanité*, 28 May: 2, available at: https://gallica.bnf.fr/ark:/12148/bpt6k4017177/f2.item.zoom.

Anon 1925b, 'Plus de quinze mille travailleurs condamnent la guerre du Riff', L'Humanité, 17 May: 1–2, available at: https://gallica.bnf.fr/ark:/12148/bpt6k401706h/f1.item.zoom.

Anon 1926a, 'Toute l'Angleterre est en grève', *L'Humanité*, 5 May: 1, available at: https://gallica.bnf.fr/ark:/12148/bpt6k402061s.

Anon 1926b, 'Les effets de la grève anglaise en France', *L'Humanité*, 9 May: 3, available at: https://gallica.bnf.fr/ark:/12148/bpt6k4020659/f3.item.zoom.

Anon 1926c, 'Les débardeurs de Marseille refusent d'embarquer le charbon à destination de l'Angleterre', *L'Humanité*, 12 May: 3, available at: https://gallica.bnf.fr/ark:/12148/bpt6k402068f/f3.item.zoom.

Anon 1936, 'Pour l'Espagne et pour leur pain 300.000 métallos ont fait grève hier', *L'Humanité*, 8 September: 1, available at: https://gallica.bnf.fr/ark:/12148/bpt6k40683oz/f1.item.zoom.

Anon 1938, 'Le peuple s'affirme contre le "diktat" de Munich', *L'Humanité*, 4 October: 4, available at: https://gallica.bnf.fr/ark:/12148/bpt6k407587p/f2.item.zoom.

Anon 1939, 'Pas de patrie!', *Clé* 1, 1 January: 1.

Anon 1945a, 'Pour mettre fin aux troubles d'Algérie', *L'Humanité*, 15 May: 1–2, available at: https://gallica.bnf.fr/ark:/12148/bpt6k47385208/f1.item.zoom.

Anon 1945b, 'Le fascisme organise la guerre civile', *L'Humanité*, 19 May: 1–2, available at: https://gallica.bnf.fr/ark:/12148/bpt6k4738524x/f2.item.zoom.

Anon 1945c, 'Oradour-sur-Glane en Algérie', *Ohé Partisans* 4, August, available at: https://www.cailloutendre.fr/2021/05/oradour-sur-glane-en-algerie-une-memoire-oubliee/.

Anon 1961–2, 'Les actualités', Socialisme ou Barbarie 33: 86, available at http://soubscan.org/pdf/soub_n33.pdf.

Aragon, Louis 1955, 'L'affiche rouge', available at http://pcf.evry.pagesperso-orange.fr/aragon.htm.

Ares, Leonard Marcel 2016, '*Under Fire*: A call for peace from the trenches', *International Socialism* 2,151 available at: http://isj.org.uk/under-fire-a-call-for-peace-from-the-trenches/.

Ashworth, Tony 1980, *Trench Warfare*, London: Macmillan.

Auclair, Marcelle 1954, *La Vie de Jean Jaurès*, Paris: Éditions du Seuil.

Ayme, Jean-Jacques 1983, 'Ces jeunesses dont leur parti ne voulait pas', *Cahiers Léon Trotsky* 16: 79–101, available at https://www.marxists.org/francais/clt/1979-1985/CLT16-Dec-1983.pdf.

Badia, Gilbert 1993, *Clara Zetkin, féministe sans frontières*, Paris: Éditions ouvrières.

Balibar, Renée and Dominique Laporte 1974, *Le Français national*, Paris: Hachette.

Bantman, Constance 2009, 'The Militant Go-between: Émile Pouget's Transnational Propaganda (1880–1914)', *Labour History Review* 74 (2): 274–87, available at: https://openresearch.surrey.ac.uk/esploro/outputs/99514213502346?institution=44SUR_IN ST&skipUsageReporting=true&recordUsage=false.

Barbusse, Henri 2007 [1916], *Le Feu*, Paris: Gallimard.

Barcia, Robert 2003, *La Véritable histoire de Lutte Ouvrière*, Paris: Denoël.

Barjonet, André 1968, *La CGT*, Paris: Éditions du Seuil.

Becker, Jean-Jacques 1973, *Le Carnet B*, Paris: Éditions Klincksieck.

Bedel, Jean 2002, *Zola assassiné*, Paris: Flammarion.

Bellanger, Claude, Jacques Godechot, Pierre Guiral and Fernand Terrou 1975, *Histoire générale de la presse française*, Volume IV, Paris: Presses universitaires de France.

Benoits, Clara and Henri 2014, *L'Algérie au coeur*, Paris: Éditions Syllepse.

Bergot, Erwan 1982, *La Coloniale du Rif au Tchad 1925–1980*, Paris: France Loisirs.

Berry, David 2002, A History of the French Anarchist Movement 1917–1945, Westport CT: Greenwood Press.

Billoux, François 1972, *Quand nous étions ministres*, Paris: Éditions sociales.

Birchall, Ian 1999, 'Neither Washington nor Moscow?', *Journal of European Studies*, XXIX: 365–404.

Birchall, Ian 2002, 'The Enigma of Kersausie: Engels in June 1848', *Revolutionary History*, 8, 2: 25–50, available at: https://www.marxists.org/history/etol/writers/birchall/200 2/xx/kersausie.html.

Birchall, Ian 2008a, 'Algeria: torture last time', *Socialist Review*, February, available at: https://socialistworker.co.uk/socialist-review-archive/algeria-torture-last-time/.

Birchall, Ian 2008b, 'Socialism and Freedom', *London Socialist Historians Group Newsletter* 32, available at: http://londonsocialisthistorians.blogspot.com/2020/01/report -socialism-and-freedom-2008.html.

Birchall, Ian 2012, 'A Note on the MNA', *Revolutionary History*, 10, 4: 156–68.

Birchall, Ian 2016, 'The General Strike Seen by the French Left', available at: http://grimanddim.org/historical-writings/2016-the-general-strike-seen-by-the-french-lef t/.

Bisoka, Aymar N, David Mwambari and Sabelo J. Ndlovu-Gatsheni 2021, 'From summit to counter-summit: imperialism, Françafrique and decolonisation', *Review of African Political Economy*, December 13, available at: https://roape.net/2021/12/13/ from-summit-to-counter-summit-imperialism-francafrique-and-decolonisation/.

Blackburn, Robin 1988, *The Overthrow of Colonial Slavery*, London: Verso.

Body, Marcel 1988, *Les Groupes communistes français de Russie 1918–1921*, Paris: Éditions Allia.

Bonte, Florimond 1931, 'L'apothéose du crime', *L'Humanité*, 6 May: 1, available at: https://gallica.bnf.fr/ark:/12148/bpt6k403891k/f1.item.zoom.

Boswell, Laird 2000, 'From Liberation to Purge Trials in the "Mythic Provinces", Recasting French Identities in Alsace and Lorraine 1918–1920', *French Historical Studies*, 23, 1: 119–52.

Boudarel, Georges 1977, *Giap*, Paris: Éditions Atlas.

Boudarel, Georges 1991, *Autobiographie*, Paris: Jacques Bertoin.

Boulangé, Antoine 2004a, *Foulard, laïcité et racisme*, Paris: L'Étincelle.

Boulangé, Antoine 2004b, 'The hijab, racism and the state', *International Socialism*, 2, 102, available at https://gallica.bnf.fr/ark:/12148/bpt6k401313g/f2.item.zoom.

Boussel, Patrice 1960, *L'Affaire Dreyfus et la presse*, Paris: Armand Colin.

Brossat, Alain and Jean-Yves Potel 1976, *Antimilitarisme et révolution*, Volume I, Paris: 10/18.

Broué, Pierre 1985, 'Trotsky et les Trotskystes face à la deuxieme guerre mondiale', *Cahiers Léon Trotsky*, 23: 35–60, available at https://www.marxists.org/francais/clt/1979-1985/CLT23-Sep-1985.pdf.

Broué, Pierre 1997, *Histoire de l'Internationale Communiste*, Paris: Fayard.

Broué, Pierre 2005, *The German Revolution, 1917–1923*, translated by John Archer, Leiden/Boston: Brill.

Bruhat, Jean 1952, *Histoire du mouvement ouvrier français*, tome I, Paris: Éditions Sociales.

Brunet, Jean-Paul 1986, *Jacques Doriot: Du communisme au fascisme*, Paris: Balland.

Bulaitis, John 2020, *Maurice Thorez*, London: I.B. Tauris.

Buonarroti, Philippe 1957 [1828], *Conspiration pour l'égalité dite de Babeuf*, Paris: Éditions Sociales.

Burns, Michael 1992, *Dreyfus: a Family Affair 1789–1945*, London: Chatto and Windus.

Busseuil, 1934, 'Défendons les Algériens de Paris', *La Révolution prolétarienne* 188, 10 December: 4, available at: https://gallica.bnf.fr/ark:/12148/bpt6k63479024/f6.item.

C.E.I. de la IVe. Internationale 1985 [1946], 'La question nationale durant la deuxième guerre impérialiste', *Cahiers Léon Trotsky* 23: 113–16, available at: https://www.marxists.org/francais/clt/1979-1985/CLT23-Sep-1985.pdf.

Cahm, Eric 1994, *L'Affaire Dreyfus*, Paris: Livre de poche.

Callinicos, Alex 2000, *Equality*, Cambridge: Polity.

Callinicos, Alex 2003, *The New Mandarins of American Power*, Cambridge: Polity.

Camus, Albert 1955, 'La bonne conscience', *L'Express*, 21 October.

Castles, Stephen and Godula Kosack 1973, *Immigrant Workers and Class Structure in Western Europe*, London: Oxford University Press.

Cazals, Rémy 2006, 'Ici les Français et les Boches parlent ensemble comme en temps de paix', in *Frères de tranchées*, edited by Marc Ferro, Paris: Perrin.

Chafer, Tony 2005, 'Chirac and "la Françafrique": No Longer a Family Affair', *Modern and Contemporary France* 13, 1: 7–23, available at: https://www.tandfonline.com/doi/full/10.1080/0963948052000341196.

Chambelland, Colette 1999, *Pierre Monatte, une autre voix syndicaliste*, Paris: Les éditions de l'Atelier/Éditions Ouvrières.

Chambelland, Maurice 1962a, 'Le compagnon Auguste Mougeot', *La Révolution prolétarienne* 468, January: 24, available at: http://cras31.info/IMG/pdf/larevolutionprolet arienne-n167.pdf.

Chambelland, Maurice 1962b, 'Discrète Marguerite', *La Révolution prolétarienne* 469, February: 1, available at: https://cras31.info/IMG/pdf/larevolutionproletarienne-n16 8.pdf.

Charby Jacques 2004, *Les Porteurs d'Espoir*, Paris: La Découverte.

Charnay, Maurice 1893, *Catéchisme du soldat*, Paris: Impr. J. Allemane.

Charnay, Maurice 1895, 'S'il disait vrai', *Le Parti ouvrier*, 7 January: 2, available at: https://gallica.bnf.fr/ark:/12148/bpt6k24060503/f2.item.

Charnay, Maurice 1898, 'L'affaire Dreyfus & les Députés socialistes', *Le Parti ouvrier*, 22 January: 3, available at: https://gallica.bnf.fr/ark:/12148/bpt6k2406408w/f3.item.

Charuel, Marc 1991, *L'Affaire Boudarel*, Paris: Éditions du Rocher.

Chaulieu, Pierre 1956–7, 'La révolution prolétarienne contre la bureaucratie', *Socialisme ou Barbarie* 20: 134–71, available at: http://soubscan.org/issue.php?slug=20.

Chauvin, Jean-René 2006, *Un Trotskiste dans l'enfer nazi*, Paris: Syllepse.

Chrisafis, Angelique 2010, 'Crackdown on "sans papiers"', *Guardian*, 16 November, available at https://www.theguardian.com/world/2010/nov/16/france-immigration-poli ce-roundups.

Chrisafis, Angelique 2015, 'Pork or Nothing', *Guardian*, 13 October.

Chuzeville, Julien 2017, *Un Court Moment Révolutionnaire: La création du parti communiste en France (1915–1924)*, Paris: Libertalia.

Chuzeville, Julien 2021, *Léo Frankel*, Montreuil: Libertalia, 2021.

Citron, Suzanne 2019 [1987], *Le Mythe national*, Paris: Les Éditions de l'Atelier.

Clayton, Anthony 1994, *The Wars of French Decolonization*, London: Longman.

Cliff, Tony 2001, 'Engels', *Selected Writings* Volume 1 *International Struggle and the Marxist Tradition*: 117–32, London: Bookmarks.

Collectif 2017, *Le Premier Congrès des Peuples de l'Orient Bakou 1920*, Paris: La Brèche & Radar.

Collin, Claude 2008, 'Le "travail allemand": origines et filiations', *Guerres mondiales et conflits contemporains*, 230: pp. 125–36.

Collin, Claude 2011, *De la Résistance à la guerre d'Indochine*, Paris: Les Indes savantes.

Collins, Henry and Chimen Abramsky 1965, *Karl Marx and the British Labour Movement*, London: Macmillan.

Comité des 20 arrondissements 1871, 'Manifeste', *Le Cri du peuple*, 27 March: 1, available at: https://gallica.bnf.fr/ark:/12148/bpt6k4683759d/f1.item.zoom.

Comité pour le RDR 1948, 'Nous sommes des millions qui cherchons le même chemin', *Franc-Tireur*, 27 February: 3, available at: https://gallica.bnf.fr/ark:/12148/bpt6k41063 55w/f3.item.zoom.

Contat, Michel and Michel Rybalka 1970, *Les Écrits de Sartre*, Paris: Gallimard.

Cortright, David 1975, *Soldiers in Revolt*, New York: Anchor Press.

Coudray, Sophie and Selim Nadi 2017, 'Decolonizing Aesthetics: French Surrealism vs Colonialism', paper at Historical Materialism Conference, London, November.

Couti, Jacqueline 2021, 'Firestarters: insurgent women in the insurrection of Southern Martinique and the Paris Commune', *The Funambulist* 34, available at: https://thefunambulist.net/magazine/the-paris-commune-and-the-world/firestarters-insurgent-women-in-the-insurrection-of-southern-martinique-and-the-paris-commune.

Craipeau, Yvan 1971, *Le Mouvement trotskyste en France*, Paris: Éditions Syros.

Craipeau, Yvan 1978, *La Libération confisquée*, Paris: Savelli.

Craipeau, Yvan 1999, *Mémoires d'un dinosaure trotskyste*, Paris: L'Harmattan.

Cratès 1909a, 'Les Dessous financiers de la guerre au Maroc', *La Vie ouvrière*, 5 October: 8–16.

Cratès 1909b, 'L'Insurrection de Barcelone', *La Vie ouvrière*, 20 October: 65–73.

Cratès 1909c, 'La Répression de Barcelone', *La Vie ouvrière*, 5 November.

Croix, Alexandre 1967, *Jaurès et ses détracteurs*, Saint-Ouen: Éditions du Vieux Saint-Ouen.

Cuenot, Alain 2011, *Clarté*, 2 volumes, L'Harmattan: Paris.

Cushion, Steve 2006, '*The 1941 miners' strike in northern France: from a dispute over soap to armed resistance*', *Socialist History* 29: 41–55.

Daix, Pierre 1976, *J'ai cru au matin*, Paris: Robert Laffont.

Daline Viktor, Armando Saitta and Albert Soboul (eds.) 1977, *Oeuvres de Babeuf: tome I*, Paris: Bibliothèque Nationale.

Dalloz, Jacques 1987. *La Guerre d'Indochine*, Paris: Éditions du Seuil.

Dalmas, Louis 1953, 'En un combat douteux', *Les Temps modernes*, August–September.

Dannat, Anton 1997, *Auf dem Floss der Medusa?*, Vienna: Marxismus 11.

Darien, Georges 1890, *Biribi*, Paris: A Savine.

Darriulat, Philippe 2001, *Les Patriotes*, Paris: Éditions du Seuil.

David, C 1926, 'Deuxième jour de grève: le mouvement s'accentue', *L'Humanité*, 6 May: 1–2, available at: https://gallica.bnf.fr/ark:/12148/bpt6k4020625/f1.item.zoom.

Davidson, Neil 2016, 'State and Nation: An Interview with Neil Davidson', *Viewpoint Magazine*, April 2016, available at: https://viewpointmag.com/2016/04/25/state-and-nation-an-interview-with-neil-davidson/.

DD 2015, 'L'Art est public'. *Radio Univers*, available at: http://www.radio-univers.com/lart-est-public-n684/.

de Beauvoir, Simone 1963, *La Force des choses*, Paris: Gallimard.

Degras, Jane (ed.) 1971 [1965], *The Communist International*, Volume III, 1929–43, London: Frank Cass.

de Massot, François 1999 [1996], 'An Interview with Jean Malaquais', *Revolutionary History* 7,2, available at: https://libcom.org/article/interview-jean-malaquais.

Derfler, Leslie 1991, *Paul Lafargue and the Founding of French Marxism, 1842–1882*, Cambridge Massachusetts: Harvard University Press.

Dérigon, Paul 1927, 'Lamine Senghor est mort', *L'Humanité*, 2 December: 2, available at: https://gallica.bnf.fr/ark:/12148/bpt6k402636h/f2.item.zoom.

Désir, Harlem 1985, *Touche pas à mon pote*, Paris: Grasset.

Devillers, Philippe 1952, *Histoire du Viêt-Nam de 1940 à 1952*, Paris: Éditions du Seuil.

Dewitte, Philippe 1985, *Les Mouvements nègres en France 1919–1939*, Paris: L'Harmattan.

Diop, David 2018, *Frère d'âme*, Paris: Éditions du Seuil.

Dominget, J. 1936, 'La grève d'une heure chez les métallos parisiens', *La Révolution prolétarienne* 231, 25 September: 11–12, available at: https://gallica.bnf.fr/ark:/12148/bpt6k62440142/f13.item.

Dommanget, Maurice 1971, *Eugène Pottier*, Paris: Études et documentation internationales.

Dommanget, Maurice 2006 [1966], *Histoire du drapeau rouge*, Marseille: Le mot et le reste.

Doriot, Jacques 1924, *L'Armée et la défense du capitalisme*, Paris: Librairie de 'l'Humanité'.

Doyon, Jacques 1973, *Les Soldats blancs de Ho Chi Minh*, Paris: Fayard.

Drake, David 1998, '*Les Temps modernes* and the French war in Indochina', *Journal of European Studies* 28, 109–10: pp. 25–41.

Drake, David 2000, 'Intellectuals, Demonisation and Exclusion in the Dreyfus Affair and L'Affaire du Foulard', in *New Perspectives on the Fin de Siècle in Nineteenth- and Twentieth-Century France*, edited by Chadwick, Kay and Timothy Unwin, Lewiston Lampeter: E. Mellen Press.

Drake, David 2006, 'The PCF, the Surrealists, Clarté and the Rif War', *French Cultural Studies*, 17, 2, June: 173–88, available at: https://citeseerx.ist.psu.edu/viewdoc/download?doi=10.1.1.870.2458&rep=rep1&type=pdf.

Drake, David 2015, *Paris at War*, Cambridge Mass.: The Belknap Press of Harvard University Press.

Drew, Allison 2014, *We Are No Longer in France*, Manchester: Manchester University Press.

Drumont, Édouard 1886, *La France juive*, Paris: Marpon et Flammarion.

Dunois, Amédée 1914, 'Un intellectuel français s'élève contre l'impérialisme', *L'Humanité*, 26 October: 1, available at: https://gallica.bnf.fr/ark:/12148/bpt6k2539880/f1.item.zoom.

Dunois, Amédée 1922, 'Le communisme en Tunisie', *L'Humanité*, 24 March: 1, available at: https://gallica.bnf.fr/ark:/12148/bpt6k4003484/f1.item.

Durgan, Andy 1999, 'Freedom fighters or Comintern army? The International Brigades in Spain', *International Socialism* 2,84, available at: https://www.marxists.org/history/etol/writers/durgan/1999/xx/intbrigades.htm.

Einaudi, Jean-Luc 1986, *Pour l'exemple*, Paris: L'Harmattan.

Einaudi, Jean-Luc 1991, *La Bataille de Paris*, Paris: Éditions du Seuil.

Einaudi, Jean-Luc 2001, *Vietnam!*, Paris: Le cherche midi.

Einaudi, Jean-Luc 2004, *Franc-Tireur*, Paris: Éditions du Sextant.

Engels, Frederick 1976 [1847], 'On Poland', *Marx and Engels Collected Works*, Volume 6, London: Lawrence and Wishart.

Engels, Frederick 2004 [1893], Letters 1893, *Marx and Engels Collected Works*, Volume 50, London: Lawrence and Wishart.

Engels, Friedrich and Paul and Laura Lafargue 1956–9, *Correspondance*, 3 volumes, Paris: Éditions sociales.

Essel, André 1985, *Je voulais changer le monde*, Paris: Stock.

Evans, Martin 1997, *The Memory of Resistance*, Oxford and New York: Berg, 1997.

Evans, Martin 2006, 'Mutiny by French troops during the Algerian war', *Socialist Worker*, 27 May, available at: https://socialistworker.co.uk/features/mutiny-by-french-troops -during-the-algerian-war.

Evans, Martin 2012, *Algeria: France's Undeclared War*, Oxford: Oxford University Press.

Fall, Bernard 1955, 'Tribulations of a party line – the French Communists and Indochina', *Foreign Affairs* 33,3, available at: https://www.foreignaffairs.com/articles/france /1955-04-01/tribulations-party-line.

Fanon, Frantz 1972, *Sociologie d'une révolution (L'an v de la révolution algérienne)*, Paris: Maspero.

Faure, Alain 1974, 'Mouvements populaires et mouvement ouvrier à Paris (1830–1834)', *Le Mouvement social* 88: 51–92.

Fauvet, Jacques 1965, *Histoire du parti communiste français* tome II, Paris: Fayard.

Fédération des bourses du travail 1902, *Le Nouveau Manuel du Soldat*, Paris: FBT.

Ferrette, François 2011, *La véritable histoire du parti communiste français*, Paris: Demopolis.

Ferro, Marc 1969, *La Grande guerre*, Paris: Gallimard.

Fèvre, Henry 1887, *Au Port d'arme*, Paris: Charpentier.

Fichaut, André 2003, *Sur le pont*, Paris: Syllepse.

Fiechter, Jean-Jacques 1965, *Le socialisme français de l'affaire Dreyfus à la grande guerre*, Geneva: Droz.

Finidori, Jean-Paul 1937, 'Une atteinte à la liberté', *La Révolution prolétarienne* 240, 10 February: 17, available at: https://gallica.bnf.fr/ark:/12148/bpt6k64683789/f21.item.

Flakin, Nathaniel 2018, *Arbeiter und Soldat: Martin Monath – Ein Berliner Jude unter Wehrmachtssoldaten*, Stuttgart: Schmetterling Verlag.

Flakin, Nathaniel 2019, *Martin Monath*, London: Pluto.

Fontenis, Georges 2000, *Changer le monde*, Paris: Alternative libertaire.

Franchet, Antonin 1903, *Le Bon Dieu laïque*, Paris: Éditions de la petite république.

Freeman Ted (ed.), Claude and Henri Martin and Henri Delmas 1998, *Drame à Toulon – Henri Martin*, Exeter: University of Exeter Press.

Fribourg, Ernest Édouard 1871, *L'Association internationale des travailleurs*, Paris: Armand Le Chevalier.

Fysh, Peter and Jim Wolfreys 1998, *The Politics of Racism in France*, London: Palgrave Macmillan.

Gallissot, René 2006, *La République française et les indigènes. Algérie colonisée, Algérie algérienne (1870–1962)*, Paris: Les Éditions de l'Atelier.

Genet, Jean 2012 [1983], 'Quatre heures à Chatila', *Le Grand Soir*, 21 September, available at: https://www.legrandsoir.info/quatre-heures-a-chatila.html.

Gervereau, Laurent, Jean-Pierre Rioux and Benjamin Stora [eds.] 1992, *La France en guerre d'Algérie*, Paris: Bibliothèque de documentation internationale contemporaine.

Gildea, Robert, James Mark and Anette Warring (eds.) 2013, *Europe's 1968: Voices of Revolt*, Oxford: Oxford University Press.

Gluckstein, Donny 1999, *The Nazis, Capitalism and the Working Class*, London: Bookmarks.

Gluckstein, Donny 2012, *A People's History of the Second World War*, London: Pluto.

Godeau, Pierre and Paule 1963, 'Une femme devant la mort', *La Révolution prolétarienne* 479, January: 11–12, available at: https://cras31.info/IMG/pdf/larevolutionproletarienne-n178.pdf.

Goebel, Michael 2015, *Anti-Imperial Metropolis: Interwar Paris and the Seeds of Third World Nationalism*, New York: Cambridge University Press.

Gopal, Priyamvada 2020, *Insurgent Empire*, London: Verso.

Gordon, Daniel 2007, 'Daniel Guérin et le mouvement des travailleurs immigrés en France après 68', in *Daniel Guérin: Révolutionnaire en mouvement(s)*, Paris: L'Harmattan.

Gordon, Daniel 2012, *Immigrants and Intellectuals*, Pontypool: Merlin.

Gottraux, Philippe 1997, 'Socialisme ou Barbarie'. Un engagement politique et intellectuel dans la France de l'après-guerre, Lausanne: Payot.

Gras, Christian 1971, *Alfred Rosmer (1877–1964) et le mouvement révolutionnaire international*, Paris: Maspero.

Gravereaux, L. 1913, *Les Discussions sur le patriotisme et le militarisme dans les congrès socialistes*, Paris: thèse de droit.

Greeman, Richard 1994, 'The Victor Serge Affair and the French Literary Left', *Revolutionary History* 5, 3, available at: https://www.marxists.org/history/etol/revhist/backiss/vol5/no3/greeman.html.

Griffuelhes, Victor 1905, 'Enquête sur l'idée de patrie et la classe ouvrière', *Le Mouvement socialiste*, August: 443.

Guérin, Daniel 1933, *La Peste brune*, Paris: Éditions L.d.T.

Guérin, Daniel 1936, *Fascisme et grand capital: Italie, Allemagne*, Paris: Gallimard.

Guérin, Daniel 1938, *Contre la guerre et l'union sacrée. Documents recueillis par Daniel Guérin*, Paris: PSOP.

Guérin, Daniel 1953, 'Pitié pour le Maghreb', *Les Temps modernes*, January–February: 1190–1219.

Guérin, Daniel 1963, *Front populaire: révolution manquée*, Paris: Julliard.

Guérin, Daniel 1964, *Un jeune homme excentrique*, Paris: René Julliard.

Guérin, Daniel 1969, *La Peste brune*, Paris: Maspero.

Guérin, Daniel 1973, *Ci-gît le colonialisme*, La Haye and Paris: Mouton.

Guérin, Daniel 1979, *Quand l'Algérie s'insurgeait*, Claix: La Pensée sauvage.

Guesde Jules and Paul Lafargue 1883, *Le Programme du Parti Ouvrier*, Paris: H. Oriol.

Guillemin, Henri 1956, *Cette curieuse guerre de 70*, Paris: Gallimard.

Guillemin, Henri 1960, *Zola Légende et Vérité*, Paris: Union Générale d'Éditions.

Guillemin, Henri 1967, *La Première Résurrection de la république*, Paris: Gallimard.

Hagnauer, Roger 1962, 'En souvenir de "la marraine" de Périgny', *La Révolution prolétarienne* 470, March: 24, available at: http://cras31.info/IMG/pdf/larevolutionproletarie nne-n169.pdf.

Hamon, Hervé and Patrick Rotman 1979, *Les Porteurs de valises*, Paris: Albin Michel, Paris.

Hamon, Hervé and Patrick Rotman 1987, *Génération tome 1: les années de rêve*, Paris: Éditions du Seuil.

Harbi, Mohanmmed 2001, *Une Vie debout*, Paris: La Découverte.

Harman, Chris 1982, *The Lost Revolution: Germany 1918 to 1923*, London: Bookmarks.

Harman, Chris 2000, 'Anti-Capitalism: Theory and Practice', International Socialism 2,88, available at: https://www.marxists.org/archive/harman/2000/xx/anticap.htm.

Hemmings, Frederick W.J. 1966, *Emile Zola*, Oxford: Clarendon.

Hirou, Jean-Pierre 1995, *Parti socialiste ou C.G.T.?*, Paris: Acratie.

Ho Chi Minh 1920, 'Discours au Congrès de Tours', available at: http://vivelepcf.over -blog.fr/article-35595523.html.

Hobsbawm, Eric J. 1977, *Revolutionaries*, London: Quartet.

Hobsbawm, Eric J. 1987, *The Age of Empire*, London: Weidenfeld and Nicolson.

Hobsbawm, Eric J. 1990, *Nations and Nationalism since 1780*, Cambridge: Cambridge University Press.

Holcroft, Thomas 1802, *Voyage à Paris*, Berlin: Voss.

Horn, Gerd-Rainer 1989, 'Le trotskysme et l'Europe pendant la deuxième guerre mondiale', *Cahiers Léon Trotsky* 39: 49–76, available at: https://www.marxists.org/francais /clt/1986-1990/CLT39- Sep-1989.pdf.

Institut Maurice Thorez 1967, *Le Parti communiste français dans la résistance*, Paris: Éditions sociales.

Isaacs, Harold Robert 2009 [1938], *The Tragedy of the Chinese Revolution*, Chicago: Haymarket.

J.F. 1948, 'La première assemblée générale du R.D.R.', *Franc-Tireur*, 13 March: 3. available at: https://gallica.bnf.fr/ark:/12148/bpt6k4106368h/f3.item.zoom.

Janvion, Émile [Anonymous], 1907, *L'École: Antichambre de caserne et de sacristie*, Aiglemont: Publications de la Colonie Communiste d'Aiglemont.

Janvion, Émile 1912, *La Franc-Maçonnerie et la classe ouvrière*, Paris: Terre Libre.

Jaurès, Jean 1898, *Les Preuves*, Paris: La Petite République.

Jaurès, Jean 1911, *L'armée nouvelle*, Paris: Jules Rouff.

Jaurès, Jean 1969 [1901–7], *Histoire Socialiste de la Révolution française*, tome VI, Paris: Éditions sociales.

Jean-Christophe, Pierre 2020, 'Martinique: l'abolition de l'esclavage et le mythe Victor Schœlcher', *Lutte ouvrière*, 27 May, available at: https://journal.lutte-ouvriere.org/2020/05/27/martinique-labolition-de-lesclavage-et-le-mythe-victor-schoelcher_148262.html.

Jeandel, Alice-Anne 2006, *Andrée Viollis*, Paris: L'Harmattan.

Jeanmichel, Lucien 1993, *Arlès-Dufour – un saint-simonien à Lyon*, Lyon: Éditions lyonnaises d'art et d'histoire.

Jeanson, Colette and Francis 1955, *L'Algérie hors la loi*, Paris: Éditions du Seuil.

Jenni, Alexis 2011, *L'Art français de la guerre*, Paris: Gallimard.

Julliard, Jacques 1965, *Clemenceau briseur de grèves*, Paris: Gallimard.

Kaddache, Mahfoud 1980, *Histoire du nationalisme algérien*, Algiers: Société Nationale d'Édition et de Diffusion.

Katz, Ethan 2012, 'Did the Paris Mosque Save Jews? A Mystery and its Memory', *The Jewish Quarterly Review*, 102, 2: 256–87.

Keiger, John 1983, *France and the Origins of the First World War*, London: Macmillan.

Kendall, Walter 1975, *The Labour Movement in Europe*, London: Allen Lane.

Kergoat, Jacques 1994, *Marceau Pivert, 'socialiste de gauche'*, Paris: Éditions ouvrières.

Kergoat, Jacques 1997, *Histoire du parti socialiste*, Paris: La Découverte.

Kidron, Michael 1962, 'Imperialism – Highest Stage but One', *International Socialism* 1, 9, available at: https://www.marxists.org/archive/kidron/works/1962/xx/imperial.htm.

Kiernan, Victor Gordon 1977, 'Colonial Africa and its Armies', in *War and Society*, edited by Brian Bond and Ian Roy, volume II, London: Croom Helm.

Kilian, Robert 1948, *Les Fusiliers marins en Indochine*, Paris: Berger-Levrault.

Köller, Heinz 1963, *Kampfbündnis an der Seine, Ruhr und Spree*, Berlin: Rütten und Loening.

Kriegel, Annie and Jean-Jacques Becker 1964, *1914, La guerre et le mouvement ouvrier*, Paris: Armand Colin.

Krivine, Alain 2004, 'Alain Krivine and Algeria' (translated from Charby 2004), available at: https://www.marxists.org/archive/krivine/1956/algeria.htm#n2.

Krivine, Alain 2011, 'Alain Krivine, l'engagé', *France Culture*, 12–16 December, available at: https://www.radiofrance.fr/franceculture/podcasts/serie-alain-krivine-l-engage.

Laborde, François [J-F. Lyotard] 1956, 'La situation en Afrique du Nord', *Socialisme ou Barbarie* 18: 87–94, available at: http://soubscan.org/issue.php?slug=18.

Laborde, François [J-F. Lyotard] 1957, 'Nouvelle phase dans la question algérienne', *Socialisme ou Barbarie* 21: 162–8, available at: http://soubscan.org/issue.php?slug= 21.

Lacour, Léon 1911, 'Le Sou du soldat', *La Vie ouvrière*, 5 October: 402–6.

Lacouture, Jean 1977, *Léon Blum*, Paris: Éditions du Seuil.

Lacroix-Riz, Annie 2006, *Le Choix de la défaite: les élites françaises dans les années 1930*, Paris: Armand Colin.

Lafargue, Paul 1885, 'La Légende de Victor Hugo', available at: https://www.marxists.org/ francais/lafargue/works/1885/06/hugo.htm.

Lafargue, Paul 1891, 'La boucherie de Fourmies du 1er mai 1891', available at: https://www .marxists.org/francais/lafargue/works/1891/05/lafargue_18910500.htm.

Lafargue, Paul 1895, 'L'idéalisme et le matérialisme dans la conception de l'histoire', *La Jeunesse socialiste* 1 and 2, available at: https://www.marxists.org/francais/lafargue/ works/1895/00/idealisme.htm.

Lafargue, Paul 1900, 'Nationalisme et socialisme', *Le Socialiste*, 27 May.

Lafargue, Paul 1970, *Textes Choisis*, Paris: Éditions sociales.

Laguiller, Arlette 1996, *C'est toute ma vie*, Paris: Plon.

Lamouchi, Noureddine 1996, *Jean-Paul Sartre et le tiers monde*, Paris: L'Harmattan.

Larue-Langlois, Françoys 2007, *Paul Lafargue*, Paris: Punctum.

Laurat, Lucien 1931, *L'Économie soviétique*, Paris: Librairie Valois.

Lazare, Bernard 1894, *L'Antisémitisme, son histoire et ses causes*, Paris: Léon Chaillet.

Lazare, Bernard 1896, *Une erreur judiciaire*, Brussels: Imprimerie Veuve Monnom.

Lazare, Bernard 1899, *Antisémitisme et Révolution*, Paris: P-V. Stock.

Le Comité Central du PCF 1925, 'Aux Ouvriers et aux Paysans de France et des Colonies', *L'Humanité*, 14 May: 1, available at: https://gallica.bnf.fr/ark:/12148/bpt6k401703c/f1 .item.zoom.

Le Cour Grandmaison, Olivier 2010, *De l'indigénat: anatomie d'un monstre juridique*, Paris: Zones.

Le Guennec, Nicole 1972, 'Le Parti communiste français et la guerre du Rif', *Le Mouvement social* 78: 39–64.

Le Madec, François 1988, *L'aubépine de mai: chronique d'une usine occupée*, Nantes: Centre de documentation du mouvement ouvrier et du travail.

Leblond, Maurice 1927, 'Les projets littéraires d'Emile Zola au moment de sa mort', *Mercure de France*, 1 October: 5–25, available at: https://www.retronews.fr/journal/ mercure-de-france/01-octobre-1927/118/4092517/7.

Lecoin, Louis 1965, *Le Cours d'une vie*, Boulogne: Union Pacifiste de France.

Lefebvre, Raymond 1919, *Le Sacrifice d'Abraham*, Paris: Flammarion.

Lefebvre, Raymond 1921, *L'Éponge de Vinaigre*, Paris: Éditions Clarté.

Lefort, Claude 1947, 'Les Pays Coloniaux', *Les Temps modernes*, March: 1068–94.

Lemaître, Maurice 1961, 'Le Tombeau', *Partisans* 1, September–October: 83.

Lenin, Vladimir 1965 [1920], *Terms of Admission into Communist International, Lenin Collected Works*, Volume 31, Moscow: Progress Publishers: 206–11.

Lenin, Vladimir 1966 [1915], *To Karl Radek, Lenin Collected Works*, Volume 36, Moscow: Progress Publishers: 334–6.

Lenin, Vladimir 1970 [1915], *Socialism and War, Lenin Collected Works*, Volume 21, Peking: Foreign Languages Press: 295–338.

Lenin, Vladimir 1974 [1915], *The Defeat of One's Own Government in the Imperialist War*, Lenin Collected Works, Volume 21, Moscow: Progress Publishers: 275–80.

Les Temps modernes 1955a, 'Refus d'obéissance', *Les Temps Modernes*, October: 385–8.

Les Temps modernes 1955b, 'L'Algérie n'est pas la France', *Les Temps Modernes*, November: 577–9.

Lévy, Bernard-Henri 1991, *Les Aventures de la liberté*, Paris: Grasset.

Liauzu, Claude 1982, *Aux Origines des tiers-mondismes*, Paris: L'Harmattan.

Liebknecht, Karl 1952, *Ausgewählte Reden und Aufsätze*, Berlin: Dietz Verlag.

Lissagaray, Prosper-Olivier 1970 [1876], *Histoire de la Commune de 1871*, Paris: Maspero.

Loez, André 2010, *Les Refus de la guerre*, Paris: Gallimard.

Loris, Marc 1985 [1942], 'La question nationale en Europe', *Cahiers Léon Trotsky* 23: 88–110, available at: https://www.marxists.org/francais/clt/1979-1985/CLT23-Sep-1985.pdf.

Lough, John 1979, *Seventeenth-Century French Drama*, Oxford: Oxford University Press.

Louis, Paul 1905, *Le Colonialisme*, Paris: Société Nouvelle de Librairie et d'Édition.

Louzon, Robert 1910, 'Cavaignac, Thiers, Briand', *La Vie ouvrière*, 5 May.

Louzon, Robert 1923, 'Une Honte', *Bulletin communiste*, 4 January: 15–16, available at: https://www.retronews.fr/journal/bulletin-communiste/04-jan-1923/1255/4526299/16.

Louzon, Robert 1925, 'Vive la République Riffaine', *La Révolution prolétarienne* 7, July: 1–9, available at: https://gallica.bnf.fr/ark:/12148/bpt6k62307673/f11.item.

Louzon, Robert 1937, 'Collectivisation ou Étatisation', *La Révolution prolétarienne* 250, 10 July: 1–3, available at: https://gallica.bnf.fr/ark:/12148/bpt6k6468388p/f3.item.

Louzon, Robert 1939, 'La "bombe"', *La Révolution prolétarienne* 301, 25 August: 6, available at: https://gallica.bnf.fr/ark:/12148/bpt6k62744912/f1.item.

Lyotard, Jean-François 1959–60, 'Le contenu sociale de la lutte algérienne', *Socialisme ou Barbarie* 29: 1–38, available at: http://soubscan.org/pdf/soub_n29.pdf.

Lyotard, Jean-François 1961–62, 'L'Algérie, sept ans après', *Socialisme ou Barbarie* 33: 10–16, available at: http://soubscan.org/issue.php?slug=33.

Lyotard, Jean-François 1963, 'L'Algérie évacuée', *Socialisme ou Barbarie* 34: 1–43, available at: http://soubscan.org/issue.php?slug=34.

Lyotard, Jean-François 1989, *La Guerre des Algériens*, Paris: Galilée.

Lyotard, Jean-François and Pierre Vidal-Naquet 1989, 'Parler encore de la guerre d'Algérie', *Libération*, 9 November.

Magraw, Roger 1970, 'The Conflict in the Villages', in *Conflicts in French Society*, edited by Theodore Zeldin, London: Allen & Unwin.

Maillard, Alain 1999, *La Communauté des égaux*, Paris: Kimé.

Maîtrejean, Rirette 2005, *Souvenirs d'anarchie*, Quimperlé: La Digitale.

Maitron, Jean 1975, *Le Mouvement anarchiste en France*, 2 volumes, Paris: Maspero.

Maitron, Jean and Claude Pennetier 1964–2023, *Dictionnaire biographique du mouvement ouvrier français*, Paris: Éditions de l'Atelier, available at: https://maitron.fr.

Malaquais, Jean 1947, *Planète sans visa*, Paris: Pré-aux Clercs.

Malaquais, Jean 1995, [1939], *Les Javanais*, Paris: Phébus.

Malye, François and Benjamin Stora 2010, *François Mitterrand et la guerre d'Algérie*, Paris: Calmann-Lévy.

Mann, Tom 1910, 'L'Arbitrage en Australie', *La Vie ouvrière*, 5 July: 1–7.

Manouchian Group, The 1944, 'The Last Letters', available at: https://www.marxists.org/history/france/resistance/manouchian/index.htm.

Marchand, René 1919, Pourquoi je me suis rallié au bolchevisme, Petrograd: Éditions de l'Internationale communiste.

Martin, Gaston 1948, *L'Abolition de l'esclavage*, Paris: Presses universitaires de France.

Martinet, Gilles 1962, *Le Marxisme de notre temps*, Paris: Julliard.

Martinet, Marcel 1919, *La Maison à l'abri*, Paris: Librairie Paul Ollendorff.

Martinet, Marcel 1923, 'Les ouvriers parisiens contre l'impérialisme', *L'Humanité*, 4 January: 1–2, available at https://gallica.bnf.fr/ark:/12148/bpt6k400632f/f1.item.zoom.

Martinet, Marcel 1934a, *Civilisation Française en Indochine*, Paris: Comité d'Amnistie et de Défense des Indochinois et des Peuples Colonisés.

Martinet, Marcel 1934b, *Où va la révolution russe? L'Affaire Victor Serge*, Paris: Librairie du travail.

Marty, André 1955, *L'Affaire Marty*, Paris: Deux Rives.

Marty, André 1999 [1929], *La Révolte de la Mer Noire*, Pantin: Le Temps des Cerises.

Marx, Karl 1985 [1864], *Inaugural Address of the Working Men's International Association, Marx and Engels Collected Works*, Volume 20, London: Lawrence & Wishart.

Marx, Karl 1989 [1875], *Critique of the Gotha Programme, Marx and Engels Collected Works*, Volume 24, London: Lawrence & Wishart.

Marx, Karl and Engels Frederick 1976 [1848], *Manifesto of the Communist Party, Marx and Engels Collected Works*, Volume 6, London: Lawrence and Wishart.

Maschino, Maurice 1961, *L'Engagement*, Paris: Maspero.

Maspero, François 1988, *Le Figuier*, Paris: Éditions du Seuil.

Mattéi, Georges 1982, *La Guerre des gusses*, Paris: Balland.

Mayoux, Marie and François 1917, *Les Instituteurs syndicalistes et la guerre*, Dignac: Fédération Nationale des Syndicats d'institutrices et d'instituteurs publics, Section de la Charente.

Mazuy, Rachel 2002, *Croire plutôt que voir*, Paris: Odile Jacob.

Mazuy, Rachel and Denis Pernot 2023, *Raymond Lefebvre La révolution et la mort*, Dijon: Éditions Universitaires de Dijon.

McGrogan, Manus 2012, 'From the Algerian War to May 1968 and After: The Roles of Left Radicals and Their Press', *Revolutionary History*, 10,4.

McKay, Claude 2020, *Romance in Marseille*, New York: Penguin.

Mélenchon, Jean-Luc 2008, *Laïcité: Réplique au discours de Nicolas Sarkozy, Chanoine de Latran*, Paris: Bruno Leprince.

Méric, Victor 1909, *Emile Zola*, Paris: Portraits d'Hier.

Merrheim, Alphonse 1911, 'L'Approche de la guerre', *La Vie ouvrière*, 5 January: 1–17; 20 January: 101–13; 5 February: 129–41; 20 February: 242–8.

Messali Hadj 1982, *Les Mémoires de Messali Hadj 1898–1938*, Paris: JC Lattès.

Miller, Paul B. 2002, *From Revolutionaries to Citizens*, Durham NC and London: Duke University Press.

Minguet, Simonne 1997, *Mes années Caudron: une usine autogérée à la Libération*, Paris: Syllepse.

Miquel, Pierre 1972, *Une énigme? L'Affaire Dreyfus*, Paris: Presses universitaires de France.

Monatte, Pierre 1909, 'Le Secrétariat International contre l'internationalisme', *La Vie ouvrière*, 20 December.

Monatte, Pierre 1925a, 'Le carnet d'un Sauvage', *La Révolution prolétarienne* 1, January: 7–8, available at: https://gallica.bnf.fr/ark:/12148/bpt6k6230761m/f18.item.zoom.

Monatte, Pierre 1925b, 'La dure leçon du 12 octobre', *La Révolution prolétarienne* 10, October: 29–30, available at: https://gallica.bnf.fr/ark:/12148/bpt6k6230770k/f32.item.

Monatte, Pierre 2018, *Lettres d'un syndicaliste sous l'uniforme 1915–1918*, edited by Julien Chuzeville, Toulouse: Smolny.

Moneta, Jakob 1971, *Le PCF et la question coloniale*, Paris: Maspero.

Monjauvis, Lucien 1971, *Jean-Pierre Timbaud*, Paris: Éditions Sociales.

Montaigne, Michel 1580, 'Des cannibales', available at: https://artflsrv03.uchicago.edu/philologic4/montessaisvilley/navigate/1/3/32/?byte=625015.

Moos Merilyn and Steve Cushion 2020, *Anti-Nazi Germans*, London: Community Languages.

Moshiri, Nazanine 2013, 'A little-known massacre in Senegal', *Al Jazeera*, 22 November, available at: https://www.aljazeera.com/features/2013/11/22/a-little-known-massacre-in-senegal.

Mothé, Daniel 1956–7, 'Chez Renault on parle de la Hongrie', *Socialisme ou Barbarie* 20: 124–33, available at: http://soubscan.org/issue.php?slug=20.

Mothé, Daniel 1957, 'Les ouvriers français et les Nord-Africains', *Socialisme ou Barbarie* 21: 146–57, available at: http://soubscan.org/issue.php?slug=21.

Mothé, Daniel 1958, 'Ce que l'on nous a dit', *Socialisme ou Barbarie* 25: 67–71, available at: http://soubscan.org/pdf/soub_n25.pdf.

Murphy, David 2020, 'When Communism Met Black Anti-Colonialism in Interwar France', *Jacobin*, 29 June, available at: https://jacobin.com/author/david-murphy.

Neale, Jonathan 2001, *The American War: Vietnam 1960–1975*, London: Bookmarks.

Neville, Peter 2007, *Britain in Vietnam*, London and New York: Routledge.

Newsinger, John 2006, *The Blood Never Dried*, London: Bookmarks.

Ngô Văn 1995, *Revolutionaries They Could Not Break*, London: Index Books.

Ngô Văn 2000, *Au Pays de la Cloche Fêlée*, Montreuil: L'Insomniaque.

Ngo Van Xuyet 1990, '*Ta Thu Thau – Vietnamese Trotskyist Leader*', *Revolutionary History* 3,2, available at: https://www.marxists.org/history/etol/revhist/backiss/vol3/no2/th au.html.

Nguyen Ai Quac 1922, 'Quelques réflexions sur la question coloniale', *L'Humanité*, 25 May: 4, available at https://gallica.bnf.fr/ark:/12148/bpt6k400409f/f4.item.zoom.

Nguyen Ai Quoc 1998 [1925], *Le Procès de la colonisation française*, Pantin: Le Temps des Cerises.

Nick, Christophe 2002, *Les trotskistes*, Paris: Fayard.

Orwell, George 1962 [1938], *Homage to Catalonia*, Penguin: Harmondsworth.

Oved, Georges 1984, *La Gauche française et le nationalisme marocain 1905–1955*, Paris: L'Harmattan.

Paizis, George 2007, *Marcel Martinet: Poet of the Revolution*, London: Francis Boutle.

Palme Dutt, Rajani 1964, *The Internationale*, London: Lawrence and Wishart.

Papayanis, Nicholas 1985, *Alphonse Merrheim: the emergence of reformism in revolutionary syndicalism, 1871–1925*, Boston: M. Nijhoff.

Pascal, Blaise 1964, [1670] *Pensées*, Paris: Garnier.

Pattieu, Sylvain 2002, *Les camarades des frères*, Paris: Syllepse.

Paz, Magdeleine 1935, 'Liberté pour Victor Serge!', *La Révolution prolétarienne*, 202, 10 July: 11–13, available at: https://gallica.bnf.fr/ark:/12148/bpt6k6348288j/f1.item.

Pedroncini, Guy 1967, *Les Mutineries de 1917*, Paris: PUF Presses Universitaires de France.

Péju, Paulette 2000, *Ratonnades à Paris*, Paris: La Découverte.

Péri, Gabriel 1926, 'Le prolétariat anglais est à la pointe d'une grande bataille ouvrière internationale', *L'Humanité*, 2 May: 3, available at: https://gallica.bnf.fr/ark:/12148/ bpt6k4020583/f3.item.zoom.

Perrault, Gilles 1984, *Un Homme à part*, Paris: Bernard Barrault.

Perry, Matt 2020, 'During the Black Sea Mutiny, French Sailors Rejected France's War on Soviet Russia', *Jacobin*, 27 December.

Peschanski, Denis 2002, *Des Étrangers dans la Résistance*, Paris: Éditions de l'Atelier.

Pisani-Ferry, Fresnette 1962, *Jules Ferry et le partage du monde*, Paris: Grasset.

Pivert, Marceau 1936, 'Tout est posible', *Le Populaire*, 27 May: 6, available at: https://gallica.bnf.fr/ark:/12148/bpt6k8223090/f6.item.zoom.

Planche, Jean-Louis 2006, *Sétif 1945*, Paris: Perrin.

Plant, John 2012, 'John Baird: A British MP Who Supported the Algerian Revolution', *Revolutionary History*, 10, 4.

Pluet-Despatin, Jacqueline 1978, *La Presse trotskiste en France de 1926 à 1968*, Grenoble: Presses universitaires.

Pottier, Eugène 1966, *Oeuvres Complètes*, Paris: Maspero.

Pouget, Émile 1976, *Le Père Peinard*, edited by R. Langlais, Paris: Galilée.

Poulaille, Henry 1935, 'Barbusse', *A Contre-Courant* 3, September.

Price, Morgan Philips 1999 [1997], *Dispatches from the Weimar Republic*, London: Pluto.

Quilliot, Roger 1972, *La S.F.I.O. et l'exercice du pouvoir 1944–1958*, Paris: Fayard.

R.S. 1948, 'Le R.D.R. tient son premier meeting', *Combat*, 20 March: 5, available at: https://gallica.bnf.fr/ark:/12148/bpt6k4749655d/f5.item.

Rabaut, Jean 1975, *L'Anti-militarisme en France 1810–1975*, Paris: Hachette.

Rapport présenté au 2e. Congrès Interfédéral Communiste de l'Afrique du Nord 1922, 'Le Communisme et la Question coloniale', *Bulletin communiste*, 7 December: 31–2, available at: https://www.retronews.fr/journal/bulletin-communiste/07-dec-1922/1255/4526433/31, *14 December:15–16*, available at: https://www.retronews.fr/journal/bulletin-communiste/14-dec-1922/1255/4526443/15.

Rayner, Ernest 1989, 'Les internationalistes du "troisième camp" en France pendant la seconde guerre mondiale', *Cahiers Léon Trotsky* 39: 23–48, available at: https://www.marxists.org/francais/clt/1986-1990/CLT39-Sep-1989.pdf.

Renton, David 2005, 'Understanding Fascism: Daniel Guérin's *Brown Plague*', *What Next?* 30, available at http://www.whatnextjournal.org.uk/Pages/Back/Wnext30/Guerin.html.

Reynaud, Paul 1931, 'Discours de Paul Reynaud sur Colonisation', 7 May, available at: https://interventions-democratiques.fr/revue-de-presse/discours-de-paul-reynaud-sur-colonisation.

Richard, Antoine 1931, 'Le cinquantenaire des lois laïques', *La Révolution prolétarienne* 117, 5 May: 7–17 available at: https://gallica.bnf.fr/ark:/12148/bpt6k62309901/f19.item.zoom.

Riddell, John (ed.) 1993, *To See the Dawn*, New York: Pathfinder.

Righi, Abdellah 2006, *Hadj-Ali Abdelkader*, Algiers: Casbah Publishers.

Risser, Nicole Dombrowski 2012, *France under Fire: German Invasion, Civilian Flight, and Family Survival during World War II*, Cambridge and New York: Cambridge University Press.

Robine, Jérémy 2006, 'Les "indigènes de la République": nation et question postcoloniale', *Hérodote* 120: 118–48, available at: https://www.cairn.info/revue-herodote-2006-1-page-118.htm.

Robrieux, Philippe 1980, *Histoire intérieure du parti communiste*, tome I, 1920–1945, Paris: Fayard.

Robrieux, Philippe 1986, *L'Affaire Manouchian*, Paris: Fayard.

Rolland, Denis 2005, *La Grève des tranchées*, Paris: Imago.

Rolland, Romain 1915, *Au-dessus de la mêlée*, Paris: Librairie Paul Ollendorff.

Rolland, Romain 1952 [1950], 'Journal des années de guerre 1914–1919', Paris: Albin Michel.

Ronsac, Charles 1988, *Trois Noms pour une vie*, Paris: Robert Laffont.

Rosen, Michael 2017, *The Disappearance of Émile Zola*, London: Faber and Faber.

Rosmer, Alfred 1921, 'Speech to the Congress of the Red International of Labour Unions in July 1921', *Bibliothek der Roten Gewerkschafts-Internationale*, Volume III, Berlin: RILU, 1921. (Translated in *Revolutionary History* 7,4, 2000–2001).

Rosmer, Alfred 1912a, 'Hervé et le hervéisme', *La Vie ouvrière*, 5 October: 74–6.

Rosmer, Alfred 1912b, 'Le Conflit des races en Orient', *La Vie ouvrière*, 20 November: 244–60.

Rosmer, Alfred 1913, 'Grève générale des Mineurs du Rand et des Ouvriers de Johannesburg', *La Vie ouvrière* 92, 20 July and 93, 5 August.

Rosmer, Alfred 1926, 'La Grève générale en Angleterre', *La Révolution prolétarienne* 17, May: 30, available at: https://gallica.bnf.fr/ark:/12148/bpt6k6235521z/f32.item.

Rosmer, Alfred 1936, *Le Mouvement ouvrier pendant la guerre* tome I, Paris: Librairie du travail.

Rosmer, Alfred 1951, 'Il y a quarante ans', *La Révolution prolétarienne* 46, January: 1–3, available at: https://cras31.info/IMG/pdf/larevolutionproletarienne-no46.pdf.

Rosmer, Alfred 1953, *Moscou sous Lénine*, Paris: Éditions Pierre Horay, available at: https://www.marxists.org/francais/rosmer/works/msl/index.htm.

Rosmer, Marguerite 1922a, 'A travers la Russie affamée', *L'Humanité*, 11 June: 1, available at: https://gallica.bnf.fr/ark:/12148/bpt6k4004260.

Rosmer, Marguerite 1922b, 'A travers la Russie affamée', *L'Humanité*, 13 June: 2, available at: https://gallica.bnf.fr/ark:/12148/bpt6k400428r/f2.item.

Ross, Kristin 2002, *May '68 and its Afterlives*, Chicago: University of Chicago Press.

Ross, Kristin 2015, *Communal Luxury: the political imaginary of the Paris Commune*, London: Verso.

Rosso, Stéphane 1910, 'Grèves et socialisme à la Guadeloupe', *La Vie ouvrière*, 20 October: 486–500.

Rousset, David 1946, *L'Univers concentrationnaire*, Paris: Éditions du Pavois.

Roy, Pierre 2004, *Pierre Brizon*, Nonette: Créer.

Rude, Fernand 1982, *Les Révoltes des canuts*, Paris: Maspero.

Ruedy, John 1992, *Modern Algeria: The Origins And Development of a Nation*, Bloomington: Indiana University Press.

Ruscio, Alain 1985, *Les Communistes français et la guerre d'Indochine*, Paris: L'Harmattan.

Sainte-Soline, Claire 1955, *D'Amour et d'anarchie*, Paris: Grasset.

Salabelle, Alfred 1912, 'Le Congrès de Chambéry', *La Vie ouvrière*, 5 September: 719–20.

Sansom, Anna 2021. ' "Proud to be colonised?": statue of French politician torn down in Martinique', *The Art Newspaper*, 10 March, available at: https://www.theartnewspape r.com/2021/03/10/proud-to-be-colonised-statue-of-french-politician-torn-down-in -martinique.

Sartre, Jean-Paul (ed.) 1953, *L'Affaire Henri Martin*, Paris: Gallimard.

Sartre, Jean-Paul 1958, 'Une Victoire', *L'Express*, 6 March.

Sartre, Jean-Paul 1964, 'Le colonialisme est un système', *Situations v*, Gallimard: Paris.

Sartre, Jean-Paul 1972, *Situations VIII*, Paris: Gallimard.

Sauvy, Alfred 1952, 'Trois mondes, une planète', *L'Observateur*, 14 August.

Saville, John 1993, *The Politics of Continuity*, London: Verso.

Schiappa, Jean-Marc 1990, 'Notes sur le dirigeant babouviste Robert François Debon', *Annales historiques de la Révolution française* 283: 93–104.

Sedgwick, Peter 1960–61, 'The Fight for Workers' Control', *International Socialism* 1,3: 18– 25, available at: https://www.marxists.org/archive/sedgwick/1960/xx/workerscontr ol.htm.

Semard, Pierre 1925, *La Guerre du Rif*, Paris: Librairie de l'Humanité.

Senghor, Lamine 1927, *La Violation d'un pays*, Paris: Bureau d'Éditions.

Senghor, Lamine 2012, *La Violation d'un pays et autres écrits anticolonialistes*, Paris: L'Harmattan.

Serge, Victor 1921a, *Pendant la guerre civile*, Paris: *Les Cahiers du travail* 6, 15 May 1921.

Serge, Victor 1921b, *Les Anarchistes et l'expérience de la révolution russe*, Paris: Les Cahiers du travail 12, 15 August 1921.

Serge, Victor 1924a, *La Ville en danger*, Paris: Librairie du travail.

Serge, Victor 1924b, 'Le Parti communiste allemand se critique lui-même', *Clarté*, 15 February.

Serge, Victor 1930, *L'an i de la révolution russe*, Paris: Librairie du travail.

Serge, Victor 1994 [1927–8], 'The Class Struggle in the Chinese Revolution', *Revolutionary History* 5,3, available at: https://www.marxists.org/archive/serge/1927/china/ index.html.

Serge, Victor 2001 [1951], *Mémoires d'un révolutionnaire*, Paris: Robert Laffont.

Serge, Victor 2012, *Carnets (1936–1947)*, Marseille: Agone.

Serge, Victor 2015a [1939], *Midnight in the Century*, translated by Richard Greeman, New York: New York Review Books.

Serge, Victor 2015b, *Anarchists Never Surrender*, edited and translated by Mitchell Abidor, Oakland CA: PM Press.

Simon, Jacques 2003, *L'Étoile Nord-Africaine*, Paris: L'Harmattan.

Slavin, David 1991, 'The French Left and the Rif War, 1924–25: Racism and the Limits of Internationalism', *Journal of Contemporary History*, 26,1: 5–32.

Smith, Leonard V 1994, *Between Mutiny and Obedience*, Princeton NJ: Princeton University Press.

Smith, T.O. 2007, *Britain and the Origins of the Vietnam War*, Basingstoke: Palgrave Macmillan.

Stil, André 1951, *Au Château d'eau*, Paris: Éditeurs français réunis.

Stoljarowa, Ruth and Peter Schmalfuss (eds.) 1990, *Briefe Deutscher an Lenin 1917–1923*, Berlin: Dietz Verlag.

Stora, Benjamin 1982, *Messali Hadj 1898–1974*, Paris: Le Sycomore.

Stora, Benjamin 1986, *Messali Hadj*, new edition, Paris: L'Harmattan.

Stora, Benjamin 1991, *La Gangrène et l'oubli*, Paris: La Découverte.

Stuart, Robert 2006, *Marxism and National Identity*, Albany: State University of New York Press.

Stutje, Jan Willem 2009, *Ernest Mandel*, London: Verso.

Surya, Michel 2004, *La révolution rêvée: pour une histoire des intellectuels et des oeuvres révolutionnaires 1944–1956*, Paris: Fayard.

Swardson, Anne 1998, 'The Dreyfus Affair's Living History', *The Washington Post*, 14 January, available at: https://www.washingtonpost.com/archive/politics/1998/01/14/the-dreyfus-affairs-living-history/d3cb9815-a7e9-4131-95a1-18d9f47f6ffd/.

Tasca, Angelo and Denis Peschanski 1986, *Vichy 1940–1944*, Milan: Annali Feltrinelli.

Tevanian, Pierre 2013, *La Haine de la religion*, Paris: La Découverte.

Thalmann, Paul and Clara 1997, *Combats pour la liberté*, Quimperlé: La Digitale.

Thompson, Edward P. 1980 [1968], *The Making of the English Working Class*, Harmondsworth: Penguin.

Thourel, Marcel 1980, *Itinéraire d'un cadre communiste*, Toulouse: Privat.

Tillon, Charles 1969, *La Révolte vient de loin*, Paris: 10/18.

Tillon, Charles 1977, *On chantait rouge*, Paris: Robert Laffont.

Tosstorff, Reiner 2004, *Profintern: Die Rote Gewerkschaftsinternationale 1920–1937*, Paderborn: Ferdinand Schoeningh.

Tran-Duc-Thao 1947, 'Sur l'interprétation trotzkyste des événements d'Indochine', *Les Temps modernes*, July: 1697–1705.

Trang-Gaspard, Thu 1992, *Ho Chi Minh à Paris 1917–1923*, Paris: L'Harmattan.

Treint, Albert 1925, 'Tous contre la guerre des banquiers', *L'Humanité*, 16 May: 1, available at: https://gallica.bnf.fr/ark:/12148/bpt6k4017054/f1.item.zoom.

Trévédy, Julien 1906, 'La Famille Limon du Timeur', *Bulletin de la société archéologique du Finistère*, tome 33: 222–46.

Trotsky, Leon 1922, 'Resolution on the French Question', *The First Five Years of the Communist International*, Volume 2, London: New Park, available at: https://www.marxists.org/archive/trotsky/1924/ffyci-2/22.htm.

Trotsky, Leon 1930, *My Life*, New York: Charles Scribner's Sons.

Trotsky, Leon 1933, 'What is National Socialism?', available at: https://www.marxists.org/archive/trotsky/germany/1933/330610.htm.

Trotsky, Leon 1936, 'Marcel Martinet', *Les Humbles*, special issue on Marcel Martinet, January–March.

Trotsky, Leon 1941 [1939], 'A Great New Writer', *Fourth International* 11, 1, February 1941: 56–8, available at: https://www.marxists.org/archive/trotsky/1939/08/writer.htm.

Trotsky, Leon 1973, *Writings of Leon Trotsky 1939–40*, New York: Pathfinder.

Trotsky, Leon and Alfred and Marguerite Rosmer 1982, *Correspondance 1929–1939*, edited by Pierre Broué, Paris: Gallimard.

Ulloa, Marie-Pierre 2001, *Francis Jeanson*, Paris: Berg.

Un jeune soldat, 1923, 'La guerre au Maroc', *La Caserne* 2, 1 July: 3, available at: https://gallica.bnf.fr/ark:/12148/bpt6k66435576/f3.item.zoom.

Un ouvrier de chez Renault [Daniel Mothé] 1956, 'Journal d'un ouvrier', *Socialisme ou Barbarie* 19: 73–100, available at: https://gallica.bnf.fr/ark:/12148/bpt6k62307673/f21.item.

Un témoin 1925, 'Mayence 1924', *La Révolution prolétarienne* 7, July: 19–26.

Vaillant-Couturier, Paul 1923, 'Trois mois de misère en Allemagne', *Clarté* 45.

Vaillant-Couturier, Paul 1925, 'Puissante grève de masses contre les tueries du Maroc', *L'Humanité*, 13 October: 1, available at: https://gallica.bnf.fr/ark:/12148/bpt6k4018555/f1.item.zoom.

Vallès, Jules 1964 [1886], *L'Insurgé*, Paris: Hachette, 1964.

van der Linden, Marcel 2007, *Western Marxism and the Soviet Union*, Leiden/Boston: Brill.

van der Motte, Franz 2009, *Jeanne Labourbe, première communiste française*, Paris: Les points sur les i.

Vétillard, Roger 2008, *Sétif, Mai 1945: Massacres en Algérie*, Versailles: Éditions de Paris.

Viollis, Andrée 2008 [1935], *Indochine S.O.S.*, Pantin: Les bons caractères.

Vitale, Roberto 1967–8, 'The Italian Left: A Report', *International Socialism* 1, 31: 33–6, available at: https://www.marxists.org/history/etol/newspape/isj/1967/no031/vitale.htm.

Vittori, Jean Pierre 1977, *Nous, les appelés d'Algérie*, Paris: Stock.

Voltaire, François-Marie 1961 [1764], *Dictionnaire Philosophique*, Paris: Garnier.

Voltaire, François-Marie 1964 [1734], *Lettres Philosophiques*, Paris: Garnier.

Vouïovitch, Voja 1924, *L'I.C.J. en lutte contre l'occupation de la Ruhr et la guerre*, Moscow: Édition du Bureau de la Presse de l'I.C.

Wald, Alan 1983, *Revolutionary Imagination: The Poetry and Politics of John Wheelwright and Sherry Mangan*, Chapel Hill: University of North Carolina Press.

Walter, Gérard 1960, *La Vie à Paris sous l'occupation 1940–1944*, Paris: Armand Colin.

Weber, Eugen 1979 *Peasants into Frenchmen*, London: Chatto and Windus.

Weber, Eugen 1985, 'La formation de l'hexagone républicain', in *Jules Ferry: fondateur de la République*, edited by François Furet, Paris: Éditions de l'école des hautes études en sciences sociales.

Weiss, Suzanne 2015, 'Welcoming refugees then and now', available at: https://johnridde ll.com/2015/10/09/welcoming-refugees-then-and-now/.

Weiss, Suzanne 2019, *Holocaust to Resistance: My Journey*, Black Point Nova Scotia: Fernwood Publishing.

Willard, Claude 1957, *La Fusillade de Fourmies*, Paris: Éditions sociales.

Willsher, Kim 2021, 'French soldiers killed Algerian lawyer in war of independence, Macron admits', *Guardian*, 3 March, available at: https://www.theguardian.com/world/2021/mar/03/french-soldiers-killed-algerian-lawyer-in-war-of-independence-macron-admits.

Wintsch, Jean 1910, 'Un modèle d'armée démocratique', *La Vie ouvrière*, 20 April: 492–501.

Wohl, Robert 1966, *French Communism in the Making*, Stanford: Stanford University Press.

Wolfreys, Jim 2015, 'After the Paris Attacks: An Islamophobic Spiral', *International Socialism* 2,146.

Wolfreys, Jim 2018, *Republic of Islamophobia*, London: Hurst and Company.

Wullens, Maurice 1939 [1920], *Pages de mon Carnet*, Paris: Les Humbles.

Zappi, Sylvia 2008, 'Yves Rocton, syndicaliste Force ouvrière et militant trotskiste', *Le Monde*, 13 October 2008, available at: https://archive.wikiwix.com/cache/index2 .php?url=https%3A%2F%2Fwww.lemonde.fr%2Fdisparitions%2Farticle%2F2008 %2F10%2F13%2Fyves-rocton-syndicaliste-de-force-ouvriere-et-militant-trotskiste _1106190_3382.html#federation=archive.wikiwix.com&tab=url.

Zeilig, Leo 2016, Frantz Fanon, London and New York: IB Tauris.

Zeldin, Theodore 1980, *Intellect and Pride*, Oxford: Oxford University Press, 1980.

Zetkin, Clara 1920, 'Le discours de Clara Zetkin', *L'Humanité*, 29 December: 1, available at: https://gallica.bnf.fr/ark:/12148/bpt6k2998978/f1.item.zoom.

Zia-Ebrahimi, Reza 2021, *Antisémitisme et Islamophobie: une histoire croisée*, Paris: Éditions Amsterdam.

Zola, Emile 1883, *Le Capitaine Burle*, Paris: Charpentier.

Zola, Émile 1896, *Nouvelle campagne*, Paris: Charpentier.

Zola, Emile 1897, *Lettre à la jeunesse*, Paris, Fasquelle.

Zola, Émile 1898, 'J'Accuse', *L'Aurore*, 13 January, available at: https://www.famous-trials .com/dreyfus/2613-j-accuse-by-emile-zola-texts-in-english-and-french.

Zola, Émile 1903, *Vérité*, La Bibliothèque électronique du Québec, available at: https:// beq.ebooksgratuits.com/vents/zola-verite.pdf.

Zola, Emile 1962 [1891], L'Argent, Paris: Fasquelle.

Index